T0135413

DIGITAL DIPLOMATICS

Archiv für Diplomatik

Schriftgeschichte
Siegel- und Wappenkunde

Begründet durch

EDMUND E. STENGEL

Herausgegeben von

WALTER KOCH und THEO KÖLZER

Beiheft 14

Digital diplomatics

The computer as a tool for the diplomatist?

Edited by

ANTONELLA AMBROSIO, SÉBASTIEN BARRET,
GEORG VOGELER

2014

BÖHLAU VERLAG KÖLN · WEIMAR · WIEN

Publication with the support of the Dipartimento di Studi Umanistici of
Università degli Studi di Napoli Federico II, as part of the ENArC Project
(EU, Culture Programme 2007–2013)

Bibliografische Information der Deutschen Nationalbibliothek:
Die Deutsche Nationalbibliothek verzeichnet diese Publikation in der
Deutschen Nationalbibliografie; detaillierte bibliografische Daten
sind im Internet über http://portal.dnb.de abrufbar.

Satz: Punkt für Punkt GmbH · Mediendesign, Düsseldorf
Druck und Bindung: Strauss, Mörlenbach
Gedruckt auf chlor- und säurefreiem Papier
Printed in the EU

ISBN 978-3-412-22280-2

Table of Content

I. Technical and theoretical models

II. Projects for the edition of texts and the publication of information

III. Digital diplomatics in the work of the historian

Appendices

Preface

This volume is the result of the work carried out during the international conference *Digital Diplomatics 2011. Tools for the Digital Diplomatist* (Naples, September 29th – October 1st, 2011). The congress was held under the patronage of the Associazione Nazionale Italiana dei Paleografi e Diplomatisti and the Commission Internationale de Diplomatique. It could be realised thanks to the financial support of the ENArC project (EU Culture Programme 2007–2013), supplied by the Dipartimento di discipline storiche of the Università degli Studi di Napoli Federico II, by the Polo delle Scienze Umane e Sociali of the same University and by ICARus (International Centre for Archival Research) to whom we express our gratitude. We especially appreciated the enthusiasm and the professionalism of the young members of the ENArC working group of the University Federico II in organizing the conference: Luca Aiello, Maria Rosaria Falcone, Alfonso Gentile, Ciro Romano, Enza Russo, Angelica Parisi, Stefania Persico, Concetta Prisco and Barbara Trenca.

We would also like to thank Vera Schwarz-Ricci for her steady hand and precise work when she helped us with the copy editing of the volume. We were lucky to find in Isabella Bolognese a trained medievalist for the proof reading of the English texts by a native speaker. The volume underwent an anonymous peer review process, and we are grateful to the reviewers for the efforts put into improving the quality of the contributions and to the authors for their positive reaction to the comments of their anonymous peers. Last but not least we extend our thanks to Theo Kölzer who accepted the volume as a Beiheft of the Archiv für Diplomatik and to Johannes van Ooyen of Böhlau for the good cooperation.

All internet addresses in the papers were checked for existence as of 2nd January 2014.

This volume is the result of a collaboration between three editors. Antonella Ambrosio was responsible in particular for the papers of Daniel Piñol Alabart, Francesca Capochiani et alii, Antonella Ghignoli, Serena Falletta, Jonathan Jarrett and Luciana Duranti, while Sébastien Barret attended to those of Camille Desenclos and Vincent Jolivet, Benoît Tock, Els De Paermentier, Nicolas Perraux, Michael Hänchen and Dominique Stutzmann, and Georg Vogeler to the papers of Richard Higgins, Gelila Tilahun et alii, Aleksandrs Ivanovs and Aleksey Varfolomeyev, Martin Roland, Žarko Vujošević et alii, and Gunter Vasold. Sébastien Barret created the basis for the glossary in the appendix. But ultimately we produced the volume as an international team – and in spite of linguistic obstacles and the struggle to coordinate three highly filled personal schedules, it was a good experience. Modern communication technologies helped a lot, so we ask for the forbearance of the readers if the editors sometimes seem to be a little too enthusiastic about the possibilities of digital tools – in the creation of books and in diplomatics.

Napoli, Orléans, Graz, autumn 2013
The editors

Digital Diplomatics

Expertise between computer science and diplomatics

ANTONELLA AMBROSIO, SÉBASTIEN BARRET,
GEORG VOGELER

Scholarship is not a matter of pencil and paper, of printed ink in leather bound books anymore. The computer has become an ubiquitous tool for humanities research and diplomatics, too. Digital Diplomatics in this sense is already a well-established field of study, as probably no diplomatist works without the help of modern information technology. This is well demonstrated by the fact that debates, which are sometimes quite heated, emerge not only between proponents of this new way of studying history, and "old-fashioned" scholars; the digital community itself is home to many a passionate discussion. This collection of the state of the art of digital diplomatics in the year 2011 can illustrate some of the battle fields.

We decided to organise the contributions in this volume in three parts: the first part collects the papers which discuss methodological and theoretical questions, like standards of charter encoding, consequences of digitally editing charters or the possibilities of transferring diplomatic questions to electronic records; the second part presents charter databases which evolved within archival contexts or in research projects, and may still be at their conceptual stage, or already realised; the final group of papers deals with charter-based research supported by digital tools, ranging from pure diplomatic research to historical, palaeographical or art-historical questions. This division in three parts is useful to highlight some common aspects of the contributions. The papers could be organised in a completely different way too. In the following we discuss a set of problems which are present – more or less extensively – in all essays, and which could serve as interpretative key to seize the new and interesting aspects on the whole and not only in their separate contexts.

A major question is, for a start, how much technical expertise is necessary to do "digital diplomatics". Some of the papers in this volume are created by "programming historians", i.e. diplomatists with a good expertise in computer sciences like Richard Higgins, Nicolas Perreaux, Gunter Vasold,

Camille Desenclos and Vincent Jolivet. Others follow a cooperative strategy involving computer scientists with diplomatic questions like Michael Gervers who cooperates with the statistics scientists Gelila Tilahun and Andrey Feuerverger, or Aleksandrs Ivanovs who has established a strong cooperation with the mathematician Aleksey Varfolomeyev.

As many problems digital diplomatics deals with have not found established technical solutions, the debate is opened to new epistemological questions. Can we detect rules in large charter corpora automatically? The question is discussed in the papers of Michael Gervers/Gelila Tilahun/Andrey Feuerverger, who are working on text statistical methods to date undated English charters in the DEEDS project, and Nicolas Perreaux who puts forward propositions for clustering the charters in a large corpus of texts from all of "Latin" Europe from the 7th to 14th century. The papers of Michael Hänchen, Jonathan Jarrett, Žarko Vujošević, Nebojša Porčić, Dragić M. Živojinović and Antonella Ghignoli can be read as considerations on the question of which answers a database can give scholars of diplomatics and which it cannot. The database seems to be a concept similar to calendars and charter editions, and shares many of the questions already asked in pre-digital terms: How can editors and collectors achieve "completeness" and what does it mean? By which criteria can diplomatists select documents to be studied?

Contrasting the statistical approach with the databases leads to another epistemological question: While the statistical approach by Els De Paermentier, Michael Hänchen, Dominique Stutzmann, Michael Gervers/Gelila Tilahun/Andrey Feuerverger or Nicolas Perreaux argues that frequent features, or at least frequent co-occurrences of features, refer to a historical reality common to the charters analysed, a database can be designed to help the researcher find individuals or single events which are documented in the charters, as Jonathan Jarrett or Martin Roland suggest. Is digital diplomatics more interested in the single charter or in a group of charters?

The transfer of these representations to databases strengthens the discussion on the structure of the description. As the applied techniques (e.g. relational databases, XML schemata) determine many of the decisions, technical skills are required for the diplomatists involved in the discussion about the methods and standards of description. Camille Desenclos and Vincent Jolivet suggest a solution for the XML encoding of charter text trying to integrate the visual appearance with the formal model. Francesca Capochiani, Chiara Leoni and Roberto Rosselli Del Turco review existing open source solutions, and suggest that the process of encoding, publishing and querying in a complex way can be done even in projects which lack the funding for the professional implementation of the necessary software.

Such an interest for the technical side, or the construction of the technical side of the matter is also perceptible in contributions presenting precise pro-

jects and the ways and means of their realisation, like the contribution of
Serena Falletta, Dominique Stutzmann or Richard Higgins and, to a lesser
extent, Aleksandrs Ivanovs' and Aleksey Varfolomeyev's. Serena Falletta discusses whether an hypertext edition is a suitable form for the digital edition
of a cartulary. Dominique Stutzmann explores some possibilities for palaeographic analysis in digital editions. Richard Higgins asks how the various
descriptions of medieval documentary holdings of an archive can be integrated into a common repository. Aleksandrs Ivanovs and Aleksey Varfolomeyev try to find a technical environment which helps to represent the
content of the charter. They show the benefits which diplomatic research can
draw from mostly technical decisions like the creation of hypertext, the
methods for encoding single letter forms, or the selection of specific repository software.

In the contributions by Benoît-Michel Tock, Luciana Duranti and Gunter
Vasold the technological part stays in the background of theoretical reflections. Benoît-Michel Tock makes an appeal for the advancement of the existing technical solutions to fit the needs of diplomatic research and to sustain
the diplomatic knowledge necessary to create the data. With that argument he
addresses the problems which can arise if technological skills are not at the
same level as diplomatics skills. Luciana Duranti's extrapolation of what can
be learned from diplomatics in its juridical tradition for the archiving of electronic records works only if the trained diplomatist understands the forensic
implications of the technologies. Gunter Vasold's model of iterative edition
requires a high level of technological skills to be implemented in computer
software to be used by the diplomatist.

Through the examples of concrete project realisations, Daniel Piñol Alabart and Jonathan Jarrett show what can be done with limited technological
resources. Other database projects, existing or *in spe*, need more technological skills. Thus, technology experts take an important part in the development
of the database of illuminated charters suggested by Martin Roland; of the
database of the charters of monasteries in the Passau diocese in the 14th century on which Michael Hänchen reports; of the database of Belgian charters
which was the base for Els De Paermentier's analysis of the Flanders chancery
in 1191–1244; of the database which will help Žarko Vujošević, Nebojša
Porčić and Dragić M. Živojinović to study the chancery of the Serbian kings;
and of the database of the early and high medieval charters of the Italian kings
presented by Antonella Ghignoli. Together with the diplomatists, these experts create databases for diplomatic research with general or hand tailored
tools. It is Jonathan Jarrett who points out that a sophisticated tool needs
more interpretational preparation of the data, while a simple description already helps in exploring the charters and detecting new connections. The discussion over where to set the limit in structuring and encoding digital charter

descriptions is still open. Do we need many databases each catering for particular research questions, like the *Italia regia* database or the database of Serbian royal charters? Or can we create a minimal description of a charter in a common charter database from which the specific research projects extract their data and enhance it, as Martin Roland proposes and Michael Hänchen does with the Monasterium.net database?

Secondly, and interestingly, most authors chose to zoom in on the methodological aspect of their research, even though they present it in a larger context. This is certainly a sign of the vitality of a research field in which technological skills and diplomatic scholarship work together, and which does not separate methodological from scholarly interpretation. Michael Hänchen's contribution is maybe the least methodological, in the sense that he draws relatively wide ranging historical interpretation of the data presented in his study – even though he stresses that his focus is primarily on methodology. The same can be said of Els De Paermentier, who describes the method by which she aims to construct a history of the chancery of the counts of Flanders: the proposed methodology has already led to convincing research results. Dominique Stutzmann's demonstration of the use of "scribal profiles" takes the opposite approach: he suggests a new palaeographical methodology adapted to a specific case, that can be transferred to other research when the digital tools become available.

Common to almost all articles is their tendency to present their subject on the methodological side, although certainly not all explicitly state their programmatic aspect. This is no doubt a result of the relative youth of the research field of digital diplomatics. Digital diplomatics is in continuous development, open for experiments, and varied, being the result of interdisciplinary efforts. The research in the field therefore mixes well established methodologies with new approaches. Even very well established undertakings like the DEEDS project or InterPARES are still evolving and revolving. We have, as a consequence, the privilege of seeing a research field developing and trying to reflect on itself – Benoît-Michel Tock's musing is a typical case of productive reevaluation after a first intense and creative phase.

Methodological questions can arise from the possibility of using digital resources in an interdisciplinary way. While the digital representation of charters can integrate images and texts, it fosters a renewed attention for the material aspects of the documents – as shown in the case of Serbian diplomatics presented by Žarko Vujošević, Nebojša Porčić and Dragić M. Živojinović – and at the same time allows the scholar to work intensely on textual aspects. Martin Roland offers us a fine example of new interdisciplinary work, when he asks for the historical value of charters carrying illuminations, and its consequence for their digital documentation. Before the creation and dissemination of images of charters became so cheap with the help of digital tools, diplomatics and art history were certainly not the first neighbouring disciplines to start interdisciplinary cooperation, even though scholars like Peter Rück had done pioneering research in that regard.

In the papers of Antonella Ghignoli, Francesca Capochiani/Chiara Leoni/ Roberto Rosselli Del Turco or Serena Falletta it also becomes apparent that digital technologies favour a new approach towards the sequence of data production, presentation and use, as well as a redefinition of the respective roles of the various scientific community members. Gunter Vasold develops this further. In his model of iterative edition he tries to fix the possibility of infinite correction and of eternal changes. Scholarly documentation and editions are then snapshots of the permanent flow of information being updated and modified – a perspective which is, from the point of view of the continuous academic search for truth, very tempting, but in particular for archival sciences potentially terrifying.

The methodological discussion stimulated by the possibilities of digital tools leads to a third observation: many of the approaches carry a kind of vintage flavour with them. Diplomatics, in the eyes of Jean Mabillon and, above all, of many of his heirs, is primarily an expertise based on classification and clustering: documents are divided into pieces and analysed on the background of models which are formulated on the basis of the observation of the whole. The study of a single charter thus requires the collection of many charters and its classification. This data collection, its comparison and its authentication is enhanced by digital technologies. Digital diplomatics can therefore lean towards a kind of new positivism (not intended as a derogatory term). This is also very explicitly defended by Luciana Duranti, who pleads for a new, contemporary *discrimen veri ac falsi*. At the same time, other methods allow for structural analysis of the texts, which is all but "positivist".

The use of a computer might give an impression of "objectivity" and clear-cut treatment of the data; but as much as electronic computing is precise and able to deal with enormous quantities of information, one should never forget two things. Firstly, the output of a computer depends on the primary input – this being the case for the data as well as for the tools used to process it. Choices and interpretations already take place at the input, in the selection of the data and in the methods of its treatment. This is, for instance, very well shown in Nicolas Perreaux's and Michael Gervers, Gelila Tilahun and Andrey Feuerverger's papers. Both of them cluster a huge amount of data with statistical methods, but with completely different aims: looking for typical word combinations for a specific time frame (Michael Gervers, Gelila Tilahun and Andrey Feuerverger), or clustering the documents into groups by issuer or region of production (Nicolas Perreaux). Secondly, the results of any digital treatment are very often still raw material awaiting its interpretation. The models proposed by Aleksandrs Ivanovs/Aleksey Varfolomeyev, Serena Falletta, Francesca Capochiani/Chiara Leoni/Roberto Rosselli Del Turco or Antonella Ghignoli should allow to present the data in a way that makes it usable for further inquiries from different perspectives, driven by the interest in the charters as sources for historical facts (Ivanovs/Varfolomeyev, Falletta), linguistic features (Capochiani/Leoni/Rosselli Del Turco) or more on the side of the external and internal features (Ghignoli). The fact that new possibilities lead to renewed reflections on diplomatics does not mean that these reflections all go in the same direction.

All in all, several paths are taking shape: there is the discussion on how to transfer the high standards of critical documentation in calendars and critical editions into digital forms. Another area of discussion certainly will be how the methods of transcription, description, edition and critical evaluation of charters will change when digital methods are applied – and which digital tools have to be developed to achieve what these methods traditionally can provide. It is still not obvious which technical skills are necessary for the diplomatist interested in doing digital diplomatics. Diplomatists will further have to learn which kind interdisciplinary work will become possible by digital representations of charters. Apart from the methodological questions, diplomatists will have to study the large corpora of documents which are now published digitally. They will have to extract new research results on practices in charter production and in use of charters, on the legal, social or linguistic particularities in time and space, or their common ground.

As many of these questions are only stimulated by digital tools, and are in the end general questions of diplomatics, it could well be that the future of diplomatics is less in debates on issues of digitisation than in debates on the subject itself. The current general consensus on the basics of diplomatics as a discipline is very much fuelled by the difficulties the discipline is going through in the universities of Europe and beyond. Establishing digital methods in diplomatics can set off discussions on the general orientation of diplomatics: shall we focus more on the visual side of the document than on the text? What do statistics of charters really tell us? Shall diplomatics dwell deeper into the single document, differentiate the description methods, and search for information on its context, or is diplomatics a science of what is common to many charters? Discussing these questions certainly will foster diplomatics scholarship, be it digital or not.

I. Technical and theoretical models

La diplomatique numérique
Une diplomatique magique?[*]

BENOÎT-MICHEL TOCK

La diplomatique d'aujourd'hui est devenue très largement numérique. Ne peut-on considérer que par là, quand on se rappelle ce qu'elle était il y a environ 25 ans, elle est devenue une diplomatique magique?

La diplomatique est devenue tellement magique ...

Il y a 25 ans, établir sa bibliographie supposait la consultation de dizaines de volumes de l'*International Medieval Bibliography*, du *Medioevo latino*, de la *Revue d'Histoire Ecclésiastique*, etc. Trouver des chartes, originales ou en copies, n'était possible qu'en se rendant dans des dépôts d'archives[1], et on y allait sans savoir ce qu'on trouverait, ni même si on y trouverait quelque chose. Photographier les actes était difficile ou coûteux, et les photocopier était strictement interdit, même si c'était parfois possible. Éditer une charte, cela voulait dire aller dans un dépôt d'archives avec un cahier et un crayon, recopier le texte, rentrer chez soi pour retaper le texte à la machine à écrire, retourner au dépôt d'archives pour vérifier la transcription ... De nos jours, tout est si facile que cela a un côté magique. Une foule de bases de données et de sites internet nous donnent accès à des inventaires ou des catalogues et numérisés, à des photos d'originaux ou de copies, à des éditions anciennes ou à des articles récents. Il est presque possible désormais d'étudier la diplomatique sans sortir de son bureau!

Nous pouvons établir nos bibliographies à partir de n'importe où, en consultant l'*International Medieval Bibliography* en ligne[2], *ITER. Gateway to the Middle Ages and the Renaissance*[3], *Mirabile. Archivio digitale della*

---

[*] Conférence inaugurale du colloque, prononcée le 29.09.2011
[1] Il est vrai cependant qu'il y avait déjà des collections de reproductions: les photographies des actes originaux allemands au Lichtbildarchiv de Marbourg, les microfilms des cartulaires français à l'Institut de Recherche et d'Histoire des Textes à Orléans.
[2] <http://www.brepolis.net/>. Tous les sites cités ont été vérifiés en août 2012.
[3] <http://www.itergateway.org/>.

cultura medievale[4] ou des sites plus spécialisés comme les pages «diplomatics» de la *Virtual Library*[5], le site internet des *Regesta imperii*[6], la base BEDE
(*Bibliographie des éditions et études de sources documentaires françaises médiévales*) de l'École des chartes[7], la bibliographie de la diplomatique due à
Horst Enzensberger (univ. Bamberg)[8] ou d'autres encore. Nous pouvons
chercher les actes dans des bases de données photographiques: la plus riche
est sans conteste *Monasterium*, qui propose 250.000 actes[9], mais, comme nous
le verrons durant ce colloque, il y en a d'autres. Dans les mêmes bases de données ou dans d'autres il est possible d'interroger aussi le texte des actes. La
base *Chartae Galliae*, par exemple, propose près de 40.000 chartes françaises
antérieures à la fin du XIIIe siècle[10].

Cette diplomatique «magique» a permis une sorte de nouvelle diplomatique. Pas seulement parce qu'il est désormais très simple d'aller dans un
dépôt d'archives, de faire des photographies numériques des documents et de
les étudier ensuite (en utilisant, évidemment, un logiciel de traitement de texte
voire même un logiciel d'édition des textes anciens). Mais les possibilités d'interrogation et de comparaison des textes permettent d'analyser, plus rapidement et de manière plus sûre, les différents usages des formules, les significations d'un mot, les relations culturelles et intellectuelles entre différents
scriptoria et chancelleries. Nous aurons d'ailleurs l'occasion, tout au long de
ce colloque, de voir à quel point les interfaces d'interrogation rendent possibles de nouvelles questions, de nouvelles recherches.

La diplomatique n'est d'ailleurs pas la seule branche de la médiévistique
qui soit devenue numérique. Mais pour la numérisation, ou plus clairement
pour la création de bases de données, la diplomatique pose des problèmes
particuliers. Chez nous, beaucoup de textes sont inédits, au moins pour le Bas
Moyen Âge, ce qui est plus rarement le cas des textes historiographiques, ha-
giographiques, littéraires ou spirituels. Nos textes sont aussi très nombreux.
Brefs, mais nombreux: ils se comptent facilement en milliers, et maintenant de
plus en plus en dizaines, ou même en centaines de milliers. Enfin, nos textes
sont souvent plus ou moins précisément datés, en tout cas assez largement
datables, et souvent aussi conservés en originaux.

---

[4]   <http://www.mirabileweb.it/>.
[5]   <http://www.vl-ghw.uni-muenchen.de/diplomatik.html>.
[6]   <http://opac.regesta-imperii.de/lang_de/>.
[7]   <http://elec.enc.sorbonne.fr/#vol12>.
[8]   <http://www.hist-hh.uni-bamberg.de/hilfswiss/diplomatik.html#diplomatik>.
[9]   <http://www.monasterium.net/>.
[10] <http://www.cn-telma.fr/chartae-galliae/index/>.

Mais on pourrait rendre la diplomatique plus magique encore!

Cependant, il est encore possible d'améliorer nos instruments de travail. D'abord en les accroissant et en les complétant. La base de données des chartes originales antérieures à 1121 conservées en France est probablement exhaustive, et donne accès à environ 5.000 actes (textes, analyses et bientôt photographies)[11]. C'est là un résultat formidable. Mais la France a sans doute conservé au total 30 à 50.000 autres chartes pour cette période, pour la plupart en copies dans des cartulaires ou des manuscrits d'érudits. Ce sera bien plus magique quand on disposera d'une base de données de l'ensemble de ces textes. Si on étend la période prise en considération jusqu'à la fin du XIIIᵉ siècle, il y a peut-être quelque 300.000 actes conservés. La base *Chartae Galliae* donne accès à environ 40.000 d'entre elles, ce qui est formidable. Mais quid de l'accès aux 260.000 autres?

Il y a moins encore d'instruments pour le Bas Moyen Âge, les XIVᵉ et XVᵉ siècles. C'est vrai pour la France, c'est vrai aussi pour la Belgique: la nouvelle version du *Thesaurus Diplomaticus*, attendue avec impatience, dépassera la fin du XIIᵉ siècle pour aller jusqu'au milieu du XIIIᵉ, mais pas plus loin. En Allemagne, le *Württembergisches Urkundenbuch online* s'arrête en 1300[12], et en Italie la plupart des volumes du *Codice diplomatico della Lombardia medievale* ne dépassent pas l'année 1200[13].

Certaines bases de données ne donnent pas accès au texte des chartes, mais seulement à une analyse. La publication de ces regestes est une première étape, importante, dans la numérisation de la diplomatique. Mais il faut bien la comprendre comme une première étape, pas comme une fin en soi, puisqu'elle ne permet pas de travailler sur les textes eux-mêmes, les mots et les formules.

Mais il est important aussi de veiller à la qualité de l'interrogation: il faut absolument disposer de champs d'interrogation séparés, qui permettent de mener des recherches sur les auteurs, les bénéficiaires, les dates, les lieux ... Et, si possible, la bibliographie, les éditions (avec l'indication de leur sources). Trop de bases de données ne donnent pas accès à ce genre d'indications, alors même qu'il est difficile d'en contester, me semble-t-il, l'intérêt en diplomatique.

On parle parfois de créer une unique base de données pour toutes les chartes européennes, ou du moins un portail d'accès unique relié à l'ensemble des bases de données de textes diplomatiques. Je ne suis pas sûr que ce soit une bonne idée: après tout, nous n'avons que rarement besoin d'interroger

---

[11] <http://www.cn-telma.fr/originaux/index/>.
[12] <http://www.wubonline.de/>.
[13] <http://cdlm.unipv.it/>.

simultanément des chartes écossaises et portugaises. Et au contraire, il est plus facile d'obtenir des financements pour la création d'une nouvelle base de données, même petite, que pour l'accroissement d'une base déjà existante. Pour moi, ce qui est vraiment important, c'est de rendre possible, dans toutes les bases de données de textes diplomatiques, les recherches les plus essentielles en diplomatique: auteur (si possible en distinguant auteur et disposant), bénéficiaire (si possible en distinguant bénéficiaire et destinataire), date, authenticité, bref résumé et texte; sans oublier une indication géographique, comme un diocèse médiéval ou une région européenne actuelle.

Dans la plupart des cas, les bases de données donnent accès à un seul texte, qui peut provenir d'éditions vieillies, incomplètes ou incorrectes. Il est vrai que, comme diplomatistes autant que comme historiens, nous utilisons ces mauvaises éditions chaque jour. Et puisque nous les utilisons comme volumes imprimés, pourquoi ne pas les utiliser aussi dans leur version numérisée? Cela n'a rien de choquant. Mais c'est moins magique. Par exemple, dans la base de données *Chartae Galliae*, j'ai repris le texte des chartes de l'abbaye de Saint-Bertin tel qu'il figure dans l'édition publiée par Haigneré[14]. Cet érudit local a fait du bon travail, mais comme souvent au XIXe siècle il n'a pas donné le texte intégral des actes qu'il éditait, omettant ce qui lui paraissait inutile. Idéalement, je devrais préparer une nouvelle édition des chartes de Saint-Bertin. Mais cela prendrait beaucoup de temps, et nombreuses sont les chartes du Nord de la France qui auraient besoin d'une nouvelle édition: pour cette seule région, de nouvelles éditions des cartulaires du chapitre cathédral d'Arras, de l'abbaye Saint-Vaast, de l'abbaye de Bergues, du prieuré d'Hesdin ou du chapitre de Béthune, par exemple, seraient nécessaires. Sans compter que pour des dizaines d'abbayes et de chapitres, il n'y a en réalité jamais eu d'édition scientifique des actes. Faudrait-il pour autant attendre ces nouvelles éditions, hypothétiques, pour inclure les actes dans des bases de données? Je ne le pense pas. Mais il est faut être clair: si la base *Chartae Galliae* permet un progrès dans l'interrogation et la lecture des chartes de Saint-Bertin, elle ne permet aucun progrès ecdotique.

Paradoxalement, je défends l'idée que, si les éditions critiques sont nécessaires, d'autres transcriptions, faites de manière plus simple et plus légère, peuvent aussi être publiées. J'ai récemment proposé de faire la différence entre les éditions critiques, qu'elles soient publiées sur papier ou en ligne, et de premières transcriptions temporaires (pouvant même être dépourvues de critique, d'identification des lieux et des personnes, et dont le texte n'est pris qu'à un seul manuscrit) publiées uniquement en ligne. Certes, cette démarche n'est pas très «scientifique», et rompt avec une progression régulière, au long d'un siècle et demi environ, des exigences ecdotiques. Mais ces transcriptions

---

[14] Les chartes de Saint-Bertin, éd. D. HAIGNERÉ, 4 vol. (1886–1899).

doivent être comprises comme une première étape, une pierre d'attente en perspective d'une édition critique à venir. Je prendrai l'exemple de l'abbaye prémontrée du Mont-Saint-Martin, au Moyen Âge dans le diocèse de Cambrai. Les chartes originales sont perdues, mais nous disposons de deux cartulaires, l'un à Paris, l'autre à Laon, et de copies d'érudits du XVIIIe siècle[15]. La presque totalité des chartes de cette abbaye est inédite. Une édition critique serait donc indispensable. Mais en attendant cette édition, dont la réalisation peut prendre des années, est-il si absurde de permettre déjà l'interrogation des actes à partir du texte de l'un des deux cartulaires?

Les reproductions des chartes sont elles aussi très importantes. Grâce à elles, il est possible de vérifier les transcriptions, voire de lire les actes s'il n'y en a pas, d'étudier les caractères externes des originaux, comme l'écriture, la mise en page, les méthodes de scellement, sans oublier les notes dorsales (si on trouve aussi une photographie du verso). En fait, nous avons besoin de plus d'une photographie par charte: si l'original est conservé, au moins une reproduction du recto, une du verso et une (ou deux) du sceau. Avec ou sans original, une photographie de chaque copie peut être utile.

Quoi qu'il en soit, les bases de données existantes donnent accès aux chartes. Ceci est évidemment très important, mais ne doit pas nous faire oublier que depuis un demi-siècle environ, les diplomatistes n'étudient pas seulement les actes, mais d'une manière générale les documents d'archives tels que les comptes, les registres ... Dans les archives du Bas Moyen Âge reposent encore des millions de documents, livres, registres, actes, qu'il sera difficile de numériser tous et étudier tous. Mais il faut y travailler!

Un autre progrès dans la diplomatique est que le travail ne porte plus seulement sur les originaux, mais aussi sur les cartulaires et autres recueils de copies. Et on sait qu'un cartulaire (mais on pourrait en dire de même d'un registre notarié) n'est pas seulement un groupe de copies distinctes, mais aussi une unité documentaire, avec sa propre structure et son propre but. La base de données des cartulaires français, due à l'Institut de Recherche et d'Histoire des Textes, est excellente[16], mais nous avons besoin d'un accès aux reproductions photographiques des manuscrits eux-mêmes.

Mais l'accès aux actes, originaux ou copies, n'est pas notre seul besoin. Nous devons aussi pouvoir élaborer nos bibliographies. Or, et malheureusement, il n'existe aucune bibliographie spécifique, courante et systématique de la diplomatique, ni imprimée, ni en ligne. Nous pouvons certes utiliser les grandes bases de données de bibliographie de la médiévistique citées ci-des-

---

[15] Sur cette abbaye voir B. Ardura, Abbayes, prieurés et monastères de l'ordre de Prémontré en France des origines à nos jours. Dictionnaire historique et bibliographique (1993) p. 388–394.

[16] <http://www.cn-telma.fr/cartulR/index/>.

sus. Et ces instruments de travail sont d'une remarquable utilité. Mais on pourrait faire mieux, par une meilleure exhaustivité, une meilleure structuration, une indexation spécifiquement diplomatique, et, pour certaines, une meilleure régularité dans les mises à jour.

Nous pourrions aussi rêver de disposer d'une base de données indiquant, pour chaque abbaye, chaque église, chaque ville, chaque seigneurie, ce qu'on a conservé comme actes (et où, bien sûr), quelles éditions existent déjà et quelles études leur ont été consacrées.

Mise à jour et pérennité

Les publications numériques, quelles qu'elles soient, posent cependant deux problèmes importants: la mise à jour et la pérennité.

Un des principaux arguments développés en faveur des publications électroniques, dès les années 1980 au moins, était qu'il est plus facile de publier des mises à jour des publications électroniques que des publications imprimées. En théorie c'est tout à fait vrai. Mais en pratique? Il faut bien avouer que les mises à jour sont assez rares. Pour des raisons financières d'une part: il est beaucoup plus facile d'obtenir de l'argent pour construire une nouvelle base de données que pour mettre à jour une base existante. En ce sens, le «management by project» sous-estime l'importance de publications structurelles, régulières et à long terme. Mais cet obstacle financier n'est pas le seul. Il faut bien avouer que la mise à jour de publications existantes pose également un problème psychologique: pour nous aussi, publier du neuf est plus motivant que revoir de l'ancien!

L'autre problème crucial est celui de la pérennité de nos bases de données. Les scribes médiévaux, les érudits des temps modernes ont dépensé beaucoup de temps et d'argent pour copier des chartes, et après plusieurs siècles, leurs travaux sont encore, de manière plus ou moins forte, utilisables. De nos jours, nous dépensons des milliers et des milliers d'euros pour créer des bases de données, mais sans être sûrs que celles-ci seront encore utilisables dans quelques décennies. Nous en sommes d'ailleurs tous bien conscients. En France, il y a quelques années, seuls les projets de bases de données garantissant un accès en ligne pérenne avaient une chance d'être financièrement soutenus. Depuis lors, c'est-à-dire en quelques années, la notion de pérennité a été étrangement raccourcie, d'abord à 50, ensuite à 30 ans. Et il est vrai que personne ne peut garantir que les systèmes informatiques d'aujourd'hui seront encore lisibles dans un demi-siècle. Mais cela interroge quant à la légitimité des dépenses actuelles en matière de bases de données; et cela incite à souligner que tout compte fait, le papier est peut-être plus pérenne que le numérique.

C'est pour cette raison qu'à mon sens, toutes les nouvelles éditions critiques de textes médiévaux (diplomatiques ou non) devraient être publiées sur papier. Et, si possible, sur support électronique, mais celui-ci me paraît moins essentiel. Le travail d'édition d'un texte est sans doute le travail le plus long, le plus difficile, mais aussi le plus utile que je connaisse en diplomatique: nous utilisons d'ailleurs toujours les éditions réalisées au XIXe, et même aux XVIIIe ou XVIIe siècle. Ceci nous permet de savoir que les livres imprimés se conservent pendant au moins quelques siècles, de sorte qu'aussi longtemps qu'il y aura des gens intéressés par les textes diplomatiques, et capables de les lire, nos éditions imprimées seront utilisables. J'espère qu'il en ira de même pour nos publications électroniques, mais je n'en suis pas sûr.

Le numérique n'est pas tout

Si la diplomatique a eu raison de s'ouvrir largement au numérique, il ne faudrait cependant pas qu'elle oublie qu'elle doit d'abord rester de la diplomatique. Que l'ordinateur doit rester une aide, un moyen, pas un but. Notre objectif reste avant tout d'éditer, dater, critiquer les actes; étudier les chancelleries, les scribes, l'usage de l'écrit ...

Je prendrai le cas de l'édition des chartes. Il va de soi qu'on ne peut plus éditer des textes médiévaux sans utiliser l'informatique. Mais est-il pour autant indispensable que les cours d'été ou les séminaires portant sur «l'édition de textes médiévaux» consacrent autant d'heures à l'édition électronique? C'est une question importante, mais pour moi le principal enjeu d'une édition critique est de donner un texte exact et bien compris, ce qui suppose d'être capable de lire, comprendre, copier et critiquer les textes et les manuscrits. Et quand je vois mes étudiants, je ne m'inquiète pas de leurs compétences informatiques (encore qu'ils semblent plus à l'aise pour naviguer sur les réseaux sociaux que pour utiliser des bases de données structurées), mais bien plus de leurs compétences en latin médiéval, en paléographie ou en ecdotique.

Conclusion

Vivons-nous réellement une époque de diplomatique magique? Oui, sans aucun doute. Notre travail est plus facile qu'il y a une génération: cependant, cela, c'est bien, mais ce n'est pas magique. Ce qui est plus important, c'est que notre travail est meilleur. Ou plutôt, que nous pouvons aujourd'hui mener des recherches qui étaient impossibles jadis. Mieux encore. Nous savons qu'à l'avenir nous pourrons sans doute de plus en plus élargir nos recherches. Et cela, c'est réellement magique!

Diple, propositions pour la convergence de schémas XML/TEI dédiés à l'édition de sources diplomatiques

CAMILLE DESENCLOS, VINCENT JOLIVET

L'École des chartes est investie depuis 2002 dans un programme d'édition électronique de sources historiques, principalement diplomatiques, prolongeant ainsi une longue tradition d'édition critique. Dès juillet 2003, le choix de la TEI s'est imposé afin de ne pas multiplier les espaces de noms pour l'encodage des éditions. Si ce choix s'est avéré excellent – le succès de la TEI en témoigne aujourd'hui –, il n'était pas encore bien maîtrisé, sans doute à cause d'une compréhension imparfaite de ce qu'est véritablement la TEI: non pas à proprement parler un schéma, mais plutôt un socle utile à la définition de différents schémas dédiés à des projets spécifiques. Cette confusion, conjuguée aux inévitables tâtonnements des premières expérimentations, s'est traduite dans nos corpus par la multiplication des solutions d'encodage arrêtées pour un même besoin. Alors même que le choix de la TEI est guidé par un impératif d'interopérabilité, il a pu conduire à la multiplication de schémas peu interopérables dans un même espace de noms. Cette situation paradoxale prévaut dans de nombreux projets aujourd'hui encore, bride les possibilités offertes par la numérisation de vastes corpus et conduit à douter de la pertinence même de l'initiative TEI pour la normalisation des documents électroniques. Les quelques 600 éléments documentés des *Guidelines* peuvent décourager le néophyte qui doit s'y confronter au commencement de son projet. La publication (HTML, ePub, LaTeX) s'avère fastidieuse et coûteuse quand il faut écrire de nouvelles XSL pour chaque nouveau corpus. L'écriture de programmes génériques d'export vers des logiciels de traitements statistiques ou de fouille de texte est rendue impossible, bridant les possibilités d'exploitation scientifique des corpus constitués. Nous perdons donc presque tout le bénéfice de l'usage d'un standard partagé, nous privant des perspectives scientifiques offertes par l'exploitation croisée de très vastes corpus.

La reprise d'un existant hétérogène à l'École des chartes a été l'occasion d'une remise à plat avec l'objectif de lever l'ensemble de ces difficultés. La méthode est bien connue, son principe simple, mais sa mise en œuvre requiert de la patience: rédiger des schémas. Cet effort de formalisation de nos pratiques éditoriales a été mené dans le cadre du développement de Diple, un logiciel de publication et de traitement des fichiers XML/TEI. Il s'agit ici de présenter ces schémas dédiés à l'édition critique de sources diplomatiques et nos méthodes de documentation. Ces schémas sont une proposition pour améliorer la convergence des pratiques d'édition des corpus diplomatiques, faciliter une réelle interopérabilité et ouvrir la voie au traitement de masse de ces corpus.

De l'expérimentation à la normalisation

L'encodage XML d'un corpus représente un effort certain: d'abord pour le choix des balises et la définition d'un modèle de document souvent complexe, ensuite pour le balisage lui-même. Le bénéfice d'un tel effort n'apparaît pas immédiatement. *A minima*, nous voudrions pouvoir lire le texte encodé, en premier lieu dans un navigateur. Aucun des éléments de l'espace de nom TEI n'étant supporté par un navigateur, la chose est impossible sans traitements (XSL) préalables, révélant certaines limites de la TEI pointées par Martin Mueller[1]: «The TEI is about encoding. [...] What about the decoding of TEI encoded documents?» TEI permet une sophistication extrême de l'encodage, mais sa sophistication précisément (600 éléments) empêche de concevoir des outils génériques qui permettraient de tirer aisément profit de la finesse de cet encodage. Les XSLT distribuées par le consortium témoignent de la difficulté à prendre en charge TEI, même avec un objectif aussi trivial que la lecture à l'écran du corpus encodé (export HTML). Cette question soulevée aujourd'hui par Martin Mueller, hier par Mark Olsen, constitue un défi pour la communauté TEI, qui doit s'y confronter pour assurer la pérennité de son «initiative.»

TEI a une philosophie permissive, proche dans ses principes du paradigme Perl: «There Is More Than One Way To Do It.» De fait, il y a plusieurs façons autorisées en TEI d'inscrire un titre ou des métadonnées, d'indiquer qu'une chaîne doit être en italique: <emph>, <emph hi="italic">, <hi rend="i"> ou <hi rend="italic">, etc. Un des aphorismes du *Zen of Python* énonce ce principe contraire à la maxime Perl: «There should be one – and preferably only one – obvious way to do it.» Martin Mueller le cite dans sa lettre et préconise que TEI fasse sienne cette devise Python.

En tant qu'utilisateur de la TEI, on ne peut que partager ce point de vue. Les fichiers TEI seraient plus faciles à prendre en charge et, surtout, le code écrit à cette fin serait plus robuste et générique. Pourtant, nous sommes

---

[1] M. MUELLER, To members of the TEI-C Board and Council (4 août 2011) <http://ariadne.northwestern.edu/mmueller/teiletter.pdf>.

conscients que ce paradigme Perl de la TEI est une des raisons de son succès: la liberté induite évite de s'enferrer dans des querelles infinies, chacun adoptant l'encodage correspondant à ses besoins et usages, et elle favorise les expérimentations concurrentes riches d'enseignements. L'ethos Perl est une incitation à l'expérimentation, à la recherche des structures les plus adaptées, tandis que l'ethos Python exprime l'exigence de repérer les structures les plus robustes et les plus génériques afin de normaliser les pratiques. Dans certains cas, il est sans doute possible, préférable même, d'arrêter une solution générique plutôt que de maintenir des solutions concurrentes. Dans le cas de l'italique, le cas est évident: une telle approche incite à s'interroger sur la nature de la chaîne en italique afin d'en désambiguïser l'usage (noms de lieux, titres, passage en langue étrangère, ...) pour lui attribuer un encodage non plus typographique mais sémantique. Seul l'italique en lui-même est encodé comme tel avec une solution dédiée (<hi rend="i">), ce qui n'empêche pas d'afficher les autres éléments en italique grâce à une XSLT et de les adapter aux usages typographiques de chaque édition. Cette double normalisation des usages favorise en aval l'interopérabilité entre les textes encodés: une entité nommée (nom de personne, de lieu, d'organisation, date, etc.) pourra immédiatement être identifiée comme telle dans l'ensemble du corpus constitué. L'expérience – c'est-à-dire la multiplication des cas – permet de dégager des solutions d'encodage pérennes et stables. C'est ce travail de normalisation que nous avons mené lors de la constitution des schémas partagés.

Des schémas dédiés

Le travail de reprise et de maintenance des éditions en ligne de l'École des chartes a été l'occasion d'évaluer chacune des solutions adoptées pour l'édition critique. Les meilleures solutions d'encodage ont été patiemment consignées dans des schémas Relax-NG[2]. Ces schémas matérialisent ce passage de l'expérimentation à la normalisation. Cela suppose bien des tâtonnements, la confrontation de nombreux cas particuliers pour dégager de manière assurée la meilleure solution d'encodage, la plus générique. Pour autant, rien n'est fixé de manière définitive: chaque nouvelle publication, en soulevant de nouveaux problèmes éditoriaux, conduit à modifier, à affiner ces schémas et contribue à les rendre plus robustes.

Le cas de l'apparat critique témoigne de l'avantage de cet effort. Si l'on se réfère au chapitre consacré à l'apparat dans les *Guidelines* de la TEI[3], on peut

---

2 <http://developpements.enc.sorbonne.fr/diple/schema/>.

3 P5: Guidelines for electronic text encoding and interchange, éd. TEI Consortium, février 2012 <http://www.tei-c.org/release/doc/tei-p5-doc/en/html/index.html>.

vite se perdre dans le nombre des possibilités d'encodage. Le seul élément <app> peut contenir jusqu'à 47 éléments. La combinatoire laisse de trop nombreuses possibilités pour permettre de concevoir un traitement générique. Aussi nos schémas ont-ils été resserrés sur les besoins spécifiques de l'édition critique de sources diplomatiques, à savoir l'expression des variantes, des leçons rejetées, des ajouts et des omissions. Les seuls éléments <lem> et <rdg>, enfants de <app>, permettent de couvrir l'ensemble de ces besoins[4]. La simplicité apparente de ce schéma résulte d'un véritable effort de modélisation des différents cas rencontrés. Cet effort permet de maîtriser très précisément le contenu des sources XML et d'écrire du code sur mesure, robuste et qui sera optimisé pour l'ensemble des nouveaux fichiers produits.

Dans le même temps, des XSLT dédiées à l'édition critique ont été développées. Un travail spécifique a été mené sur les titres et la table des matières, les notes, mais aussi le tableau de la tradition. Cet affichage, fidèle aux conventions de l'édition critique, est garanti pour tous les corpus encodés conformément aux schémas. De la même manière, il devient possible de composer des feuilles d'export génériques vers des outils statistiques ou de fouille (par exemple Lexico3, R ou Weka). La rationalisation des pratiques d'encodage facilite ainsi la mise en écran et les exploitations scientifiques.

Un travail similaire portant sur les métadonnées en TEI est également nécessaire pour faciliter le partage entre corpus. L'École des chartes édite de très nombreuses chartes tandis que le Centre d'Études Supérieures de la Renaissance de Tours, en partenariat avec le CRN Telma[5], poursuit un ambitieux programme de publication de minutes notariales. L'objectif serait de permettre aux chercheurs de se constituer un corpus de recherche en couplant les deux bases. Les métadonnées doivent permettre un tel échange. Ce principe évident est cependant difficile à mettre en œuvre avec une TEI qui offre de nombreuses possibilités pour l'encodage des métadonnées sans contraindre une manière commune indispensable au couplage des corpus.

Les métadonnées de date illustrent bien cette difficulté. Il existe plusieurs manières de les encoder et la structure imbriquée de TEI rend leur localisation plus difficile encore. Rien ne permet de déterminer de manière assurée la localisation de la date de l'acte ou de la minute édités: dans le <teiHeader> ou dans le corps du texte (<text>), dans un élément <date>, au sein d'un <doc-Date>, lui-même contenu dans un <body> ou dans un <front>? Pour l'ensemble des métadonnées, nous partageons l'appréciation de Martin Mueller[6]

---

[4] <http://developpements.enc.sorbonne.fr/diple/schema/app>.

[5] Centre de Ressources Numériques, axe des sources historiques manuscrites, <http://www.cn-telma.fr/>.

[6] M. MUELLER, To members of the TEI-C Board and Council.

qui reprend à son compte un autre aphorisme du *Zen of Python:* «Flat is better than nested». Dans cette optique, le <teiHeader> nous semble inutilement complexe et ne permet pas d'échanger efficacement des textes – et ne parlons pas du cas où chaque composant du fichier source XML doit être identifié et daté. Une liste plate de métadonnées Dublin Core s'avère plus efficace pour les traitements, du moins pour les métadonnées les plus communément partagées (auteur, date, couverture spatiale, langue).

La normalisation des pratiques d'encodage des métadonnées nous semble donc nécessaire, sous peine d'en perdre l'utilité. Nos schémas spécifient l'obligation de déclarer les métadonnées de date dans un élément <date> lui-même inséré dans front/docDate. Bien sûr, d'autres conventions peuvent être adoptées, mais la solution, quelle qu'elle soit, n'a de valeur que si elle est partagée.

À ces considérations sur l'interopérabilité des corpus s'ajoute la question du traitement de ces métadonnées et donc de leur format d'inscription. Héritière de TEI et de son «approche Perl», CEI documente ainsi l'élément <date>: «contains date in any format»[7]. La consigne est à la fois suffisamment ouverte pour couvrir tous les cas possibles et trop imprécise pour les traitements. Pour permettre les extractions en fonction de critères chronologiques, chaque type de date (date de temps, date de lieu, intervalle, date approximative, *terminus a quo* ou *ante quem*) doit être exprimé de la même manière. Comme pour l'apparat critique, nous avons consigné nos solutions dans un schéma; elles constituent des propositions de départ à même d'être améliorées au gré des corpus et des collaborations.

Ces schémas ne sont pas conçus comme une nouvelle norme que chacun devrait adopter telle quelle, mais plutôt comme un ensemble de préconisations, adaptables en fonction des contraintes et objectifs de chaque projet. Il existe des mécanismes de surcharge et de redéfinition des motifs d'encodage qui permettent ces adaptations. Ces schémas Relax-NG font office de réservoir (*library*) de motifs nommés (*named patterns*) dédiés à l'encodage des composantes de l'édition critique (tableau de la tradition, apparat critique, datation, etc.). Y figurent également quelques propositions utiles pour l'encodage de certains motifs diplomatiques (comme le repérage des parties du discours). L'éditeur compose son propre schéma en assemblant les motifs utiles à l'édition et en y ajoutant ceux qui servent son projet scientifique (par exemple un encodage diplomatique, paléographique ou linguistique).

---

[7] Charters Encoding Initiative <http://www.cei.lmu.de/>.

Documenter

Le consortium TEI, par le biais de ROMA, permet déjà de personnaliser simplement des schémas, mais la documentation générée grâce à cette application reste générique et attachée à l'ontologie TEI, alors que nous avons besoin de consigner des problèmes et des solutions bien précis d'encodage. Reste la possibilité d'écrire directement, sans passer par ROMA, un fichier ODD dont la syntaxe permet aussi d'établir des spécifications fines et bien documentées. Mais considérant que ce problème de la spécification des schémas et de leur documentation est un problème générique à XML et non propre à TEI, nous avons préféré privilégier un langage de schéma plus standard et mieux partagé, Relax-NG, plutôt que d'introduire une nouvelle syntaxe dédiée telle que ODD.

Cependant ces schémas sont difficiles à lire. Aussi, avons-nous développé un module spécifique, le module XREM de Diple, afin de les visualiser sous la forme d'une documentation textuelle navigable. Une telle documentation est un repère utile pour l'éditeur scientifique qui n'est pas nécessairement familier des techniques XML. Elle consigne les règles d'encodage de l'édition, précise son projet scientifique et permet surtout, grâce à la validation XML, de s'assurer que le fichier TEI est bien conforme à ces mêmes règles. Nous n'avons plus d'un côté un schéma et de l'autre un guide pratique d'encodage mais un seul et même fichier, le schéma Relax-NG, qui, de manière performative, déclare des règles, les documente et impose de les respecter, par le processus de validation.

La validation, par l'homogénéité de l'encodage qu'elle implique, atteste de la qualité d'édition de la source inscrite dans le fichier TEI, qualité d'autant plus appréciable que la documentation explicite cet encodage. De plus, le recours aux schémas et au processus de validation constitue une première étape dans le processus de validation scientifique: créer une documentation structurée nécessite de préciser plus finement les composantes classiques de l'édition critique. Ainsi, pour l'apparat, il a fallu entrer dans le cœur des notes pour en dégager une typologie plus précise et mieux maîtrisée: lemmes et variantes, corrections éditoriales, lacunes, additions et suppressions. Ce travail de définition n'est pas toujours fait dans les publications imprimées dont les normes déjà anciennes sont considérées comme des évidences. Pour autant, il ne s'agit pas de réinventer les conventions éditoriales, bien au contraire, la documentation de nos schémas s'appuie sur des pratiques éditoriales reconnues[8]. Le passage à l'outil informatique implique cependant une adaptation de ces conven-

---

[8] Conseils pour l'édition des textes médiévaux, coord. O. GUYOTJEANNIN/F. VIELLIARD (2001).

tions. Il ne s'agit plus de transcrire tel mot en italique ou entre crochets droits, mais d'expliciter la raison de cette mise en forme: mot rétabli par l'éditeur, lecture incertaine, etc. Cette réflexion sur le sens même des usages typographiques et leur spécification au sein de la documentation nous apparaissent être un excellent garant de la validité scientifique du projet éditorial. À ce titre, ils peuvent favoriser la reconnaissance institutionnelle de l'édition électronique.

* * *

Le succès de la TEI repose en grande partie sur un parti pris permissif revendiqué, adapté à la diversité des projets et des pratiques: ne pas contraindre les motifs d'encodage. La TEI, et c'est sa première qualité, permet l'élaboration de schémas sur mesure pour chaque projet. Pour autant, la liberté induite a un revers: elle autorise la multiplication des solutions d'encodage pour un même besoin et interdit de concevoir des traitements véritablement génériques. Cette difficulté peut être ressentie de manière négative, comme en témoignent les nombreux messages postés sur les listes de diffusion réclamant des outils (logiciels) pour exploiter un encodage qui représente souvent un lourd investissement. Les étudiants, dont le besoin essentiel reste le rendu d'un mémoire imprimé, sont eux aussi réticents à utiliser TEI pour leurs éditions de sources: comment leur garantir qu'ils pourront bénéficier d'une sortie papier de leur encodage, conforme aux standards universitaires? Répondre à ce besoin en apparence simple de l'édition papier n'est pas trivial quand on connaît la complexité et la singularité de chaque encodage TEI. Il est irresponsable d'inciter les étudiants à investir dans TEI en prétendant que des rudiments XSLT suffisent. Dès lors, on comprend qu'ils privilégient l'utilisation de LaTeX, très bien adapté leurs besoins, tout en regrettant que la masse importante des sources éditées ne soit pas immédiatement exploitable en TEI.

La communauté TEI doit être en mesure de répondre à ce type de besoin, tant pour une publication imprimée que pour une publication HTML. L'émergence d'initiatives communautaires pour la conception d'outils génériques se heurte à la multitude des partis-pris d'encodage adoptés dans chaque projet scientifique. S'entendre sur certains motifs partagés, dédiés à des besoins bien identifiés tels que l'édition critique, est donc un préalable nécessaire. Une telle entente ne constitue nullement un appauvrissement des possibilités offertes par TEI; bien au contraire, elle suppose d'identifier très précisément des besoins partagés et de se concentrer d'abord sur leur résolution logicielle. Placer ainsi au centre de la réflexion, non pas l'encodage en tant que tel, mais son exploitation, permet de résoudre cette tension révélée par Martin Mueller entre *encoding* et *decoding*. La définition de ces schémas partagés doit s'accompagner systématiquement d'outils de traitements adaptés à la prise en charge des motifs d'encodage définis. Diple témoigne de cette démarche, en associant systématiquement à ses schémas d'édition critique des outils de conversion pour l'écran, le papier ou les traitements.

Ces schémas sont une proposition que de nouveaux cas éditoriaux conduiront à réévaluer et à modifier. Mais cette rationalisation des pratiques d'encodage offre à l'usage un gain de temps considérable – en capitalisant les solutions d'encodage, on s'évite de «réinventer la roue» à chaque nouveau projet et on dispose de code éprouvé, utile à leur prise en charge – et cela permet de se concentrer sur la spécificité de chaque nouveau corpus.

Outre un gain de temps évident et la valorisation facilitée des projets TEI, cette démarche peut fédérer une partie de la communauté autour d'un projet partagé. En offrant un bénéfice immédiat en contrepartie de l'effort d'encodage, elle peut contribuer à attirer de nouveaux contributeurs TEI, à augmenter ainsi la masse des corpus disponibles et ouvrir la voie à l'exploitation croisée de très vastes corpus.

Codifica, pubblicazione e interrogazione sul web di *corpora* diplomatici per mezzo di strumenti *open source*

FRANCESCA CAPOCHIANI, CHIARA LEONI,
ROBERTO ROSSELLI DEL TURCO

Premessa

L'uso del Web come piattaforma preferenziale per la pubblicazione di documenti scientifici di ogni tipo riguarda anche le discipline archivistiche e diplomatiche: sono sempre più frequenti i progetti che intendono divulgare i corpora documentali, a volte di dimensioni non trascurabili, per mezzo di questo strumento. Tra i percorsi possibili inizia a riscuotere un crescente successo la codifica di testi diplomatici con linguaggio di markup XML: rispetto a soluzioni proprietarie, che spesso presentano problemi di costi, conservazione e migrazione dei dati, la creazione di corpora codificati risulta più debole per quanto riguarda la visualizzazione e l'accessibilità (interrogazione, ricerca) dei dati, in quanto la marcatura dei testi rappresenta soltanto un primo, sia pure essenziale, passo in vista di una loro fruizione sul web.

Questo articolo si propone di mostrare come, grazie all'uso di software *open source*, il singolo studioso o un piccolo team di ricercatori possa digitalizzare un corpus di documenti usando il formato TEI (<http://www.tei-c.org/>), pubblicarlo sul web e inserire nell'interfaccia un motore di ricerca come eXist (<http://exist-db.org/>) o XTF (<http://xtf.cdlib.org/>) per effettuare ricerche complesse. Descriveremo quindi in dettaglio tre diverse fasi per la creazione e pubblicazione di documenti diplomatici: la codifica dei testi, la visualizzazione e la ricerca.

1. La codifica

1.1 La TEI

La *Text Encoding Initiative* (TEI) è un'associazione internazionale nata nel 1987 con l'obiettivo di creare uno standard di codifica per la digitalizzazione dei testi (in particolare di tipo umanistico-letterario) indipendente da specifiche applicazioni software, in modo da permettere lo scambio di documenti tra piattaforme informatiche differenti.

Dopo due versioni preliminari degli schemi di codifica e della relativa documentazione, nel maggio del 1994 viene pubblicata la prima versione ufficiale (TEI P3) basata sul linguaggio SGML. Nel gennaio del 1999 è stato costituito il *TEI Consortium*, un'organizzazione internazionale senza scopo di lucro con il fine di mantenere, sviluppare e promuovere lo standard TEI. Il Consorzio ha pubblicato la versione P4 nel giugno 2002 introducendo il pieno supporto a XML, scelta che ha portato nuova energia e sviluppo al progetto TEI. L'ultima versione, la P5, è del novembre 2007 e ha introdotto importanti novità in molte aree[1].

Gli schema di codifica TEI XML sono modulari, estensibili e personalizzabili, corredati da una dettagliata documentazione[2] e disponibili sotto una licenza *open source*. La possibilità di personalizzare gli schemi di codifica, infatti, è una caratteristica fondamentale in quanto permette sia la modifica dell'esistente per motivi specifici, sia l'estensione (nuovi elementi e attributi) in modo da poterli usare in ambiti di cui la TEI ancora non si è occupata.

Oggi gli schemi di codifica TEI sono riconosciuti a livello internazionale come uno strumento di fondamentale importanza come standard per la codifica dei testi e per la loro conservazione a lungo termine. Il successo della TEI ha aperto la strada a una migliore conservazione e diffusione del patrimonio culturale che, grazie alla digitalizzazione e al web, potrà essere disponibile per tutti, non solo per gli accademici.

1.2 I moduli TEI utili per la diplomatica

La TEI non dispone, ancora, di elementi specifici per la codifica di documenti di natura diplomatica e archivistica, ma grazie alla modularità dei suoi schemi è possibile creare una buona struttura di partenza per la codifica di questo tipo di documenti[3].

---

[1] Sono di particolare interesse per i nostri scopi le innovazioni introdotte per quanto riguarda la codifica dei caratteri, la descrizione di manoscritti e il collegamento testo-immagine.

[2] TEI CONSORTIUM, TEI P5: Guidelines for Electronic Text Encoding and Interchange (2007). <http://www.tei-c.org/Guidelines/P5/>.

[3] Gli schemi TEI non sono l'unico linguaggio XML che è possibile impiegare nel campo dell'archivistica e della diplomatica: al contrario, uno standard come l'Encoded Archival Description (EAD) è molto diffuso e utilizzato, si tratta tuttavia di uno schema di codifica che riguarda i metadati relativi ai documenti catalogati, mentre gli schemi TEI, pur comprendendo una sezione riservata ai metadati (l'elemento <tei Header>), sono finalizzati alla trascrizione dei documenti stessi; nulla vieta, in ogni

Oltre ai moduli base necessari per tutti i documenti TEI XML (*tei, core, header, textstructure*), i moduli utili per la creazione di un corpus di documenti diplomatici sono:

- *corpus:* grazie all'elemento radice *<teiCorpus>* permette di inserire i testi che compongono il corpus in altrettanti elementi *<TEI>*;
- *msdescription:* offre elementi (come *<msDesc>*) che possono essere utilizzati per registrare informazioni dettagliate su un manoscritto;
- *namesdates:* può essere usato per codificare nomi e date in maniera più dettagliata di quanto sia possibile con i soli elementi messi a disposizione dal modulo *core*;
- *textcrit* per includere la codifica dell'apparato critico di un testo;
- *transcr* per la trascrizione di risorse primarie, come manoscritti o altre fonti primarie;
- *figures* per includere nella codifica non solo testo, ma anche immagini, tabelle e formule matematiche;
- *gaiji* per la codifica di caratteri o glifi non standard.

La possibilità di personalizzare gli schemi di codifica è un aspetto fondamentale di tutto il *framework* TEI: il metodo più semplice per creare il proprio schema di codifica personalizzato è usare l'applicazione web Roma[4], ma se necessario è possibile modificare direttamente un documento di tipo ODD[5].

1.3 Il modulo *transcr* e <facsimile>

Nella codifica dei manoscritti la visualizzazione delle immagini non è una caratteristica indispensabile, soprattutto se lo scopo principale è quello di fare delle ricerche testuali, ma in alcuni casi potrebbe essere utile includere le scansioni, ad esempio per la conservazione e protezione di documenti rari o per la visualizzazione di parti danneggiate o difficilmente leggibili, che potrebbero addirittura essere integrate con un restauro virtuale.

Come accennato in precedenza, la versione P5 delle norme TEI apporta numerosi miglioramenti, soprattutto per quanto riguarda la codifica di trascrizioni ed edizioni diplomatiche di manoscritti, permettendo di includere

---

caso, che EAD e TEI possano convivere, ad esempio nel caso che le capacità descrittive dei metadati TEI vengano reputate insufficienti. Per un'introduzione a EAD e al più recente EAC (Encoded Archival Context) si veda A. C. THURMAN, Metadata Standards for Archival Control: An Introduction to EAD and EAC, in: Cataloging & Classification Quarterly 40,3–4 (2005) p. 183–212.

[4] Il sito ufficiale è <http://www.tei-c.org/Roma/>.

[5] Acronimo per "One Document Does it all", un linguaggio di programmazione "literate" per la creazione di schemi XML.

anche le immagini frutto di un'eventuale scansione. Includendo il modulo *transcr* all'interno di uno schema di codifica TEI, infatti, è possibile creare, oltre a una normale edizione ipertestuale, un facsimile digitale (edizione composta dalle sole immagini del documento) o un'edizione digitale basata su immagini (edizione diplomatica affiancata dalle immagini del manoscritto) grazie ai nuovi elementi e attributi introdotti.

L'elemento *<facsimile>* contiene un facsimile digitale di una qualsiasi fonte scritta, composto dalle immagini digitali della fonte stessa. Questo elemento è di tipo strutturale e si trova allo stesso livello gerarchico dell'elemento *<text>*, quindi oltre a sostituirlo può anche affiancarlo, pertanto è possibile creare un documento TEI in maniera flessibile, combinando gli elementi desiderati: un *<teiHeader>* e un *<text>* per una edizione solo testuale; un *<teiHeader>* e un *<facsimile>* per creare un facsimile digitale con le sole immagini del documento; un *<teiHeader>*, un *<facsimile>* e un *<text>* per creare un'edizione digitale che comprenda sia il testo e le immagini, e la possibilità di collegarli tra loro.

Questo modulo, infatti, mette a disposizione un attributo globale *@facs*, che può essere inserito in qualsiasi tipo di elemento testuale per collegare il suo contenuto a una immagine. Tuttavia per creare collegamenti più complessi tra testo e immagine è necessario utilizzare altri due elementi introdotti nel modulo *transcr*: *<surface>* e *<zone>*. Quando si deve annotare solo una parte di un'immagine, come una riga o una singola parola, è indispensabile ricorrere all'utilizzo di questi elementi perché permettono di definire delle aree all'interno delle immagini e di creare collegamenti diretti fra il testo trascritto e le immagini. L'elemento *<surface>* definisce l'area di scrittura di un'immagine, o l'intera immagine, come un'area rettangolare e il collegamento testo-immagine viene creato inserendo all'interno di *<surface>* uno o più elementi *<graphic>* contenenti il link all'immagine. L'elemento *<zone>* definisce una qualsiasi area d'interesse, sempre di forma rettangolare, all'interno dello stesso piano cartesiano di un elemento *<surface>*. Recentemente (aprile 2010) è stato aggiunto un attributo *@points* per questi due elementi per definire aree non rettangolari e superare così questo limite.

Dopo aver compreso l'utilizzo di questi elementi creare il reale collegamento tra testo e immagine è piuttosto semplice: prima di tutto è necessario assegnare a ogni elemento che compone il documento un id univoco usando l'attributo *@xml:id*; quindi inserire negli elementi testuali l'attributo *@facs* con il valore dell'id dell'immagine corrispondente al testo, mentre nelle immagini l'attributo *@start* con il valore dell'id dell'elemento testuale che è contenuto nell'immagine.

Figura 1 – L'utilizzo degli elementi <surface> e <zone> su un manoscritto.

1.4 Strumenti *open source* per la gestione d'immagini e testi

La parte più laboriosa in questo tipo di codifica è l'inserimento delle coordinate come valori dei vari attributi: per farlo possiamo utilizzare dei comuni programmi di grafica oppure affidarci ad alcuni strumenti specifici.

Uno di questi è lo **UVic IMT**[6] (Image Markup Tool), sviluppato da Martin Holmes presso la University of Victoria (California): questo strumento per-

---

[6] The UVic Image Markup Tool Project: <http://www.tapor.uvic.ca/~mholmes/image_markup/>.

mette all'utente di definire aree rettangolari e annotarle con l'ausilio di un'interfaccia grafica intuitiva e di facile utilizzo. Non sono necessarie conoscenze approfondite di XML o degli schemi di codifica TEI, infatti i dati del progetto vengono salvati automaticamente in un documento XML già conforme allo standard TEI P5.

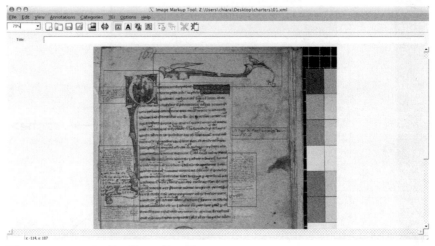

Figura 2 – Esempio di utilizzo di IMT.

In un qualsiasi momento è possibile creare dal file XML una versione HTML, utile per la visualizzazione in un navigatore web; oltre a generare la pagina HTML, il programma si occupa del codice Javascript necessario per collegare testo e immagini.

Nonostante la sua efficacia, questo strumento presenta alcune limitazioni: può lavorare solo su un'immagine alla volta, rendendo meno agevole quindi l'annotazione o la trascrizione di un intero manoscritto; il file deve essere integrato successivamente con la trascrizione del testo, per cui è necessario l'utilizzo di un editor XML.

Un altro strumento simile è **Tile**[7], sviluppato dal *Maryland Institute for Technologies in the Humanities* per creare e modificare edizioni basate su immagini. Contiene uno strumento per annotare le immagini e un riconoscitore semi-automatico che annota le aree di testo all'interno di un'immagine; può essere usato direttamente sul web oppure essere scaricato per una installazione locale.

---

[7] URL del sito web ufficiale: <http://mith.umd.edu/tile/>.

Figura 3 – Il Text Image Linking Environment.

Presenta i seguenti strumenti e funzionalità:
- *Image Markup Tool*. Permette di annotare parti di un'immagine disegnando rettangoli, poligoni e ellissi, di applicare etichette alle selezioni e creare manualmente i collegamenti tra le sezioni di un'immagine e le righe di testo trascritto;
- *Importing and exporting tools*. Permette di importare dati di TEI P5 o JSON direttamente in TILE e di creare uno script per importare da vari formati XML; permette, inoltre, di esportare i propri dati, come TEI o JSON, o di usare degli script per salvarli come file XML, HTML o txt. Possono essere aggiunti altri strumenti di importazione ed esportazione, attraverso l'utilizzo di plugin;
- *Semi-automated line recognizer*. Un riconoscitore semi-automatico, implementato in Javascript, che annota le immagini individuando le singole righe su di esse e che seleziona le parti di un'immagine basandosi su quelle righe;
- *Plugin architecture*. La particolare struttura a plugin di TILE permette all'utente di creare plugin che possono modificare l'interfaccia, filtrare e processare i dati o connettere altri strumenti.

Un ultimo esempio è **TextGridLab**[8], uno strumento che fa parte di un ampio progetto di ricerca tedesco, il TextGrid, che mira alla creazione di un am-

---

[8] TextGrid – Virtual Research Environment for the Humanities: <http://www.textgrid.de/en/startseite.html>.

biente di ricerca virtuale per la modifica, l'annotazione, l'analisi e la pubblicazione collaborativa di testi; il Text Grid Laboratory è l'interfaccia che permette di accedere agli strumenti e ai servizi di questo ambiente virtuale attraverso un software intuitivo.

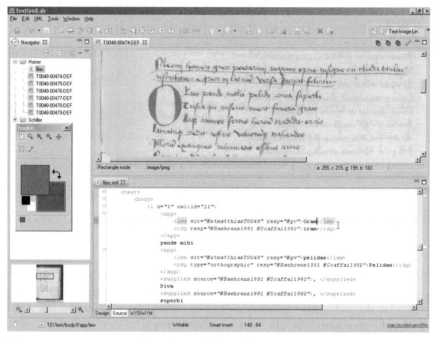

Figura 4 – Un esempio di utilizzo del tool di annotazione delle immagini di TextGridLab.

Questo software presenta una serie di strumenti utili alla gestione dei documenti: un editor XML in cui gli utenti possono scegliere tra una visuale più tecnica con tag e attributi e una visuale più semplice che mostra chiaramente la struttura del file; un *Text-Image-Link Editor* per creare i collegamenti tra una sezione di un'immagine e un testo, simile a IMT; uno strumento di ricerca all'interno di diversi dizionari presenti nell'ambiente virtuale di TextGrid; *DigiLib*[9], uno strumento web per visualizzare le immagini che permette di creare una galleria con la possibilità di fare zoom, di ridimensionare e di annotare; il *Workflow Tool* per l'elaborazione semi-automatica dei dati; il *Lemmatizer* per la lemmatizzazione automatica delle parole; COSMAS II (Corpus Search, Management and Analysis System), uno strumento per effettuare ricerche nei database di corpora tedeschi che permette, inoltre, di fare ricerche personalizzate in testi e corpora basati su TextGrid; LEXUS (Lan-

---

[9] Per maggiori informazioni: <http://digilib.berlios.de/>.

guage Archiving Technology), uno strumento di creazione, analisi e visualizzazione del lessico di un testo.

1.5 Progetti basati su corpora XML

Sono molti i progetti basati su linguaggio XML: alcuni di questi si affidano a schemi di codifica creati appositamente, come il *Codice Diplomatico della Lombardia Medievale*[10], avviato dall'Università di Pavia nel 2000, o il *Documents of Early English Data Set*[11], avviato dalla University of Toronto nel 1975.

Ma la progressiva diffusione e il costante miglioramento degli schemi di codifica TEI rendono sempre meno conveniente questa scelta: fra i progetti basati su TEI possiamo citare le *Editions en ligne de l'École des chartes*[12], *Chartae Burgundiae Medii Aevi*[13], *Digital Monumenta Germaniae Historica*[14] e *Anglo-Saxon Charters*[15].

1.6 La CEI

Ciascuno dei progetti sopra menzionati ha individuato una propria via, basata sugli schemi TEI XML, per la codifica diplomatica, ma il risultato è una certa frammentazione e, soprattutto, la mancanza di strumenti specifici condivisi per marcare questo tipo di documenti. Per risolvere questo problema una rappresentanza di studiosi impegnati in questo ambito si è riunita nell'aprile del 2004 a Monaco per cercare di far confluire esperienze e idee in un unico progetto, ampliando gli schemi di codifica TEI in modo da creare uno standard di codifica per i documenti di natura diplomatica e archivistica: nasce così un gruppo di lavoro chiamato *Charters Encoding Initiative*.

1.7 Elementi CEI utili alla codifica di *charters*

Per raggiungere i propri obiettivi la CEI cerca di soddisfare le esigenze di tutte le discipline coinvolte nello studio di questo tipo di documenti, come l'archivistica, la diplomatica e la biblioteconomia. Ognuna di queste aree di ricerca ha le sue necessità di codifica, ma è anche possibile trovare molti ele-

---

[10] CDLM: <http://cdlm.unipv.it/>.
[11] DEEDS: <http://deeds.library.utoronto.ca/>.
[12] ELEC: <http://elec.enc.sorbonne.fr/>.
[13] Sito ufficiale <http://www.artehis-cbma.eu/>.
[14] Consultabile all'indirizzo <http://www.dmgh.de/>.
[15] Sito web <http://www.ascluster.org/>.

menti in comune. Il punto di partenza sono gli schemi di codifica TEI, affiancati da nuovi elementi e attributi specifici.

Prima di tutto è fondamentale che ogni documento sia definito come unità base, al cui interno si possano trovare i metadati (*<chDesc>*) e il testo (*<tenor>*) vero e proprio. L'elemento radice di una codifica CEI è *<cei>* e può contenere il *<teiHeader>* e un singolo testo (*<text>*) oppure un *<group>* di testi.

1.7.1 I metadati

I metadati sono necessari nella codifica e sono racchiusi nell'elemento *<chDesc>* (prima chiamato *<regestum>*) che appunto è una descrizione della "carta". Per una descrizione più dettagliata è necessario utilizzare gli elementi che *<chDesc>* può contenere:

- **: un riassunto dell'atto e altri elementi che specificano la persona a cui è intitolato l'atto (*<issuer>*), il luogo in cui è stato scritto (*<placeName>*), la persona a cui è indirizzato (*<recipient>*) e la persona che fisicamente lo deve ricevere, se differente dal *<recipient>* (*<addressee>*);
- *<issuePlace>*: il nome del luogo dove è stato emesso l'atto;
- *<issueDate>*: la data di emissione dell'atto, scritta in qualsiasi formato (può essere usato anche l'elemento *<date>* che usato come figlio diretto dell'elemento *<chDesc>* si riferisce proprio alla data di emissione dell'atto);
- *<issued>*: un contenitore per la data (*<date>*) e il luogo (*<placeName>*) dell'emissione del documento;
- *<witList>* contiene una lista di tutti i testimoni (a loro volta inseriti negli elementi *<witness>*) che troviamo nell'apparato critico dentro gli elementi *<wit>*;
- *<diplomaticAnalisys>*: un'analisi diplomatica del documento, la critica formale della forma e del contenuto, contiene riferimenti ad altre edizioni o a studi sul documento, inseriti in elementi specifici (*<prints>*, *<regesta>*, *<facsimiles>* e *<studies>*);
- *<class>* utilizzato per una classificazione formale o testuale del documento, ad esempio *writ, preceptum*, mandato, *Bulle, oblatio, transsumptum*, etc.;
- *<datatio>* serve ad inserire il documento nel suo contesto storico, attraverso l'annotazione di formule tipiche per la datazione.

Può essere inserita anche una completa descrizione fisica del documento con l'elemento *<physicalDesc>* (utilizzabile all'interno dell'elemento *<witness>*), che riprende la maggior parte degli elementi da *<physDesc>*[16] (possiamo notare delle modifiche nel nome di alcuni elementi) del modulo *msdescription* degli schemi di codifica TEI P5. Gli elementi che troviamo solo nella codifica CEI sono:

---

[16] La descrizione del modulo e dell'elemento può essere letta nelle *Guidelines* della TEI P5 al link <http://www.tei-c.org/release/doc/tei-p5-doc/en/html/MS.html#msph>.

⅄ *<handList>* contiene una serie di elementi, elencando i diversi scribi o stili di scrittura, inseriti negli elementi *<hand>*;

⅄ *<authDesc>* descrive il tipo di autenticazione utilizzato per il documento;

⅄ *<rubrum>* contiene una classificazione del documento;

⅄ *<scribe>* identifica (con il nome o con un'abbreviazione) lo scriba della "carta".

1.7.2 Il testo

Una caratteristica peculiare degli atti è la loro struttura linguistica: nelle cancellerie e negli studi legali, infatti, esistevano delle parti di discorso predefinite e formalizzate in formule che spesso erano uguali per gli stessi tipi di documento. Risulta dunque fondamentale annotare in maniera esatta queste parti del discorso.

Il testo del documento, inserito all'interno dell'elemento *<tenor>*, è suddiviso in 3 sezioni principali (che danno anche il nome agli elementi che le contengono):

⅄ *<protocol>*: la parte iniziale formale del documento;

⅄ *<context>* annota quella parte del documento che dal CID (Commission Internationale de Diplomatique[17]) viene descritta come il testo vero e proprio che si rapporta direttamente all'atto giuridico messo per scritto;

⅄ *<eschatocol>*: la parte finale del documento contenente alcune frasi stereotipate.

L'elemento *<tenor>* può contenere molti elementi strutturali per il testo che sono ripresi esattamente dagli schemi di codifica TEI; gli elementi che sono stati introdotti appositamente per la codifica di questi documenti sono: *<nota>*, *<pict>* (per le parti illustrate nel documento, come Cristogrammi, croci prefisse a sottoscrizioni, simboli, etc. ...), *<elongata>* (per annotare le lettere allungate rispetto alle altre, utilizzate da alcune cancellerie nella scrittura), *<notariusSign>* (per annotare il simbolo notarile), *<notariusSub>* (contiene la sottoscrizione di un notaio) e *<datatio>*.

Andando ancora più a fondo nell'analisi diplomatica delle "carte", il testo principale può essere ulteriormente analizzato e suddiviso; quindi all'interno di *<context>* possiamo trovare elementi che prendono il nome dalle parti di discorso che contengono:

⅄ *<publicatio>*: una formula per la quale ciò che segue è portato alla conoscenza di tutti;

⅄ *<arenga>*: il preambolo, quella parte di discorso che giustifica in maniera generale il testo con considerazioni giuridiche, religiose, morali o semplicemente di convenienza;

---

[17] Si veda il sito ufficiale <http://cidipl.org/>.

➤ <*petitio*>: la richiesta motivata per cui è stato scritto il documento e per il quale deve essere presa una decisione;

➤ <*dispositio*>: la parte fondamentale del documento dove l'autore manifesta la sua volontà, fa nascere l'atto giuridico e ne determina la sua natura;

➤ <*sanctio*>: le clausole penali inserite nell'atto per assicurarne l'esecuzione;

➤ <*corroboratio*>: in questa clausola sono annunciati i segni di validazione dell'atto, cioè quelli che sono stati apposti per donargli validità;

➤ <*testes*>: la lista dei nomi dei testimoni che costatano l'esistenza dell'atto e danno il loro consenso.[18]

1.8 Progetti che usano CEI

Tra i progetti basati sugli schemi di codifica CEI citiamo *MGH Constitutiones et acta publica imperatorum et regorum 1357–1378*[19], una parte del progetto *Monumenta Germaniae Historica*; una lista di immagini di "carte" di re europei prima del 1200[20], codificate da Irmgard Fees e Peter Worm, con la possibilità di esportarle in CEI; MOM-CA[21], l'archivio collaborativo di Monasterium.net[22] che utilizza gli standard preliminari della CEI.

1.9 Sviluppi futuri

La mancanza di uno schema di codifica specifico per la diplomatica e l'archivistica ha stimolato la ricerca di possibili soluzioni al problema, i progetti citati sopra ne sono un esempio. Fortunatamente gli schemi di codifica TEI sono molto flessibili e modulabili, in quest'ottica persino gli schemi CEI rappresentano una personalizzazione assai sofisticata e complessa. Possiamo concludere che la creazione della CEI è solo il primo passo, anche se fondamentale, verso uno standard per la codifica di documenti di questo tipo: la soluzione ottimale è una vera e propria integrazione degli elementi CEI all'interno degli schemi di codifica TEI, in modo da avere un unico standard XML per la codifica di documenti che permetta di digitalizzare anche documenti importanti dal punto di vista storico, diplomatico e archivistico, molto complessi nella loro struttura e quindi nella loro annotazione.

Una delle possibilità più interessanti è creare un SIG (Special Interest Group) per creare un modulo specifico per la diplomatica all'interno della TEI, dando così la possibilità agli studiosi interessati di condividere idee e necessità per i loro progetti direttamente con gli editor degli schemi di codi-

---

[18] Tutte le definizioni sono prese da M. M. C. Ortí, Vocabulaire international de la diplomatique (1997).

[19] Consultabili al sito <http://telota.bbaw.de/constitutiones/>.

[20] Si possono trovare al link <http://www.hgw-online.net/abbildungsverzeichnis/>.

[21] Sito ufficiale <http://www.mom-wiki.uni-koeln.de/>.

[22] Maggiori informazioni al sito <http://www.monasterium.net/>.

fica. Ad esempio esiste già un SIG per la codifica di manoscritti[23], con l'obiettivo di creare un modulo specifico per la Critica Genetica[24], che contiene, comunque, elementi interessanti anche dal punto di vista diplomatico.

2. La visualizzazione

Se alcune iniziative relative alla pubblicazione di documenti XML (in particolare TEI XML) sul Web si sono fermate prima di raggiungere un punto di sviluppo soddisfacente[25], altre vengono avviate e succedono alle prime, a riprova di una necessità fondamentale per chi si occupa di codifica di testi[26]. Tuttavia non esiste ancora una soluzione matura per soddisfare tale necessità: il software esistente è ancora troppo giovane, o limitato, o entrambe le cose. In questa seconda sezione vi presenteremo un programma di visualizzazione che, per quanto nato in ambito diverso (navigazione di edizioni digitali basate su immagini), si presta benissimo a gestire un corpus di documenti diplomatici.

2.1 Il progetto EVT

Il progetto EVT (acronimo per *Edition Visualization Technology*), nato nell'ambito del progetto *Vercelli Book Digitale*[27] e attualmente sviluppato presso l'Università degli Studi di Pisa, ha come obiettivo la realizzazione di un software di visualizzazione di edizioni digitali basate su immagini, in modo da permettere la consultazione online dei contenuti del manoscritto.

Il software si presenta come un set di strumenti flessibile e personalizzabile sviluppato per consentire agli utenti di visualizzare, leggere e confrontare le edizioni in un ambiente elettronico. La sua disponibilità online e la facilità d'uso, anche per utenti con competenze informatiche di medio o basso livello, permettono di raggiungere il grande pubblico. Il software implementato consente di accedere ai contenuti testuali e alle riproduzioni fotografiche in facsimile del manoscritto originale fornendo, in aggiunta, una serie di funzionalità supplementari: strumenti per la manipolazione delle immagini (zoom, applicazione di filtri alle immagini), per il confronto testuale (edizione diplomatica, ed. critica, traduzioni) e per la ricerca nei testi.

---

[23] Visualizzabile all'indirizzo: <http://www.tei-c.org/SIG/Manuscripts/>.

[24] È possibile trovare le linee guida di questo modulo al link <http://www.tei-c.org/SIG/Manuscripts/genetic.html>.

[25] Si veda ad esempio il progetto TEIViewer (<http://teiviewer.org/>), purtroppo abbandonato.

[26] Molto promettente, anche in considerazione dello stretto rapporto con gli editor TEI, il progetto TEI Boilerplate (<http://dcl.slis.indiana.edu/teibp/>).

[27] Si veda il sito <http://vbd.humnet.unipi.it/>.

Per quanto non sviluppato specificamente per la visualizzazione di testi diplomatici, EVT è uno strumento più che adeguato per tale scopo, sia come strumento per la visualizzazione di un corpus di documenti in TEI XML, sia perché consente di visualizzare e studiare le immagini dei manoscritti strettamente connessi con i documenti del corpus.

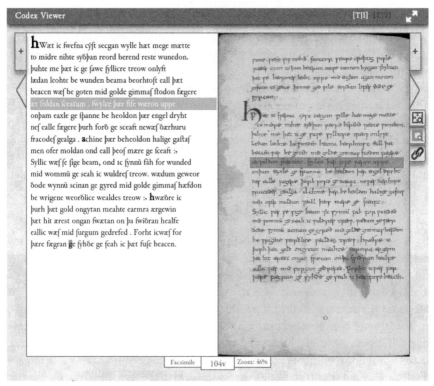

Figura 5 – La modalità di visualizzazione immagine-testo (UI provvisoria).

2.2 Funzionalità di EVT

Le funzioni attualmente implementate si basano sui principi fondamentali della disciplina Human Computer Interaction (HCI) e tengono conto di numerosi aspetti: da quelli strettamente collegati ai criteri di programmazione al comportamento degli utenti. Caratteristiche indispensabili sono una buona funzionalità ipertestuale, la definizione di strumenti di manipolazione delle immagini e la funzionalità di ricerca avanzata, aspetto che tratteremo con maggior dettaglio nel corso dell'articolo[28]. In futuro, infatti, EVT verrà inte-

---

[28] Si veda la terza sezione dell'articolo.

grato con il motore di ricerca XML eXist-Db in modo da consentire ricerche semplici e complesse sui testi che compongono l'edizione.

EVT presenta un layout estensibile, con capacità di nidificazione e compatibilità con widget UI dei maggiori *framework* Javascript per le interfacce GUI. Attualmente sono previste, e in parte già implementate, le seguenti funzionalità:

1. *immagini e testo presenti in frame separati*: solo immagini, solo testo, immagine e testo, immagine e immagine (recto-verso, *hotspot*, immagine del manoscritto con zoom), testo e testo (traduzione ed edizioni varie);

2. *diversi livelli di fruizione nel frame di testo*: l'utente deve poter scegliere tra un'edizione diplomatica o semi-diplomatica, o diverse modalità di visualizzazione per le caratteristiche testuali (abbreviazioni, ampliamenti, aggiunte, cancellazioni, lacune, danni, etc.);

3. *collegamento testo-immagine*: cliccando su una parola del testo dell'edizione si passa alla corrispondente area dell'immagine del manoscritto, e viceversa;

4. *zoom in / out per le immagini del manoscritto*: questo può essere attuato in diversi modi, ad esempio l'*Electronic Junius*[29] offre due lenti di ingrandimento separate, una per una superficie quadrata e l'altra per tutta la riga di testo: quest'ultima appare ingrandita in un riquadro distinto;

5. *strumenti di elaborazione delle immagini*: una serie di semplici filtri da applicare a un'immagine o a parti specifiche della stessa;

6. *salvataggio delle impostazioni*: l'utente deve essere in grado di salvare il risultato del filtro applicato in modo da replicare esattamente lo stesso processo in un momento successivo;

7. *segnalibri*: per accelerare la navigazione del testo e dell'immagine gli utenti possono collocare dei segnalibri temporanei e selezionarli in modo da accedere rapidamente al punto indicato.

8. *note di testo (sticky notes):* gli utenti dovrebbero essere in grado di prendere appunti e annotare le loro osservazioni su parti specifiche della edizione (un dettaglio in un'immagine, una parola dell'edizione diplomatica, etc.);

9. *l'uso di un righello e altri strumenti grafici per capire le dimensioni reali di un'immagine*;

10. un riquadro separato che contiene le immagini in miniatura di tutti i fogli del manoscritto in modo che l'utente possa scegliere direttamente l'immagine da aprire;

11. gli *hotspot* per presentare i dettagli più interessanti del manoscritto.

L'accesso all'applicazione avviene attraverso una semplice pagina di presentazione grafica, tutta la navigazione e gli strumenti del software invece vengono presentati tramite un'unica vista principale, così strutturata:

---

[29] Electronic Junius Manuscript: <http://omacl.org/Junius/>.

- la modalità immagine/testo è considerata la modalità di *default* dell'applicazione, quella disponibile al momento dell'avvio;
- la modalità immagine/immagine presenta due immagini affiancate, utile per edizioni che offrono versioni diverse di una stessa immagine, legate magari a qualche particolare tipo di elaborazione;
- la modalità testo/testo mostra due testi affiancati, utile per presentare edizioni diverse dello stesso testo, o la relativa traduzione.

La struttura dell'interfaccia grafica cambia a seconda delle esigenze dell'utente: tutti i pannelli utilizzati potranno essere collassati o aperti a schermo intero così che l'utente visualizza i contenuti utilizzando lo spazio che ritiene più consono alle sue esigenze.

Il software è stato progettato per un utilizzo ottimale con navigatori moderni, come Chrome o Firefox. Essendo concepito esclusivamente per la visualizzazione e ricerca di dati in formato TEI XML, EVT non comprende alcuna funzionalità di editing, pertanto è necessario affiancargli un buon editor XML per la codifica dei testi, e un software come Image Markup Tool o TextGrid per l'elaborazione delle immagini.

2.3 Aderenza agli standard e distribuzione del software

Gli standard utilizzati per la codifica dei testi sono stati XHTML 1.0, XML 1.0 e CSS 2.0 per le impostazioni grafiche delle pagine. Per quanto concerne i formati di memorizzazione delle immagini sono stati utilizzati i formati più comuni (JPEG, GIF e PNG), evitando accuratamente ogni formato proprietario. La programmazione del software fa un ricorso estensivo di Javascript, tecnologie DHTML che utilizzano lo standard W3C DOM, AJAX e la libreria jQuery. Il software e l'interfaccia grafica utilizzati nella realizzazione di EVT sono state realizzati tenendo presente le indicazioni riguardanti gli standard internazionali del W3C, i vantaggi e le disposizioni per utilizzare e creare codice *open source* e le regole di accessibilità.

Creare un software *open source* permette numerosi vantaggi: la disponibilità di accesso ai codici sorgenti; la possibilità di apportare continui miglioramenti al programma attraverso il lavoro delle comunità di sviluppatori; una garanzia di sicurezza. Un codice *open source* è garanzia di trasparenza dal momento che è costantemente sottoposto a verifica da parte di centinaia di utenti (è quindi più semplice individuare e correggere gli errori). Il futuro di un programma non è legato all'azienda che ne detiene il controllo, ma dipende dal lavoro e dal dialogo tra sviluppatori, utenti, aziende e istituzioni.

Per consentire un futuro lavoro di integrazione e riprogettazione del codice, si è deciso di commentare ogni funzionalità messa a punto, compresa la parte di codice che riguarda l'utilizzo della libreria jQuery. Il progetto è aperto alla collaborazione con altri studenti e studiosi, sarà infatti distribuito su uno dei siti che raccolgono software *open source* come Sourceforge[30].

2.4 Stato attuale e sviluppi futuri

Per la versione 1.0 del software, prevista per la fine del 2013, sono previste funzionalità "d'ampio raggio" che riteniamo indispensabili per qualunque ambiente di visualizzazione di edizioni digitali; altro requisito fondamentale è una stabilità più che buona. Tra gli obiettivi di sviluppo ricordiamo in particolare l'ampliamento degli strumenti di manipolazione delle immagini, l'integrazione con un motore di ricerca e la gestione semplificata dei documenti del corpus. Per quanto riguarda quest'ultimo punto, infatti, EVT prevede che l'utente possa caricare in maniera semplice documenti codificati secondo gli schemi di codifica TEI XML, senza un intervento diretto di programmazione. Per quanto riguarda la visualizzazione delle immagini EVT presenta già caratteristiche interessanti quali le funzionalità di *pan & scan*, lente d'ingrandimento e zoom.

Quanto all'integrazione con un motore di ricerca, EVT dovrà offrire differenti modalità di ricerca: la prima consente di cercare parole all'interno dei documenti (ricerca semplice), la seconda permette di costruire interrogazioni anche di tipo strutturale, cioè sugli elementi della marcatura, attraverso un'interfaccia grafica (ricerca avanzata).

3. La ricerca

3.1 La conservazione digitale nei database XML

Una volta che il manoscritto è stato codificato e digitalizzato in base alle norme contenute nello schema di codifica, la collezione di documenti XML risultanti costituirà di fatto un database testuale: sarà pertanto necessario definire un metodo di ricerca efficace sulla base delle caratteristiche di questo tipo di dati. Se prendiamo come modello d'esempio il ricco mark-up TEI, infatti, noteremo che esso non si presta bene ad essere usato immediatamente con qualsiasi software per database, in quanto molti di essi per funzionare al meglio hanno bisogno di una struttura essenziale e rigidamente organizzata.

Al momento i database restano ancora lo strumento principale per gestire l'informazione strutturata e quasi sicuramente manterranno questo ruolo an-

---

30 Documento disponibile all'indirizzo <http://www.opensource.org/docs/definition.php>.

cora per molto tempo, data la maggiore anzianità sul campo, la diffusione tra gli sviluppatori e la velocità delle operazioni. Per fortuna il supporto a XML è stato integrato nei software più recenti: la maggior parte dei database relazionali, infatti, si presentano come *XML-enabled*, sono quindi in grado di gestire il formato XML mappandolo con il proprio modello; negli ultimi anni, tuttavia, si è assistito alla crescente diffusione dei *native XML database* (NXD), basi di dati il cui modello interno è quello gerarchico. Un database XML nativo fornisce un elevato grado di flessibilità per quanto riguarda la struttura dei dati in esso contenuti; tali dati possono essere *document-centric* (altamente irregolari) o *data-centric* (rigidamente strutturati).

Il nucleo del problema, pertanto, risiede nella scelta della tipologia di database ai fini di un corretto utilizzo. Di seguito vengono forniti alcuni strumenti d'analisi per la definizione di un database XML atto a soddisfare le richieste di un software di visualizzazione per le edizioni digitali e, più in generale, per l'implementazione di archivi rivolti alla consultazione digitale.

3.2 Criteri per la scelta del tipo di database

Sembra lecito ritenere che l'archiviazione e l'interrogazione di un corpus annotato in un database XML sia una procedura semplice. In realtà non è così. Vi sono diversi aspetti che devono essere considerati prima di scegliere come memorizzare un corpus in un database XML. Ad esempio: quali strutture deve fornire un database per essere adatto per la memorizzazione e l'interrogazione? Le attuali basi di dati XML offrono queste strutture, e, se non le offrono, possono essere aggiunte?

Sembra questo il caso per gli *XML enabled database* (Oracle DB, MS SQL Server), diffusi a partire dagli anni Novanta: essi hanno sempre mantenuto integra la propria architettura estendendola con funzionalità necessarie alla gestione di documenti XML, ma facendo sempre ricorso a estensioni per il trasferimento di dati tra documenti XML e strutture di dati propri. Questa limitazione è stata superata dai "neonati" modelli *native XML database*, i quali memorizzano le informazioni provenienti da dati non strutturati. Entrambe queste categorie di database da tempo si confrontano come Davide e Golia[31] in diversi scenari di sviluppo. Come nella Bibbia, le sorti della battaglia sembrano ormai segnate: infatti ci sono numerose buone ragioni per utilizzare un *native XML database*.

La prima è ricorrere ad essi quando i dati sono semi-strutturati; difatti se i database *XML enabled* sono tipicamente relazionali e *object-oriented*, quelli

---

[31] Si veda A. SERNA/J. K. GERRIKAGOITIA, David & Goliath: A Comparison Of XML-Enabled And Native XML Data Management Techniques, in: XML Journal (2005), <http://xml.sys-con.com/node/104980>.

nativi basano il proprio modello dei dati su XML, un vantaggio che influenza notevolmente i tempi di risposta di una query effettuata sul calcolatore. Una seconda ragione è la velocità di *retrieval* dei dati: a seconda di come il database XML nativo memorizza i dati, potrebbe essere capace di recuperare i dati più velocemente di un database relazionale permettendo il *retrieving* dei documenti senza la necessità di ricorrere a *join* logici eseguiti dai database relazionali.

La gestione della ricerca nel campo delle edizioni digitali sembra quindi trovare una soluzione appropriata grazie ai *native XML database*, i cui risultati, sebbene non siano ancora estremamente diffusi per motivi commerciali[32], sono ormai largamente noti.

3.3 Database XML Nativi: il panorama internazionale

In una prospettiva d'ampio raggio, il database ideale ai fini di un progetto di ricerca (archiviazione o costruzione di un software di visualizzazione) deve essere *open source*, ben documentato, aggiornato, *TEI-based* e con una gestione *document centric*. Nel mondo del software libero i database più utilizzati che garantiscono buoni standard di accessibilità, usabilità e compatibilità con gli schemi TEI sono elencati qui di seguito (Tabella 1).

	Native Database Solutions	Database usage
Commercial	eXcelon XIS	10 %
	Tamino	70 %
	TEXTML	30 %
	GoXML DB	35 %
open source	Philologic	22 %
	BaseX	51 %
	Berkeley	63 %
	Xaira	72 %
	XTF	78 %
	eXist-DB	80 %

Tabella 1 – Selezione di database XML proprietari e open source.

Esiste una grande varietà di sistemi in differenti stadi di sviluppo e con differenti gradi di maturità. Come si può evincere dalla tabella, basata sull'analisi dei progetti attivi riportati sul sito della TEI (<http://www.tei-c.org/Activi-

---

[32] I database più diffusi restano, per il momento, quelli relazionali, si veda l'articolo di U. WESTERMANN e W. KLAS, An Analysis of XML Database Solutions for the Management, in: ACM Computing Surveys 35 (2003) p. 331–373.

ties/Projects/>), XTF[33] ed eXist-db[34] sono i prodotti più utilizzati; seguono i database Berkeley[35] e BaseX[36], impiegati come valida alternativa a eXist-db; quanto a Xaira[37], invece, è l'evoluzione di SARA, database utilizzato, tra l'altro, dal *British National Corpus*[38]. Stranamente Philologic[39] sembra in assoluto il database meno adottato in questo settore di ricerca, forse per i suoi limiti operativi (nasce per gestire documenti in TEI P4 Lite).

Tra i database XML nativi *open source* molto interessante è il caso di eXist-db, che può vantare una comunità di sviluppatori e utenti estremamente dinamica. Essendo un database XML nativo la struttura delle informazioni è estremamente diversa da quella tipica dei DBMS relazionali, basata sulla triangolazione [schema-record-tabelle]: eXist-db non gestisce i dati come tabelle, ma come collezioni di dati, in maniera simile al modello di un *file system* dove le *collections* corrispondono agli schemi e tabelle relazionali, le *resources* sono paragonabili ai record relazionali e il *service* è un sistema che fornisce l'accesso a tutte le funzionalità avanzate del DBMS.

eXist-db supporta molti standard Web 2.0: WebDav, Javascript, Ajax e XHTML. Quando si scarica il software, la pagina di *index* è la stessa del sito ufficiale, ma si lavora in localhost. eXist-db inoltre gestisce la manipolazione dei documenti memorizzati tramite XQuery e può essere integrato in architetture software di ampio raggio.

Quanto ad Apache Xindice, che non rientra nel campione di ricerca effettuato, è un *model-based* scritto interamente in Java – quindi deve essere ospitato da una Java Virtual Machine – nato come proseguimento di un progetto denominato dbXML Core[40]. Va comunque segnalato per la buona flessibilità riguardo l'organizzazione delle collezioni di documenti: ogni collezione, eccetto quella principale, può contenere delle sotto-collezioni, ovvero documenti XML e XMLObjects, una struttura, ancora una volta, che ricalca quella di un *file system*.

L'elenco complessivo delle tecnologie e delle specifiche relative a questa categoria di database *open source* ne include molte di più di quelle citate fin

---

[33] The eXtensible Text Framework (*XTF*): <http://xtf.cdlib.org/>.

[34] Questo progetto fornisce un'eccellente documentazione reperibile a questo indirizzo: <http://exist-db.org/exist/apps/doc/documentation.xml/> e numerosi esempi di applicazioni a questa URL: http://exist-db.org/exist/apps/demo/index.html/.

[35] Berkeley-db: <http://www.oracle.com/technetwork/database/database-technologies/berkeleydb/overview/index.html>.

[36] BaseX: <http://basex.org/>.

[37] Xaira-db: <http://www.oucs.ox.ac.uk/rts/xaira/>.

[38] British National Corpus: <http://www.natcorp.ox.ac.uk/>.

[39] Il database PhiloLogic, un progetto sviluppato dall'Università di Chicago, è disponibile alla URL: <http://www.lib.uchicago.edu/efts/ARTFL/philologic/>.

[40] Per la consultazione del progetto si veda: https://lists.sourceforge.net/lists/listinfo/dbxml-core-announce/>.

ora[41]. Da questa ricerca è possibile ricavare una tendenza d'utilizzo: si passa da casi di grande diffusione (eXist-db) a tecnologie abbastanza rare per quanto riguarda l'implementazione concreta (BaseX).

3.4 Integrazione della ricerca nell'interfaccia Web

Le tecnologie più adottate per la creazione dell'interfaccia web di ricerca vanno dal semplice XHTML all'uso di Javascript con tecniche AJAX: l'obiettivo principale nell'implementazione di tale interfaccia è quello di rendere la ricerca fruibile da tutti pur mantenendo la potenza e l'espressività di linguaggi di interrogazione complessi. In questo senso il database nativo XTF permette di implementare un'interfaccia di ricerca e di visualizzazione flessibile, seppur con qualche limitazione.

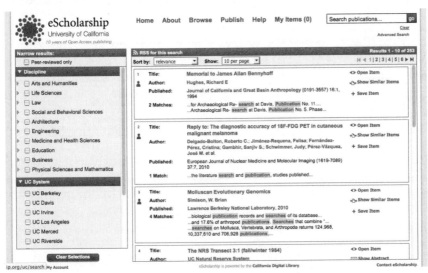

Figura 6 – Risultato di una ricerca avanzata nel portale *eScholarship*.

Un esempio significativo è la modalità di ricerca avanzata "search and display" del progetto *eScholarship*[42], sviluppato dall'Università della California. L'utente non ha bisogno di effettuare il login e può subito scegliere tra due alternative di ricerca *full-text*: un modulo di *simple query* e un modulo per l'*advanced query*, quest'ultima implementata attraverso la scelta di filtri e preferenze varie (fig. 6). Nonostante il notevole livello di dettaglio della ricerca, la limitazione che questo sistema presenta è la mancata possibilità d'u-

---

[41] Per una lista di prodotti XML-DB si consulti <http://www.rpbourret.com/xml>.
[42] Web site URL: <http://www.escholarship.org/>.

tilizzo delle espressioni regolari, che renderebbero molto più accurati e dinamici i risultati della ricerca.

Il progetto ARTFL[43] (*Project for American and French Research on the Tresaury of the French Language*), a cura del Centre National de la Recherche Scientifique e dell'Università di Chicago, attivo dal 1982, risponde a questa esigenza implementando un'interfaccia di ricerca estremamente articolata (fig. 7). Sono disponibili vari formati di visualizzazione che richiamano i contenuti inseriti nel database (Philologic): informazioni bibliografiche, il numero di pagina per ogni occorrenza, il riordino dei risultati sullo schermo per data, il nome dell'autore e le parole chiave.

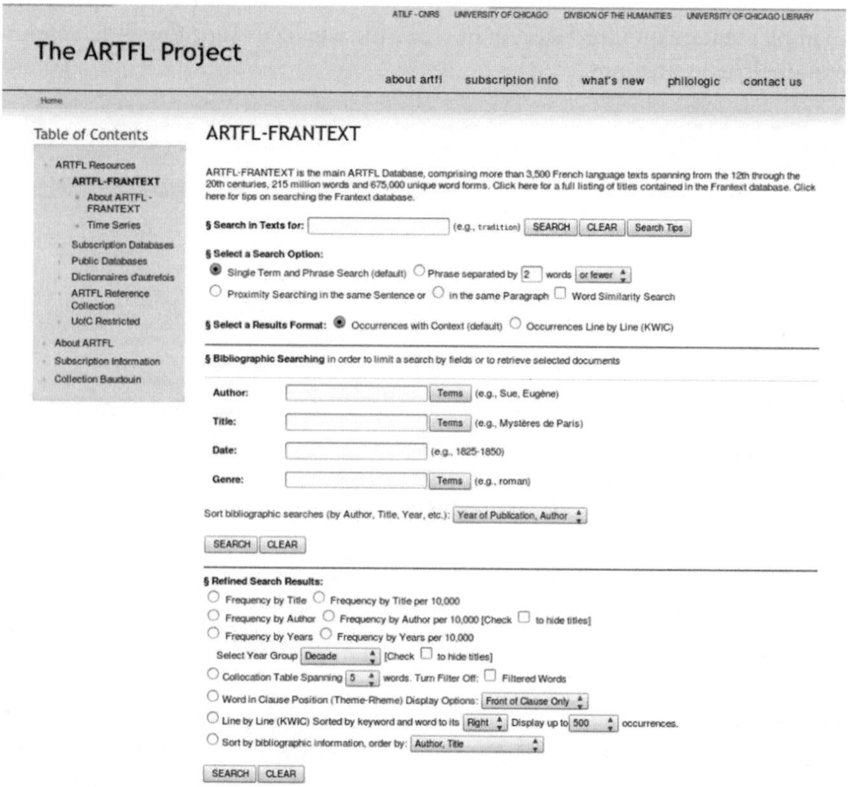

Figura 7 – Esempio di Advanced Query nel progetto *ARTFL*

Il livello di presentazione con XTF è maggiormente personalizzabile tramite XSLT, come si può evincere dalla consultazione del *Mark Twain Project*[44]. Il progetto MTP è un'applicazione Web che utilizza gli standard TEI le cui fun-

---

[43] The ARTFL Project: <http://artfl-project.uchicago.edu/>.
[44] Mark Twain Project: <http://www.marktwainproject.org/>.

zionalità principali riguardano la ricerca di un oggetto, la navigazione per gli oggetti, l'accesso, la manipolazione del apparato testuale di un oggetto e la creazione di liste personalizzate, il tutto tramite un *parser query*.

3.5 XTF e eXist-db: progetti TEI-based a confronto

È sorprendente notare la quantità di progetti reperibili sul Web che utilizzano il database XTF per molti servizi che richiedono un alto livello di implementazione. Oltre al sopra citato progetto *eScholarship* sono catalogabili come progetti TEI-based: *The Chemistry of Isaac Newton*[45], *The Online Archive of California* (OAC)[46], *Calisphere*[47], *The California Digital Library*[48]. Altre implementazioni altamente personalizzate sono *The OAPEN Library*[49], *The Indiana University Board of Trustees Minutes*[50] e *The Encyclopedia of Chicago*[51], una collaborazione tra la Chicago Historical Society e la Biblioteca Newberry.

In generale questi progetti sono accomunati dalla visualizzazione e ricerca di immagini e testi attraverso una robusta interfaccia di ricerca. I progetti basati su eXist-db, invece, presentano un panorama ben diverso e molto più articolato. Oltre a garantire un'implementazione più specifica nella sezione di ricerca, ogni progetto emerge e si contraddistingue per una maggior interattività. Ad esempio, *The interactive album of Medieval Paleography*[52] è una raccolta di esercizi interattivi riguardanti la trascrizione di manoscritti medievali, per un totale di 27 esercizi (22 in latino medievale, 5 in francese antico) creati con IMT, i file XML-TEI così generati vengono poi caricati sul database eXist-db. Gli esercizi sono *computer mark assisted* (CMA): è possibile selezionare una riga, scrivere la parola nella casella, e se la risposta al quesito è corretta la casella diventa verde, altrimenti il risultato sarà restituito con il colore rosso; un'interessante esperienza applicabile anche al campo dell'*e-learning*.

Altri progetti presi in esame che ricorrono all'utilizzo di eXist-db, quali *Diary of Robert Graves*[53], *The Opera Liber*[54], *The Anglo-Norman Dictio-*

---

[45] Disponibile all'indirizzo: <http://webapp1.dlib.indiana.edu/newton/>.

[46] Si veda: <http://www.oac.cdlib.org/>.

[47] Consultabile a: <http://www.calisphere.universityofcalifornia.edu/>.

[48] Web site URL: <http://www.cdlib.org/>.

[49] Open Access Publishing in European Networks: <http://www.oapen.org/>.

[50] Disponibile sul sito <http://webapp1.dlib.indiana.edu/iubot/about.do>.

[51] Disponibile sul sito <http://encyclopedia.chicagohistory.org/>.

[52] Interactive Album of Mediaeval Palaeography: <http://ciham.ish-lyon.cnrs.fr/paleographie/index.php?l=en>.

[53] Progetto attivo su: <http://graves.uvic.ca/graves/site/index.xml>.

[54] The Opera Liber Project: <http://193.204.255.27/operaliber/index.php?page=/operaLiber/home>.

nary[55], *Le mariage sous l'Ancien Régime*[56], *Early Americans Digital Archives*[57], *Corpus Pieter Willems*[58], *Sermones.net*[59], *Colonial Despatches*[60], *Vienna-Oxford International Corpus of English*[61], *Digital Quaker Collection*[62], si contraddistinguono rispetto al modello XTF in quanto:

- supportano i seguenti protocolli di rete: XML-RPC, XML:DB API, SOAP, WebDAV, Atom Publishing Protocol.
- fanno uso di numerosi linguaggi di ricerca: XQuery, XQuery Update facility, XSLT, XPath, XUpdate.
- interagiscono con l'interfaccia di ricerca: XML:DB, RESTful Web API attraverso il protocollo HTTP, DOM e SAX.

3.6 I database XML nativi come sistemi online di *information retrieval*

L'esame dei documenti immagazzinati nei database XML nativi si basa su due funzionalità: *ranking* e *browsing*. Il primo è la presentazione dei risultati in ordine di rilevanza, nozione basilare nei sistemi di information retrieval[63], il secondo è il raggruppamento dei documenti in classi di somiglianza che permette all'utente di sfogliare i risultati della ricerca in ordine logico. L'ordine di rilevanza di un documento si definisce a partire da quattro categorie riassunti nella tabella seguente:

	Documenti rilevanti (R)	Documenti non rilevanti (NR)
Documenti recuperati (r)	rR	rNR
Documenti non recuperati (nr)	nrR	nrNR

Tabella 2 – Rapporto tra ordini di rilevanza.

Esso viene effettuato attraverso quattro parametri di valutazione: il grado di precisione dei documenti rilevanti, detto *Precisione* (rR / (rR + rNR)), il cor-

---

[55] Website URL: <http://www.anglo-norman.net/>.

[56] Le mariage sous l'Ancien Régime: <http://mariage.uvic.ca/>.

[57] Disponibile sul sito del MITH: <http://mith.umd.edu/eada/intro.php/>.

[58] Un'edizione di ricerca olandese: <http://ctb.kantl.be/corpora/CPWNL/>.

[59] Sermones.net: éditions électroniques de sermons latins médiévaux: <http://www.sermones.net/content/jacques-de-voragine/>.

[60] Colonial Despatches: the colonial despatches of Vancouver Island and British Columbia 1846–1871. <http://bcgenesis.uvic.ca/>.

[61] Vienna-Oxford International Corpus of English: a corpus of transcripts of spoken ELF interactions in TEI format: <http://voice.univie.ac.at/>.

[62] Earlham School of Religion – Digital Quaker Collection: <http://esr.earlham.edu/dqc/>.

[63] Si veda K. SPARCK JONES/P. WILLETT, Readings in Information Retrieval (1997).

rispettivo opposto, detto *Recall (rR / (rR+nrR))* che definisce la capacità di rigettare documenti non rilevanti. Il *Silenzio* (nrR / (rR + nrR)) è invece la percentuale di documenti rilevanti non recuperati sul totale dei documenti rilevanti presenti nell'insieme, mentre il *Rumore* (rNR / (rR + rNR)) è la percentuale di documenti non rilevanti sul totale dei documenti recuperati. Oltre a queste misure di efficacia, non va dimenticato che l'elemento principale per la valutazione della rilevanza sono gli utenti in relazione ai limiti posti all'interrogazione .

L'architettura di XTF presenta uno dei più articolati sistemi di *retrieval* delle informazioni tra i modelli *open source*. Esso è composto di servlet Java e strumenti che consentono agli utenti di eseguire la ricerca *web-based* e recupero dei documenti elettronici. Il recupero dei documenti inizia con una query *web-based* effettuata da un utente: il servlet *crossQuery* controlla la query e produce un elenco di documenti corrispondenti per la visualizzazione in un browser web. La selezione di un documento ottenuto dalla pagina dei risultati della ricerca invoca il *servlet dynaXML*, che recupera e formatta il documento effettivo per la visualizzazione in un browser web. Lo strumento *textIndexer* visualizzato nella parte inferiore come risultato di ricerca viene utilizzato per aggiornare l'indice di ricerca del documento ogni volta che i documenti vengono aggiunti, rimossi o aggiornati.

Un altro caso interessante è l'architettura di Xaira: come impostazione di default, Xaira indicizza tutti gli elementi codificati, dal file XML caricato viene creato un indice (il quale verrà utilizzato come database) che dovrà essere rigenerato a ogni modifica del file (altrimenti i dati non saranno aggiornati).

3.7 La produzione dei metadati

I metadati agevolano l'identificazione delle risorse elettroniche e rappresentano un punto di ancoraggio essenziale per i database. Si distinguono metadati *nativi*, ovvero quelli che si trovano nel documento al momento della sua creazione, e metadati *aggiuntivi*, i quali vengono creati da terzi per incrementare il valore della risorsa. Precisi schemi di metadati descrittivi sono stati standardizzati nel settore delle Digital Libraries (si ricordano i *records* della Library of Congress in *Machine-Readable Cataloging* – MARC[64] – o progetti annotati tramite Dublin Core[65]) e nell'archivistica (EAD)[66]. Quanto ai metadati riguardanti manoscritti digitalizzati, essi vengono elaborati in misura maggiore attraverso il sistema di codifica TEI P5 per consentire ricerche complete e libere

---

[64] Un'ampia documentazione è disponibile online: B. Furrie, Understanding MARC (2009), <http://www.loc.gov/marc/umb/>.

[65] Dublin Core Metadata Initiative: <http://www.ietf.org/rfc/rfc2413.txt>.

[66] Si veda la nota n. 3.

da parte dell'utente ed essere consultabili con un browser. Ancora una volta, quindi, la scelta di un buon database rimane il requisito basilare per il lavoro di ricerca. Questi dati infatti dovranno essere conservati in un sistema di gestione dei documenti basato su un database, e non su una semplice struttura di file.

Un utilizzo estensivo dei metadati strutturati secondo lo standard TEI P5 è presente nel Progetto *eCodices*[67] (fig. 8) dove ciascun manoscritto digitalizzato è corredato della più recente descrizione scientifica disponibile, riproposta in maniera tale da rispecchiare il più possibile la descrizione a stampa. I file possono inoltre essere visualizzati nel formato XML conforme a TEI-P5 e in formato PDF nel caso sia presente una versione a stampa e si disponga delle autorizzazioni necessarie.

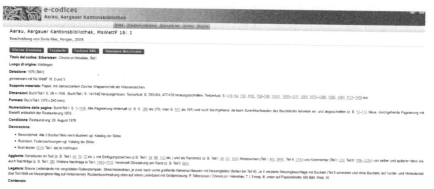

Figura 8 – Elenco dei metadati estratti da un manoscritto digitalizzato sul portale *e-codices*.

Altrettanto interessante è il sistema di gestione dei metadati del progetto BibIt[68] , basato sul framework METS[69]. A partire dai metadati archiviati nei *record* METS i metadati vengono generati mediante procedure automatiche in formato TEI Header e inseriti nei file TEI XML dei testi. Per ciascun testo il servizio online BibIt fornisce sia i metadati descrittivi, sia i puntatori alle diverse modalità di accesso diretto al testo; tali modalità consistono nella possibilità di scaricare il file XML originale e nella visualizzare on-line della pagina in formato HTML generato dinamicamente.

[67] *E-codices*: <http://www.e-codices.unifr.ch/it/>.
[68] *La Biblioteca Italiana*: <http://www.bibliotecaitaliana.it/>.
[69] METS: <http://www.loc.gov/standards/mets/>.

3.8 La gestione di una banca dati testuale

Un progetto autorevole sviluppato presso la sede universitaria dell'*Oxford University Computing Services* (OUCS) è il sistema di archiviazione *Oxford Text Archive*[70], il quale ha consacrato la TEI Lite come comune punto di partenza per l'archiviazione di testi elettronici. L'archivio è costituito da 1300 testi elettronici, risorse che provengono da centri di ricerca di tutto il mondo. Anche l'*Electronic Text Center*[71] (ETC) possiede un archivio i cui testi sono tutti memorizzati in formato TEI SGML, garantendo un alto livello scientifico della base di dati. Tra i grandi archivi anglosassoni ricordiamo anche lo *Women Writers Project*[72], sviluppato dalla Brown University[73], il quale raccoglie testi della letteratura femminile dal 1300 all'epoca Vittoriana, anch'essi in formato TEI.

Ma come vengono gestiti questi archivi? Esistono dei punti in comune? Nel corso dell'articolo abbiamo visto che esiste una notevole differenziazione in riferimento alla tipologia di database utilizzato. Tuttavia i progetti sopra elencati presentano dei parametri comuni per la gestione dell'architettura dell'archivio. Difatti il sistema deve essere facilmente accessibile per la comunità scientifica, fornire ai ricercatori uno strumento facile ed efficace da usare, essere implementato su un database più versatile possibile.

Prendiamo adesso come "caso di studio" il progetto "*Colonial Despatches – The colonial despatches of Vancouver Island and British Columbia 1846–1871*[74]" analizzando a fondo ciò che è stato fatto ai fini della gestione dell'archivio.

Il sito si basa sul database XML eXist che contiene tutti i documenti della collezione codificati in TEI XML (P5). L'applicazione è basata su software *open source* e può essere eseguita su Linux, OSX, Windows o qualsiasi altro sistema operativo con una macchina virtuale Java. I documenti vengono recuperati tramite XQuery inviate al motore di ricerca che restituisce i risultati sotto forma di frammenti o documenti XML. Questi risultati vengono poi elaborati utilizzando XSLT per creare pagine web XHTML/CSS che vengono, in ultima istanza, inviate al browser. Questo diagramma può essere riassunto nella struttura visibile sotto (fig. 9).

---

[70] Oxford University Computing Services: <http://ota.ahds.ac.uk/>.
[71] University of Virginia Library: <http://www2.lib.virginia.edu/etext/index.html/>.
[72] The Brown University, *Women Writers Project*: <http://www.wwp.brown.edu/>.
[73] The Brown University: <http://www.brown.edu/>.
[74] Website URL: <http://bcgenesis.uvic.ca/>.

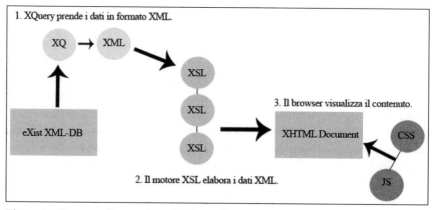

Figura 9 – Processo di estrazione dei dati nel progetto *Colonial Despatches*.

Il lavoro sui database XML prosegue ininterrottamente aggiungendo ogni volta nuovi tasselli e diventando una tecnologia *cutting-edge*. Tuttavia lo sforzo di garantire l'interoperabilità, l'indipendenza da una particolare piatta-forma, la condivisione dei dati e lo sviluppo degli standard aperti, dovranno continuare ad essere le linee guida che, ormai più di dieci anni fa, spinsero verso la nascita del linguaggio di marcatura XML.

Conclusioni

Lo standard XML è nato con la grande ambizione di essere il nuovo linguag-gio del Web: malgrado questo obiettivo non sia stato raggiunto, XML e le numerose tecnologie ad esso collegate si sono comunque guadagnati una po-sizione centrale per quanto riguarda la codifica dei dati testuali, la loro elabo-razione, la pubblicazione sul Web e la ricerca dei contenuti. XML è alla base di tutte le fasi relative alla creazione di un corpus di documenti che abbiamo fin qui descritto (codifica dei testi, visualizzazione, ricerca) ed è soprattutto fondamentale per il funzionamento di EVT, il software che integra visualizza-zione e ricerca. Anche software potenti come eXist e XTF sono strettamente collegati al Web, inteso come output naturale dei risultati delle ricerche, in-fatti possono creare in maniera dinamica pagine HTML per visualizzare i ri-sultati delle query.

L'integrazione di dati in formato XML in un *framework* complesso come questi potenti database, tuttavia, non è operazione tra le più agevoli: poter disporre gratuitamente di tecnologie così sofisticate è una vittoria di Pirro se le competenze richieste per implementare un sito completo sono tali da im-porre la spesa di risorse non trascurabili, affidando la gestione del corpus di documenti e la creazione del sito a tecnici specializzati. Con lo sviluppo di

EVT intendiamo fornire uno strumento efficace, ma per quanto possibile *user-friendly*, alla portata di studiosi e ricercatori che abbiano le competenze minime per installarlo e utilizzarlo.

BIBLIOGRAFIA / WEBLIOGRAFIA

Codifica basata su XML

Charters Encoding Initiative. <http://www.cei.lmu.de/>.

TEI CONSORTIUM, TEI P5: Guidelines for Electronic Text Encoding and Interchange, (2007). [Versione 2.3.0. Ultimo aggiornamento il 17 gennaio 2013] <http://www.tei-c.org/Guidelines/P5/>.

XML recommendation sul sito del consorzio W3C: <http://www.w3c.org/TR/REC-xml/>.

G. VOGELER, Towards a standard of encoding medieval charters with XML, in: Literary and Linguistic Computing (2005) p. 269–280. <http://his.library.nenu.edu.cn/upload/soft/haopdf/83/TowardsaStandardofEncodingMedievalCharterswithXML.pdf>.

Documentazione su EVT

F. FIORENTINI, EVT: Edition Visualization Technology; Progettazione e sviluppo un software per la consultazione di edizioni digitali. <http://etd.adm.unipi.it/theses/available/etd-09132008-133733/>.

Progetto Vercelli Book Digitale: <http://islp.di.unipi.it/bifrost/vbd/>.

R. ROSSELLI DEL TURCO, La digitalizzazione di testi letterari di area germanica: problemi e proposte, in: Digital philology and medieval texts. Atti del Seminario internazionale, Arezzo, 19–21 Gennaio 2006, a cura di A. CIULA/F. STELLA (2007) p. 187–213.

R. ROSSELLI DEL TURCO, After the editing is done: designing a Graphic User Interface for Digital Editions, in: Digital Medievalist Journal 7 (2011). <http://digitalmedievalist.org/journal/7/rosselliDelTurco/>.

Database e ricerca: enabled XML database e database XML nativi

B. BOS, XML representation of a relational database (1997). <http://www.w3.org/XML/RDB.html>.

R. BOURRET, Consulting, writing, and research in XML and databases (2005) URL: <http://www.rpbourret.com/xml/XMLAndDatabases.htm>.

R. BOURRET, XML Database Products (2010). <http://www.rpbourret.com/xml/XMLDatabaseProds.htm>.

M. GRAVES, Designing XML Databases (2002).

A. SERNA, J. K. GERRIKAGOITIA, David & Goliath: A Comparison Of XML-Enabled And Native XML Data Management Techniques, in: XML Journal (2005). <http://xml.sys-con.com/node/104980>.

W. SHELDON, Getting started with eXist and Xquery, in: LTER Databits (2009). <http://databits.lternet.edu/node/52>.

TEI Projects: <http://www.tei-c.org/Activities/Projects/>.

W3C. XQuery and XPath Full Text 1.0. W3C candidate recommendation (May 2008). <http://www.w3.org/TR/2008/CR-xpath-full-text-10-20080516/>.

W3C. Extensible Markup Language (XML) 1.0 (Fourth Edition). W3C recommendation (September 2006). <http://www.w3.org/TR/2006/REC-xml-20060816/>.

W3C. XML Path Language (XPath) Version 2.0. W3C recommendation (November 2007). <http://www.w3.org/TR/2007/REC-xpath20-20070123/>.

W3C. XQuery 1.0: An XML Query Language. W3C recommendation (January 2007). <http://www.w3.org/TR/2007/REC-xquery-20070123/>.

U. WESTERMANN/W. KLAS, An Analysis of XML Database Solutions for the Management, in: ACM Computing Surveys 35 (2003) p. 331–373.

XML:DB Initiative. XML:DB Database API. Working draft, XML:DB Initiative, (September 2001). <http://xmldb-org.sourceforge.net/xapi/xapi-draft.html>.

Open Source Native XML-DB Software

XTF Docs: <http://xtf.wiki.sourceforge.net/>.

Xaira: <http://www.oucs.ox.ac.uk/rts/xaira/>.

Xindice: <http://xml.apache.org/xindice/>.

eXist-DB: <http://exist-db.org/>.

K. STAKEN, Introduction to Native XML Databases: <http://www.xml.com/lpt/a/2001/10/31/nativexmldb.html>.

eXist – TEIWiki <http://wiki.tei-c.org/index.php/EXist>.

Berkeley DBXML website: <http://www.oracle.com/technetwork/database/database-technologies/berkeleydb/overview/index.html>.

XML: DB Initiative website: <http://xmldb-org.sourceforge.net/>.

Dalla carta al bit
Note metodologiche sull'edizione digitale
di un cartulario medievale

SERENA FALLETTA

Il progetto di edizione digitale del codice Vat. Lat. 3880

Il passaggio dalla carta al bit caratteristico dell'ultimo decennio ha imposto alla comunità degli storici uno sforzo interpretativo sulle potenzialità degli strumenti tecnologici e una verifica critica sullo stato delle discipline coinvolte nella transizione. La convergenza al digitale ha infatti investito sostanzialmente tutti i campi in cui tradizionalmente si muove la pratica storiografica: l'archiviazione e la conservazione dei dati, l'ormai classica analisi quantitativa sulle fonti seriali e non ultima, la diffusione dei risultati della ricerca su internet[1]. Il rapporto tra storici e oggetti della riflessione storica è stato dunque profondamente modificato dall'avvento delle tecnologie informatiche, che hanno offerto vie di accesso a risorse utili al lavoro ma anche una strumentazione adeguata per individuare – con precisione maggiore rispetto a quella consentita dalle metodologie tradizionali – le risorse che costituiscono la base della ricerca e se possibile, attraverso un passaggio ricco di implicazioni epistemologiche, di averne edizioni fruibili anche a distanza. Per il medievista si sono aperte nuove possibilità, sia ecdotiche che ermeneutiche, tutte legate a specifiche risorse digitali e tutte in grado di sviluppare innovativi metodi di indagine, applicabili all'esegesi e all'edizione delle fonti, all'apertura multidisciplinare e al vaglio critico dei risultati, inducendo profonde mutazioni di linguaggio e prassi.

Da queste considerazioni è nato il progetto di edizione digitale del codice Vat. Lat. 3880, avviato nell'ambito del Dottorato in Storia dell'Europa Medi-

---

[1] Questi tre approcci sono stati sintetizzati da Peppino Ortoleva nel suo ormai classico P. Ortoleva, Presi nella rete? Circolazione del sapere storico e tecnologie informatiche, in: Storia & Computer. Alla ricerca del passato con l'informatica, a cura di S. Soldani/L. Tomassini (1996) p. 64–82.

terranea, promosso dall'Università degli Studi di Palermo e conclusosi nell'-
aprile del 2009[2]. La ricerca ha preso le mosse dalla volontà di sperimentare
una pratica storiografica mediata e accompagnata dalle tecnologie digitali, in
cui a mutare non fossero esclusivamente le modalità della pubblicazione, ma
lo stesso punto d'origine della ricerca: la fonte storica come risorsa in grado di
determinare suggestioni, produrre stimoli ed interessi, creare riflessioni.

Lo scopo dichiarato del progetto di edizione digitale è stato quello di mettere a disposizione degli studiosi il testo di una fonte inedita, in una forma
aperta alla costruzione e alla revisione delle ipotesi interpretative. I tre temi su
cui si è sviluppata la costruzione informatica sono stati quindi: la pubblicazione in rete del codice Vat. Lat. 3880, l'elaborazione di una codifica informatica per la conservazione e la gestione dei dati, l'elaborazione di un modello
storiografico che utilizzasse materiali digitali non solo nella fase della ricerca,
ma anche in quella della scrittura, permettendone l'accesso al lettore in varia
misura e con differenti modalità. La proposta dell'edizione digitale di un manoscritto medievale è stata insomma costruita perseguendo l'obiettivo di non
approdare alla semplice trascrizione testuale in formato elettronico, ma ricreare un laboratorio virtuale all'interno del quale trovassero spazio tutta una
gamma di strumenti d'indagine (regesti, inventari, saggi, bibliografie, motore
di ricerca etc.) in grado di arricchire i testi e favorirne nuovi modi di fruizione.

Ai fini della sperimentazione si è scelta una tipologia di fonti manoscritte –
quella dei cartulari monastici – recentemente rivalutata dalla critica storica.
Per la Sicilia, uno dei testi più rilevanti in tal senso è il *Liber Privilegiorum
Sanctae Montis Regalis Ecclesiae,* registro contenente i documenti storici più
significativi dell'arcidiocesi di Monreale, progettato dall'arcivescovo Arnaldo
di Rassach nel XIV secolo per tutelare e rivendicare i diritti della sua Chiesa[3].
Secondo la tradizione riferita da Carlo Alberto Garufi nel suo *Catalogo illustrato del Tabulario di Santa Maria Nuova in Monreale*, il testo fu approntato
in quattro copie di cui la più autorevole, per chiarezza e completezza, è il testimone attualmente conservato presso la Biblioteca Apostolica Vaticana con
la segnatura Vat. Lat. 3880[4].

---

[2] S. FALLETTA, L'edizione digitale del Liber Privilegiorum Sanctae Montis Regalis
Ecclesiae, 2007–2009, <http://vatlat3880.altervista.org/>.

[3] Sull'arcivescovo Arnaldo di Rassach v. M. DEL GIUDICE, Descrizione del tempio e
monasterio di S. Maria Nuova di Monreale. Vite dei suoi Arcivescovi, Abbati e Signori
col Sommario dei Privilegi, della detta Santa Chiesa di Giovan Luigi Lello. Ristampata
ad opera del padre Don Michele Del Giudice priore cassinese (1702) p. 29.

[4] Cfr. C. A. GARUFI, Catalogo illustrato del Tabulario di Santa Maria Nuova in
Monreale (1902). L'esame paleografico e codicologico condotti sul codice Vat. Lat.
3880 hanno mostrato come il manoscritto sia stato invece composto successivamente,
quasi a ridosso del XVI secolo, come confermerebbe anche un dato interno sfuggito

Si tratta di un codice cartaceo in buono stato di conservazione e dalla fattura molto semplice[5], scritto da unica mano su due colonne in una gotica indulgente alla semigotica di piccolo formato, omogenea e identica nel modulo e nel tratteggio, con iniziali calligrafiche e titoli di colore rosso. Nella sua concezione originaria il *liber* conteneva divisi *in partes quatuor*, 26 diplomi reali, 22 pontifici, 14 concessioni e donazioni di prelati e 22 altri documenti fra atti pubblici, lettere, sentenze, per un totale di 84 documenti: il testimone vaticano ne raccoglie invece 90, comprendendone 6 successivi alla morte di Arnaldo di Rassach. Molti privilegi contenuti nel *liber* sono noti alla critica attraverso pubblicazioni successive, anche se ormai datate e condotte sulle singole testimonianze fornite dal Tabulario della chiesa: da qui, l'esigenza di pubblicare l'intero cartulario, inquadrandolo all'interno dell'ambito storico e sociale di produzione, con particolare attenzione alla comunità che lo ha gestito e trasmesso.

Un pretesto valido per sperimentare soluzioni informatiche nel trattamento dei dati storici è stato poi fornito dalle stesse caratteristiche strutturali e concettuali del volume, che contiene documentazione diplomatica contraddistinta da un alto grado di connettività interna ed esterna. Fine principale del progetto è stato infatti ricreare in ambiente digitale il *corpus* documentario incluso all'interno del codice monrealese, adottando un linguaggio di codifica calibrato sulle caratteristiche dei diplomi ma anche sulle esigenze – le categorie di analisi critica – della ricerca storico-diplomatistica. In questa direzione, l'obiettivo perseguito è stato non tanto testare soluzioni inedite o mirabo-

all'attenzione degli studiosi che finora – occupandosi più o meno indirettamente del Liber Privilegiorum di Monreale – hanno citato questo testimone: l'ultimo documento in esso riportato è infatti datato 4 Dicembre 1464. Il testimone vaticano potrebbe dunque essere stato trascritto sotto le direttive dell'arcivescovo Ausias de Spuig. Delle altre tre copie, mentre una risulta dispersa, le altre due si conservano entrambe in Sicilia: il testimone XX E 8 presso la Biblioteca del Seminario Arcivescovile di Monreale, mentre la Biblioteca Regionale della Regione Siciliana custodisce il manoscritto frammentario F.M.5, che è probabilmente il testo originario voluto dal Rassach. Sul De Spuig v. L. Boglino, La Sicilia e i suoi cardinali (1884) p. 26; Del Giudice, Descrizione p. 49; C. Eubel, Hierarchia Catholica Medii Aevi sive Summorum Pontificum, S. R. E. Cardinalium, Ecclesiarum antistitum series, ab anno 1431 usque ad annum1503 perducta, et documentis Tabularii praesertim Vaticani collecta, digesta, edita (1914) p. 196.

[5] Codice di mm. 310,5×210, formato da cc. 56, con numerazione moderna eseguita ad inchiostro nero, composto da quattro fascicoli settenioni e rigato foglio per foglio a penna; le righe per pagina sono 40 da c.1r a c.17r, 42 da c.17v a c.53v. La filigrana riproduce una mano che tiene una stella, la cui lunghezza è di 80,5 mm. che, secondo le indicazioni di Gerhard Piccard, fu utilizzata a Neuenburg, in Svizzera, nel 1494, cfr. G. Piccard, Die Wasserzeichenkartei Piccard im Haupstaatsarchiv Stuttgart 17: Wasserzeichen Hand & Handschuh (1997).

lanti, bensì l'individuazione e il disvelamento delle potenzialità che le tecnologie telematiche hanno reso disponibili per migliorare la qualità della ricerca e dei suoi risultati.

Il fattore X: l'eXtensible Markup Language

In ambito storico, la questione fondamentale della rappresentazione informatica dei documenti è la salvaguardia della loro identità senza che ciò vada a discapito della possibilità di compiere elaborazioni e ricerche sui singoli segmenti che contengono informazioni e dati omogenei. Il problema in sostanza, è quello di conservare un rapporto stretto fra il dato e il contesto nel quale esso si inscrive: opzione impossibile all'interno di un database, in cui i singoli frammenti informativi sono estratti dall'ambito di appartenenza, decontestualizzati, proprio per essere più efficacemente manipolati.

L'esplorazione delle strutture informative presenti nei dati storici, il loro recupero, riordino e l'aggregazione secondo i punti di vista suggeriti dalle ipotesi di ricerca, attivando o evidenziando connessioni prima sconosciute o scarsamente evidenti ma al contempo mantenendone l'integrità sono del resto esigenze di vecchia data. Nel 1975, nel corso della *Table Ronde CNRS* organizzata dall'École Française de Rome e dall'Istituto di Storia Medievale di Pisa, Alessandro Pratesi ed Ermanno Califano – dando voce all'allora diffusa diffidenza nei confronti dell'uso del computer in analisi storiche – denunciavano infatti come risposte soddisfacenti dal trattamento informatico delle fonti documentarie medievali si sarebbero potute conseguire soltanto con la memorizzazione dei documenti *in extenso*, sottolineando come l'alternativa tra *full-text* e immissione di dati significativi in un *database* rappresentasse una scelta fondamentale tra informazione globale e diretta ed informazione preselezionata da altri, senza possibilità di un raffronto immediato con il documento originario[6].

---

[6] v. A. Pratesi, Limiti e difficoltà dell'uso dell'informatica per lo studio della forma diplomatica e giuridica dei documenti medievali, in: Informatique et Histoire Médiévale. Communications et débats de la Table Ronde CNRS, organisée par l'École française de Rome et l'Institut d'Histoire Médiévale de l'Université de Pise, Rome, 20–22 mai 1975, prés. par L. Fossier/A. Vauchez/C. Violante (1977) p. 187–190; E. Califano, Registrazione diretta e integrale dei documenti. Utilizzazione di regesti, ibid. p. 253–256, in particolare p. 254. Il concetto è stato ribadito, negli anni Novanta, da Joacquim Carvalho: "I migliori metodi per l'input dei dati forniti da fonti storiche sono quelli che preservano la struttura originaria dell'informazione; un'unica fonte dovrebbe essere registrata come un unico file; la successione dei diversi elementi di informazione nel file dovrebbe seguire fedelmente la successione con cui sono riportati nella fonte originaria", J. Carvalho, Soluzioni informatiche per microstorici, in: Quaderni Storici, ns. 78 (1991) p. 761–791, in particolare p. 777.

L'esigenza metodologica di rispettare la natura eminentemente contestuale dell'informazione contenuta nelle fonti storiche e, parallelamente, esserne in grado di valutare il contesto di produzione, senza tralasciare nessun dato utile a confermare le ipotesi di ricerca proposte, ha trovato nell'ultimo decennio una risposta nella codifica informatica dei testi attraverso i linguaggi di marcatura, che identificano le strutture e le relazioni intercorrenti tra i dati all'interno dello stesso testo codificato, arricchendolo anche di informazioni relative alle sue caratteristiche strutturali e intrinseche[7]. Attraverso un linguaggio di marcatura l'informazione è dunque scomponibile in dimensioni realmente minime: ad ogni livello, dal più elevato – l'intero documento – al minore – il paragrafo, la frase, la parola, la singola lettera – è infatti possibile riconoscere e assegnare un valore semantico. In questo senso anche il termine codice assume un significato diverso e, forse, più ampio: non solo strumento per trasferire informazioni da un sistema all'altro, da una lingua all'altra, ma complesso meccanismo che modella la (e si modella sulla) materia trattata[8].

Tra i *markup language*, la scelta è ricaduta su XML, standard di pubblico dominio indipendente da qualunque piattaforma hardware o software, da sistemi di archiviazione e visualizzazione, la cui natura standardizzata e l'ampia diffusione in progetti editoriali di stampo simile ha consentito di raccogliere e definire la struttura semantica completa del codice Vat. Lat. 3880, lasciando spazio a future specializzazioni e raffinamenti nella marcatura[9]. In tale prospettiva XML ha rappresentato un versatile intermediario per la comprensione e l'approccio ai numerosi progetti editoriali esaminati nella fase iniziale di questo studio, ma anche per il superamento dei diversi stadi redazionali del lavoro proposto e più in generale di un percorso evolutivo che ha richiesto il

---

[7] I presupposti teorici dei linguaggi di marcatura vanno rintracciati nella teoria dell'informazione di Shannon v. C. E. SHANNON/W. WEAVER, The mathematical theory of communication (1949).

[8] Cfr. G. GIGLIOZZI, Codice, testo, interpretazione, in: Studi di codifica e trattamento automatico di testi, a cura di G. GIGLIOZZI (1987) p. 65–84, in particolare p. 66.

[9] Appartenente alla famiglia dei linguaggi dichiarativi SGML e sviluppato dal W3C nel 1998 con lo scopo di proporre alla comunità accademica una codifica dichiarativa per la rappresentazione degli elementi costituenti e delle relazioni intercorrenti all'interno di un documento, XML è "a common syntax for expressive structure in data". Per la storia del linguaggio di marcatura, cfr. F. MESCHINI, Dieci anni di XML, in: Da XML all'elaborazione di conoscenza: approcci professionali e uso sociale della rete. Atti del Seminario AIDA (Roma, Centro Congressi Frentani, 30 marzo 2007), in: AIDAinformazioni 25,1–2 (2007) p. 56–70. Per le sue molteplici applicazioni v. invece S. ST. LAURENT, Monastic XML: an ascetic view of XML best practices, 2002, <http://monasticxml.org>. Per le caratteristiche e i vantaggi dell'utilizzo di XML nel trattamento di documenti storici si rimanda infine anche ad un mio recente contributo: S. FALLETTA, Linguaggi di marcatura nel trattamento informatico delle fonti storiche: l'edizione digitale del codice Vat. Lat. 3880, in: Schede Medievali 48 (2010) p. 253–271.

continuo rimaneggiamento degli elementi inizialmente concepiti. Il vantaggio di conservare tutte le informazioni selezionate in etichette XML e la sua capacità di espansione infinita degli attributi, hanno rappresentato dunque la chiave di volta di un progetto la cui vocazione è stata, sin dall'inizio, la volontà di rinnovarsi senza che questa scelta comportasse necessariamente la perdita degli obiettivi iniziali della ricerca in atto.

La codifica a scopo scientifico e interpretativo apre comunque un mondo fatto di decisioni, teoriche e operative. Ciò che si vuole codificare è ciò che si vuole conservare, ovvero ciò che si ritiene importante: "memorizzare e codificare un testo, farne un'edizione – così come in passato – significa introdurre una nostra griglia interpretativa tra le sue pieghe: rompere i legami che in esso ci appaiono naturali per disporre le sue parti (quelle parti che siamo riusciti ad individuare) in un ordine diverso"[10]. Un documento storico veicola, ovviamente, una serie di contenuti testuali, di informazioni su eventi, luoghi, persone, oggetti del mondo materiale, concetti, idee: riconoscerli, poterli ritrovare, passare dall'uno all'altro, collegarli fra loro costituisce un esperimento euristico che i linguaggi di marcatura consentono e che evidentemente fa slittare l'operazione di codifica di un testo dai suoi aspetti puramente linguistici, formali o strutturali a quelli relativi al suo contenuto informativo e ai più complessi significati di cui esso è portatore. Introdursi in un universo così complesso – almeno apparentemente – ha significato, pragmaticamente, operare delle scelte.

Oltre gli standard: un modello di codifica per le fonti storiche

Nel caso prospettato la prima decisione da prendere ha riguardato l'eventuale adozione o meno di un modello di marcatura preesistente. In effetti, nonostante l'assenza di precise linee guida per la codifica informatica di fonti storiche e il frequente impiego di scelte poco rispettose delle tradizionali formulazioni metodologiche e operative o, al contrario, eccessivamente prudenti e conservative[11], non è mancata negli ultimi anni – all'interno della comunità umanistica attenta alle tecnologie elettroniche – una spinta alla definizione di modelli e procedure condivisibili per l'edizione dei testi.

---

[10] G. Gigliozzi, Il testo e il computer. Manuale di informatica per gli studi letterari (1997) p. 209.

[11] Un esempio su tutti: gli MGH online, 2010, <http://www.dmgh.de>: pubblicazione su supporto digitale, in formato HTML ma senza caratteristiche di sofisticata elaborazione, di materiali scientificamente elaborati secondo i parametri della grande scuola tedesca.

In particolare, esistono alcune esperienze di notevole qualità che sono state quindi assunte ad autorevoli punti di riferimento[12]: tra di esse merita un richiamo – per il ruolo di riferimento assunto nell'ambito del progetto – il *Codice Diplomatico Digitale della Lombardia Medievale*, progetto che ha consorziato le università lombarde diretto da Michele Ansani e ispirato a criteri di rigore scientifico[13]. Il lavoro è stato in grado di dimostrare come la validità di un'edizione elettronica non coincida con la maggiore rapidità nelle procedure di pubblicazione o consultazione, ma piuttosto nella trasparenza dell'iter critico, la maggiore consapevolezza e responsabilità dell'editore, nonché la possibilità di contemperare molteplici livelli di accesso alla documentazione calibrati tanto sulle esigenze della ricerca quanto sulle strutture documentarie.

In relazione allo standard XML da adottare, all'epoca del progetto la TEI, oggi riconosciuta come uno strumento di fondamentale importanza al livello internazionale per la conservazione a lungo termine dei dati elettronici in vari ambiti disciplinari, non aveva ancora elaborato *guidelines* che includessero soluzioni rispondenti alle necessità sottese alla codifica di fonti storiche, di una marcatura cioè forgiata sulla semantica e le specificità storico-territoriali dei documenti[14]. Si è optato quindi per la creazione di un modello specifico, che pur introducendo elementi di interpretazione personale, è stato bilanciato dalla presenza del testo integrale e da una metodologia che ha proceduto per gradi successivi di raffinamento, passando necessariamente da uno schema di

---

[12] Tra i lavori più significativi, nonostante ormai datati, v. I. H. KROPAČ, Fontes Civitatis Ratisponensis, (1996) – 1999–2006, <http://bhgw20.kfunigraz.ac.at/>; ÉCOLE NATIONALE DES CHARTES/O. GUYOTJEANNIN, Chartes de l'abbaye de Saint-Denis (VIIᵉ–XIIIᵉ siècles), 2010–2012, <http://saint-denis.enc.sorbonne.fr/>. In ambito italiano va citato il Vercelli Book Digitale, edizione del codice 107 della Biblioteca Capitolare di Vercelli – un manoscritto di 136 carte ben conservate che contiene 23 omelie in prosa e sei poemi allitterativi anglosassoni, redatto alla fine del X secolo e portato a Vercelli nell'XI probabilmente come dono di un pellegrino – da segnalare per la molteplicità delle forme di visualizzazione e di consultazione dei materiali previsti, cfr. R. ROSSELLI DEL TURCO, Vercelli Book Digitale, 2000–2013, <http://vbd.humnet.unipi.it/>. Per una lista aggiornata di edizioni digitali di fonti storiche v. P. SAHLE, A catalog of Digital Scholarly Editions, 2008–2013, <http://www.digitale-edition.de/vlet_histo.html>.

[13] M. ANSANI, Codice Diplomatico Digitale della Lombardia Medievale, 2000–2013, <http://cdlm.unipv.it/>.

[14] A seguito di numerose operazioni di raffinamento e aggiornamento, le *P5 Guidelines* possono invece attualmente essere prese a modello e utilizzate anche in ambito storico, cfr. TEI, *Text Encoding Initiative. P5 Guidelines*, 2007–2013, < http://www. tei-c.org/Guidelines/P5/>. Anche la CEI, standard di codifica per diplomi medievali e moderni utilizzato ad esempio all'interno del progetto *Monasterium*, è diventata negli ultimi anni un ottimo modello di riferimento per la codifica di documentazione storica, cfr. Monasterium.Net, 2013 <http://www.mom-wiki.uni-koeln.de/CEI/>.

codifica iniziale a maglie larghe ad uno più dettagliato, in relazione al procedere dello studio analitico e storico-diplomatistico dei documenti.

Per elaborare il modello di codifica si è proceduto quindi allo spoglio fisico dei documenti, con lo scopo di estrapolarne non solo la struttura comune riconducibile alle caratteristiche della diplomatica medievale, ma anche di evidenziare gli elementi aggiuntivi, integrabili con gli attributi stabiliti dai canoni editoriali e in grado di approfondirne il significato[15]. Questo approccio ha contribuito in maniera determinante a fissare in partenza gli elementi descrittivi e analitici delle informazioni storiche perseguite. Il lavoro ha infatti previsto il recupero di dati di livello superiore rispetto alla tradizionale descrizione archivistico-diplomatica, riformulandone la funzione di indicatori/qualificatori del contenuto dei documenti censiti.

La codifica è stata articolata su due macro-blocchi: quello delle metainformazioni di apparato, e quello delle metainformazioni di testo, relative alla struttura e al contenuto del documento.

Le metainformazioni di apparato, poste in apertura ad ogni documento, hanno incluso la sua posizione all'interno del cartulario, l'indicazione dei documenti precedenti e successivi all'interno dell'edizione, permettendo la navigazione sequenziale al suo interno, le informazioni editoriali (data topica e cronica), il numero delle carte di riferimento nel manoscritto. Sono stati inoltre inseriti gli elementi propri dell'apparato e cioè la tradizione del testo in relazione agli originali[16] e le copie[17], le eventuali edizioni critiche, i regesti, le notizie bibliografiche. Attraverso questa sezione della marcatura sono stati dunque delineati i metadati archivistici, elementi del profilo che accompagnano ogni entità documentaria a prescindere dal supporto specifico di memorizzazione, includendo tutte le informazioni utili alla sua identificazione e interpretazione.

I marcatori che definiscono l'articolazione del discorso documentario sono stati strutturati secondo una griglia che, riflettendo in linea di massima la tradizionale analisi formale dei documenti medievali, non ha prescritto però regole di inclusione rigidamente preordinate, consentendo numerose eccezioni nel rispetto della prassi documentaria analizzata.

---

[15] "L'*horse-texte*, ciò che è fuori dal testo, è anche *dentro* il testo, si annida tra le sue pieghe: bisogna scoprirlo, e farlo parlare", ha giustamente detto Carlo Ginzburg ricordando come, nel valutare le proprie prove, gli storici dovrebbero sempre spazzolare la storia contropelo, imparando a leggere le testimonianze al di là delle intenzioni di chi le ha prodotte, cfr. C. GINZBURG, Rapporti di forza. Storia, retorica, prova (2000) p. 46.

[16] es. <ORIGIN entecons="BCRS" fondo="FM" segn="Balsamo 29" dim="mm. 850+36590">

[17] es. <COP entecons="BSEM" segn="XX.E.8">

Sono stati infatti previsti dei marcatori di struttura, attenti alla disposizione materiale del testo e alla sua articolazione logica, riconoscendone l'importanza fondamentale in documentazione di natura giuridica, emanata da cancellerie pubbliche, all'intero della quale era d'obbligo individuare una definita struttura diplomatica finalizzata a corroborarne il valore legale. Ciascuna delle articolazioni principali del documento medievale (protocollo, testo, escatocollo) ha incluso ovviamente delle sottopartizioni (tenore, sottoelementi del protocollo quali invocazione, intitolazione, inscrizione, data, *apprecatio,* formule di perpetuità e quelli relativi al testo, ovvero preambolo, narrazione, dichiarazione, disposizione, sanzione e autenticazione; dell'escatocollo sono stati marcati rote e relative legende, date, ricognizione cancelleresca, sottoscrizioni, elenco dei testimoni e *complectio* del notaio).

Relativamente alle informazioni storiche deducibili dalla documentazione esaminata, sono stati marcati: i nomi di luogo, cui sono stati assegnati alcuni attributi obbligatori (normalizzazione del nome, identificazione, tipo e subtipo, ubicazione)[18]; le persone, con attributi obbligatori (normalizzazione del nome, identificazione della persona) e facoltativi (eventuali attributi del nome, di parentela, titolo, carica, qualifica o mestiere)[19]; le istituzioni ecclesiastiche, rendendo obbligatori gli attributi di normalizzazione e identificazione dell'istituzione, subtipo (tipologia dell'istituzione) e ubicazione[20]. Infine, sono stati introdotti anche i tags <BENIMM/> per gli elenchi e le descrizioni di beni, e i tag <SCRIPT/> e <TT/>, a marcare rispettivamente il redattore del documento e gli eventuali testimoni.

Il modello di codifica proposto è stato dunque calibrato sulle specificità storiche e territoriali della documentazione, introducendo una marcatura semantica con palesi – ma palesati – elementi di interpretazione storica, nella convinzione che la possibilità offerta dall'utilizzo di XML di restituire un testo comunque integrale fosse in grado di ridurre al minimo i pericoli connessi nella dichiarata soggettività dell'operazione[21]. L'atteggiamento seguito è stato quello di adeguare via via il lavoro ai problemi nuovi che sono sorti nel

---

[18] Es. <TOP nm="Albesi, fontes" id="Sorgente Alvano" tipo="el geografico" subtipo="fonte" ub="Contrada Alvano, Monte Genuardo, Cl">fontes Albesi</TOP>.

[19] Es. <PERSONA nm="Silvester" attr="comes Marsici" id="Silvestro, conte di Marsico" tit="comes" fil="Guillelmus, comes Marsici">Silvestri comitis Marsici</PERSONA>.

[20] Es. <ECCL nm="Montis Regalis, ecclesia" id="Chiesa di S. Maria Nova di Monreale" subtipo="chiesa" ub="Comune di Monreale, Pa">Montis Regalis ecclesie</ECCL>.

[21] Per la descrizione dettagliata degli elementi e attributi progettati per la codifica e numerosi esempi di come si è operato si rimanda alla sezione del sito <http://vat-lat3880.altervista.org/index_storia_e_informatica.html>. La marcatura XML di tutti documenti editi del codice Vat. Lat. 3880 è liberamente accessibile a chiunque desideri

corso dell'analisi, predisponendo una codifica iniziale debole che si riservasse
la possibilità di intervenire sul testo, man mano che emergevano nuovi inter-
rogativi o che la documentazione studiata andava acquisendo maggiore consi-
stenza. Tali presupposti si sono rivelati efficaci ancor più nell'ambito di un
progetto di ricerca che, per definizione, non ha voluto prevedere fin dall'inizio i suoi possibili sviluppi, rimandando – anche nel modello di codifica proposto – aperto a successive ridefinizioni, alla luce di nuovi dati o di una diversa interpretazione di quelli esistenti.

Work in progress. Il *Liber Privilegiorum* on line

La codifica informatica di fonti storiche presuppone non solo il trasferimento
tecnico dal supporto cartaceo a quello elettronico ma anche, e soprattutto, la
creazione di un habitat digitale all'interno del quale non smarrire le tradizionali bussole che orientano la ricerca e garantiscono l'uso corretto dei documenti.

Nell'ottica di una ricerca finalizzata alla creazione di un laboratorio di in-
tersezione tra elementi tecnologici, storici ed espositivi innovativi, la dimensione ipertestuale è sembrata la soluzione più adatta per rendere visivamente
disponibili anche gli approfondimenti scientifici successivi che hanno guidato
il lavoro di edizione, creando contemporaneamente i presupposti per una
maggiore trasparenza della metodologia critica utilizzata e la possibilità di
ottenere molteplici livelli di accesso alla documentazione: un ipertesto come
strumento euristico in grado di integrare fonte e ricerca, superando i limiti
obbliganti di una pubblicazione cartacea attraverso blocchi testuali legati ma
privi di gerarchie, capace di stabilire connessioni inedite tra idee o dati simili
attraverso semplici collegamenti elettronici. L'output finale dell'edizione è
stato dunque concepito in una forma ipertestuale aperta, con lo scopo finale
di rappresentare l'apologia del 'montaggio' come principio conoscitivo e co-
municativo interno alla narrazione stessa della storia e delle sue fonti.

La preferenza accordata alla forma ipertestuale come canale rappresenta-
tivo è stata incoraggiata anche dalle suggestioni derivate dalle proprietà del
discorso storico, ovvero dal largo spazio in esso occupato dalla narrazione,
dall'esemplificazione, da procedimenti indiziari più che probatori e il suo
svolgimento contemporaneo su diversi piani d'indagine. Caratteristiche che,
sul piano formale, si traducono nella compresenza di numerosi livelli di let-
tura: dalla sintesi interpretativa alla minuta analisi filologica e che "sembrano

---

consultarla: per visualizzare il file sorgente basta infatti scegliere dal menu del browser
Visualizza>Sorgente pagina oppure Visualizza>*HTML* in Internet Explorer.

rendere l'idea base dell'ipertestualità particolarmente adeguata al saggio storico"[22].

La cornice ipertestuale dell'edizione digitale del *Liber* è stata dunque concepita come uno strumento euristico in grado di integrare la fonte e la ricerca condotta, superando i limiti obbliganti di una pubblicazione cartacea attraverso la messa in scena di blocchi testuali collegati elettronicamente, legati tra loro ma privi di gerarchie e funzionali a stabilire connessioni inedite tra idee o dati simili. La possibilità di incardinare i diplomi del *Liber*, attraverso semplici strumenti di collegamento, ai materiali critici prodotti, ha permesso di superare la consueta sussidiarietà del dato documentario rispetto all'analisi o alla narrazione e di valorizzare "l'interoperabilità fra testi e informazioni, che il mezzo digitale consente di mettere direttamente in relazione, al di là dell'allusione descrittiva che ha caratterizzato la tradizione"[23].

L'impiego dell'ipertestualità ha permesso infine di ricreare un dialogo effettivo tra la fonte e la sua esegesi e costruire tragitti interpretativi capaci di attraversare il racconto e le testimonianze: l'ipertesto è stato infatti costruito come un discorso storico che, seguendo il modello classico degli *Essais* di Montaigne, proponesse un itinerario mentale attraverso la fonte primaria e i saggi di corredo. La ricerca ha subito l'effetto benefico di un accrescimento esponenziale, grazie ad una periferia informativa che si è aggiunta all'edizione vera e propria, allargandone i confini e rivelandone la ricchezza: ad emergere sono stati i dintorni del testo e – ciò che sembra ancora più interessante – un orizzonte nel quale la stessa soggettività dello studioso è necessariamente arretrata, tralasciando l'interpretazione compiuta in favore di percorsi percorribili ma non necessariamente precostituiti.

Anche la possibilità di rappresentazione non lineare dei saggi e degli apparati e la parallela ricaduta sul rapporto intrattenuto dall'editore con la sua fonte, sono stati indicatori aggiuntivi di importanza nella scelta della forma ipertestuale, in particolare nell'ambito delle soluzioni pratiche da adottare per far fronte a questioni finora impostate come teoriche e metodologiche. Concretamente infatti, la scelta ipertestuale ha risolto il problema dell'ordinamento dei novanta documenti contenuti nel cartulario, che sono stati trasposti sul supporto informatico mantenendo l'autonomia del pezzo singolo, ma sono però divenuti raggiungibili da diversi punti di accesso. Realizzando

---

[22] P. Corrao, *Saggio storico, forma digitale: trasformazione o integrazione?* Abstract della relazione presentata a Medium-evo. Gli studi medievali e il mutamento digitale, I Workshop Nazionale di studi medievali e cultura digitale (Firenze, 21–22 giugno 2001).

[23] P. Corrao, *Pieno e Basso Medioevo: metodologia della ricerca e modelli interpretativi*, in: Storia dell'Europa e del Mediterraneo, diretta da A. Barbero. Dal Medioevo all'età della globalizzazione. IV: Il Medioevo (secoli V-XV), a cura di S. Carocci, 8: Popoli, poteri, dinamiche (2006) p. 361–408, in particolare p. 374.

un'edizione cartacea, si sarebbe infatti dovuta scegliere obbligatoriamente l'organizzazione della fonte – ad esempio si sarebbe dovuta mantenere la divisione originale per *partes* proposta dal manoscritto – e questa disposizione sarebbe stata l'unica possibile porta d'ingresso alla documentazione contenuta nel *Liber*. La composizione ipertestuale dei documenti ha stemperato invece a monte qualsiasi problema di ordinamento ispirato a criteri di pertinenza e provenienza, poiché l'autonomia dei singoli documenti ne ha determinato il riposizionamento virtuale in sequenze tipologiche diverse da cui accedere, a seconda delle esigenze espresse dal fruitore, al singolo documento.

Nel contempo, la prospettiva offerta dall'integrazione della fonte elettronica con altri testi, strumenti, informazioni – tutti simultaneamente disponibili su un'unica schermata – tramutando l'edizione in una metafonte, ha permesso l'annullamento delle canoniche partizioni disciplinari, fondendole in una dimensione editoriale nuova, le cui caratteristiche sono derivate dalla stessa natura ibrida e generativa della scrittura elettronica.

Ad un livello superiore, l'ipertesto ha creato infine la possibilità di realizzare le cornici in cui inquadrare le informazioni tratte dai documenti, la cui varietà concettuale si è intrecciata alla realizzazione di tragitti storici uniti dal filo conduttore dell'istituzione di appartenenza ma separabili a seconda delle esigenze della consultazione. In questo senso si sono tenute in considerazione le indicazioni di Silvio D'Arco Avalle, che ha più volte rimarcato la necessità di studiare i testi medievali senza isolarli artificialmente dal contesto caratterizzante dei codici che li conservano, recuperando il valore scientifico di tutti i tratti – anche quelli culturali – di ogni testimonianza manoscritta[24]. In questo modo ha preso vita un modello di edizione testuale in forma di *hypertext document system*, una *hyperedition* che ricalca, in qualche modo, le indicazioni già fornite da C. B. Faulhaber nel saggio *Textual criticism in the 21st Century*[25]: un meccanismo in grado di collegare tra loro i documenti o parti di documenti e di assemblare in un ambiente che funziona grazie al concorso del mezzo informatico, tutti gli ingredienti di un'edizione seriamente condotta.

---

[24] Cfr. S. D'Arco Avalle, Le procedure informatiche nelle scienze umane, in: Macchine per leggere. Tradizioni e nuove tecnologie per comprendere i testi. Atti del Convegno di studio della fondazione Ezio Franceschini e della fondazione IBM Italia (Certosa del Galluzzo, 19 novembre 1993), a cura di C. Leonardi/M. Morelli/F. Santi (1993) p. 3–6.

[25] Lo studioso ha proposto, agli inizi degli anni Novanta del Novecento, una tecnica di organizzazione di materiali testuali supportata dall'ipertesto, cfr. C. B. Faulhaber, Textual criticism in the 21st Century, in: Romance Philology 45 (1991) p. 123–148.

Tempo di bilanci

Passeggiando per le strade di Roma, può capitare di incontrare un ironico graffito che recita: "Il futuro non è più quello di una volta!". La frase, che sembra vantare antiche origini[26], ben si adatta alla prospettiva in cui va inquadrato il progetto di edizione digitale presentato: una dimensione operativa nella quale il procedimento informatico con cui lo storico mette a disposizione della comunità scientifica i propri materiali di lavoro, non si è configurato semplicemente come una strumentazione comoda e rapida per l'accesso alla documentazione analizzata, ma ha implicato una profonda ridefinizione dei modi in cui le analisi e le pratiche storiografiche possono essere condotte.

Oggi il campo della ricerca storica, profondamente investito dall'avvento delle tecnologie informatiche, sembra dover necessariamente ridiscutere il monumentale compito che ogni studioso, a diversi livelli, ha da sempre affrontato: la trascrizione del passato nel presente. Una trascrizione che implica sia la re-iscrizione e la conservazione dei contenuti centrali delle discipline storico-filologiche nei nuovi formati offerti dell'infrastruttura informatica sia l'integrazione di tecnologie e tecniche emergenti nel lavoro e nelle pratiche essenziali delle scienze umanistiche. Si tratta di doveri dialettici, che richiedono la simultanea elaborazione di nuovi paradigmi funzionali e interpretativi ma soprattutto, esigono la sperimentazione pragmatica di tecniche e programmi finalizzati a realizzare forme di elaborazione, comunicazione e diffusione della cultura più adatti agli attuali canali informativi.

Sebbene la ricerca storica sia ancora percepita come atto eminentemente solitario e saldamente legato ad una forte idea di autorialità, la Rete sta divenendo – proprio negli ultimi anni – il luogo ideale dove realizzare proficui scambi intellettuali fra studiosi di formazione e provenienze differenti in direzione di una cultura convergente e partecipativa, fermo restando il controllo critico e rigoroso dei procedimenti scientifici e il rifiuto energico della interdisciplinarietà fine a se stessa[27]. In questa direzione sembrano andare le sempre più numerose esperienze condotte sul Web nel settore umanistico, dove l'utilizzo ponderato dell'informatica si è significativamente misurato con la capacità di produrre informazione di qualità strutturata, arricchita da metadati, aggiornata e certificata, ma soprattutto in grado di configurarsi come offerta – per lo storico ma anche per qualunque utente interessato – di servizi e risorse alla ricerca. Come ha sintetizzato Franco Carlini, "che gli piaccia o

---

[26] V. Graffiti latini. Scrivere sui muri a Roma antica, a cura di L. CANALI/G. CAVALLO (2001) p. 102.

[27] V. H. JENKINS, Cultura convergente. Dove i vecchi e i nuovi media collidono (2007).

no, l'intellettuale deve imparare a usare questo mezzo, intanto come strumento di ricerca. Esso è fonte"[28].

Utilizzando metodologie informatiche resta rilevante – anzi acquisisce peso – la capacità di sintesi e comparazione propria della storia e della critica delle fonti, mentre si rinnova la capacità di disvelamento dei meccanismi materiali e delle scelte culturali e funzionali che presiedono tutti i passaggi, tecnici e non, della costruzione interpretativa. Il testo elettronico sotto forma di un archivio estensibile, rivedibile, partecipabile, offre grandi vantaggi riguardo alla completezza dei dati, pur non presentando – naturalmente – la piacevole leggibilità di un libro o la gratificante narratività dell'esposizione storica che è parte qualificante della rielaborazione storica.

In attesa che la multimedialità e gli ipertesti, il Web e le pratiche in evoluzione riconfigurino metodologie ed epistemologie, dando vita ad un'etica e ad uno stile della produzione scientifica definitivamente post-moderne e soprattutto post-gutenberghiane, in questo frattempo segnato da difficili convivenze l'atteggiamento maggiormente proficuo resta dunque quello di saggiare palmo a palmo il terreno, conquistarlo un passo alla volta, cercando una sperimentazione sostenibile e impatti rassicuranti. A fronte di un universo in cui la scrittura e il testo mutano, virando verso il digitale, il primo dovere dell'umanista sembra essere – forse – quello di riappropriarsi dei propri strumenti di produzione, di quegli arnesi che sono in grado di illuminare e al contempo scuotere il senso profondo di una indagine storica, producendo un riflesso sulle forme comunicative che colpisce al cuore i modi, gli sguardi e le metodologie del sistema di valori cui lo storico è abituato. Il risultato finale sarà un curioso andirivieni fra un nuovo, che alletta e spinge a rivisitare i saperi e le conoscenze acquisite e un vecchio – ma senz'altro sarebbe meglio dire: una tradizione – che traccia un sentiero da non perdere mai di vista, per non correre il rischio di smarrirsi.

---

[28] F. CARLINI, Lo stile del Web. Parole e immagini nella comunicazione di rete (1999) p. 169.

Progressive Editionen als multidimensionale Informationsräume

GUNTER VASOLD

Digitale Editionen werden vordergründig als alternative Publikationskanäle wahrgenommen, die eine Reihe von Einschränkungen klassischer, das heißt gedruckter Editionen aufheben. Häufig genannte Vorteile aus Sicht der Editoren sind etwa der Wegfall von durch Druckkosten auferlegten Mengenbegrenzungen, die „Multimedialität", die sich im Regelfall durch die Bereitstellung digitaler Faksimiles manifestiert, sowie die Einbettung in einen Hyperraum, die eine unmittelbarere Verlinkung mit anderen Ressourcen erlaubt. Aus Sicht der Benutzer digitaler Editionen steht wohl die Verfügbarkeit und bequeme Zugänglichkeit solcher Editionen im Vordergrund.

Die Möglichkeiten digitaler Edition gehen jedoch weit über diese Vorteile hinaus. Digitale Edition führt, wenn sie entsprechend gedacht und umgesetzt wird, zu einer Transmedialisierung, deren wesentliches Merkmal die über den Zeitpunkt der Publikation hinaus mögliche Trennung von Inhalt und Form ist, wodurch beispielsweise individuelle Sichtweisen auf Inhalte oder die Rekontextualisierung von Inhalten erleichtert werden[1]. Diese Unterscheidung zwischen definierten Modellen folgenden Daten (Repräsentationen) und davon weitgehend entkoppelten Darstellungsformen (Präsentationen) als Sichtweisen auf die Daten eröffnen Möglichkeiten, die längerfristig zu einer Neufassung zentraler editorischer Konzepte führen werden, beispielsweise zu einem veränderten Textbegriff.

Ein anderer, bisher nur wenig untersuchter Aspekt digitaler Edition liegt in der Möglichkeit diese zu dynamisieren. An Stelle einer statischen, zum Zeitpunkt ihrer Publikation erstarrten Edition könnte ein Ansatz treten, der Edition als offenen, jederzeit veränderbaren und wachsenden Informations-

---

[1] P. SAHLE, Digitale Editionsformen. Zum Umgang mit der Überlieferung unter den Bedingungen des Medienwandels, Teil 2: Befunde, Theorie und Methodik (Schriften des Instituts für Dokumentologie und Editorik 8, 2013); in komprimierter Form: DERS., Digitale Editionstechniken, in: Digitale Arbeitstechniken für die Geistes- und Kulturwissenschaften, hg. v. M. GASTEINER und P. HABER (2010), S. 231–249; DERS., Zwischen Mediengebundenheit und Transmedialisierung, in: Editio – Internationales Jahrbuch für Editionswissenschaft 24 (2010) S. 23–36.

raum versteht. Dadurch werden jedoch Konzepte und Mechanismen in Frage
gestellt, die darauf basieren, daß Editionen einen oder einige wenige verant-
wortliche Editoren haben und daß deren Arbeitsergebnisse langfristig stabil
bleiben. Dabei geht es beispielsweise um die Rolle des Editors, aber auch um
Qualitätskriterien, für die typischerweise die Person des Editors, des Heraus-
gebers und die dahinter stehende Institution als Indikatoren herangezogen
werden. Es geht aber auch um Fragen wie Zitierbarkeit, den Verlust autorita-
tiver Textfassungen oder, aus der Sicht der Editoren, um den Nachweis editorischer Tätigkeit in Hinblick auf wissenschaftliche Credits. Im folgenden sollen einige daraus entstehende zentrale Probleme herausgearbeitet und ein
möglicher Lösungsweg skizziert werden.[2]

Eine dynamische Edition bietet eine Reihe von Vorteilen. Sie erlaubt beispielsweise nachträgliche Korrekturen. Während in einer gedruckten Edition
spät gefundene Fehler bestenfalls in einer beigelegten Liste von Errata richtig
gestellt werden, können zentral auf einem Server vorgehaltene digitale Editionen jederzeit verbessert und somit verändert werden[3].

Aus der nachträglichen Veränderbarkeit ergibt sich die Möglichkeit, die
mit der Erarbeitung einer Edition verbundene Dynamik über den Zeitpunkt
ihrer Publikation hinaus fortzuführen. Die Erarbeitung einer Urkundenedition ist eine iterative und rekursive Abfolge von heuristischen Prozessen, Be-
arbeitungs-, Transformations- und Interpretationsprozessen. In mehreren
Arbeitsschritten werden Textfassungen erstellt, kollationiert, überarbeitet
und schließlich fixiert, es werden Regesten geschrieben, Textzeugen und Literatur eingearbeitet sowie eine Reihe weiterer erschließender Tätigkeiten
durchgeführt. Alle Zwischenergebnisse erfahren Überprüfungen und Über-
arbeitungen, ehe sie Publikationsreife erreichen. Damit verbunden ist eine
fortwährende Kommunikation im weitesten Sinne: der Austausch mit Mitar-
beitern und Fachkollegen, aber natürlich auch die (erneute) Konsultation der
Originale, von Literatur, Datenbanken usw.

Mit dem Zeitpunkt ihrer Publikation verliert eine Edition – und das gilt
auch für die meisten digitalen Editionen – diese Dynamik. Sie wird zu einer
statischen Ressource. Bei genauerer Betrachtung wird jedoch deutlich, daß
die mit dem Entstehungsprozeß der Edition verbundene Dynamik nicht un-
terbrochen, sondern nur verlagert wird. Sie findet nicht mehr im Kontext der

---

[2] Ich arbeite an einer Dissertation mit dem Arbeitstitel „Edition als Prozess", die
den Ansatz einer nicht-statischen und kontinuierlich fortschreitenden digitalen Edition analysiert und konzeptionelle sowie technische Voraussetzungen dafür untersucht.

[3] Wobei bereits hier darauf hingewiesen werden muß, daß stillschweigend vorge-
nommene Verbesserungen vor allem in Hinblick auf die Zitierbarkeit problematisch
sind.

Edition statt, sondern in anderen Publikationen. Dies läßt sich etwa am Beispiel der Edition der Urkunden Friedrichs II. zeigen. Als erste Edition mit einem umfassenden Anspruch erschien zwischen 1852 und 1861 die von Huillard-Bréholles besorgte Sammlung der Urkunden des Staufers. Julius Ficker publizierte aus dem Nachlaß Böhmers 1870 die Acta Imperii Selecta mit 56 Urkunden Friedrichs II. Die beiden Acta Imperii Bände Eduard Winkelmanns erschienen 1880 bis 1885. Sie enthalten weitere 371 Urkunden und Briefe, teilweise ediert, teilweise als Regesten. Danach vergingen mehr als hundert Jahre, bis 2002 der erste Band der systematischen Neuedition von Walter Koch im Rahmen der MGH publiziert wurde[4]. In den Jahren dazwischen erschienen, verstreut in Aufsätzen, Konferenzbeiträgen und Festschriften eine Reihe von Vorabeditionen, Arbeitsberichten und Studien, die das Wissen über die Urkunden Friedrichs erweiterten[5]. Parallel dazu wurden die Urkunden Friedrichs auch von den Regesta Imperii bearbeitet. In drei Bänden erschienen wieder aus dem Nachlaß Johann Friedrich Böhmers die von Ficker und Eduard Winkelmann besorgte Ausgabe zwischen 1881 und 1901, ergänzt durch den 1983 erschienenen Band mit Nachträgen und Ergänzungen von Paul Zinsmaier[6].

---

[4] Historia diplomatica Frederici secundi sive Constitutiones, privilegia, mandata, instrumenta quae supersunt istius imperatoris et filiorum eius, hg. v. J-L-A. HUILLARD-BRÉHOLLES, 12 Bde. (1852–1861); Acta imperii selecta, ges. v. J.H. BÖHMER, hg. aus dem Nachlasse von J. FICKER (1870); Acta imperii inedita saeculi XIII. Urkunden und Briefe zur Geschichte des Kaiserreichs und des Königreichs Sicilien in den Jahren 1198–1273, hg. v. E. WINKELMANN, 2. Bde. (1880–1885); Die Urkunden Friedrichs II., bearbeitet v. W. KOCH, MGH Diplomata XIV.1 (2002).

[5] Beispielhaft seien hier erwähnt: S. BERNICOLI, Eine ungedruckte Urkunde Friedrichs II. für S. Giovanni Evangelista zu Ravenna, NA 26 (1901) S. 203–206; L. GENUARDI, Documenti inediti di Federico II., in: QFIAB 12 (1909) S. 236–243; F. HAUSMANN, Zwei unbekannte Diplome Kaiser Friedrichs II. für die letzten Markgrafen von Vohburg-Hohenburg, in: MIÖG 78 (1970) S. 250–259; G. ANTONUCCI, Un mandato inedito di Federico II, in: ASCL 12 (1942) S. 217–220; K. HÖFLINGER und J. SPIEGEL, Ungedruckte Stauferurkunden für S. Giovanni in Fiore, in: DA 49 (1993) S. 75–11; M. THUMSER, Eine unbekannte Originalurkunde Friedrichs II. aus dem Archiv der Sforza in Rom (1231), in: DA 50 (1994) S. 199–204. Weitere Beispiele in W. KOCH, Urkunden Friedrichs II., S. XIII f., Anm. 17 und 18.

[6] Die Regesten des Kaiserreichs unter Philipp, Otto IV., Friedrich II., Heinrich (VII.), Conrad IV., Heinrich Raspe, Wilhelm und Richard. 1198–1272, Bd. 1–3, bearb. von J. FICKER und E. WINKELMANN (1881–1901); Die Regesten des Kaiserreichs unter Philipp, Otto IV., Friedrich II., Heinrich (VII.), Conrad IV., Heinrich Raspe, Wilhelm und Richard. 1198–1272. Nachträge und Ergänzungen, bearb. von P. ZINSMAIER, P.-J. HEINIG und M. KARST (1983).

Ihre Veröffentlichung macht also eine statische Edition zu einem latent alternden Element in einer sich verändernden Umwelt[7]. Eine offene und dynamische Edition dagegen bietet die Möglichkeit, nachträglich erzielte Erkenntnisse und Ergebnisse direkt an die Edition anzulagern und dort zentral verfügbar zu machen, entweder durch eine einfache Verzeichnung bzw. Verlinkung, oder als direkte Ergänzung der Edition. Dadurch werden Diskussionsergebnisse und neue Erkenntnisse für Benutzer der Edition unmittelbar sichtbar. Wieder am Beispiel Friedrich II. wird deutlich, daß der Erkenntnisstand einer Edition stark zeitabhängig ist. Walter Koch hat errechnet, daß die Editionen Huillard-Bréholles und Winkelmanns zusammen nur knapp 70 Prozent der in der MGH-Edition edierten Urkunden verzeichnen[8]. Dazu kommen noch neu entdeckte kopiale Überlieferungen und die jährlich wachsende Literatur[9].

Ein solches Überarbeiten bestehender Ergebnisse erscheint auch angesichts der sich verändernden Umwelt einer Edition sinnvoll. Dies können physische Kontexte sein, etwa wenn Originale durch Katastrophen zerstört werden oder wenn sich ihr Lagerort ändert. Archive werden zusammengelegt oder Archivbestände reorganisiert, wodurch sich Archivsignaturen verändern können[10]. Auch historisch-wissenschaftliche Kontexte ändern sich. Hier ist etwa das sich wandelnde Wissen über eine Quelle, deren Verursacher, die Entstehungszeit und Wirkung zu berücksichtigen, aber auch ein Wandel des Erkenntnisinteresses und damit der anhand der Edition zu klärenden Fragestellungen und Methoden. Der Vergleich der aktuellen Merowinger-Edition der MGH mit der von Pertz besorgten Edition von 1872 zeigt erstaunliche Unterschiede[11]. Diese betreffen nicht nur die absolute Zahl der verzeichneten Urkunden und Fälschungen, sondern in noch stärkerem Ausmaß das *discrimen veri ac falsi*, das eine Neubewertung rund eines Drittels der Urkunden

---

[7] Vgl. K. SUTHERLAND, Being Critical: Paper-based Editing and the Digital Environment, in: Text Editing, Print and the Digital World, hg. V. D. DEEGAN und K. SUTHERLAND (2009) S. 13–25, hier S. 15 f.

[8] KOCH, Friedrich II. (wie Anm. 4), S. IX.

[9] Vgl. ebd. S. XII. Hier findet sich auch der Hinweis auf mögliche weitere Funde: „[...] man wird sich auch nie ausschließen können, dies oder jenes übersehen zu haben" mit der Bitte um Meldung von Neufunden, damit diese „gegebenenfalls in einem Folgeband nach[ge]tragen" werden können.

[10] Während der Arbeit an den Fontes Civitatis Ratisponensis. Geschichtsquellen der Stadt Regensburg online, hg. v. I. KROPAČ (2005ff.) <http://www.fcr-online.com> war es nötig, einen beträchtlichen Teil der in den beiden Bänden des Regensburger Urkundenbuchs verzeichneten Archivsignaturen zu überarbeiten, weil diese sich nach Publikation der Edition verändert hatten.

[11] Diplomata regum Francorum e stirpe Merovingica, hg. v. K. A. F. PERTZ, MGH Diplomata I (1872); Die Urkunden der Merowinger, hg. v. T. KÖLZER, MGH Diplomata I.1 (2001).

zur Folge hatte[12]. Eine traditionelle Edition stellt im wissenschaftlichen Diskurs einen zwar stabilen, jedoch gleichzeitig statischen Bezugspunkt dar, der auf Grundlage eines bestimmten Paradigmas und mit einem bestimmten Fokus erstellt wurde[13]. Das impliziert jedoch auch, daß eine solche Edition im Laufe der Zeit altert und neuen Ansprüchen, die sich aus veränderten Fragestellungen und Methoden ergeben, nicht mehr genügen kann.

In einer zunehmend digitalisierten Umwelt steigt die Wahrscheinlichkeit, daß eine (digitale) Edition zum Ausgangspunkt für davon abgeleitete neue Erscheinungs- und Erschließungsformen wird. Damit meine ich Transformationen bzw. Anreicherungen der publizierten Daten durch Dritte im Rahmen ihrer Forschung. Dies können beispielsweise Bildmanipulationen am digitalen Faksimile sein, das Explizitmachen bestimmter Strukturen – etwa des Urkundenformulars – durch Markup oder das Erschließen und Anreichern einer Quelle durch zusätzliche Metadaten. Es können sogar ganz neue, aus der Edition abgeleitete Repräsentationsformen entstehen, beispielsweise die Kodierung bestimmter Inhalte in Form statistischer Daten oder als Set von RDF-Tripeln. In diesen Anreicherungen und zusätzlichen Repräsentationsformen steckt viel Arbeit und Wissen, sie werden jedoch vorwiegend nur intern verwendet und nicht allgemein verfügbar gemacht. Darunter leidet die Nachvollziehbarkeit von Ergebnissen, aber auch die Chance diese nachzunutzen. In einer offenen Edition können diese Erweiterungen, Ergänzungen oder Neuinterpretationen in die Edition zurückfließen und so den Informationsraum der Edition erweitern und zum Ausgangspunkt weiterer Untersuchungen werden[14].

Ein anderes Argument für dynamische Editionsformen liefert die zunehmend schwierige Finanzierungssituation für Editionsprojekte und das Problem der Edition von Massenquellen. Wenn traditionelle Editionen darauf bedacht sind, in Hinblick auf die Auswahl der Quellen, deren Aufbereitung und Erschließung der später darauf aufbauenden Forschung möglichst nützlich zu sein, so ist dies eine Gratwanderung. Zum einen bedeutet die Auswahl der Quellen eine Filterung, zum anderen ist eine möglichst allgemein nutzbare Aufbereitung zeit- und damit kostenintensiv. Ein möglicher Ausweg aus dieser Schere zwischen Quantität und Qualität könnte in einem Modell lie-

---

[12] Vgl. KÖLZER, Merowinger (wie Anm. 11) S. XII.

[13] Man denke etwa nur an die unterschiedlichen Ansprüche an eine Edition aus geschichtswissenschaftlicher und philologischer Perspektive. Vgl. dazu K. KRANICH-HOFBAUER, Editionswissenschaft als interdisziplinäre Grundwissenschaft, in: Jahrbuch der Oswald von Wolkensteingesellschaft 12 (2000) S. 49–64.

[14] Ähnlich: G. CRANE, Give us editors! Re-inventing the edition and re-thinking the humanities, in: Proceedings of Online Humanities Scholarship: The Shape of Things to Come, Conference held at the University of Virginia on March 26–28, 2010, hg. v. J. McGANN (2010) S. 81–97, hier S. 83 f. <http://cnx.org/content/col11199/1.1/>.

gen, bei dem Quellen zunächst in einem nur geringen Erschließungsgrad (digitales Faksimile, Kopfregest) bereitgestellt werden. Bei entsprechendem Forschungsinteresse bzw. nach Maßgabe der verfügbaren Mittel kann eine solche Edition nachträglich weitergeführt werden; eine vollständige Edition ist jedoch nicht das vordergründige Ziel[15].

Ein Vor- und Zwischenergebnisse verfügbar machender Ansatz kann auch für Editionen sinnvoll sein, die von Beginn an auf eine vollständige Edition nach den hohen editorischen Vorgaben klassischer kritischer Editionen ausgerichtet sind. Da bis zur Publikation einer solchen Edition mitunter Jahrzehnte vergehen, diese manchmal sogar überhaupt unterbleibt, erscheint die – klar als solche gekennzeichnete – Vorabpublikation von Zwischenergebnissen, etwa von digitalen Faksimiles oder von vorläufigen Transkription vorteilhaft[16]. Voraussetzung dafür ist aber die Akzeptanz einer Editionsform, die ein solches iteratives Vorgehen unterstützt.

Wenn eine Edition schrittweise erstellt und veröffentlicht werden kann, so erleichtert dies ein arbeitsteiliges Vorgehen, weil einzelnen Bearbeitern unterschiedliche Aufgaben mit vorgegebenen Zielen zugewiesen werden können. Eine solche kooperative Vorgehensweise scheint mir angesichts der für die Erstellung einer Urkundenedition benötigten Fachkenntnisse aus verschiedenen Bereichen der Geschichte, der Paläographie, Diplomatik, Sphragistik, Prosopographie, Toponomastik usw. sinnvoll, zumal für digitale Editionen noch zusätzliche Kenntnisse etwa im Bereich der Datenmodellierung, -transformation und -aufbereitung erforderlich sind.

Man kann eine kooperativ erstelle Edition sogar so weit denken, daß Benutzer in den Editionsprozeß integriert werden. Dieser Ansatz wird seit einigen Jahren verstärkt diskutiert. In Anlehnung an das fallweise als „Mitmachweb" bezeichnete Web 2.0, wurden solche Editionsformen als *Edition 2.0*

[15] Vgl. I. H. Kropač, Work in Progress: Vom Digitalisat zum edierten Text, in: Editionswissenschaftliche Kolloquien 2005/2007, hg. v. M. Thumser und J. Tandecki (2008) S. 167–183; M. Thaller, Wie ist es eigentlich gewesen, wenn das Gedächtnis virtuell wird?, in: Forschung in der digitalen Welt, hg. v. R. Hering, J. Sarnowsky, Ch. Schäfer und U. Schäfer (Veröffentlichungen aus dem Staatsarchiv der Freien und Hansestadt Hamburg 20, 2006) S. 13–28, hier S. 17–24. Aus archivarischer Sicht wurde mehrfach auf den ökonomischen Aspekt eines solchen Ansatzes verwiesen. Vgl. K. Uhde, Urkunden im Internet – Neue Präsentationsformen alter Archivalien, in: AD 45 (1999), S. 441–464; Ders., Der Archivar als Dienstleister der Diplomatiker, in: Digitale Diplomatik, hg. v. G. Vogeler (AfD Beiheft 12, 2009) S. 188–199; F. Roberg, Findbuch – Regest – Edition – Abbildung, in: Der Archivar 64/2 (2011) S. 174–180.

[16] Vgl. G. Schmitz, ‚Unvollendet' – ‚Eingestampft' – ‚Kassiert', in: Zur Geschichte und Arbeit der Monumenta Germaniae Historica, hg. v. A. Gawlik (1996) S. 64–73. Zum selben Problem und potentiellen Lösungen M. W. Küster, Ch. Ludwig und A. Aschenbrenner, TextGrid: eScholarship und vernetzte Angebote, in: IT – Information Technology 51/4 (2009) S. 183–190, hier S. 183 f.

oder *Social Edition* bezeichnet[17]. Das Spektrum der Benutzerbeteiligung reicht dabei von der Möglichkeit, Kommentare zu hinterlassen, bis hin zum Crowdsourcing, also der Auslagerung bestimmter editorischer Tätigkeiten an die Benutzer durch Bereitstellung entsprechender Online-Werkzeuge[18].

Progressive Edition

In der Literatur finden sich Überlegungen zu und ansatzweise auch konkrete Beispiele für dynamische Editionsformen. Die Ziele und Ansätze sind dabei so unterschiedlich wie die dafür gewählten Bezeichnungen[19]. Die meisten dieser Ansätze nutzen die Möglichkeiten eines mehrstufigen Editionsprozesses, fokussieren aber letztlich auf eine am Ende des Prozesses stehende, weitgehend stabile, d. h. abgeschlossene Edition als „Produkt".

Bei genauerer Betrachtung eines mehrstufigen und offenen Editionsmodells stellt sich jedoch die Frage, ob es nicht konsequent und sinnvoll wäre, die damit verbundene Dynamik als implizite Eigenschaft einer Edition zu denken. In einem solchen Modell ist eine Edition weniger ein aus dem Editionsprozeß

---

[17] P. Boot und J. v. Zundert, The Digital Editions 2.0 and The Digital Library: Services, not Resources, in: Bibliothek und Wissenschaft 44 (2001) S. 141–152; R. Siemens, M. Timney, C. Leitch, C. Koolen und A. Garnett, Toward Modeling the Social Edition: An Approach to Understanding the Electronic Scholarly Edition in the Context of New and Emerging Social Media, in: Literary and Linguistic Computing 27/4 (2012) S. 445–461.

[18] Bei der Edition der Matrikelbücher der Akademie der Bildenden Künste München (http://matrikel.adbk.de/) hat sich die Kommentarfunktion als sehr fruchtbar erwiesen. Vgl. B Jooss, Die Digitale Edition der Matrikelbücher der Akademie der Bildenden Künste Schriften des Instituts für Dokumentologie und Editorik 4, 2011). Das vielleicht bekannteste Beispiel für ein erfolgreiches Crowdsourcing-Projekt ist Transcribe Bentham (http://www.ucl.ac.uk/transcribe-bentham/).

[19] Um nur einige zu nennen: *Dynamische Edition, Schichtenedition, Work-in-Progress-Edition, Living Edition, Edition 2.0, Fluent Edition* oder *Social Edition*. Vgl. A. Hofmeister, Das Konzept einer „Dynamischen Edition" dargestellt an der Erstausgabe des „Brixner Dommesnerbuches" von Veit Feichter (Mitte 16. Jh.) (2003); I. H. Kropač, Theorien, Methoden und Strategien für multimediale Archive und Editionen, in: Mediaevistik und neue Medien, hg. v. K. v. Eickels, R. Weichselbaumer und I. Bennewitz (2004) S. 295–316; Ders., Work in Progress (wie Anm. 15); M. Thaller, Digital Manuscripts as Base Line for Dynamic Editions, in: Digital Technology and Philological Disciplines, hg. v. A. Bozzi, L. Cigoni und J.-L. Lebrave (2004) S. 489–511; Ders., Reproduktion, Erschließung, Edition, Interpretation: Ihre Beziehung in einer digitalen Welt, in: Vom Nutzen des Edierens, hg. v. B. Merta, A. Sommerlechner und H. Weigl (MIÖG Ergänzungsband 47, 2005) S. 205–227. R. Siemens, Social Edition (wie Anm. 17); G. Crane, Give us Editors! (wie Anm. 14); P. Boot und J. v. Zundert, Digital Editions 2.0 (wie Anm. 17).

hervorgehendes Produkt als ein ständig fortschreitender Prozeß, aus dem zeit-
und interessensabhängige, grundsätzlich nur temporär gültige, aber langfristig
verfügbare „Produkte" als Sichtweisen ableitbar sind (Abbildung 1). Ich be-
zeichne eine solche Editionsform als progressive Edition, weil damit ausge-
drückt wird, daß die Edition keinen Endpunkt erreichen kann, der Editionsprozeß also nie beendet wird.

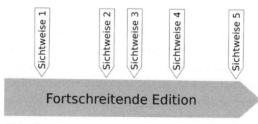

Abbildung 1

Eine progressive Edition ist also per definitionem niemals fertig. Sie kann jederzeit erweitert, angereichert und modifiziert werden. Dabei lagert sich im
Lauf der Zeit zusätzliches Wissen über die edierte Quelle und ihre Kontexte
an und steht späteren Benutzern der Edition zur Verfügung. Eine progressive
Edition erlaubt es aber auch, jede Zwischenstufe als Ausgangspunkt für eigene Forschungen zu verwenden, neue Richtungen einzuschlagen oder exi-
stierende Deutungen zu variieren. Sich daraus ergebende Resultate können
wieder in die Edition zurückgeführt oder zumindest dort referenziert werden. In einer solchen Edition sind damit auch parallele, einander widerspre-
chende Repräsentationsformen möglich.

Voraussetzungen

Voraussetzung für eine solche Editionsform ist, daß sie als Menge von aus
distinkten Arbeitsschritten hervorgehenden Resultaten gesehen wird, die jeweils eindeutig einem verantwortlichen Bearbeiter zugeordnet werden können. Diese klare organisatorische Abgrenzung einzelner Aufgaben hat den
Vorteil, daß daraus konkrete Arbeitsschritte mit definierten Ergebnissen ableitbar sind. Sie ermöglicht die Zuweisung von Verantwortungsbereichen und
erleichtert somit eine kooperative Arbeitsweise. Bei Bedarf können einzelne
Arbeitsschritte in Teilaufgaben unterteilt und damit projektspezifische Work-
flows geplant und abgebildet werden[20]. Gerade in einem kooperativen Szena-

---

[20] Eine solche vorab erfolgte Planung und Festlegung kann dazu beitragen, ein Edi-
tionsprojekt in vorgegebenen Bahnen zu halten oder bestimmte Arbeitsschritte zu

rio können dadurch einzelnen Beteiligten nicht nur Aufgaben, sondern auch damit verknüpfte Rollen zugewiesen werden, was wiederum die Delegierung bestimmter Tätigkeiten an Hilfskräfte oder Spezialisten erleichtert. Gleichzeitig kann damit aber deren Beitrag, weil er als Teil der Edition dokumentiert ist, als eigenständige Teilleistung gewürdigt werden. Bearbeiter müssen dadurch konkrete Verantwortung für ihren Part übernehmen, können aber auch wissenschaftliche Credits erwerben. Die Resultate von Teilaufgaben stehen in einer transparenten, zitierbaren Form bereit, was ihre Überprüfbarkeit erleichtert und gleichzeitig ihre Referenzierbarkeit im Diskurs ermöglicht.

Damit sind die Voraussetzungen zu einem Verständnis von Edition als offenem Wissensraum geschaffen, in dem die Editoren zwar die Oberhoheit haben, wo sich jedoch unabhängig von diesen und klar als solches erkennbar, auch externes Wissen anlagern kann. Dadurch verschiebt sich die Grenze zwischen Editor und Nutzer. Jeder Nutzer ist ein potentieller „Miteditor", der sein Wissen beispielsweise als Kommentar hinterlassen oder sogar editorische Teilaufgaben übernehmen kann.

Eine progressive Edition ist nicht zwingend mit einer Crowdsourcing-Edition gleichzusetzen, zu der jeder beitragen kann. Wie oben bereits skizziert, kann eine solche Edition auch auf einen oder einige wenige beitragende Editoren eingeschränkt werden, welche die Edition iterativ erarbeiten und zugänglich machen. Auch hier sind vorgegebene Arbeitsschritte zu absolvieren, und es stellt sich das Problem von sich im Lauf der Zeit verändernden Daten. Sinnvoll sind vermutlich Mischformen, bei denen zentrale Teile der Edition von deklarierten Editoren erarbeitet werden, um die sich, deutlich von der Kernedition unterscheidbar, externe Anreicherungen anlagern[21].

Ein multidimensionaler Informationsraum

Eine progressive Edition stellt einen multidimensionalen Informationsraum dar. In diesem ist das Nebeneinander, aber auch das Fehlen einzelner Repräsentationsformen einer Quelle noch relativ übersichtlich und einfach zu verwalten, wie dies etwa Ingo Kropač im Konzept der Integrierten Computergestützten Edition oder Patrick Sahle als zentrales Element transmedialer Editionen beschrieben haben[22]. Die Daten der Edition liegen dabei in mehre-

priorisieren. Gleichzeitig kann sie auch als Werkzeug zur Projektsteuerung und sogar zur Qualitätskontrolle dienen.

[21] Eine explizite Übernahme editorischer Teilaufgaben durch Externe könnte etwa bedeuten, daß die Lokalisierung topographischer Angaben durch Lokal- oder Regionalhistoriker vor Ort durchgeführt wird.

[22] I. H. Kropač, Theorien (wie Anm.19); zu Sahle: siehe Anm. 1.

ren, parallel vorgehaltenen (Teil)Objekten vor, in Abbildung 2 symbolisiert durch die vier beispielhaft gewählten Repräsentationsformen digitales Faksimile, (graphematische oder graphetische) Transkription, normalisierter Text und Überlieferung(sdokumentation).

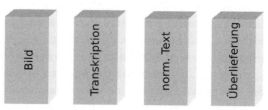

Abbildung 2: Repräsentationsformen

Allerdings existiert jede dieser Repräsentationsformen in einem Beziehungsgeflecht, dessen Berücksichtigung besondere Ansprüche an den Benutzer, aber auch an das zur Speicherung und Verwaltung verwendete System stellt. Die einzelnen Repräsentationsformen existieren also nicht einfach gleichberechtigt nebeneinander, sondern stehen in vielfältigen Beziehungen zueinander und zu anderen internen und externen Objekten (Abbildung 3). Eine Form kann etwa unmittelbar von einer anderen Form abgleitet sein. Eine Form kann eine andere Form näher beschreiben oder erschließen. Eine Form kann durch einen Bearbeiter erstellt worden sein, der auch andere Formen erstellt, bearbeitet oder kommentiert hat.

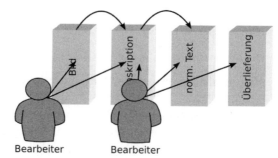

Abbildung 3: Beziehungen

Diese an sich schon recht komplexe Struktur wird noch deutlich verkompliziert, wenn – und das ist für eine progressive Edition unumgänglich – jede Repräsentationsform in beliebig vielen Versionen existieren kann (Abbildung 4)[23]. Dadurch wird nämlich nicht nur eine zusätzliche Dimension eingeführt, sondern es kann auch zu Seiteneffekten kommen, die sich aus den Be-

---

[23] Hinsichtlich der Versionierung können sich sogar noch, in Abbildung 4 nicht dargestellte zusätzliche Dimensionen auftun, wenn man unterschiedliche Arten von

ziehungen der Repräsentationsformen zueinander ergeben und auf diese wieder zurückwirken.

Dies läßt sich an einem trivialen Beispiel zeigen: Nehmen wir an, daß von einer Transkription weitere Textformen abgeleitet wurden. Wenn nun nachträglich in der Transkription ein Lesefehler festgestellt und korrigiert wird, so ist davon nicht nur die Transkription selbst betroffen, sondern auch alle von dieser Transkription abgeleiteten Formen, möglicherweise bis hin zum Register. Es entsteht also nicht nur eine neue Version dieser einen Repräsentationsform, sondern gleichzeitig eine mitunter beträchtliche Zahl von neuen Beziehungen. Diese bestehen nicht nur zwischen den einzelnen Versionen einer Repräsentationsform und zwischen den verschiedenen Repräsentationsformen einer Quelle, sondern auch als „Nicht-Beziehungen", die etwa dokumentieren, daß der normalisierte Editionstext nicht mehr von der aktuellsten Version der Transkription abstammt und nachgezogen werden sollte[24].

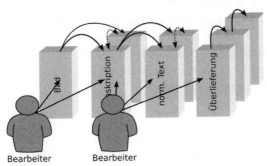

Abbildung 4: Versionen

Prozeßdaten

Die Beziehungen lassen sich nur verwalten, wenn zusätzlich zu den eigentlichen Daten auch Prozeßdaten generiert werden, die alle Änderungen an der Edition dokumentieren. Diese halten Akteure, Zeitpunkt, Anfangs- und Endpunkt sowie die durchgeführten Änderungen fest: *Version n einer be-*

Versionen unterscheidet: etwa vorläufige, nicht öffentlich zugängliche Arbeitsversionen, abgeschlossene aber nicht überprüfte oder approbierte Versionen.

[24] Der Konjunktiv wurde hier bewußt gewählt, weil ein solches Nachziehen anderer Repräsentationsformen zwar grundsätzlich wünschenswert ist, jedoch nicht als freiwillige Leistung Dritter vorausgesetzt werden kann. Allerdings sollte für Bearbeiter und Benutzer sichtbar sein, daß eine Nachbearbeitung der verwendeten Repräsentationsform nötig ist. Sinnvoll erscheint mir, daß vom System automatisch eine Nachricht (etwa in Form einer E-Mail) generiert wird, die Editoren darauf hinweist, daß ein Eingreifen erforderlich wäre.

stimmten Repräsentationsform x wurde zu einem bestimmten Datum von Person A auf Basis der Version m der Repräsentationsform y erstellt und zu einem anderen Zeitpunkt von Person B überprüft und für korrekt befunden.

Eine dynamische, sich beständig weiterentwickelnde Editionsform kann also nur funktionieren, wenn diese nicht nur Ergebnisse, sondern auch die zu diesen Ergebnissen führenden Prozesse sichtbar macht, weil dadurch Benutzern, aber auch späteren Editoren Mittel an die Hand gegeben werden sich in diesem komplexen Informationsraum zu orientieren, Entscheidungen nachzuvollziehen und Teile ein- bzw. auszublenden[25]. Man kann diese Daten auch als Teil des Diskurses über die Quelle verstehen. Daher müssen in einer progressiven Edition die Prozeßdaten als wichtiger Teil der Edition verstanden werden.

Es ist evident, daß eine progressive Edition nur mit Hilfe entsprechender Software sinnvoll realisierbar ist. Diese muß in der Lage sein, 1) parallel vorliegende Repräsentationsformen getrennt voneinander vorzuhalten und zugänglich zu machen, 2) zu jeder Repräsentationsform beliebig viele Varianten in Form von Versionen zu speichern, 3) die vielfältigen Beziehungen zwischen diesen Entitäten zu verwalten und 4) jede Änderung an der Edition teilautomatisiert zu protokollieren.

Darstellungsformen

Neben der Verwaltung der transmedialen Editionsdaten stellt deren Darstellung in einer dem Benutzer nachvollziehbaren und nutzbaren Weise eine weitere Hürde dar. Meiner Ansicht nach muß diese Darstellung weitgehend unabhängig von den dahinter stehenden Daten gedacht werden, weil nur dadurch jene Unabhängigkeit zwischen Repräsentation und Präsentation erreicht werden kann, die es erlaubt, flexibel auf Änderungen im Erkenntnisinteresse oder auch nur auf veränderte gestalterische Moden zu reagieren. Darstellungsformen sind also nur austauschbare, relativ kurzlebige Sichtweisen auf die dahinter stehenden Daten. Dennoch gilt es auch hier einige grundsätzliche Fragen, wie etwa die der Zitierbarkeit einer sich verändernden Edition oder einer sinnvollen Datenselektion zu lösen.

---

[25] Aus editorischer Sicht können die Prozeßdaten dazu verwendet werden, die Arbeit zu organisieren und vor allem einen Überblick über bereits geleistete Teilaufgaben zu bewahren. Sie sind damit auch Grundlage einer (mächtigeren) elektronischen Alternative zu den von Walter Koch als wichtig für die Edition der Urkunden Friedrichs II. beschriebenen, projektintern verwendeten Arbeitsbögen. Vgl. KOCH, Friedrich II. (wie Anm. 4) S. XII.

Das Problem der Zitierbarkeit läßt sich dadurch lösen, daß nicht die Edition als Ganzes, sondern eine bestimmte Version der Edition zitiert wird. Hier bietet sich ein Konzept an, das im Bereich der Softwareentwicklung weit verbreitet ist. Jede Änderung an den Daten führt zu einer fortlaufenden Versionsnummer, über die dann eine bestimmte Version abgerufen werden kann[26]. Alternativ kann dazu auch ein Datum verwendet werden, wobei im Hintergrund die zu diesem Datum aktuellste Version ermittelt und diese ausgegeben wird. Zusätzlich scheint mir auch Tagging von Versionen als ein für Edition sinnvolles Mittel. Dabei kann einer bestimmten Version zusätzlich zu ihrer Versionsnummer ein bedeutungstragendes Etikett zugewiesen werden, um einen bestimmten Zustand zu bezeichnen. Ein solches Etikett erfüllt dann eine ähnliche Funktion wie die Angabe einer Auflage eines gedruckten Werkes.

Je mehr Daten sich in der Edition anlagern und je komplexer sich der Informationsraum gestaltet, umso schwieriger wird es, diese Daten in einer Form aufzubereiten, die für Benutzer nachvollziehbar und mit Gewinn verwendbar ist. Da sich während der letzten 15 Jahre gezeigt hat, daß nicht nur die formale Gestaltung von webbasierten Benutzerschnittstellen starken Veränderungen unterliegt, sondern auch dahinter stehende Muster der Benutzerführung, ist es nahezu unmöglich, hier längerfristig gültige Lösungen zu entwickeln. Als zentrale Forderung muß gelten, den Benutzer nicht zu überfordern. Das kann bedeuten, daß dem Benutzer standardmäßig eine von den Editoren also solche zu kennzeichnende Auswahl der zentralen Repräsentationsformen der Edition, also quasi eine Leitform in der jeweils aktuellsten Version angeboten wird. Gleichzeitig muß sichergestellt sein, daß dem Benutzer bei Bedarf zusätzliche Informationen, etwa alternative Repräsentationsformen, frühere Versionen, die zur einer Version gehörenden Prozeßdaten, abgeleitete Formen oder Kommentare zugänglich gemacht werden.

Résumé

Auf den ersten Blick wirkt ein solches Konstrukt möglicherweise unnötig kompliziert und kaum realisierbar. Die bewußte Entscheidung für einen solchen Ansatz bietet aber Lösungen für viele Probleme, die in Zusammenhang mit dynamischen Editionen bisher offen geblieben sind. Nur wenn explizite Bearbeitungsstufen definiert sind, wenn deren Ergebnisse langfristig verfügbar und eindeutig adressierbar bleiben und wenn zusätzlich noch Prozeß-

---

[26] Ein ähnliches Konzept verfolgt die Wikipedia mit den als Permalinks zitierbaren Versionen.

daten vorhanden sind, aus denen die Genese der einzelnen Resultate ableitbar ist, wird eine solche, ständig im Fluß befindliche, potentiell aus vielen Quellen gespeiste Form von Edition sinnvoll realisierbar und nutzbar.

The return of diplomatics as a forensic discipline

LUCIANA DURANTI

Diplomatics was developed in the 17th century as a methodology for establishing the authenticity of records attesting to patrimonial rights. It developed as a study of the nature, genesis, formal characteristics, structure, transmission, and legal consequences of records for the purpose of understanding their true nature, meaning, and effects[1]. The diplomatic interpretation of authenticity based on the form of a document (its extrinsic and intrinsic elements) and its transmission across space and through time became the foundation of the law of evidence, and is still perfectly consistent with the legal principles we hold today in both common law and civil law systems; thus, it could be used to establish legal authenticity and to protect it over time for general records management and archival purposes. However, diplomatists as a profession have increasingly used their knowledge to support purposes related to historical research, turning away from the "bella diplomatica" that made them so popular a few centuries ago[2].

Today, as the world is confronted with the challenges presented by digital records, it would be very useful to governments, public and private organizations and individuals if diplomatists turned their attention back to where their discipline began, and rediscovered those concepts, principles and methods that allowed them to establish the identity and trustworthiness of records of unknown origin. This is not to say that professionals calling themselves "diplomatists" should abandon their historical outlook or the use of diplomatic criticism for historical purposes, but they are encouraged to offer the benefit of their knowledge, rooted in centuries-old consolidated concepts and principles, to support the creation, maintenance and preservation of current documents so that our present will have a future, and the future will have a trustworthy documentary past to study, and from which to learn.

If diplomatics is a science rather than a historical methodology, it should be treated as such, rather than simply as an auxiliary discipline of history, and this

---

[1] L. DURANTI, Diplomatics: New Uses For An Old Science, in: Archivaria 28 (1989) p. 7–27.

[2] DURANTI, Diplomatics p. 13.

involves developing it in light of changes in the context and characteristics of the documentary output of society, and using it not only to analyse charters but to understand documents of all times and types. Such a perspective also involves using diplomatics not only retrospectively – to know the past – but also prospectively – to determine how the documents we create should look like and should be maintained for their authenticity to be proven in the future. Does this imply a rejection of traditional diplomatics? This author does not think so. Just like the physics of Newton continues to live together with that of Einstein, there is no reason why diplomatics of medieval records cannot live together with diplomatics of modern and contemporary records. Admittedly, the greatest objection to this position comes from those who do not believe that diplomatics is a science, with a body of theory, methods and practices constituting an internally consistent system of knowledge that can grow over time when confronted with different realities. However, usually, these writers do not define themselves as professional diplomatists, but either as historians or archivists, and use diplomatic methodology for historical or archival purposes. Rather than indulging in a literature review of their position, and debating their point of view, I will present the arguments supporting the tenets of this article, which are not based on scholarly discourse alone, but on research findings[3].

Following the publication of a series of articles in which this author identified the fundamental concepts, principles and methods of diplomatics that are applicable to contemporary documents[4], she decided to test these ideas in a research project conducted in collaboration with the Department of Defense

---

[3] This does not mean that there has not been scholarly discourse supporting the development of a diplomatics of contemporary records. See for example: P. Carucci, Il documento contemporaneo (1987); J. Turner, Experimenting with New Tools: Special Diplomatics and the Study of Authority in the United Church of Canada, in: Archivaria 30 (1990) p. 91–103; J. P. Sigmond, Form, Function and Archival Value, in: Archivaria 33 (1991–1992) p. 141–147; O. Guyotjeannin, The expansion of diplomatics as a discipline, in: American Archivist 59 (1996) p. 414–421; B. Barbiche, Diplomatics of Modern Official Documents (Sixteenth–Eighteenth Centuries): Evaluation and Perspectives, in: American Archivist 59 (1996) p. 422–436; B. Delmas, Manifesto for a Contemporary Diplomatics: From Institutional Documents to Organic Information, in: American Archivist (1996) p. 438–452; F. Blouin, A Framework for a Consideration of Diplomatics in the Electronic Environment, in: American Archivist (1996) p. 466–479; E. Parinet, Diplomatics and Institutional Photos, in: American Archivist (1996) p. 480–485; H. MacNeil, Trusting records: legal, historical, and diplomatic perspectives (2000); M. Guercio, Archivistica Informatica (2002); Exportations de la diplomatique, II, Documents contemporains, ed. O. Guyotjeannin, in: BECh 161 (2003) p. 493–623.

[4] L. Duranti, Diplomatics: New Uses For An Old Science, in: Archivaria 28–33 (1989–1992), later reprint in a book with a new Introduction Chapter: L. Duranti, Diplomatics: New Uses For An Old Science (1998).

of the United States, and known as the UBC-DOD project. Its purposes were to 1. design a digital record-keeping system using the concepts and principles of diplomatics to determine records structure, intrinsic and extrinsic elements, procedures, etc., relying on a diplomatic understanding of the paper records produced by the Department of Defense; and 2. establish controls on such a system allowing for the records in it to be considered authentic on the basis of a diplomatic analysis. The project was so successful that it resulted in the Department of Defence standard DOD 5015.2, which is today the United States federal standard for record-keeping systems, and the foundation on which other standards, like MoReq2, have been designed[5].

On the wave of the success of this first use of diplomatics in relation to the digital environment, this author decided to start a new project using diplomatics to develop methods of digital preservation based on the protection of the essential characteristics of digital records identified in the course of the UBC-DOD Project. This was the first phase of the InterPARES Project, which resulted – among several other things – in requirements for the authenticity of digital records that are now embedded in all kinds of digital systems for records maintenance and preservation[6]. It is important to note that, with the birth of the InterPARES Project, this author's research team had become international and interdisciplinary, including researchers from five continents and in a variety of allied disciplines, such as law and computer science. After the conclusion of InterPARES 1, the research team realised that the material it was looking at was very similar to traditional records, that is, static in form and behaviour. It was therefore essential to test the validity of the findings on interactive documentary material and, if necessary, to develop additional concepts, principles and methodologies. This was the spirit that led the research team to the second phase of InterPARES, focusing on experiential, dynamic

---

[5] L. DURANTI/T. EASTWOOD/H. MACNEIL, Preservation of the Integrity of Electronic Records (2002); US DEPARTMENT OF DEFENSE, DoD 5015.2 STD, Design Criteria Standard for Electronic Records Management Software Applications, <http://www.dtic.mil/whs/directives/corres/pdf/501502std.pdf> (DoD 5015.2-STD, 1997, updated April 2007); EUROPEAN COMMISSION, Model Requirements for the Management of Electronic Records (MoReq2), <http://www.project-consult.net/Files/MoReq2_body_v1_0.pdf> (2008).

[6] H. MACNEIL, Providing grounds for trust: developing conceptual requirements for the long-term preservation of authentic electronic records, in: Archivaria 50 (2000) p. 52–78; L. DURANTI, Concepts, Principles and Methods for the Management of Electronic Records, in: The Information Society: An International Journal 17 (2001) p. 271–279; H. MACNEIL, Providing Grounds for Trust II: The Findings of the Authenticity Task Force of InterPARES, in: Archivaria 54 (2002) p. 24–58. For other relevant products of InterPARES 1 go to <http://www.interpares.org/ip1/ip1_documents.cfm?cat=atf>.

and interactive systems. It was during the five years of this project that the greatest advances were made in developing a new body of knowledge that was defined "digital diplomatics" because it was based on and consistent with what the team began to call "classic diplomatics"[7].

One of the conclusions of the second phase of the InterPARES project was that, as digital technology had separated the content and structure of documents/records from form, it is no longer possible to determine their authenticity on the basis of the form of the object-record, which is composite and permanently new[8], but it is necessary to make an inference of authenticity from its environment. For this reason diplomatics needs the help of a relatively new body of knowledge, Digital Forensics. In fact, record professionals are increasingly called to act as forensics experts, for example, by being asked to ensure the identity and integrity of digital records through time and attest to it, and to acquire digital records, often from obsolete systems or portable media, without altering them in the process. Also digital forensic experts are called to act as records professionals, for example, when they are asked to identify what digital materials fall under the definition of records, and to keep them intact for as long as needed. Moreover, they are asked to attest to the integrity of digital systems, to provide quality assurance for digital systems that produce, contain or preserve records, to assess whether spoliation (i.e., fraudulent disposal) has occurred, and to ensure that e-discovery requirements are fulfilled. It is clear that both records professionals and digital forensics experts need to be educated in diplomatics, but it is equally clear that diplomatists concerned with digital records need to be educated in digital forensics. In fact, digital technology has changed the traditional object of the diplomatist's attention, the document/record, into an entity which might have different manifested and stored (documentary presentation and digital presentation) versions and lack stability, and the authenticity of which depends entirely on the environment in which it exists. For this reason, this author began a new project, entitled "Digital Records Forensics", which involved records and law professionals and digital forensics experts, and aimed to merge the theory of digital diplomatics with the practice of digital forensics[9].

---

[7] L. DURANTI, Diplomatics, in: Encyclopedia of Library and Information Science, ed. M. BATES/M. N. MAACK/M. DRAKE (2009); EAD., InterPARES.

[8] We know from research that we cannot keep digital records, but only maintain the ability to reproduce them, which are therefore always new objects, made up of several digital components. L. DURANTI/K. THIBODEAU, The Concept of Record in Interactive, Experiential, and Dynamic Environments: the View of InterPARES, in: Archival Science 6 (2006) p. 13–68. Online: <http://dx.doi.org/10.1007/s10502-006-9021-7>.

[9] See Digital Records Forensics at <www.digitalrecordsforensics.org>. This change of direction in research to reach out to another discipline is discussed in L. DURANTI,

Digital forensics is defined as "the use of scientifically derived and proven methods toward the collection, validation, identification, analysis, interpretation, documentation, and presentation of digital evidence derived from digital sources for the purpose of facilitating or furthering the reconstruction of events, or helping to anticipate unauthorised or inappropriate actions"[10]. Clearly, the purposes of digital forensics are the same that determined the origin and development of traditional diplomatics. Although its methods are based on conceptual assumptions about records, trustworthiness, and record-keeping which are slightly different from the archival and diplomatic ones, they are not necessarily conflicting with them. This article focuses on the assumptions regarding trustworthiness and, specifically, integrity.

In the archival view, records trustworthiness is composed of three qualities: reliability, accuracy and authenticity. Reliability is defined as the trustworthiness of a record[11] as a statement of fact, based on the competence of its author, its completeness, and the controls on its creation; accuracy is defined as the correctness and precision of a record's content, based on the above **and** on the controls on content recording and transmission; and authenticity is defined as the trustworthiness of a record that is what it purports to be, untampered with, and uncorrupted, based on its identity and integrity, and on the reliability of the records system in which it resides. Authenticity is in turn composed of identity and integrity, where identity is the whole of the attributes of a record that characterise it as unique and distinguish it from other records (e.g. date, author, addressee, subject, classification code), and integrity is the quality of a record that is capable of transmitting exactly the message it is meant to communicate in order to achieve its purpose (e.g. text and form fidelity, absence of technical changes)[12]. Both identity and integrity are assessed in context, that is, in light of the administrative-juridical, provenencial, procedural, documentary and technological environment in which the record was created (i.e., made or received and set aside for further action or reference) and used over time[13].

From Digital Diplomatics To Digital Records Forensics, in: Archivaria 68 (2009) p. 39–66; and L. DURANTI/B. ENDICOTT-POPOVSKY, Digital Records Forensics: A New Science and Academic Program for Forensic Readiness, in: Journal of Digital Forensics, Security and Law 5,2 (2010) p. 45–63.

[10] Digital Forensics Research Workshop, 2001, online at <http://www.dfrws.org/2001/dfrws-rm-final.pdf>, p. 16.

[11] In the context and for the purposes of this article the terms record and archival document are used interchangeably.

[12] See InterPARES Project Terminology Database, Glossary, at <http://www.inter-pares.org/ip2/display_file.cfm?doc=ip2_glossary.pdf&CFID=1865090&CFTOKEN=66432882>.

[13] MACNEIL, Providing Grounds for Trust p. 52–78.

In contrast with the archival view, the digital forensics view of trustworthiness is linked to the type of document that is the object of its consideration. Digital forensics divides documents into three groups: 1) Computer Stored Documents, which contain human statements, and, if created in the course of business, are records (e.g. e-mail messages, word processing documents) and can be used in a court of law as substantive evidence; 2) Computer Generated Documents, which do not contain human statements, but are the output of a computer programme designed to process input following a defined algorithm (e.g. server log-in records from Internet service providers, ATM records) and in a court of law can only be used as demonstrative evidence[14]; and 3) Computer Stored & Generated Documents, which are a combination of the two (e.g. a spreadsheet that has received human input followed by computer processing, that is, by the mathematical operations of the spreadsheet programme) and can be used in a court of law in either way.

According to digital forensics, reliability is the trustworthiness of a record as to its *source*, defined in a way that points to either a reliable person (for computer stored documents) or a reliable software (for computer generated documents), or both. If the source is a software, it should be open source, because the processes of records creation and maintenance can be forensically authenticated either by describing a process or system used to produce a result, or by showing that the process or system produces an accurate result, and open source allows for both types of authentication.

Accuracy is instead a component of authenticity and, specifically, integrity. Digital entities are guaranteed to be accurate if they are repeatable, that is, if the same process carried out on them produces the same outcome. Repeatability, which is one of the fundamental precepts of digital forensics practice, is supported by the documentation of each and every action carried out on the digital evidence. Open source software is also the best choice for assessing accuracy, especially when conversion or migration occur, because it allows for a practical demonstration that nothing could be altered, lost, planted, or destroyed in the process.

Authenticity, to digital forensics experts, means that the data or content of the record are what they purport to be, and were produced by or came from the source they are claimed to have been produced by or come from. Again, the term "source" is used to refer to a person (physical or juridical), a system, software, or a piece of hardware. As in the archival concept, authenticity implies integrity, but the opposite is not true, that is, integrity does not imply authenticity (because identity must also be certain). In fact, the digital foren-

---

[14] The difference between substantive and demonstrative evidence is that the former is admitted for its content, while the latter only for the mere fact of its existence, in support of other substantive evidence.

sics view of integrity is much more nuanced than the archival view, for which integrity is simply the quality of being complete and unaltered in all essential respects, a definition that equally applies to data, documents, records, copies, or records systems.

In digital forensics, integrity is divided into several types. The first type is data integrity, which is the fact that data are not modified either intentionally or accidentally "without proper authorisation," and is based on bitwise integrity, that is, on the fidelity not only of the bits, but of their order. To clarify, in the analogue environment, a document may fade to the point of being unreadable but maintains the same content/data in the same order in which they were first affixed to the medium. In contrast, in the digital world, if the original bits are, for example, 101, the value conveyed is 5, but if we change the order to 110, the value is 6, and, if we change again to 011, the value is 3. The same bits have different value if their order changes. Thus, loss of fidelity implies different content. Records professionals are today responsible for preventing loss of data integrity. How can they do that? Intentional alteration is preventable through permission and access controls, but accidental alteration avoidance requires that additional hardware and/or software be in place. Both types of alteration require, in addition to methods for preventing them, methods of determining whether the record has been altered, maliciously or otherwise. For this we cannot rely on file size, dates or other file properties, but need audit logs and strong methods like Checksum and HASH Algorithms.

A second type of integrity digital forensics experts are concerned with is duplication integrity, that is, the fact that, given a data set, the process of creating a duplicate of the data does not modify the data either intentionally or accidentally, and the duplicate is an exact bit copy of the original data set. This type of integrity is extremely important to archivists because we can only preserve digital records by reproducing them. However, when archivists – like diplomatists – talk about duplication, they usually refer to making "copies", while forensic experts refer to "taking images". The difference is fundamental.

A copy is a selective duplicate of files. One can only copy what one can see. Therefore copying provides an incomplete picture of the digital device. Furthermore, it rarely includes confirmation of completeness and it mostly involves moving individual files. In contrast, an image is a bit by bit reproduction of the storage medium, a full disk copy of the data on a storage device – regardless of operating system or storage technology – made prior to performing any analysis of the disk. Creating a disk image is important in forensics to ensure that disk information is not inadvertently changed, to reproduce forensic test results on the original evidence, and to capture information normally invisible to the operating system when in use (including memory, page files, boot sector, BIOS). In addition, digital forensics experts link duplication integrity to time, and have considered the use of time stamps for that purpose. The reason is that every time one accesses a computer, something changes, thus, no two images taken at different times – even in a close sequence – are identical.

Whether one chooses a reproduction process involving copying or imaging in order to preserve digital records must depend not only on the technological advantages presented by the one or the other method, but also and foremost on professional considerations, such as those embedded in deontological codes, considering that the imaging involves reproducing also deleted files. Thus, while duplication integrity, as well as all other types of integrity, is a concept archivists as well as diplomatists need to appropriate and use, as is the case with all concepts taken from other disciplines, they need to bring it to bear on their own discipline by adapting it to the scientific, ethical and social context in which they carry out their functions.

Another type of integrity is computer integrity, which means that the computer produces accurate results when used and operated properly, and that it was so employed when the evidence was generated. Very similar is the concept of system integrity, which means that the system in question would perform its intended function in an unimpaired manner, free from unauthorised manipulation, whether intentional or accidental. Both integrities imply hardware and software integrity. To be able to establish computer and system integrity one needs to verify that 1) sufficient security measures are in place to prevent unauthorised or untracked access to the computers, networks, devices, or storage, and 2) stable physical devices will maintain the value they were given until authorised to change: users/permissions, passwords, firewalls, and system logs. The latter are sets of files *automatically* created to track the actions taken, services run, or files accessed or modified, at what time, by whom and from where. They are categorised in Web logs (Client IP Address, Request Date/Time, Page Requested, HTTP Code, Bytes Sent, Browser Type, etc.), Access logs (User account ID, User IP address, File Descriptor, Actions taken upon record, Unbind record, Closed connection), Transaction logs (History of actions taken on a system to ensure Atomicity, Consistency, Isolation, Durability; Sequence number; Link to previous log; Transaction ID; Type; Updates, commits, aborts, completes), and Auditing logs. The latter are increasingly required by law to demonstrate the integrity of the system and, when properly configured and restricted, they provide checks and balances, they are able to determine effective security policies, to trap errors that occur, to provide instantaneous notification of events, to monitor many systems and devices through 'dashboards,' to support the determination of the accountability of people, to provide the necessary snapshot for post-event reconstruction ('black-box'), and to answer Who-What-Where-When questions, but only if retained for sufficient time.

Regardless of the elements of the computer/system that are examined to verify it, computer/system integrity can be inferred on the basis of repeatability, verifiability, objectivity and transparency. More generically, an inference of system integrity can be made if the theory, procedure or process on which the system design is based 1) has been tested or cannot be tampered with; 2) has been subjected to peer review or publication (standard); 3) has an acceptable known or potential error rate; and 4) is generally accepted within the relevant scientific community.

The final type of integrity is process integrity, that is, the respect of formalised legal requirements for the collection, recovery, interpretation and presentation of digital evidence. The assessment of process integrity is based on two fundamental principles: the principle of non-interference and the principle of identifiable interference. The former means that the method used to gather and analyse [or acquire and preserve] digital data or records does not change the digital entities; the latter means that, if the method used does alter the entities, the changes are identifiable. These principles, which embody the ethical and professional stance of digital forensics experts, are consistent with the traditional impartial stance of archivists and diplomatists, as well as with their responsibility of neutral third party, or trusted custodian[15].

If trustworthiness embodies the qualities of reliability, accuracy, and authenticity (with its sub-qualities of identity and integrity), its assessment gives origin to authentication. To archivists and diplomatists, authentication is a means of declaring the authenticity of a record at one particular moment in time. In the digital environment authentication is often entrusted to a digital signature. The digital signature is functionally equivalent to seals rather than to signatures (i.e. it is an extrinsic element of form rather than an intrinsic one) in that it verifies origin (identity), certifies intactness (integrity), and makes a record indisputable and incontestable (non-repudiation). However, seals are associated with a person while digital signatures are associated with a person and a record.

Also, for digital forensics, authentication is proof of authenticity by means of an authoritative declaration, but such declaration is provided by a witness who can testify to the existence and/or substance of the record on the basis of his/her familiarity with it. In the absence of such person, the declaration of authenticity is provided by a digital forensics expert showing that the computer process or system produces accurate results when used and operated properly, and that it was so employed when the evidence was generated. In digital forensics, the strength of circumstantial digital evidence could be increased by metadata which record 1) the exact dates and times of any document sent or received, 2) which computer(s) actually created them, and 3)

---

[15] L. DURANTI, From Digital Diplomatics to Digital Records Forensics p. 60–61.

which computer(s) received them. A chain of legitimate custody is grounds for inferring authenticity and authenticating a record, and so is a digital chain of custody, that is, the information preserved about the record and its changes showing that specific data was in a particular state at a given date and time. Additionally, a declaration made by an expert who bases it on the trustworthiness of the record-keeping system and of the procedures controlling it (quality assurance) is recognised as valid authentication, and so is circumstantial evidence that a system would perform its intended function in an unimpaired manner, free from unauthorised manipulation of the system, whether intentional or accidental. Biometric identification systems and cryptography are not considered by digital forensics the most reliable means of authentication.

Clearly there are several concepts, methods and practices related to the determination of the trustworthiness of digital records that can be taken from digital forensics and integrated with the traditional archival and diplomatic knowledge. The documentary world is becoming increasingly digital. It is vital to governments, businesses, citizens, the courts, and the scholars of the future to be able to trust the documentary by-product of activities conducted in the digital environment. The theoretical core of classic diplomatics is the foundation of its subsequent development as a methodology of analysis in the digital environment, as demonstrated by research like that conducted by the InterPARES Project[16], but both theory and methodology need to be integrated with other knowledge and further developed to be able to meet the digital challenge[17]. Only diplomatics scholars can accomplish this and should do it before our digital documentary heritage is lost to future generations. If not they, who? If not now, when?

---

[16] The InterPARES Projects, which started in 1998, is funded by the Social Sciences and Humanities Research Council of Canada till 2019. Under the direction of this author it has gone through three phases, and has just started a fourth phase, called InterPARES Trust, the goal of which is to ensure that records generated and/or kept online can be maintained and proven authentic throughout their life. In other words, this fourth phase is about diplomatics of records in the Cloud. For the first three phases of the project, see <http://www.interpares.org/>. The website of the fourth phase, InterPARES Trust, will be found on the website of the Centre for the International Study of Contemporary Records and Archives: <http://www.ciscra.org/>.

[17] L. DURANTI/C. ROGERS, Educating for Trust, in Archival Science 11 (2011) p. 373–390. Also available electronically on SpringerLink DOI: 10.1007/s10502-011-9152-3. See <http://www.springerlink.com/openurl.asp?genre=article&id=doi:10.1007/s10502-011-9152-3>; DURANTI/ENDICOTT-POPOVSKY, Digital Records Forensics p. 45–63; DURANTI, Diplomatics.

II. Projects for the edition of texts and the publication of information

Proyecto ARQUIBANC – Digitalización de archivos privados catalanes
Una herramienta para la investigación

DANIEL PIÑOL ALABART

Introducción

En este trabajo se exponen las líneas generales de dos proyectos de investigación que tienen como eje central el trabajo con los archivos privados. Los dos proyectos, uno financiado por el Ministerio de Innovación y Ciencia y el otro por la Universidad de Barcelona quedan englobados bajo el nombre ARQUIBANC[1]. Este responde al mueble presente en muchas casas catalanas y en el que se guardaba la ropa de casa y, en la mayoría de casos, se utilizaba para guardar la documentación. El mueble al que nos referimos era un arcón con respaldo y servía también para sentarse delante de la chimenea, que era el centro vital de cualquier casa en tiempos pretéritos. En ambos proyectos participa profesorado de la universidad y se trabaja en colaboración con instituciones archivísticas y con algunos de los propietarios de documentación privada. Los objetivos marcados quieren poner de manifiesto la importancia que tiene la documentación privada para la construcción de la Historia y cómo es necesario el poder acceder a esta documentación para poder investigar.

En la mayoría de los casos la documentación privada se conserva en manos privadas, es decir, en manos de aquellas familias que generaron dichos archivos. En otras ocasiones la documentación se conserva en archivos públicos. Pero unos y otros casos la documentación debe de estar bien conservada y debe de poder ser accesible a los investigadores tal como manda la legislación archivística.

---

[1] Proyecto PGIR 08-09, de la Universitat de Barcelona. Proyecto de investigación HAR2008-01748 del Ministerio de Innovación y Ciencia.

El proyecto ARQUIBANC y la documentación privada catalana.

Cuando se diseñaron las líneas principales de la investigación el punto de partida se situaba en un conocimiento amplio de la situación de los archivos privados en Cataluña[2]. A partir del estudio previo basado en la bibliografía existente, en informes de la administración y en la propia experiencia, se fijaron los cuatro objetivos principales del proyecto: localizar archivos; recuperar la documentación; organizar los archivos en los que fuera necesario; difundir los archivos privados entre la comunidad científica.

En la actualidad nadie duda de la importancia que tiene el patrimonio documental privado en Cataluña para la investigación histórica. Así se constató en el *Coloquio internacional: Los archivos patrimoniales, situación actual y retos de futuro* celebrado en los días 1 y 2 de junio en la Universidad de Barcelona. El coloquio, centrado en los archivos patrimoniales, concluyó que la documentación privada en general y la de los archivos patrimoniales es fundamental para la construcción de la Historia. Entre los archivos privados debemos contar con los archivos patrimoniales, los familiares – a veces es difícil diferenciar unos de otros-, empresariales, entidades de derecho privado, y personales[3]. Pero de todos estos archivos los que más nos han interesado son los patrimoniales por la importancia capital que tienen para poder entender el desarrollo histórico, económico, social y cultural de Cataluña. Estos archivos se han creado para la gestión de patrimonios y de empresas familiares, han servido para fijar la memoria de las familias que los generaron y también para gestionar el ámbito más íntimo y personal.

Algunos de los archivos privados catalanes se conservan en instituciones. Los ingresos de archivos privados en archivos públicos son habituales y forman parte de la política de preservación del patrimonio documental privado que lleva a cabo la administración catalana. Así, entre los años 2002–2008 se calcula que se conservan en archivos públicos un total de 6.069 fondos privados (asociaciones, comerciales y empresas, patrimoniales, personales)[4]. Uno de los archivos que lidera la recuperación y depósito de archivos privados es el Arxiu Nacional de Catalunya, que ingresa archivos empresariales[5],

---

[2] P. Gifre/J. Matas/S. Soler, Els arxius patrimonials (2002).

[3] J. Boadas et al., Conceptes i tipologies de fons privats, in: Lligall. Revista catalana d'Arxivística 16 (2000) p. 299–301.

[4] Generalitat de Catalunya, Departament de Cultura, Estadística d'Arxius 2008, versión on-line <http://www20.gencat.cat/docs/CulturaDepartament/SSCC/GT/Arxius%20GT/arxius%202008.pdf>.

[5] Como ejemplo de esta iniciativa ver J. Fernández Trabal, Los archivos empresariales en Cataluña. Balance de 15 años de actuación del Arxiu Nacional de Catalunya, in: Revista de Historia Industrial 9 (1996) p. 183–98.

archivos personales y archivos patrimoniales[6]. De todos estos archivos privados 682 son archivos patrimoniales, conservados en archivos públicos, según datos de 2010[7].

Pero la mayoría de fondos se conservan en manos de sus propietarios. No disponemos de datos ya que no existe un inventario general del patrimonio archivístico privado pero sí que sabemos que, en el año 2002 el 70 % de los archivos patrimoniales de la provincia de Girona estaba en manos privadas[8]. Si bien los datos se refieren únicamente a los archivos patrimoniales, podemos pensar que los datos son extrapolables a las otras tipologías citadas anteriormente.

La legislación se ocupa de los archivos privados. Así, la Ley 9/1993 de 30 de septiembre, del Patrimonio Cultural Catalán[9], en el artículo 19.2/b es especifica que los documentos privados forman parte del patrimonio documental catalán. Y la Ley 10/2001, de 13 de julio, de Archivos y Documentos[10], remarca que su ámbito de actuación incluye los archivos privados. El artículo 13 de la Ley establece una serie de disposiciones para los propietarios a través de las cuales obligan a éstos a tener inventarios de sus archivos y a facilitar el acceso a los investigadores.

Localización

A partir de estas consideraciones previas se vio que el punto de partida que debía llevar a facilitar el acceso de los investigadores a la documentación era localizar los archivos. Este primer paso, relacionado con el primer objetivo, supone un trabajo complejo ya que no existe un censo de archivos. A pesar de esta carencia hemos encontrado vías para poder acceder a algunos de los archivos que se conservan en manos privadas. La primera, y la más importante, es el contacto directo con los propietarios. Algunos de ellos se acercan a la universidad para pedir información sobre sus documentos o para solicitar alguna transcripción paleográfica. Por esta vía se han podido localizar documentos interesantes como una libreta de censos enfitéuticos del siglo XIV perteneciente al Mas Ferrer, en Sitges, documento con el que se ha podido

---

[6] J. FERNÁNDEZ TRABAL, Aproximació al contingut dels arxius nobiliaris i el seu interès per a la investigació, in: Butlletí de l'Arxiu Nacional de Catalunya 28 (2011) p. 2–8.

[7] Generalitat de Catalunya, Departament de Cultura. "Estadística d'Arxius, Informe 2010", versión on line, <http://www20.gencat.cat/docs/CulturaDepartament/SSCC/GT/Arxius%20GT/Informe_Arxius_2010_def2.pdf>.

[8] GIFRE/MATAS /SOLER, Arxius p. 99–103.

[9] Diari Oficial de la Generalitat de Catalunya (DOGC), n. 1807, 11/10/1993.

[10] DOGC, n. 3437, 24/07/2001.

realizar un estudio de una comunidad rural en la época medieval[11]. Del mismo modo ha llegado hasta nosotros el *Llibre de la Baronia d'Eramprunyà*, un cartulario de los siglos XIV-XV con copias de documentación de la antigua Baronía de Eramprunyà, que estaba en manos de la familia Marc. La importancia de este cartulario llevó a su actual propietario a pedir una transcripción y un estudio diplomático del mismo. Este trabajo ha permitido saber que el cartulario estuvo desaparecido durante gran parte del siglo XX aunque se tenían noticias de su existencia. El cartulario ha sido editado y publicado recientemente[12].

Otra vía importante para localizar archivos es la contraria, es decir, cuando los investigadores vamos en búsqueda de los propietarios para que permitan investigar en sus en sus archivos. Ello pide un conocimiento previo que indique a qué persona, familiar o lugar debemos dirigirnos para conseguir ver un archivo. Así hemos accedido al notable archivo Fontcuberta, un conjunto documental formado por tres fondos archivísticos independientes, con fechas que van desde mediados del siglo X hasta el siglo XXI.

También debemos considerar los trabajos de los alumnos dentro del Grado de Historia o del Máster en Culturas Medievales. Son trabajos basados en documentación que los alumnos conservan en sus casas. Por ejemplo se han podido localizar más de una cuarentena de archivos privados de la comarca catalana de Osona. Pero estos archivos representan, no obstante, una pequeña parte de los archivos patrimoniales conservados en dicha comarca. También se ha realizado un trabajo de inventario de los archivos patrimoniales en la localidad barcelonesa de Sant Cugat del Vallès y la posteriors elaboración de una base de datos[13]. Otro trabajo ha utilizado documentación conservada en el Castell del Papiol, en Barcelona, para poder realizar la biografía de uno de los señores feudales de este castillo, en el siglo XIV[14].

Ya se ha hecho referencia a los archivos privados conservados en archivos públicos, y éstos también son objeto de nuestra atención. Se trata de los archivos comarcales catalanes, el Arxiu Nacional de Catalunya o el Archivo de la Corona de Aragón en Barcelona en los que se constata que el ingreso de fondos privados es constante[15]. De esta manera se han localizado más de 300 ar-

---

[11] C. MUNTANER ALSINA, Els Milà Ferreres de Sitges (Barcelona, Cataluña): un ejemplo de pequeño archivo familiar en el seno de una comunidad rural, in: Arquivos de família, séculos XIII-XX: que presente, que futuro (en prensa).

[12] El Llibre de la Baronia d'Eramprunyà, ed. E. CANTARELL/M. COMAS/C. MUNTANER (2011).

[13] F. GIMÉNEZ, Els arxius de les masies de Sant Cugat del Vallès (septiembre de 2011).

[14] A. ORIVE, Galceran de Papiol (1285–1318): senyor del Castell de Papiol (enero de 2011).

[15] Los trabajos presentados se publicaron in: Lligall. Revista Catalana d'Arxivística 16 (2000).

chivos privados conservados en archivos públicos, aunque se ha trabajado con datos del año 2009.

Recuperación

Somos conscientes que los archivos privados, en ocasiones, pueden ser objeto de expolios, dispersiones, ventas o destrucciones. Por ello creemos que el segundo paso en la investigación es la recuperación de archivos, aunque algunos de ellos están en condiciones de conservación muy óptimas, y cuentan con instrumentos de descripción adecuados. Pero también hay algunos que se conservan de forma deficientes. Desde el punto de vista de la investigación se trata de recuperar archivos privados por su valor historiográfico. Los miembros del equipo de investigación creemos en la obligación que tenemos de recuperar esta documentación y poner al alcance de la comunidad investigadora.

Organización

La mayoría de archivos privados tienen un sistema de organización realizado en siglos pasados pero que todavía resulta útil, aunque no esté dentro de los parámetros de la archivística actual. Cuando en un archivo que localizamos no encontramos un sistema de clasificación seguimos el modelo del cuadro de clasificación de los archivos patrimoniales conservados en el Arxiu Nacional de Catalunya. Uno de los archivos en los que hemos centrado más nuestra atención es el ya citado archivo Fontcuberta. En este archivo existen unos índices elaborados en 1887 que contienen la fecha, el regesto de cada uno de los documentos, con la fecha, el nombre del notario que validó el documento y todos los datos de su ubicación física en el archivo. Este archivo reúne tres fondos patrimoniales completamente independientes y procedentes de tres patrimonios diferentes: el fondo Fontcuberta (siglos XIII-XXI), representa la rama principal a la que se han agregado los otros dos, pero sin mezclarse; el fondo Perramon (siglos XIII-XIX); i el fondo Sentmenat (siglos X-XIX).

Difusión

Los pasos anteriores llevan a este último de la difusión. El objetivo último del proyecto es facilitar a los investigadores que puedan consultar los archivos. El acceso a los archivos privados queda garantizado, en teoría, por la legislación archivística. Pero el acceso generalmente no se hace efectivo ni se traduce en una accesibilidad práctica[16]. Por un lado faltan facilidades por parte de los propietarios para que los investigadores accedan a los documentos; por otro no existen instrumentos de descripción que permitan conocer la documentación conservada en cada caso, excepto en aquellos archivos en los que sí que existen. Por ello nuestro proyecto quiere acercar los archivos privados a los investigadores. Una de las estrategias seguidas es la digitalización de la documentación, aunque esto solamente se puede llevar a cabo cuando los propietarios accedan a este proceso. Para llevar a cabo la digitalización se tienen en cuenta algunas consideraciones para no procurar no cometer algunos de los errores que son habituales. Por ejemplo queremos evitar realizar una digitalización indiscriminada y seguir algunos criterios que permitan racionalizar el proceso[17]. Para ello la digitalización comienza con la preparación de los documentos (elección de los que se van a digitalizar – anteriores al siglo XVII –; comprobación de los índices antiguos; indicaciones a la empresa externa ...)[18]. Dentro del proceso de digitalización somos conscientes de cuestiones que nos llevan a la reflexión. Por ejemplo, pensamos que la digitalización, tan en auge en los últimos años, no debería ser el objetivo, sino un medio. ¿Por qué digitalizamos? No para conservar, puesto que se conserva mucho mejor un pergamino medieval que un archivo electrónico. La conservación era una de las primeras intenciones cuando la Archivística hablaba de digitalizar documentos, sobre todo documentos privados[19]. Pero después se ha visto que la utilidad de la digitalización estaba destinada a la difusión, entendiéndola ésta dentro de diferentes ámbitos, por ejemplo, en la Paleografía y la Diplomática, ciencias para las que las ilustraciones y las reproducciones de documentos son fundamentales. Las publicaciones de Paleografía y los materiales dedicados a la docencia tienen que ir siempre acompañadas por imágenes de documentos. La digitalización es pues una solución para las publicaciones pero también para la docencia ya que la mayoría de miembros del equipo de investigación somos docentes en Paleografía y Diplomática.

La digitalización se realiza a través de una empresa externa a la universidad y financiada a través del presupuesto del proyecto. A la empresa se le indica qué documentos hay que digitalizar y con qué calidad. Por ejemplo, se realiza una copia de calidad alta en formato TIFF para poder conservar las imágenes en discos duros externos; se realiza una segunda copia de baja resolución en formato JPG para poder insertarla en la base de datos a través de la que se

---

[16] E. Yakel, Els arxius a l'era de l'accessibilitat, in: Lligall. Revista Catalana d'Arxivística 23 (2005) p. 117–34.

[17] E. Serra, Digitalització? Parlem-ne, in: BID. Textos universitaris de biblioteconomia i documentació 24 (2010), publicació on-line <http://bid.ub.edu/24/serra1.htm>

[18] M. Day, Preparing Collection for Digitization (2011).

[19] R. E. Seton, The Preservation and Administration of Private Archives. A RAMP Study (1984).

puede consultar. Si la resolución fuera muy alta el manejo de la base de datos sería deficiente y se generarían problemas en la visualización de las imágenes. El formato JPG permite la búsqueda rápida, el acceso fácil y la lectura óptima de los documentos.

Los mismos criterios en lo que a formato se refiere se siguen cuando la digitalización la realizan miembros del equipo en el caso de archivos que no se pueden trasladar hasta la sede de la empresa digitalizadora. Entonces el proceso se realiza mediante una cámara digital en los mismos archivos o con un escáner en aquellos casos en que los documentos son llevados a la Universidad.

Una vez se han digitalizado los documentos se conservan en discos duros externos y se insertan en una base de datos alojada en el servidor de la Universitat de Barcelona. De hecho existen dos bases de datos. Una que recoge documentos sueltos o conjuntos documentales privados de poca entidad (base de datos Memoria); la otra base de datos (Scripta) incluye, por el momento, documentos procedentes del Arxiu Fontcuberta a causa de la gran cantidad de documentación conservada en este archivo (55 metros lineales). Esta base de datos contiene las fichas de descripción de cada unidad documental y en todas ellas hay un campo en el que se incluye el regesto y otro con la imagen de la mayoría de documentos. Las fichas de las bases de datos siguen las directrices marcadas por la norma internacional de descripción archivística ISAD(G), aunque con variaciones notables sugeridas por Pere Puig para la descripción de los pergaminos documentales[20]. Se prevé incluir un campo con la transcripción en aquellos casos en que la imagen no sea lo suficientemente óptima para ser leída a través de la pantalla o que no se haya podido digitalizar por diferentes motivos (falta de autorización del propietario, estado muy deficiente de conservación ...). Los otros campos incluyen datos de descripción como por ejemplo la cronología, la lengua, soporte, tradición documental, tipología documental, formato, notario ... Las búsquedas se pueden realizar por palabras a través de todos estos campos y se pueden listar los documentos por todos los campos excepto por el regesto. Todo el equipo de investigación participa en la elaboración de las fichas, en definitiva, en la descripción archivística de los documentos. Para que todos los colaboradores en esta tarea sigan los mismos criterios se incluye un libro de estilo en las notas de edición de la base de datos.

Esta base de datos está incluida en una página web que también permite la difusión de los resultados de investigación[21]. Uno de los elementos presentes en la base de datos es el formulario para solicitar la autorización para la consulta de la base de datos. En un principio se prevé que únicamente la persona

---

[20] P. Puig, Los pergaminos. Qué son y cómo se tratan (2008).
[21] <http://www.ub.edu/arquibanc/home.html>.

interesada en utilizar la base de datos con los documentos para llevar a cabo una investigación pueda acceder a ella después de solicitar la autorización. Los archivos que no pueden ser digitalizados se citan en la web también como una forma de dar difusión a estos archivos y que los investigadores tengan conocimiento de su existencia. Se incluyen también enlaces a los archivos públicos que conservan fondos privados.

Pero esta difusión a través de la red nos lleva a otra reflexión. Ciertamente que es importante encontrar información sobre documentos privados en Internet y poder recuperar esta información rápidamente[22]. Pero cabría preguntarse si es necesario que las imágenes sean accesibles a todo el mundo o hay que establecer alguna restricción. En el proyecto se ha decidido controlar el acceso a través del mecanismo del formulario de solicitud de la autorización. Habría que reflexionar también en torno a la cuestión de quién debe ser el primer usuario de la base de datos y de las imágenes. Y somos conscientes, después de reconducir el último objetivo de la difusión, que la base de datos va dirigida, en un primer lugar, a los miembros del equipo de investigación. Las imágenes se incluyen en la base de datos para que los investigadores del equipo puedan trabajar más cómodamente, sin necesidad de acudir a los archivos privados, en la realización de trabajo de investigación.

También reflexionamos sobre la difusión en la red, que es importante, pero la tendencia actual nos lleva a olvidar otras formas de difusión que no pueden ser dejadas de lado en ningún caso. Nos referimos a la publicación y edición de fuentes como elemento básico para poder difundir documentos privados entre los investigadores. En el ámbito de las ciencias auxiliares de la Historia existen numerosas iniciativas de edición de fuentes. Por ejemplo citamos el proyecto de la *Catalunya carolíngia* que edita documentos catalanes anteriores al año 1000. O la Fundació Noguera que publica ediciones de fuentes notariales procedentes de los importantes y notables archivos notariales catalanes. Nuestro proyecto ha localizado el ya citado *Llibre de la Baronia d'Eramprunyà* y ha llevado a cabo su edición con la financiación del propietario y se ha iniciado recientemente el trabajo de edición de otro cartulario perteneciente a la misma baronía.

Desde el punto de vista de la historiografía los archivos patrimoniales son importantes para poder realizar monografías locales y pensamos que también estas monografías, con la inclusión de apéndices documentales, pueden ser otra vía para difusión de documentación privada. Pero sobre todo la historiografía local es muy importante porque acerca la Historia fuera del ámbito

---

[22] V. GIMÉNEZ CHORNET, La recuperació de la informació en els arxius en línia, in: BID. Textos universitaris de biblioteconomia i documentació 27 (2011), publicación on-line <http://bid.ub.edu/27/gimenez1.htm>.

académico y estas publicaciones pueden ser una forma de visualizar el uso de los archivos en general, y de los privados en particular, para la construcción del pasado.

* * *

Si una pequeña parte de los numerosos archivos privados conservados en Cataluña puede ser consultada por los investigadores o si las herramientas diseñadas permiten conocer la existencia de estos archivos, el proyecto habrá cumplido con los objetivos marcados. Acercando los archivos a la comunidad científica cumplimos con la obligación que nos impone la sociedad de trabajar en beneficio de quién financia la investigación. Y cumplimos un poco también con la obligación de hacer avanzar el conocimiento de nuestro pasado, para el que los archivos privados son una fuente inagotable de información.

Sources and persons of public power in 7th–11th-century Italy
The idea of *Italia Regia* and the *Italia Regia* project[1]

ANTONELLA GHIGNOLI

1. *Italia Regia* as a framework

The idea of *Italia Regia* has been in existence for quite some time, during which the complexity of its nature has significantly increased[2]. *Italia Regia* has become a point of aggregation and collaboration between scholars[3] and, at the same time, a heuristic framework for research projects, to which the book series "Italia Regia" is dedicated[4]. It has also become a method of studying not only the documentation issued by the royal power or by public agents, but also the recipients of preserved public documents and the individuals involved in the genesis of public writings at any level, with or without

---

[1] Arguments and considerations expressed in this paper come from a long-term collaboration between François Bougard, Antonella Ghignoli and Wolfgang Huschner: the three editors and scientific coordinators of the project *Italia Regia*.

[2] An overview, from the ‚invention' of *Italia Regia* as conceptualised by François Bougard, when he was *Directeur des Études médiévales* at the *École Française de Rome*, to the completion of the database, in A. GHIGNOLI, Le ricerche sui diplomi regi e imperiali dell'Archivio arcivescovile e dell'Archivio capitolare di Lucca, in: Il patrimonio documentario della chiesa di Lucca. Prospettive di ricerca. Atti del Convegno Internazionale di Studi (Lucca, Archivio Arcivescovile, 14–15 novembre 2008), a cura di S. PAGANO/P. PIATTI (Toscana Sacra 2, 2010) p. 109–129.

[3] In addition to the three editors (see above note 1) there is a scientific committee for *Italia Regia*: Giulia Barone, Stefano Gasparri, Flavia De Rubeis.

[4] At the publisher Eudora Verlag, Leipzig: Europäische Herrscher und die Toskana im Spiegel der urkundlichen Überlieferung. I sovrani europei e la Toscana nel riflesso della tradizione documentaria (800–1100), hg. von F. BOUGARD/A. GHIGNOLI/W. HUSCHNER, unter Mitarbeit von S. Roebert und K. Viehmann (Italia Regia, 1), in press; Herrscherurkunden für Empfänger in Lothringen, Oberitalien und Sachsen (9.–12. Jahrhundert). Diplomatische und historische Forschung, hg. von W. HUSCHNER/TH. KÖLZER, unter Mitarbeit von K. Viehmann (Italia Regia, 2), forthcoming in 2014.

an official title. *Italia Regia* is also a digital tool, and it is on this aspect that the short presentation below will focus[5].

Since early and high medieval kingdoms of Latin Europe were not based upon institutional but on personal structures, the monarchs had to cooperate with the secular and clerical nobility who exercised an autonomous or nearly independent rule in their territories. The communication between both parties took place in situations of proximity and distance via oral, symbolic, and script-based forms. As a script-based form, the royal charter represents the principal source for the investigation of the modes of relation and 'communication' between representatives of the social *élites*. Another mode of relation of no less importance is represented by the record of legal disputes (*notitia iudicati, placitum*). Due to its history of research and its uniquely rich documentary tradition, Italy is a perfect regional case study with around 1200 royal charters for Italian recipients and 600 *placita*.

From around 1970, the diplomatic analysis of the royal charters has shifted from traditional questions of legal and constitutional history to aspects of communication, ritual and social history[6]. Nevertheless, the old as well as the new approaches judge the charters almost exclusively from the perspective of the monarch, in evident contradiction to the political structure of early and high medieval realms. The records of legal disputes, however, as part of the system of the documentation, need a more complex approach[7]. The Italian tradition allows for the investigation of the manifold connections between legal and royal charters as well as their differences with respect to various evaluation criteria[8].

---

[5] See also A. Ghignoli/U. Parrini, Il sistema informatico del progetto "Italia Regia". Risultati per la Toscana, in: Europäische Herrscher und die Toskana (see note 4).

[6] It is sufficient here to mention the studies of Heinrich Fichtenau, Hagen Keller, Peter Rück. On the wide range of subjects, that international research has been dealing with over the last five decades by investigating the scope of meaning of early and high medieval royal charters in the orally dominated societies of Latin Europe, see Th. Kölzer, Diplomatik, in: AfD 55 (2009) p. 405–424, here p. 412, 416–421.

[7] See as starting point F. Bougard, La justice dans le royaume d'Italie de la fin du VIIIᵉ siècle au début du XIᵉ siècle (Bibliothèque des Écoles françaises d'Athènes et de Rome 291, 1995); and also ID., Écrire le procès: le compte rendu judiciaire entre VIIIᵉ et XIᵉ siècle, in: Médiévales 56 (printemps 2009) p. 23–40.

[8] F. Bougard, Diplômes et notices de plaid: dialogue et convergence, in: Europäische Herrscher und die Toskana (see note 4). Moreover, use as evidence in legal disputes was an exceptionally important function of the royal charters from the point of view of successive generations of recipients. Legal charters could precede, accompany or follow royal charters. The text of royal charters was often included in legal charters, thus being transferred into a different document type, written, or, in other cases, authenticated by judges and notaries.

Within the framework of the 'idea' conceptualised in *Italia Regia*, the co-ordinators thought a database to be the best digital tool to connect together royal charters, *placita* and persons involved in the written world of early medieval *Regnum Italiae*. The database becomes an essential starting point for the study of: 1) the royal charters from four different and equivalent perspectives of recipient, mediator, issuer and scribe, as well as in the three stages of its 'biography', that is genesis, importance during the lifetime of participating individuals and importance for later generations; 2) the records of legal disputes. In both cases, documents are investigated according to proper methods of diplomatic analysis, with a clear focus on questions of textual tradition[9], and connecting them (*diplomata* and *placita*) to each other, with the aim of understanding the structure of public power *sub specie scripturarum*.

2. *Italia Regia* Database

The Data Base Management System used is MySQL. The server http (Apache) is located at the Scuola Normale Superiore (SNS) of Pisa[10]: the cgi-bin pro-

---

[9] The question of text transmission is crucial in any case – as we know – in historical research. It assumes particular weight in this project and particularly for the royal charters. The project aims to examine systematically documents of different issuers (imperial, pontifical, episcopal, princely and legal charters etc.) as well as counterfeits which were issued earlier, simultaneously or later, and which are directly or indirectly linked with the corresponding royal charter concerning contents or graphic design. Therefore, the project aims also to consider the variously shaped copies of royal charters as independent carriers of meaning. This leads to the question of the intentions of the party ordering a copy, and of the representation of the intention of the copyist. With respect to the "afterlife" of the (original) diplomas, it is also relevant to note which of the elaborately designed exterior characteristics had been copied, emphasised or ignored by copyists of successive generations. Another question relates to determining the function and usage period of copies which not only imitated the exact content of the original, but also its exterior design. The examination of each royal charter within three stages of its 'biography' allows for the identification of earlier documents as graphic models, the analysis of the scope of meaning of the exterior characteristics in the period of the document's origin as well as determining which characteristics continued or shifted in successive generations.

[10] The SNS server has been used because of the acquired experiences with information technology (IT) applications targeted to the communication and management of cultural heritage and resources at that institution. IR-Database is a creation of LARTTE (*Laboratorio per l'Analisi, la Ricerca, la Tutela, le Tecnologie e l'Economia del patrimonio culturale*), the Interdisciplinary centre for the research, planning and management of cultural Heritage, which has been one of the research centres of the Faculty of Arts of the SNS since 2004: <http://lartte.sns.it/>. It developed in response to the transformations taking place both on a national and international level, which have produced nu-

The table of Fig. 1 shows the structure designed for the *Italia Regia* Database
(IR-Database).

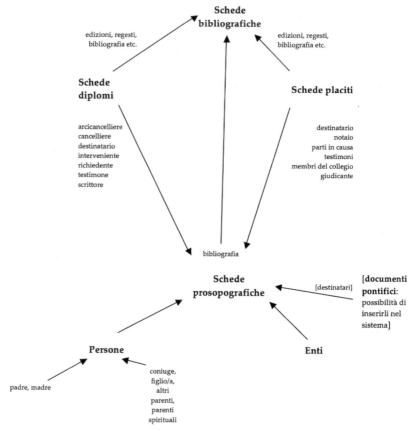

Fig. 1. Structure of IR-Database

grams written in Perl programming language are run to generate html pages
dynamically. It is a relational and dynamic database enabling corrections and
amendments at any time. The registered collaborators of the project work
online in internet[11]. Under the supervision of the editors, collaborators can

merous areas of interest for the laboratory: history of archaeology, history of art, history of collections, legislation on cultural heritage, IT applications for cultural heritage,
protection, management, communication and best use of cultural heritage. Various multidisciplinary research groups are currently operating within LARTTE and developing
research projects at a national and international level, and continuing collaborations
with museums, directorates, archives, libraries and research institutes. For the collaboration with our project, *Italia Regia*, see: <http://lartte.sns.it/index.php?id=87>.

[11] At the following internet address: <http://lartte.sns.it/scriba/>.

complete the 'forms' of the database with information or textual passages that result from the research undertaken on a particular document. They can also search the forms completed by other colleagues; in this way a collaborator may compare or query any documents held within the ever-growing database, thus increasing new results for documents still in preparation. In other words, the database functions as a storage of data and, at the same time, as a dynamic tool. Fig. 2 shows the homepage of IR-database, the digital desk of our research project.

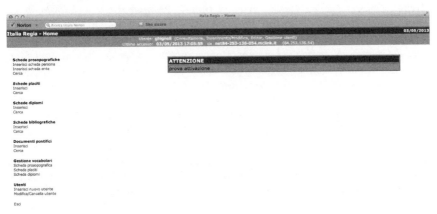

Fig. 2. Homepage of IR-Database

Despite the international composition of the research group, the working language of the database is Italian. The research fellows, however, can use German as well as French when communicating with each other.

The forms for royal charters ("Scheda diplomi") and records of legal disputes ("Scheda placiti") are conceived according to a problem-oriented diplomatic question pattern[12]. The operation of completing a form requires an in-

---

[12] The structure of the database is also ready to include data from papal documents (see above Fig. 1 and Fig. 2: "Documenti pontifici"). To have an idea of the structure and since it is not possible to reproduce the image of the whole *scheda*, here is the articulated series of data fields in the "Scheda Diplomi": *Inserito, Modificata, Stato* (fields concerning the status of the form), *Provincia, Diocesi, Autore, Destinatario, Chiave Destinatario, Note Destinatario, Data (testo), Data da (anno), Data a (anno), Data Note, Luogo, Regesto, Segnatura archivistica, Tradizione diplomatistica, Note tradizione, Note dorsali, Dimensioni, Stato di conservazione, Note stato di conservazione, Arcicancelliere, Chiave scheda arcicancelliere, Interveniente, Chiave interveniente, Note interveniente, Petente, Chiva petente, Note petente, Tetimone, Chiave testimone, Note testimone, Scriba, Chiave scriba, Note scriba, Numero righe, Rigatura, Misura interlinea, Marginatura, Descrizione della scrittura, Invocazione simbolica, Invocazione verbale, Note invocazione verbale, Intitulatio, Note intitulatio,*

depth analysis of the document[13] – in its external[14] and internal features – which could take place in an archive, in a library or indeed in the collaborator's own home: a not-insignificant collection of digital photos of charters is at the project's disposal.

A prosopographic section ("Schede prosopografiche") is added for systematically recording the persons named in a charter or involved in any way in its genesis, as well as to record their positions and ranks, and their interre-

---

Arenga (num), Arenga (testo), Arenga (note), Promulgatio / Inscriptio, Note Promulgatio /Inscriptio, Narratio, Note narratio, Formula di immunità, Note formula di immunità, Formula di Pena, Note formula di pena, Corroboratio, Note corroboratio, Riga del signum, Note riga del signum, Monogramma, Signum speciale, Ricognizione, Note ricognizione, Signum recognitionis, Datazione, Note datazione, Apprecatio, Note apprecatio, Sigillo, Documento anteriore, Note documento anteriore, Documento posteriore, Note documento posteriore, MGH, FSI, Altre edizioni, Note edizione, Regesta imperii, Citazione in altri documenti, Riproduzioni, Traduzione, Bibliografia. The series of data fields in the "Scheda placiti" is as follows: *Inserito, Modificata, Stato* (fields concerning the status of the form), *Provincia, Diocesi, Data (testo), Data da (anno), Data a (anno), Data Note, Luogo dell'azione giudiziaria, Note luogo, Luogo di redazione del placito, Note luogo, Definizione del documento, Parti in causa, Chiave parti in causa, Destinatario, Chiave destinatario, Note destinatario, Regesto, Segnatura archivistica, Tradizione diplomatistica, Note tradizione, Note dorsali, Dimensioni, Descrizione della scrittura, Impaginazione, Tipo di formulario, Note tipo formulario, Componente del collegio giudiziario, Qualifica componente collegio, Chiave componente collegio, Numero udienze, Note numero udienze, Procedura, Note procedura, Prova, Testo/Note prova, Sentenza /decisione, Citazioni o riferimenti giuridici, Compromesso, Citazioni o riferimenti giuridici, Pena pecuniaria, Citazioni o riferimenti giuridici, Pena spirituale, Citazioni o riferimenti giuridici, Ordine di documentazione, Testimone giudiziario, Chiave scheda testimone, Note testimone, Sacramentalis, Chiave scheda sacramentalis, Note sacramentalis, Notaio, Chiave scheda notaio, Note notaio, Testimone, Chiave scheda testimone, Note testimone, Citazione in altri documenti, Note, Edizione, Bibliografia.*

[13] Furthermore, the evaluation of one individual charter (*diploma* or *placitum*) needs the examination of approximately seven or eight further preceding, contemporary or later documents by different issuers, of different kinds and transmission forms.

[14] The external features of the charters, especially for the diplomas, which have only been considered as "decorative" elements and therefore often ignored, are examined systematically and equally in combination with the internal features of originals, copies and counterfeits. The project studies the effect of different types of scripts (diplomatic minuscule, capitalis, use of uncial letters) or elaboration of scripts (*litterae elongatae*), their hierarchy and the features of the authentication means (wax seals, lead seals) over large or short viewing distances as well as the entire composition of the charter image. The role of symbols for Christ, the Virgin Mary and other saints in different places of the charters may be of great importance. Determining the potential range of meaning for the usage of the letter combination (*Nexus litterarum*) is one further objective of the project as well as potential influences of the Byzantine praxis.

lations reflected in the document. A third section ("Schede bibliografiche") is dedicated to references to other sources and literature. These four principal tables (Schede) are related through common fields ("key-fields"). Accurate completion of the forms is an essential requirement for the IR-Database to be a dynamic and functional network of interrelated information: the collaborators have to follow specific guidelines.

Fig. 3 and 4 show respectively the beginning of a "Scheda Placiti", and its final part (printing the whole Scheda would mean 10 A4-size pages): this is a *placitum* dated 1st July 997, Lucca.

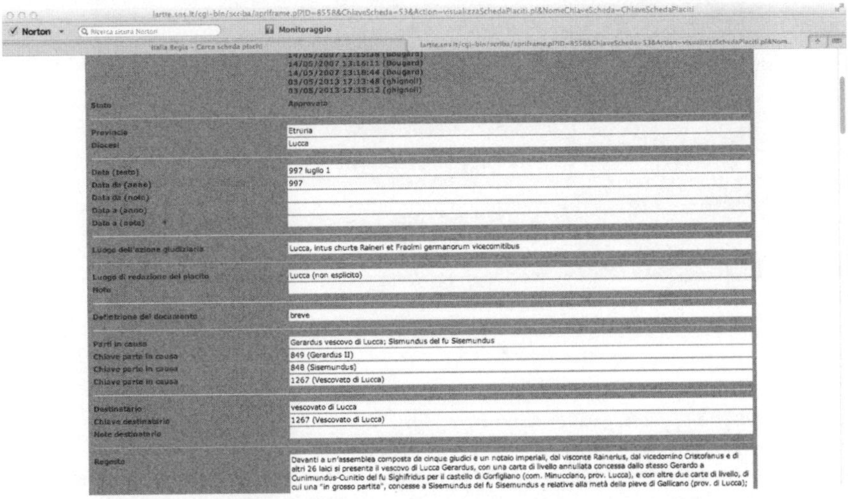

Fig. 3

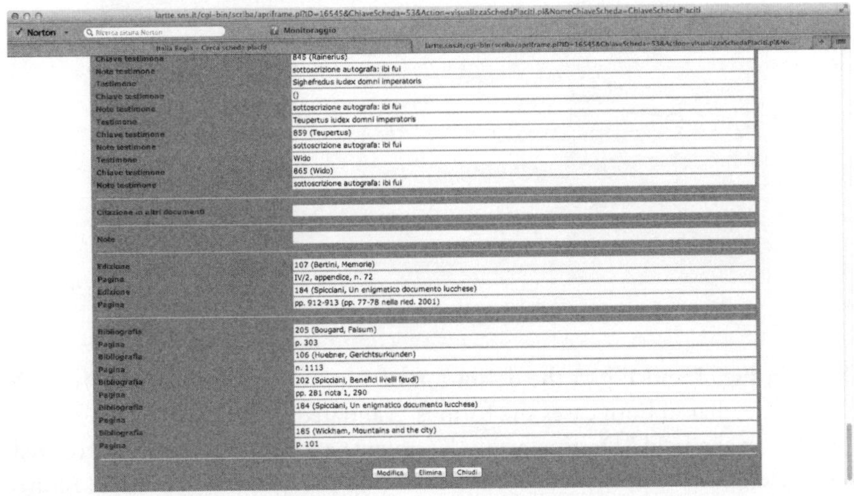

Fig. 4

Fig. 5 and 6 show respectively the initial fields of a "Scheda diplomi", and the fields of the middle of the form: this is the D O II 239 dated 31st December 980, Ravenna.

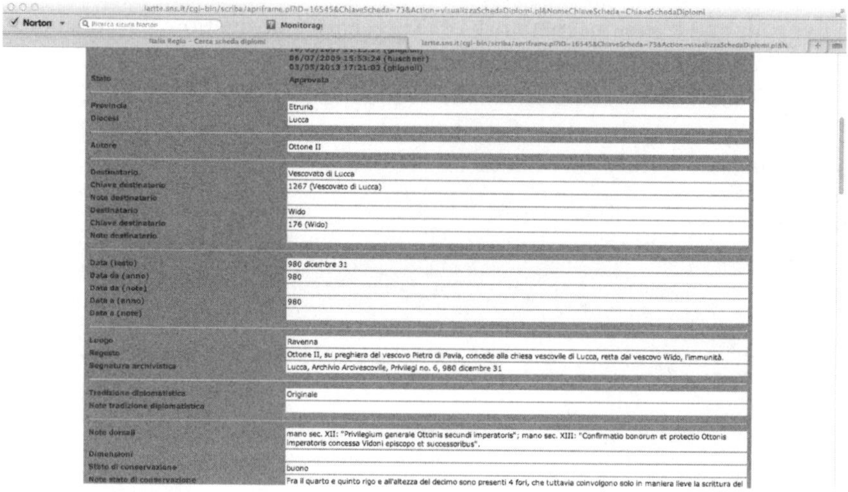

	06/07/2009 15:53:24 (huschner) 03/05/2013 17:21:03 (ghignoli)
Stato	Approvata
Provincia	Etruria
Diocesi	Lucca
Autore	Ottone II
Destinatario	Vescovato di Lucca
Chiave destinatario	1267 (Vescovato di Lucca)
Note destinatario	
Destinatario	Wido
Chiave destinatario	176 (Wido)
Note destinatario	
Data (testo)	980 dicembre 31
Data da (anno)	980
Data da (note)	
Data a (anno)	980
Data a (note)	
Luogo	Ravenna
Regesto	Ottone II, su preghiera del vescovo Pietro di Pavia, concede alla chiesa vescovile di Lucca, retta dal vescovo Wido, l'immunità.
Segnatura archivistica	Lucca, Archivio Arcivescovile, Privilegi no. 6, 980 dicembre 31
Tradizione diplomatistica	Originale
Note tradizione diplomatistica	
Note dorsali	mano sec. XII: "Privilegium generale Ottonis secundi imperatoris"; mano sec. XIII: "Confirmatio bonorum et protectio Ottonis imperatoris concessa Vidoni episcopo et successoribus".
Dimensioni	
Stato di conservazione	buono
Note stato di conservazione	Fra il quarto e quinto rigo e all'altezza del decimo sono presenti 4 fori, che tuttavia coinvolgono solo in maniera lieve la scrittura del

Fig. 5

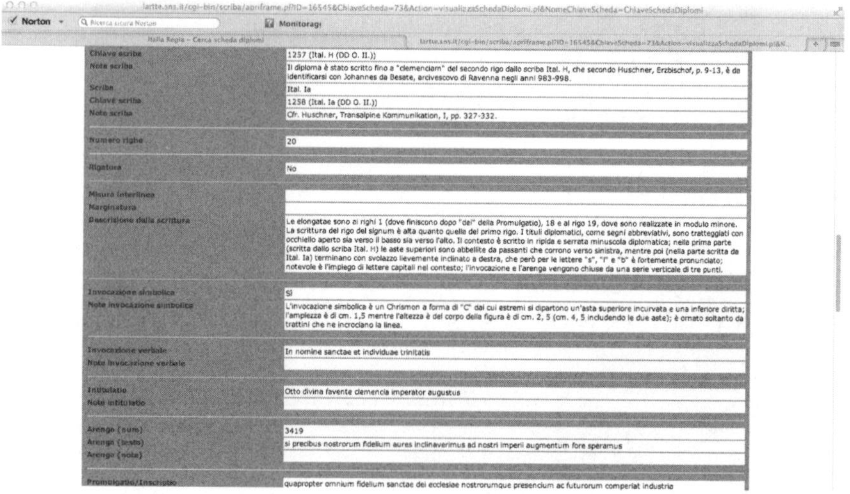

Chiave scriba	1257 (Ital. H (DD O. II.))
Note scriba	Il diploma è stato scritto fino a "clemenciam" del secondo rigo dallo scriba Ital. H, che secondo Huschner, Erzbischof, p. 9-13, è da identificarsi con Johannes da Besate, arcivescovo di Ravenna negli anni 983-998.
Scriba	Ital. Ia
Chiave scriba	1258 (Ital. Ia (DD O. II.))
Note scriba	Cfr. Huschner, Transalpine Kommunikation, I, pp. 327-332.
Numero righe	20
Rigatura	No
Misura interlinea	
Marginatura	
Descrizione della scrittura	Le elongatae sono ai righi 1 (dove finiscono dopo "dei" della Promulgatio), 18 e al rigo 19, dove sono realizzate in modulo minore. La scrittura del rigo del signum è alta quanto quella del primo rigo. I tituli diplomatici, come segni abbreviativi, sono tratteggiati con occhiello aperto sia verso il basso sia verso l'alto. Il contesto è scritto in ripida e serrata minuscola diplomatica; nella prima parte (scritta dallo scriba Ital. H) le aste superiori sono abbellite da passanti che corrono verso sinistra, mentre poi (nella parte scritta da Ital. Ia) terminano con svolazzo lievemente inclinato a destra, che però per le lettere "s", "l" e "b" è fortemente pronunciato; notevole è l'impiego di lettere capitali nel contesto; l'invocazione e l'arenga vengono chiuse da una serie verticale di tre punti.
Invocazione simbolica	Sì
Note invocazione simbolica	L'invocazione simbolica è un Chrismon a forma di "C" dai cui estremi si dipartono un'asta superiore incurvata e una inferiore diritta; l'ampiezza è di cm. 1,5 mentre l'altezza è del corpo della figura è di cm. 2, 5 (cm. 4, 5 includendo le due aste); è ornato soltanto da trattini che ne incrociano la linea.
Invocazione verbale	In nomine sanctae et individuae trinitatis
Note invocazione verbale	
Intitulatio	Otto divina favente clemencia imperator augustus
Note intitulatio	
Arenga (num)	3419
Arenga (testo)	si precibus nostrorum fidelium aures inclinaverimus ad nostri imperii augmentum fore speramus
Arenga (note)	
Promulgatio/Inscriptio	quapropter omnium fidelium sanctae dei ecclesiae nostrorumque presencium ac futurorum comperiat industria

Fig. 6

Note in Fig. 3 and Fig. 5 the definition of "approvata" in the field "stato": this means that in both cases the form is "validated". Note in Fig. 5 the name "Wido" in the field "Destinatario" (Recipient) and its presence in the related key-field "Chiave destinatario", which allows the queries — we shall return to this name later.

The structure of the relational and dynamic IR-Database allows also the possibility of interrelating images of scripts and symbols[15].

3. *Italia Regia* website

The *Italia Regia* Project also has an open-access website. Fig. 7 shows the homepage of the IR-Website[16], where the logo of the "Istituto storico italiano per il medio evo" is clearly visible: the project has been under the aegis of this national research Institute since 2009.

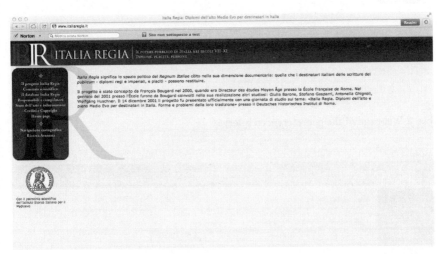

Fig. 7 Homepage of IR-Website

The website is conceived for the publication of all those data that are recorded in the IR-Database in validated forms, for example, the "schede" of the documents we saw above (see Fig. 3 and Fig. 5). From the pages of the IR-Website, external users can freely search data, explore a georeferenced map or use the

---

[15] This particular function – allowed, as we said, by the architecture of the database – is nevertheless still being discussed. The database shall offer images of the entire charter (recto and verso), close-ups and images of references to relevant preceding, simultaneous and later documents which are directly linked to the transmission of the corresponding charter. Graphic symbols, prominent writing samples and seals shall be included as details. If the archive has already released images for the internet, corresponding links should be established. An individual database category should be assigned to the images of subscriptions. The individual signatures, if available, could be linked to the respective prosopographic database entry of the corresponding person.

[16] At the internet address: <http://www.italiaregia.it>.

advanced queries page for specific searches. Fig. 8 illustrates the website data search, and Fig. 9 shows the page for advanced queries.

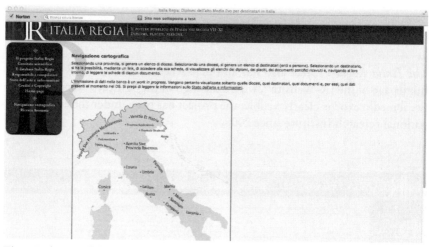

Fig. 8 Webpage of the georeferenced query

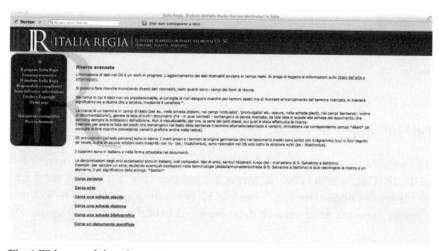

Fig. 9 Webpage of the advanced query

In Fig. 10 we can see what happens by searching, for example, for the person "Wido", seen in Fig. 5, in the form of the advanced query: the query generates a list.

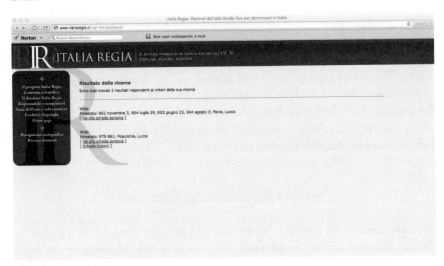

Fig. 10

Clicking the third link ("Scheda diploma") of the list displays the page shown in Fig. 11.

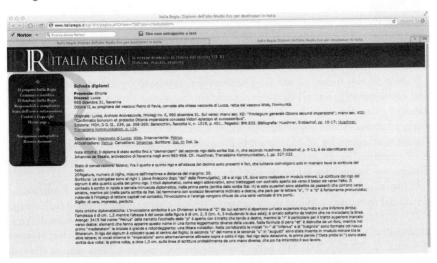

Fig. 11

It is the page in which all the information contained in the database about D O II 239 (see above Fig. 5 and Fig. 6) is combined together.

The role and architecture of the external structure of the IR-Database are nevertheless under discussion again within the research group, particularly with regards to the free access by anybody to the results of the project through the mechanism of queries[17]. In a not too distant future the *Italia Regia* website shall include a category in which material (scientific articles and papers of the members of the group, applied terminology, a methodological basis of the project, for example) is available as separate PDF files as well as direct links to the entries of editing and cataloguing projects (Codice diplomatico della Lombardia medievale, dMGH, Regesta Imperii). The homepage shall also offer key information about the project in languages other than Italian (almost certainly French and German, and of course English) to increase the effectiveness of the project.

4. *Italia Regia* at the present time

We have studied all charters (*diplomata* and *placita*) spatially distributed by Tuscan dioceses and by recipients[18], which means that the work of the *Italia Regia* team concerning the *provincia Etruria* is complete[19]. The project now intends to cover the *provincia Aemilia*[20], with the hope, in the future, of covering the whole of northern Italy (the main region of the Italian kingdom), in

---

[17] For example, particular problems concern the images of charters: to preserve the rights of the respective archives, external users should not be allowed to download any images.

[18] On the modeling suggestion of the structure of Kehr's *Italia Pontificia*, see again GHIGNOLI, Le ricerche sui diplomi regi p. 110–111 (see note 2).

[19] Not all the forms of the IR-Database are validated by the editors, however, and consequently, not all data concerning the *provincia Etruria* are searchable by external users through the *Italia Regia* website at the present time, for the reason declared above. Some important results, however, of this first phase are published in the form of essays by W. Huschner, F. Bougard, A. Ghignoli, G. Barone, S. Roebert, K. Viehmann, N. D'Acunto, and A. Verardi in: Europäische Herrscher und die Toskana im Spiegel der urkundlichen Überlieferung (see note 4).

[20] Initial publications concerning this new phase are: A. GHIGNOLI, Tradizione e critica del testo, una variante documentaria: il diploma di Ottone I per il fedele Ingo (D O. I. 371), in: Sit liber gratus, quem servulus est operatus. Studi in onore di Alessandro Pratesi per il suo 90° compleanno, a cura di P. CHERUBINI/G. NICOLAJ (Littera Antiqua 19, 2012) p. 231–247; EAD., Diplomi dei Salii per la Chiesa arcivescovile di Ravenna e critica del testo nel lavoro dello storico, in: Herrscherurkunden für Empfänger in Lothringen (see note 4); F. BOUGARD, Les diplômes des fonds ecclésiastiques de Plaisance, ibid.; K. VIEHMANN, Diplome des 9. und 10. Jh. für die bischöfliche Kirche von Parma, ibid.; M. SCHMIDT, Die Diplome Berengars I. für Bischof Petrus von Reggio Emilia (900–915) und seine Kirche, ibid.

order to give access to new information concerning all public documents during the period.

In conclusion, we conceived the IR-Database as a practical tool to support diplomatic, palaeographical and historical research within the framework of *Italia Regia*. Its digital dimension makes it an exceptionally versatile tool[21], with a high degree of potential, especially when considering the possibility to cross reference data and results and digital images[22]. However we do not intend the innovative nature of our project to be limited merely to the digital dimension. There are several other aspects of the 'idea' of *Italia Regia* that reflect the innovations of the project, of which we will mention only two in this paper. First, the traditional restriction on the perspective of the ruler is overcome, as the perspectives of all parties involved in the documentation – recipient, mediator, issuer and scribe – are systematically examined. Second, the common model of the chancellery, based on the modern idea of a chancellery, is rejected as a firmed assumption or an irrefutable guide-concept to study the political structure of this period[23]. For these two aspects – and for the others not mentioned here[24] – it is not required that the diplomatist and palaeographer or – as we prefer – the medievalist coming to grips with early medieval charters should necessarily be 'digital'.

In the case of *Italia Regia*, the digital tool – and its development with implied modifications – will have to run dependent on the success or failure of ideas and methods of historians, diplomatists and palaeographers.

---

[21] The IR-Database is an ongoing project and as such a work in progress; we acknowledge that much more can be done to fulfill the potential offered by this tool.

[22] That digital images represent a real innovation from the digital world of diplomatic research is stressed in M. ANSANI/A. GHIGNOLI, Testi digitali: nuovi media e documenti medievali, in: Les historiens et l'informatique: un métier à réinventer. Actes de l'atelier ATHIS VII organisé par l'École française de Rome avec le concours de l'ANR, Rome, 4–6 décembre 2008, études réunies par J.-PH. GENET/A. ZORZI (Collection de l'École française de Rome 444, 2010) p. 73–86.

[23] On this argument see W. HUSCHNER, Transalpine Kommunikation im Mittelalter. Diplomatische, kulturelle und politische Wechselwirkungen zwischen Italien und dem nordalpinen Reich (9. bis 11. Jahrhundert), (MGH Schriften 52, 2003); ID., Die ottonische Kanzlei in neuem Licht, in: AfD 52 (2006) p. 353–370; ID., L'idea della "cancelleria imperiale" nella ricerca diplomatica. Diplomi ottoniani per destinatari in Toscana, in: La Tuscia nell'alto e pieno medioevo. In memoria di Wilhelm Kurze, a cura di M. MARROCCHI/C. PREZZOLINO (2007) p. 183–197.

[24] For example, the number of data fields required for each "Scheda" or the quantity of documents analysed in each evaluation, see above notes 12 and 13.

The Repository view
Opening up medieval charters

RICHARD HIGGINS

The cataloguing of the manuscript collections now in the care of Durham University Library[1] has a long and complex history, reflecting the activities of a wide range of individuals and institutions. It remains in something of a state of flux, as it attempts to assimilate not just retroconversion of old lists, but also to cope with the arrival of new material and even the processing of collections on the behalf of other institutions for whom we provide archival services. In the interests of being able to train new archivists, and to avoid constant re-designing of stylesheets and web interfaces, it is important to follow consistent rules for the content and structure of descriptions of all material within the collections.

An archival repository can potentially look after any type of document, ranging from the most formal record sequence to undecipherable fragments, on any medium from papyrus to floppy disk. It is necessary to catalogue these all within one data structure, not just to make it feasible to run a cataloguing operation but also to be able to provide a coherent search and display system. Whereas the charter specialist may be able to assemble their metadata in a format designed solely with the charter format in mind, a repository needs a structure that can be adapted to many genres of document, with the potential to complement the rigor needed to organise data with the flexibility to accommodate the various depths of description befitting the items described. In English repositories, many collections of family papers will contain a few medieval charters, although nearly all the documents are from 18th to 20th century. The range of material and document types across even a single collection can be broad; when all these collections are considered together the breadth of material that has to be coped with is vast.

---

[1] For further information on the Library's Special Collections, see <http://www.dur.ac.uk/library/asc/>.

One of the major collections in the care of Durham University Library's Special Collections is the Durham Cathedral Archive[2]. This contains the records collected by the cathedral in the last thousand years, forming a continuous record of the physical buildings, the institutions that were based within it and the estates, rights and privileges that maintained it. The medieval part of this is the archive of Durham Priory, a well-preserved group of the records of the Benedictine house, its obedientiaries and daughter cells from the late 11th century until the dissolution of that institution at the end of 1539 and immediate refounding as Durham Cathedral. This has been being organised and catalogued for nearly as long as the building has been in existence, and preserves many features of medieval archival practice. The archive is indeed interesting not just for the content of the documents, but as a record of how records were made, retained and organised throughout the last millennium.

This is only one of some five hundred collections: few are as complex or contain documents requiring such detailed item level description, but each has peculiar characteristics that should be accommodated within the cataloguing process. Any descriptive metadata format suitable for this varied task needs to be elastic, adaptable and deployable. Elastic, because it may be used in the most summary manner to describe entire groups of material, or to analyse each separate document in great depth. Adaptable, in that it describes objects within collections that vary from homogeneous runs of similar material to the strange, isolated occurrences that can only be regarded as the survivals of circumstance (such as the 18th century wig worn by one bibliophile that accompanied his library into our collections). Most of all, it must be deployable, as it is pointless to expend any effort creating catalogues that cannot be effectively used. In this respect EAD[3] was ahead of the technology available when it first appeared. At the outset it used SGML, and relied upon either a downloadable viewer or software aimed at the giants of the military and aviation industry (the former still a strange concept in the early evolution of the World Wide Web, the latter priced to match a richer market than the archive repository). The expansion of the Web and the development of XML from SGML has now produced a choice of software from a range of mature products which, as will be seen, now enable the potential versatility of XML data to be exploited to many different purposes.

---

[2] For a description of this collection see <http://www.dur.ac.uk/library/asc/collection_information/cldload/?collno=41>.

[3] EAD is a standard in the care of the Library of Congress, homepage: <http://www.loc.gov/ead/>.

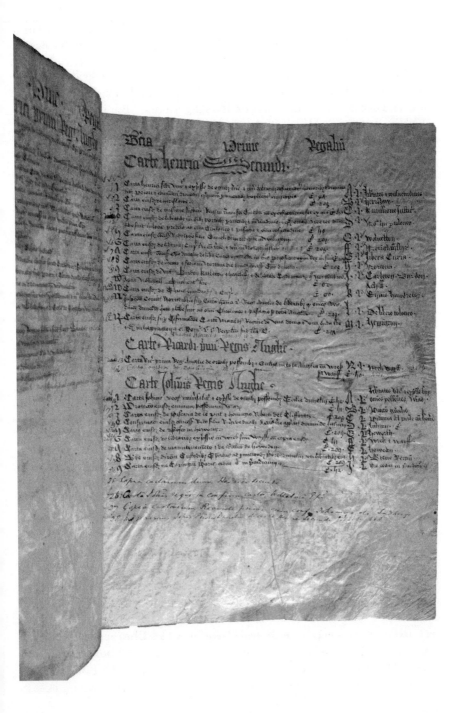

This page from the Repertorium Magnum, compiled in the mid-15th century and used as a finding aid to the collection until the 19th century, lists the section of the Regalia class (royal charters) issued by Henry II, Richard I and John.

EAD has proven a most flexible metadata format for describing collections at Durham. As a member of the UK Archives Hub[4] Durham has used it for over a decade to create collection level descriptions, but it is the ease with which it allows varied levels of detail to be incorporated into one system that really proves the value of the format. It enables material to be described at series or item level, and where a brief description of a group of documents has been given it is simple to expand this by adding extra information as the opportunity arises. Thus even when a charter has not yet been catalogued, it is possible to create blank entries that only contain the identifying reference numbers for the sequence of documents and to add a note to indicate those which have not survived. The next phase, having identified these empty sequences, is to expand the description with additional EAD elements containing descriptive text as and when resources become available.

The class of Miscellaneous Charters (as the name implies) was a post-medieval creation that served as a general category for all charters, including most of the post-medieval ones, that did not seem to form part of a sequence. Later comparison with medieval repertories and cartularies has enabled some original document groupings to be recreated, but the class remains a mixture in which some patterns can be discerned amongst the general flow of isolated documents. Apart from a 19th century manuscript slip catalogue (in Latin) there is no complete list describing all the documents. Material that had been identified as of specific interest, such as a scattered group that includes many of the earliest surviving Scottish royal charters, had more recent descriptions which have been added to the EAD catalogue, but this remains the section of the archive requiring the most work. That work is being done item by item, by adding to the existing EAD file.

The facility within EAD for linking between descriptions enables the concise recording of the complex relationships between archival documents. Thus the first three charters in the first compartment of the first box of the Eboracensia class of charters (broadly covering property held south of County Durham), although none of them physically exist at this location, are described thus, using the nested EAD <c0...> container to encode the hierarchical relationship between the documents:

```
<c01 level="series"><did><unittitle type="head" id="Eb">Eboracensia</unittitle>
</did><c02 level="file"><did><unittitle type="head" id="Eb-1">1.Eboracensia</unittitle></did><c03 level="item"><did><unitid id="Eb-1-1-1">1.1.Ebor.1</unitid>
</did><custodhist><p>= <archref altrender="endure" href="http://endure.dur.ac.uk:8080/
```

---

4 <http://archiveshub.ac.uk/>.

fedora/get/UkDhU:EADCatalogue.0071" xpointer="A-4-1-1">**4.1.Archiep.1**</archref>
</p></custodhist></c03><c03 level="item"><did><unitid id="Eb-1-1-2">**1.1.Ebor.2**</unitid></did><custodhist><p>= <archref altrender="endure" href="http://endure.dur.ac.uk:8080/ fedora/get/UkDhU:EADCatalogue.0091" xpointer="P-1-1-22">**1.1.Pap.22**</archref> (missing).</p></custodhist></c03><c03 level="item"><did><unitid id="Eb-1-1-3">**1.1.Ebor.3**</unitid></did><scopecontent><p>**Agreement between the prior and convent of Durham and the hospital of Allerton.**</p></scopecontent><custodhist><p>**Missing.**</p></custodhist><altformavail><p>**Copy:** <archref altrender="endure" href="http://endure.dur.ac.uk:8080/fedora/get/ UkDhU:EADCatalogue.0074" xpointer="ct3-44">**DCD Cart. III, f.81v–82r**</archref></p></altformavail></c03>

The first document is kept within the Archiepiscopalia class (charters issued by Archbishops) – a hyperlink connects to the description of it in that catalogue; the second would be in the Papalia class (charters issued by Popes) – although the document itself is missing a hyperlink connects to that catalogue, whence another link connects to the description of the document made from the earliest extant cartulary copy; the third document does not survive, but a link connects to the catalogue of the cartulary in which a copy exists, where it is described.

The previous example showed how EAD can describe documents that are not present; the hyperlinks used each connected to a detailed description of a single charter. Aside from the basic descriptive elements of reference number, date, physical characteristics, content and cross-references to later copies, transcriptions, digitised versions and bibliographical citations, it is also possible to use EAD to enhance the description of the charter, either to format the description in a meaningful way or to allow for semantic analysis of a corpus of descriptions.

<c03 level="item"><did><unitid countrycode="GB" repositorycode="GB-UkDhU" id="A-2-1-1">**2.1.Archiep.1**</unitid> <unitdate normal="12250124">**9 Kal. February, 10 [Walter Gray] [24 January 1225]**</unitdate><physdesc><physfacet type="seal">(<arc href href="http://endure.dur.ac.uk:8080/fedora/get/UkDhU:EADCatalogue.0184" xpointer="GB-3222" altrender="endure">**G&B 3222**</archref>) **Attached by double tag through folded foot of document.**</physfacet></physdesc></did> <scopecontent><p><genreform>**Charter**</genreform> of <persname role="grantor">**Walter [Gray] archbishop of York**</persname> **granting and confirming to the** <corpname role="grantee">**prior and convent of Durham**</corpname> **the due and ancient pensions that have been accustomed to receive from the churches in their gift in his diocese, namely from** <corpname>**Rounton**</corpname> **3 marks,** <corpname>**Kirby Sigston**</corpname> **10 marks,** <corpname>**St. Peter the Less, York**</corpname>, **1 mark,** <corpname>**All Saints York and Holtby**</corpname> **50s.,** <corpname>**Skipwith**</corpname> **1 mark,**

\<corpname>**Hemingbrough**\</corpname> **3 marks,** \<corpname>**Howden**\</corpname> **5 marks,** \<corpname>**Brantingham and the chapel of Blacktoft**\</corpname> **10 marks,** \<corpname>**Welton**\</corpname> **3 marks,** corpname>**Walkington** \</corpname> **100s.,** and \<corpname>**Normanton-on-Soar**\</corpname> **1 mark.**\</p>
\<p altrender="ddcwit">**Witnesses:** \<persname role="witness">**N[icholas] formerly bishop of Man and the Isles**\</persname>; < persname role="witness">**Richard the archbishop's chaplain**\</persname> **and** < persname role="witness">**Brother John the bishop's chaplain**\</persname>; \<persname role="witness">**Richard de Bereford**\</persname>; \<persname role="witness">**William de Vescy**\</persname>; \<persname role="witness">**Robert of Witton**\</persname>; < persname role="witness">**Odo of Richmond**\</persname> **and** < persname role="witness">**Reginald of Stowe**\</persname>, **clerks.**\</p>\<p>**Dated:** \<geogname role="issue">**Otley**\</geogname>.\</p>
\</scopecontent>\<altformavail>\<p>**Printed: Hutchinson,** \<title render="italic">**History of Durham**\</title>, **II, 79n**\</p>\</altformavail>\<altformavail>\<p>**Printed:** \<abbr> **RWaGry**\</abbr> **p.153 (Appx I No.XXIX) (from Cart. III)**\</p>\</altformavail>
\<altformavail>\<p>**Copied in** \<archref href="http://endure.dur.ac.uk:8080/fedora/get/ UkDhU:EADCatalogue.0078" xpointer="ke068" altrender="endure">**DCD Cham.Cart. f.5r**\</archref>, **with variations and omissions and** \<archref altrender="endure" xpointer="dcdaddun-169" href="http://endure.dur.ac.uk:8080/fedora/get/UkDhU:EADCatalo gue.0069">**1.2.Archid.Dunelm.7(xvi)**\</archref>.\</p>\</altformavail>\</c03>

This description of charter 2.1.Archiep.1 shows how a layer of analysis can be added in EAD if required. The \<physfacet> element, when qualified with a type attribute, can be used to mark any physical characteristic of the charter for which a specific EAD element does not already exist, and the indexing elements \<genreform>, \<persname>, \<corpname> and \<geogname> can be used to similar purpose. These also have an authfilenumber attribute which can be used to establish a link to external authority lists, or Linked Data syntax could be used. Features built into EAD can also be used to elucidate the function of the document within the archive. Once there are EAD catalogues for all the classes of documents and all the recensions in which they occur (such as cartulary copies, modifications and re-issues) it is possible to hyperlink these occurrences together. In the example above, the document was later copied into the Chamberlain's Cartulary and was cited in a charter relating to property within the Archdeaconry of Durham. There is also a link to the separate early 20th century catalogue of seals attached to documents within the archive (reference GB 3222): both this and the links back from later versions of the document means that only a single description of each item need be given in full.

As stated earlier, all of this metadata is to no purpose if it cannot be communicated to the researcher in formats that can be understood and easily viewed. Although the raw XML EAD file is available, and uses for this will be shown later, it is necessary to present the content in simple standard ways, most of which are delivered via the web. At present, none of these fully exploit the detailed charter-specific markup used within the EAD, but this will be developed in the future. The additional analytical elements currently remain invisible in the output, which caters for the simpler level of EAD markup common to all. Like Javascript, the additional markup is designed to degrade gracefully or rather have to no apparent effect in the more basic distributions. There are now open-source tools available to create various outputs from XML data which are generally developing more quickly and with better response to the requirements of the user than commercial products, which tend to have a very slow pace of development. It seems many of the risks are common to both sectors: either one has a very specialised product with the constant risk that development will cease altogether, or you are one small voice lost in a global cacophony of clients trying to attract the attention of the developer to get your required feature built into the next version. In this situation, at least with the open-source system you can make your own improvements, and you are left with a foundation from which to work if the developers move on to new products.

As EAD is simply XML data there are now many tools available with which to develop applications. At Durham XEP, XTF, METS Navigator and Fedora Commons are all used. XEP[5], by RenderX, is a formatting engine that uses XSL-FO stylesheets to produce PDFs from XML. This produces the format that was present before EAD, the hardcopy printout on the shelf of the repository search room, but also provides one means of distributing the catalogue as a single digital file that can be read, searched, copied and printed from on a wide range of electronic devices. Previous experience with producing PDFs on-the-fly showed that this placed very intensive loads on the server, so it has proven more effective to generate a new PDF each time a substantial change is made to a catalogue and to store that static file.

XTF[6], developed by the California Digital Library, provides a versatile search and display system for all the EAD data created at Durham. Although it supports other formats, it is primarily the ease with which it manages com-

---

[5] Although XEP is a commercial product, RenderX generously provide free desktop licences on application to academic users – <http://www.renderx.com/download/academic.html>.

[6] <http://xtf.cdlib.org/>.

plex XML documents that makes it invaluable. Within the XTF framework it is possible to control several features provided by Java servlets, largely through XSL files. In addition to creating the visual interface within the web browser, XSL files control the conversion from XML to HTML and so govern how the EAD files are displayed to the searcher. A further series of XSL files control what is indexed (performed by the Lucene library) and what search interfaces are provided to those indexes. A highly useful bonus is that the HTML files output by XTF are all harvested by search engines such as Google, ensuring that catalogue data is being searched by inquirers who would have had no intention to search your particular archive.

Although these tools have evolved, they provide much the same catalogue service that was in place a decade ago. What has really transformed the way in which the catalogues can be developed is the addition of a framework with all the flexibility and adaptability of EAD itself, the Fedora-Commons digital repository software[7]. This has been designed as a generic content-agnostic system – it will function with most digital material if the programming skills to connect the packages are available; working with XML is straightforward.

All digital objects loaded into the Fedora repository are identified by a unique permanent reference (known as the PID) which can be defined by the hosts. Any object may have a series of named datastreams which could be XML metadata, digital images or redirects to external resources. Each of these datastreams can have tracked versions, enabling each significant change to the catalogue to be retained and recorded. Returning to the EAD examples given above, it can be seen that all the hyperlinks to other catalogues contain href attributes similar to <http://endure.dur.ac.uk:8080/fedora/get/UkDhU: EADCatalogue.0093/>. Here the PID of the catalogue "UkDhU:EAD Catalogue.0093" is combined with the base URL of the repository and the "get" command. This command alone would retrieve a list of available information about this digital object, the list of datastreams within this indicates that such datastreams as EAD, PDF and XTF are available. When the URLs to these are constructed[8] they in turn download the XML EAD file, download the pre-created PDF file or use a URL redirect to hyperlink to the XTF display of the EAD file. Where a link is required to a specific item within a catalogue, the unique id attribute of that description also needs to be supplied in the xpointer attribute. Giving these two values separately means that one

---

[7] <http://www.fedora-commons.org/>.

[8] In turn the URLs are <http://endure.dur.ac.uk:8080/fedora/objects/UkDhU: EADCatalogue.0093/datastreams/EAD/content> <http://endure.dur.ac.uk:8080/ fedora/objects/UkDhU:EADCatalogue.0093/datastreams/PDF/content> <http:// endure.dur.ac.uk:8080/fedora/objects/UkDhU:EADCatalogue.0093/datastreams/XTF/ content/> the pattern, and potential for substitution, is clear.

stylesheet can create a PDF while another produces HTML: the different syntaxes for creating links in each can be assembled for the specific target format.

Patterns of behaviour can be defined to create web services which perform functions. By associating XSL transformations with digital objects using Fedora's Content Model Architecture[9] it is possible, for example, to create a URL that when passed the two variables of a PID identifying an EAD catalogue and the id attribute of the description of a single document within it will output that description as a fragment of the whole file. In fact, most manipulations of digital objects within the Fedora repository can be expressed as structured URLs, which can be built from a combination of supplied variables and fixed strings.

This leads on to the integration of digital images of charters with their EAD descriptions, all of which are digital objects stored within Fedora. The title of this piece was partly chosen to reflect current work on the collection. As mentioned previously, the Miscellaneous Charters class is not yet fully catalogued. A large group of tightly folded medieval documents was identified within the class, which it was decided to record in both the folded and unfolded states, also photographing any visible text and seals attached. The images preserve a possibly significant method of storage, but were also then used in a colleague's palaeography teaching as practical exercises in interpretation. This produced a set of descriptions of the documents which were added to the catalogue.

Presenting these online raised a problem. While it is relatively easy to display a single image with the relevant catalogue entry, what was produced in this exercise was an unpredictable number of images, each of which might require a description extracted from a different catalogue. The solution arrived at was based on existing work developing page-turning software for some printed reports from Durham's Sudan Archive. This had used METS Navigator[10], which derives the page sequence from a separate METS metadata file[11] which it loads and processes. In response to complaints about the varying page sizes of the different series of reports, a Javascript-based zooming capability was added to the software which now allows close examination of the charter text. For each digitised object an XML METS file is created to define the sequence of images displayed. The METS Navigator software loads this METS file (stored in Fedora as a datastream) and constructs from this a series of "pages". As each "page" is viewed, a check is made to see if there is a catalogue entry for the item in the image by testing for the presence of a

---

[9] <https://wiki.duraspace.org/display/FEDORA34/Content+Model+Architecture>.
[10] Developed by Indiana Digital Library <http://metsnavigator.sourceforge.net/>.
[11] Maintained by the Library of Congress <http://www.loc.gov/standards/mets/>.

particular datastream. Where this is found the description is loaded into the web page within an iframe as XML, having been extracted from the relevant catalogue using XSL. A simple example, Miscellaneous Charter 3601[12], has 4 "pages": the document folded, unfolded front and dorse, and a single seal. The description of the seal is derived from a different EAD catalogue. Miscellaneous Charter 3650[13] is similar, but has two seals.

The ability to store and display different datastreams within the structured Fedora repository, and to build consistent URLs to access digital versions of objects such as charters makes it possible to build web-based disseminators that combine all the information that is currently available on each object, while ensuring that any revisions or additions made to that metadata will automatically be incorporated into the view currently available to the researcher. Combined with the capacity of EAD to record very fine detail about individual items such as charters, this creates a highly flexible system that can be used to open up the contents of a medieval archive and elucidate the relationship between the documents, extant or transcribed, contained within it. The Fedora repository and METS metadata structure allows any number of relevant images to be referenced and presented to the researcher: the same structure can also be used to present images of the relevant pages of printed editions of the work or the text of transcriptions, should these be available. The fact that this method is ultimately generic, and can be used in large repositories to interpret and display any material, not just charters, means that the effort of developing the system can be justified as relevant to the whole repository, which in turn helps to ensure that it is regularly maintained and migrated as web technologies evolve, rather than being treated as a project that has been completed and is now no longer the priority of any current staff. The long term future of EAD seems as assured as any standard, maintained and revised on a regular cycle and now adopted around the world for storing archival catalogues, so using it to store and organise the catalogues of Durham Cathedral's archives should ensure that the descriptions are available to current researchers, and will be easily migrated into whatever format succeeds EAD.

---

[12] <http://endure.dur.ac.uk:8080/fedora/objects/UkDhU:DCD_Misc.Ch.3601/datastreams/DAO/content>.

[13] <http://endure.dur.ac.uk:8080/fedora/objects/UkDhU:DCD_Misc.Ch.3650/datastreams/DAO/content>.

Das serbische Kanzleiwesen
Die Herausforderung der digitalen Diplomatik[*]

ŽARKO VUJOŠEVIĆ, NEBOJŠA PORČIĆ, DRAGIĆ M. ŽIVOJINOVIĆ

In den letzten Jahrzehnten entwickeln sich in der Diplomatik zwei Tenden-zen, die zu den wichtigsten Neuheiten seit deren Etablierung als wissen-schaftliche Disziplin im 19. Jahrhundert gehören. Im Bereich der Urkunden-darstellung ist die Rede von der elektronischen Datenverarbeitung sowie der Digitalisierung; im Bereich der Erschließung geht es um die Überprüfung der überkommenen Vorstellungen über den Entstehungsprozess der Dokumente, bzw. das Konstrukt „(Herrscher)kanzlei". Unter dem ersten Punkt sind die immer zahlreicheren und umfassenderen digitalen Sammlungen sowohl re-trodigitalisierter als auch „born digital" Urkundeneditionen gemeint, deren Auflistung hier wohl nicht vonnöten ist. Es sei nur erwähnt, daß mehrere Beispiele deutlich zeigen, in welchem Maße das Analysenpotenzial solcher Urkundenkorpora in letzter Zeit zugenommen hat und fortwährend zu-nimmt: Ressourcen von den dMGH bis zu den XML-kodierten und somit für die unterschiedlichsten Suchanfragen nutzbaren neueren Datenbanken eröff-nen der Diplomatik neue Wege und Forschungsaspekte[1]. Die Möglichkeiten, die das digitale Zeitalter mit sich bringt, könnten gerade mit Blick auf die er-wähnte zweite Tendenz – die Neubewertung der Kanzlei – außerordentlich fruchtbar sein, insbesondere hinsichtlich der Entwicklung neuer Verständnis-modelle, die das klassische Bild von der „bürokratisch" und streng hierar-

---

[*] Dieser Aufsatz ist das Ergebnis der Arbeit an den Projekten Nr. 177003 und 177029, die vom Wissenschaftsministerium der Republik Serbien unterstützt werden.
[1] Zu erwähnen sind u. a. die aus einer elektronischen Datenbank – den eMGH – erwachsenen dMGH <http://www.dmgh.de>, die zum diplomatischen Informations-system gewordenen „Anglo-Saxon Charters" (http://www.aschart.kcl.ac.uk), die online-Editionen der „École des Chartes" <http://elec.enc.sorbonne.fr>, das Urkundenbuch der Lombardei <http://cdlm.unipv.it>, das virtuelle Urkundenarchiv Monasterium <http://www.monasterium.net> und das kanadische DEEDS-Projekt <http://deeds.library.utoronto.ca/>.

chisch eingerichteten Herrscherkanzlei (von Sickel, Bresslau) stark relativiert haben[2].

Die serbische Diplomatik befindet sich angesichts der genannten Tendenzen in einer besonderen Lage, bedingt durch die spezifischen Umstände, in denen sie sich entwickelt hat. Der Bestand der serbischen mittelalterlichen Dokumente, die erst seit der zweiten Hälfte des 12. Jhs. erhalten sind, ist verhältnismäßig klein – grob geschätzt, handelt es sich um nicht mehr als ca. 600 Stück[3]. Es ist aber von sehr vielfältigem Material die Rede, wofür die Tatsache spricht, daß es Dokumente von mehr als 80 Ausstellern in drei Sprachen sind (Serbisch, Latein, Griechisch). Obwohl mit der Edition dieses Materials schon in der ersten Hälfte des 19. Jhs. begonnen wurde, gewährt keine von den bisherigen ungefähr 15 größeren Sammelbänden einen vollständigen Überblick über die Quellenlage[4]. Die mit der Verfügbarkeit in Editionen in Verbindung stehenden Schwierigkeiten sind umso schwerwiegender, da sie mit einem anderen Problem einhergehen – der großen Streuung der erhaltenen Originale und Abschriften (siehe Karten – Abb. 1 und 2). Von den erwähnten rund 600 Einheiten kann der serbische Diplomatiker kaum 20 in seinem eigenen Land konsultieren, während der Großteil des Materials (ca.

---

[2] So stellt W. Huschner, Transalpine Kommunikation im Mittelalter. Diplomatische, kulturelle und politische Wechselwirkungen zwischen Italien und dem nordalpinen Reich (9.–11. Jahrhundert) (2003); Ders., Die ottonische Kanzlei in neuem Licht, in: AfD 52 (2006) S. 353–370. das Konzept der „Kanzleimäßigkeit" in Frage, indem er einen viel höheren Anteil der Empfängerausfertigungen in den Kaiserurkunden des 9–11. Jhs. als bislang gedacht ermittelt (ähnliches H.-H. Kortüm, Zur päpstlichen Urkundensprache im frühen Mittelalter. Die päpstlichen Privilegien 896–1046 (1995) für die Papsturkunden vor 1046) und von einer geistigen Elite (Bischöfe, Äbte), deren Vetreter am Hof bei Gelegenheit im Namen sowohl des Herrschers als auch des Empfängers als Urkundenverfasser und -schreiber tätig waren, spricht. Mit der eher eigenwilligen Darstellung der R. McKitterick, Charlemagne. The Formation of a European Identity (2008) S. 204–212, die im Reich Karls des Großen ein „Netzwerk von Pfalznotaren" vermutet, wäre selbst der Begriff „Kanzlei" schon als völlig passée zu verstehen.

[3] Diese Zahl ist zwar auf Dokumente der Aussteller aus dem serbischen mittelalterlichen Staat begrenzt. Im weitesten Sinne, als Gesamtheit der erhaltenen diplomatischen Produktion Serbiens und Bosniens, samt Dokumenten dubrovniker (ragusanischer), albanischer, ungarischer und türkischer Abstammung in slawischer/serbischer Sprache, würde ein „serbischbezogener" Bestand rund 1500 Stücke umfassen (vgl. Ž. Vujošević, Diplomatik in Serbien und Montenegro, in: AfD 52 (2006) S. 533).

[4] Während manche Dokumente in rund einem Dutzend verschiedener und vom Standpunkt der modernen Diplomatik mehr oder weniger überholten Sammelbände zu finden sind, sind mehr als 20 % nur unikal ediert, und immer noch gibt es einige Stücke, die bislang gar nicht oder nur im Auszug ediert worden sind (zur Editionspraxis siehe Ž. Vujošević, Diplomatik S. 533–537).

65 %) an zwei Orten im Ausland lagert: in Dubrovnik (Kroatien) und in den Klöstern des Mönchsstaates auf der griechischen Halbinsel Athos[5].

Abb. 1: Streuung der erhaltenen Originale und Abschriften in Serbien und Montenegro

Die unbefriedigende Editionslage sowie die erschwerte Zugänglichkeit zu den Beständen haben die serbische Diplomatik behindert, ihre Hauptaufgaben zu bewältigen, nämlich die Urkunden auf ihre Echtheit zu überprüfen und somit ihren Quellenwert zu ermitteln. Wegen fehlender Möglichkeiten, einen Überblick über die Gesamtheit des Bestands zu gewinnen, blieb die Festlegung allgemeiner Echtheitskriterien bislang aus. Folglich ist auch der Inhalt des Begriffs „Kanzlei" immer noch unklar und umstritten. Es ist doch unter dem Einfluß von Auffassungen, die in der europäischen Diplomatik

---

[5] Die sich in Serbien befindenden Stücke liegen in fünf verschiedenen Einrichtungen in drei Standorten (Archiv Serbiens, Archiv der Serbischen Akademie der Wissenschaften und Künste, das Museum des Serbischen Orthodoxen Kirche – alles in Belgrad; vier Urkunden sind an den Wänden der Klöster Žiča und Gračanica aufbewahrt). Im Staatsarchiv Dubrovnik finden sich 209 (inzwischen als eine Sammlung mit Bildern und diplomatischem Kommentar auf dem Portal Monasterium verfügbar: <http://www.mom-ca.uni-koeln.de/mom/SerbianRoyalDocumentsDubrovnik/collection>) und auf Athos 175 Stücke – davon 98 im serbischen Kloster Hilandar, während der Rest ziemlich unausgeglichen in zehn weiteren Klöstern verteilt ist. Ein Viertel der serbischen Urkunden ist über beinahe 25 Standorten europaweit zerstreut – eine ist sogar nach New York gelangt. Der Vollständigkeit halber sei angemerkt, daß man bei 38 Dokumenten, die zerstört wurden oder verloren gingen, nachdem sie der Forschung bekannt worden waren, nur noch über den Text verfügt.

vorherrschend waren, üblich geworden, von einer „serbischen mittelalterlichen Kanzlei" als einem institutionalisierten Träger der Produktion der Dokumente zu sprechen[6].

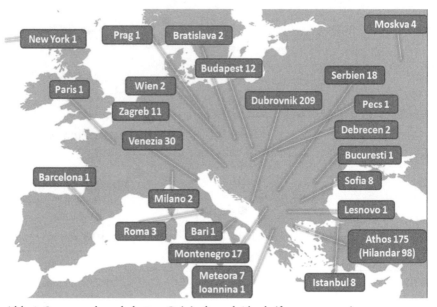

Abb. 2: Streuung der erhaltenen Originale und Abschriften europaweit

Die Forschungsprobleme lassen sich am Beispiel der Urkunden Stefan Dušans (König 1331–46, Kaiser 1346–55) veranschaulichen. Die nicht allzu große Menge des erhaltenen Materials erlaubte die Erstellung einer nahezu vollständigen kommentierten Edition der griechischen Urkunden serbischer Aussteller und eines Regestenwerks der serbischen Urkunden des genannten Herrschers[7]. Während das erste Vorhaben eine große Uniformität der griechischen Diplome Stefan Dušans vor Augen geführt hat, was vor allem auf die konsequente Übernahme byzantinischer Vorbilder zurückzuführen ist, zeigte die Betrachtung aller von ihm ausgestellten serbischen Dokumente eine unerwartete Vielgestaltigkeit: Sowohl in Bezug auf die innere als auch auf die äußere Form der Urkunden ließen sich große Unterschiede feststellen. Umso

---

[6] In diesem Sinne erscheint der Begriff „Kanzlei" in zahlreichen Veröffentlichungen, u. a. F. Dölger, Die byzantinische und die mittelalterliche serbische Herrscherkanzlei, in: XIIᵉ Congrès International des Études Byzantines, Rapports IV (1961) S. 83–103; Lj. Maksimović, Das Kanzleiwesen der serbischen Herrscher, in: Kanzleiwesen und Kanzleisprachen im östlichen Europa, hg. von C. Hannick (AfD Beiheft 6, 1999) S. 25–54.

[7] A. Solovjev/V. Mošin, Grčke povelje srpskih vladara (1936); L. Slaveva/V. Mošin, Srpski gramoti od Dušanovo vreme (1988).

mehr war und ist dies für die Forschung zur serbischen Diplomatik verwirrend, da das Konzept „Kanzleimäßigkeit" immer noch vorherrschend ist, wobei den Empfängern bislang kein wesentlicher Einfluß auf die Urkundenproduktion zubilligt wurde[8].

Angesichts der genannten Probleme und Unklarheiten müssen die Urkunden in einer vollständigen und einheitlichen Sammlung von kritischen Editionen besser zugänglich und einheitlich erschlossen werden[9]. Mit der zunehmenden Anwendung von Informationstechnologien in der Diplomatik stellt sich die Frage, ob die Entscheidung zugunsten der Herstellung eines „born digital" Urkundenkorpus, dessen Ergebnis eine vollständige Urkundendatenbank mit kritischen Editionen, ausführlichem Kommentar und hochqualitativen farbigen Lichtbildern sein sollte, statt einer traditionellen gedruckten Edition die bessere Lösung wäre. Eine solche Datenbank empfiehlt sich im serbischen Fall auch wegen der oben dargestellten Überlieferungslage, die eine tiefere diplomatische Bewertung jedes einzelnen Stücks (und nicht „nur" ein virtuelles Archiv der etwa mit Regesten versehenen Digitalisate) erlaubt.

Welche besonderen Vorteile hätte eine Datenbank für die Erforschung der Kanzlei? Als eine „Einrichtung", die in einem gewissen Grad regelhaft arbeiten sollte, besitzt die Kanzlei die Neigung, die gleiche Form in verschiedenen Kontexten zu verwenden. Die digitale Darstellung der Urkunden ermöglicht eine einfachere, schnellere und zuverlässigere Überprüfung dieser „bürokratischen" Wiederholbarkeit in den verhältnismäßig umfangreicheren Korpora diplomatischen Materials, wenn die Urkundenmerkmale, in denen die erwähnte Eigenschaft der Kanzlei erkennbar wäre, in getrennten Rubriken ausgesondert, hervorgehoben und durchsuchbar werden. So würde die Datenbank neben dem kritisch edierten Text, dem Kommentar und den Angaben

---

[8] Vgl. etwa S. Ćirković, Hilandarski iguman Jovan (Problem akata srpske carske kancelarije), in: Osam vekova Hilandara. Istorija, duhovni život, književnost, umetnost i arhitektura (2000) S. 59–70. Die kanzleibezogene Untersuchung wird auch durch die Tatsache erschwert, daß es in Serbien keine erhaltene Register gibt. Möglicherweise hat es auch keine gegeben. So *erinnert sich* König Stefan Dečanski (1321–31) in einem Brief an Venedig von 1330, daß er der Republik *einmal* gewisse Privilegien schriftlich gegeben hat (Monumenta spectantia historiam Slavorum meridionalium 1, hg. von S. Ljubić (1868) S. 377, Nr. 552), während Kaiser Stefan Dušan in einer Diplom an Hilandar von 1355 unbestimmt auf eine erhaltene Vorurkunde hinweist – *die Urkunde aus der Zeit meines Königtums* (B. Korablev, Actes de Chilandar II. Actes serbes, in: Vizantijskij vremennik, priloženie k 19. tomu (1915; Nachdr. 1975) S. 477, Nr. 33).

[9] Es ist gerade der lang erwartete Sammelband Zbornik srednjovekovnih ćiriličkih povelja i pisama Srbije, Bosne i Dubrovnika I (1186–1321), hg. von V. Mošin/S. Ćirković/D. Sindik (2011) erschienen, der nur ca. 15 % des gesamten (zwar nur ursprünglich serbischsprachigen) diplomatischen Materials durch Edition und knappen Kommentar darstellt.

zu den früheren Editionen, Literatur, Abbildungen usw. folgende Kategorien anbieten, deren formalisierter Inhalt durch das ganze Urkundenkorpus durchsuchbar sein soll:

Dokumentname	*Datum (Format jjjj-mm-tt mit ggf. taq, byz [für „byzantinisches Jahr", Sept – Aug], tpq, cca, ?) – Aussteller – (laufende Nummer).*
Aussteller	*Formalisierte kürzeste Form (z. B. Stefan Dečanski und nicht König Stefan Uroš III. Dečanski).*
Empfänger	*Formalisierte kürzeste Form (z. B. Hilandar und nicht das Kloster Hilandar).*
Kurzregest *(erscheint nur im Verzeichnis, ebenfalls durchsuchbar)*	*Was (Dokumenttyp), wer, wem, wovon; in Klammern Datum und Ort in heutiger Form.* *Beispiel:* <u>*Urkunde des Kaisers Uroš dem Kloster Hilandar über das Geschenk des Mönchs Roman (11. März 1365, Priština).*</u>
Vollregest	*Wer (voller Name samt Titel) – was (bestimmte Zeitwörter zur Beschreibung des Geschäfts: schenkt, bestätigt, bekanntmacht …) – wem – Rechtstitel/Betreff – ggf. zusätzliche Bemerkungen/Erklärungen.*
Überlieferung	<u>*Original (Original?)*</u> <u>*Abschrift (Abschrift?)*</u> *, darauf ggf. Verfasser, Ort, Zeit. Weitere diplomatische Erklärungen zur Überlieferungsart werden in freier Form im Kommentar mitgeteilt.* <u>*Fälschung (Fälschung?)*</u> *Wenn mehrere: A, B, C … untereinander.*
Selbstbezeichnung des Dokuments	*Übersetzt (transkribiert), Zeilenangabe.* <u>*Nicht vorhanden*</u> *(der Text im ganzen bekannt, die Angabe fehlt).* <u>*Unzugänglich*</u> *(keine Hinweise in den Quellen/der Literatur aber die Angabe könnte aus dem momentan nicht vorliegenden Dokument erschloßen werden).* <u>*Keine Angaben*</u> *(keine Hinweise, das Dokument verloren gegangen).*
Aufbewahrungsort	*Ort – Archiv-/Klostername – Signatur* <u>*Verschollen.*</u> <u>*Vernichtet.*</u> *In beiden Fällen gefolgt durch: „der letzte bekannte Aufbewahrungsort …", ggf. mit Signatur. Umstände in freier Form unter Geschichte des Dokuments.*
Beschreibstoff	<u>*Pergament, Papier, Mauer*</u> *(ggf. in freier Form Spezifika und Schäden, die das Lesen beeinträchtigen – z. B. Kodex von 10 Blättern; letzte Zeile verblasst).* <u>*Unzugänglich; Keine Angaben.*</u> *Bei Register- oder Chartularabschriften – leeres Feld.*
Maße	*Länge x Breite in mm, ggf. Hinweis zu Änderungen durch Schäden, geklappte Plica u.ä.* <u>*Unzugänglich; Keine Angaben.*</u> *Bei Register- oder Chartularabschriften – leeres Feld.*

Wasserzeichen	*Kürzeste Bezeichnung, Belegjahr(en), Literaturhinweis.* *Nicht vorhanden; Unzugänglich; Keine Angaben.*
Sprache	*Serbisch, Griechisch, Latein, Italienisch (ggf. mit Kommentar, z. B.: Italienisch – ursprünglich Serbisch).*
Schrift	*Kyrillisch, Griechisch, Lateinisch; Schriftart (z. B.: Schnellschrift).*
Besonders gefärbte Buchstaben/Zeichen	*Farbe, Beschreibung (welche, was, wo, wie).* *Keine; Unzugänglich; Keine Angaben.* *Wenn nach Überlieferungsart solche Elemente nicht zu erwarten sind – leeres Feld.*
Graphische Symbole und Verzierungen	*Kurze Beschreibung, siehe oben.*
Siegel	*Kurze Beschreibung.* *Reste, ggf. Beschreibung.* *Spuren, ggf. Beschreibung.* *Beschreibung (bei Transsumpte, Übersetzungen, Corroboratio).* *Erwähnung (wie oben).* *Nicht vorhanden; Unzugänglich;Keine Angaben.*
Unterschrift	*Übersetzung, Zeilenangabe, ggf. knapper Kommentar.* *Nicht vorhanden; Unzugänglich; Keine Angaben.*
Logos-Formel	*Übersetzung, Zeilenangabe, ggf. knapper Kommentar.* *Unzugänglich; Keine Angaben (wenn erwartet aber nicht vorhanden, sonst leeres Feld).*
Zeugen	*Wie oben.*
Dorsualnotizen	*Position, Charakter (Regest, Bemerkung ...), Verfasser, Ort, Zeit (nach Bedarf knapper Kommentar). Der Wortlaut wird unter dem Urkundentext wiedergegeben.* *Keine; Unzugänglich; Keine Angaben.*
Ausstellungsort	*Übersetzt (transkribiert), Zeilenangabe.* *Nicht vorhanden im Text (darauf mittelbare Schließung mit Kommentar).* *Keine Angaben (wenn im Text nicht vorhanden und mittelbar nicht zu schließen ist).* *Unzugänglich.*
Ausstellungszeit	*Wie oben.*
Schreibervermerk; Beurkundungsbefehl	*Übersetzt (transkribiert), Zeilenangabe.* *Nicht vorhanden im Text; Keine Angaben; Unzugänglich.*
Vorurkunden und ggf. andere erwähnten Dokumente	*Chronologisch, ggf. Hinweis auf Deperdita.*

Neben den allgemeinen Vorteilen, die eine solche Urkundendatenbank mit sich bringt (bessere Zugänglichkeit sowie Übersichtlichkeit, Durchsuchbarkeit, Aktualisierbarkeit), ist diese auch als ein starkes Werkzeug für die Kanzleiforschung zu betrachten. Ihr Analysenpotenzial wäre insbesondere bei Klärung vieler offenen Fragen sowie Überprüfung herkömmlicher und nicht immer zuverlässiger Äußerungen in der serbischen Diplomatik zu nutzen.

Diese betreffen zuerst die charakteristischen Merkmale in den Urkunden, die vermeintlich die für eine „Kanzleimäßigkeit" sprechenden Regelhaftigkeiten aufweisen. Es folgen einige Beispiele der Unklarheiten, die sich auf die äußeren Urkundenmerkmale beziehen und durch vergleichende Analyse, die innerhalb der Datenbank einfach und schnell durch kombinierte Katergoriensuche durchzuführen wäre, zu lösen sind (zum Verfahren siehe die Abb. 3 und 4 – kombinierte Suche der Formen der Beglaubigung).

Zum Beschreibstoff wird angenommen, daß Pergament, das in Serbien seit Anfang des 14. Jhs. abwechselnd mit Papier verwendet wurde, den feierlichen Schenkungen und Bestätigungen in den Klösterurkunden vorbehalten war, während „weniger bedeutenden" Schreiben (etwa Briefe, Prostagmata) auf Papier angefertigt wurden[10]. Eine kombinierte Suche der betreffenden Kategorien könnte die Feststellung sowohl einer eventuellen typologisch bezogenen Differenzierung als auch der Präferenzen einzelner Aussteller ermöglichen („Kurzregest" mit dem Dokumenttyp als erstes Wort – „Beschreibstoff" bzw. „Aussteller" – „Beschreibstoff").

Was die Schrift betrifft, soll die Datenbank eine übersichtliche Gruppierung der kyrillischen Urkunden ermöglichen. Wegen der möglicherweise chronologischen Entwicklung der Schriftart (Unziale – diplomatische Minuskel – Halbunziale des 15. Jhs.) wäre dies bei Datierung mancher (von vielen) undatierten Urkunden nützlich. Es wäre durch eine kombinierte Suche der Rubriken „Schrift" und „Empfänger" auch mit größerer Sicherheit zu überprüfen, ob die Unziale bei Urkunden für Klöster charakteristisch war, was in der Forschung manchmal behauptet wird[11]. Wenn ja, könnte dies auch als ein weiterer Hinweis auf einen höheren Anteil der Empfängerausfertigungen verstanden werden, da in den Klosterskriptorien fast ausschließlich die genannte Schriftart verwendet wurde[12]. Mit den hochqualitativen Urkundenabbildungen, die die Datenbank anbieten soll, sind auch bessere Ergebnisse der Untersuchungen der Evolution der Orthographie zu erwarten, die anhand der Verwendung von bestimmten Sonderzeichen sowie den Auswirkungen

---

[10] Allerdings gelte dies nur für einen bestimmten Zeitraum: G. Čremošnik, Studije za srednjovjekovnu diplomatiku i sigilografiju Južnih Slavena (1976) S. 19–26.

[11] Vgl. für die Urkunden des Königs Milutin (1282–1321) V. Mošin, Povelje kralja Milutina – diplomatička analiza, in: Istorijski časopis 18 (1971) S. 84–85.

[12] Zu diesem Phänomen siehe P. Đorđić, Istorija srpske ćirilice. Paleografsko-filološki prilozi (1971) S. 258–265, 284–286, 289–298, 303–311; D. Bogdanović, Katalog ćirilskih rukopisa manastira Hilandara. Paleografski album (1978) S. 3–116. Für griechische und lateinische Urkunden ist hier die Schriftart bedeutungslos – denn in diesen sind ausschließlich byzantinische Kanzleischrift bzw. gotische Minuskel vertreten: F. Dölger/J. Karayannopulos, Byzantinische Urkundenlehre 1. Die Kaiserurkunden (1968) S. 31–34; V. Novak, Latinska paleografija (1952) S. 231–256.

der sog. „Reform von Resava" (15. Jh.) auch in dem diplomatischen Material erkennbar ist[13].

Weitere Forschungsprobleme beziehen sich auf die verschiedenen Formen der Beglaubigung, zu denen neben Siegel auch Logos-Formel, Unterschrift und eventuell Besonders gefärbte Buchstaben sowie Zeichen gehören sollen[14]. Umstritten ist, welche Rolle dem Siegel für serbische Urkunden zukam: diente es nur/überhaupt als Beglaubigung oder als Herrscherpräsentation oder beides? Durch vergleichende Analyse, die innerhalb der Datenbankdurch kombinierte Suche der Rubrik „Siegel" mit den anderen oben genannten Kategorien durchzuführen wäre, ließe sich diese wichtige Frage klären (siehe Abb. 3 und 4).

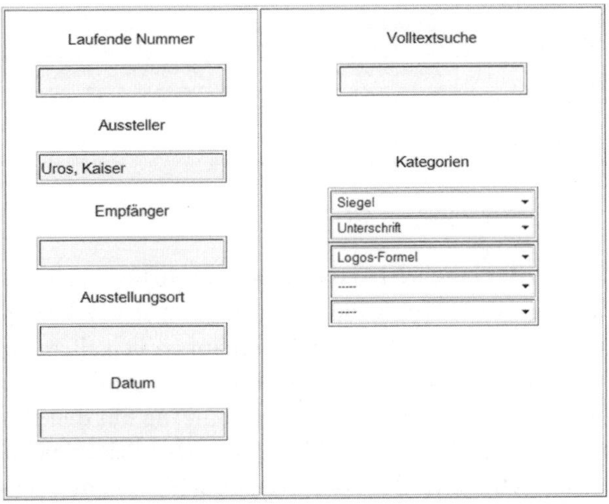

Abb. 3: Kombinierte Kategoriensuche, Schritt 1: Suchinterface

---

[13] Über die Entwicklung der serbischen Schrift in den Urkunden G. ČREMOŠNIK, Studije iz srpske paleografije i diplomatike, in: Glasnik Skopskog naučnog društva 21 (1940) S. 3–8; DERS., Die serbische diplomatische Minuskel, in: Wiener Archiv für Geschichte des Slawentums und Osteuropas 3: Studien zur älteren Geschichte Osteuropas (1959) S. 103–110; V. JERKOVIĆ, „Poluustav" u srpskim poveljama od kraja XIV i tokom XV veka, in: Zbornik Matice srpske za filologiju i lingvistiku 42 (1999) S. 89–111. Über die Unklarheiten in der Evolution der Orthographie B. JOVANOVIĆ-STIPČEVIĆ, O sređivanju srpskoslovenskog pravopisa u prvim decenijama XIV veka, in: Arhiepiskop Danilo II i njegovo doba (1991) S. 265–280.

[14] Die farbigen Buchstaben erscheinen in den serbischen Urkunden unter byzantinischem Einfluß, wobei Rot vor allem für Herrscherunterschrift und Logos-Formel, Grün für die Unterschriften der kirchlichen Oberhäupter verwendet wurde: F. DÖLGER, Herrscherkanzlei S. 84, 93; V. MOŠIN, Samodržavni Stefan knez Lazar i tradicija Nemanjićkog suvereniteta od Marice do Kosova, in: O knezu Lazaru (1975) S. 30. Im Unterschied zu Byzanz ist die Verwendung der roten Tinte deutlich weniger konsequent und auch mehrdeutig, da sie nicht nur als Beglaubigung (Unterschrift, Logos-Formel), sondern auch als Hervorhebung und Verzierung vorkommt.

1356-05-xx Урош	
	Трагови, помен (Назив документа).
Печат [Siegel]	На широком простору између датума и белешке о записивању видљива су четири правоугаоно распоређена процепа, можда предвиђена за висећи печат – златни, судећи по називу документа (по мишљењу Д. Синдика, Српска акта, 51. прорези су међусобно толико размакнути, да није сигурно да ли су били намењени печаћењу; Р. Михаљчић, ССА 2, 92. констатује да „хрисовуља није оверена печатом", без помена трагова).
Потпис [Unterschrift]	У Христа Бога благоверни Стефан Урош, цар Србима и Грцима (ред 59).
Логос-формула [Logos-Formel]	ЦАР (ред 11), СЛОВОМ (ред 40), ХРИСОВУЉУ (ред 56).
1360-10-15 Урош	
Печат [Siegel]	Помен (Изворни назив; короборација „wбразумъ и знаменикмь царьскимь", ред 26).
	Трагови печаћења нису уочени. Судећи по називу документа, очекивала би се овера златним печатом.
Потпис [Unterschrift]	Стефан Урош, у Христа Бога верни цар Србима и Грцима (ред 28).
Логос-формула [Logos-Formel]	ЦАР (ред 5), ХРИСОВУЉ (ред 11), СЛОВО (ред 24), СЛОВО (ред 26).
1363-07-15 Урош	
Печат [Siegel]	Нема.
Потпис [Unterschrift]	Стефан Урош, верни цар Србима и Грцима (ред 24).
Логос-формула [Logos-Formel]	Нема.
1365-03-11 Урош	
Печат [Siegel]	Златни висећи печат пречника 34 мм на црвеној врпци, причвршћен са задње стране на начин који на снимку није видљив. На аверсу је стојећи лик владара са легендом у пољу, на реверсу стојећи лик св. Стефана, такође са легендом у пољу. Према Д. Синдику, Српска акта, 58. (Српски печати, 234-235.) печат је оригиналан, али „није добро причвршћен (покретљив је на врпци)", што дозвољава могућност да је премештен са другог документа (уп. Р. Михаљчић, ССА 5, 143-144; од старијих издавача печат помиње само Миклошич – према Аврамовићу, в. Издања).
Потпис [Unterschrift]	Стефан Урош, верни цар Србима и Грцима (ред 23).
Логос-формула [Logos-Formel]	Цару (ред 7), хрисовуљ (ред 11), слово (ред 21).

Abb. 4: Kombinierte Kategoriensuche, Schritt 2: Suchergebnis

Neben der beschriebenen Kategoriensuche würde die vorgeschlagene Datenbank gewisse Möglichkeiten zur Analyse der Urkundentexte anbieten. Die textstatistischen Methoden beschränken sich allerdings zur Zeit auf ein Stichwortregister (keyword in context) und „multiple word search" (mehrfache Wortsuche, MWS), die aber den Umgang mit den Problemen der Urkundensprache und der inneren Merkmale erheblich erleichtern können.

Die charakteristische Mehrsprachigkeit der serbischen Urkunden (ca. 12 % des Bestands sind ursprünglich Latein und 8 % auf Griechisch verfasst) ließ Jahrzehnte lang die Frage der Existenz einer lateinischen und einer griechischen Kanzlei am serbischen Königs- und Kaiserhof offen[15]. Mehr als eine allgemeine Tendenz zu einer positiven Antwort war bislang nicht möglich. Doch die Umstände, in denen die beiden vermuteten Kanzleien funktionierten, ihre Formulare sowie Personal bleiben unbekannt. Eine Erörterung dieser Fragen wird noch auf eine mit dem Stichwortregister oder durch das MWS-Verfahren durchzuführende vergleichende Analyse innerhalb einer mit verwandtem Material (etwa ungarische und byzantinische Urkunden)

---

[15] Vgl. vor allem die Dölger – Mošin Diskussion: F. DÖLGER, Byzantinische Diplomatik. 20 Aufsätze zum Urkundenwesen der Byzantiner (1956) S. 75–101, 152–175, 302–324; V. MOŠIN, Gab es unter den serbischen Herrschern des Mittelalters eine griechische Hofkanzlei, in: AUF 13 (1935) S. 183–197; DERS., Akti iz Svetogorskih arhiva, in: Spomenik Srpske kraljevske akademije 91 (1939) S. 219–260; DERS., Povelje cara Dušana i Jovana Paleologa Pantelejmonovom manastiru, in: Zgodovinski časopis 6–7 (1952–1953) S. 402–416.

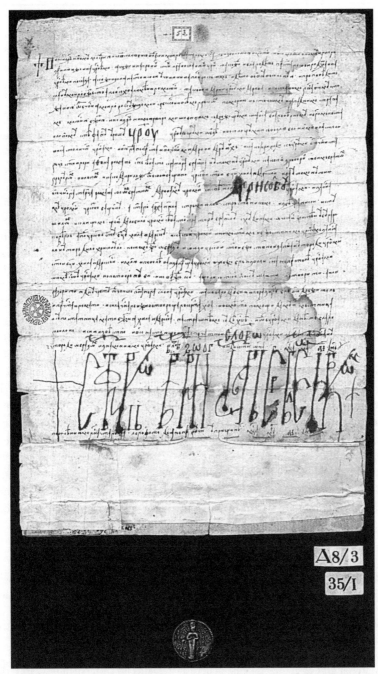

Abb. 5: Formen der Beglaubigung: Urkunde des Kaisers Uroš vom
11. März 1365 mit dem Siegel, der Unterschrift und der Logos-Formel
(Foto: Arhiv Srbije, Belgrad).

versehenen Datenbank warten müssen. Solche Methoden wären auch bei der Untersuchung des in den serbischsprachigen Urkunden vorhandenen Phänomen der abwechselnden Verwendung der „Gelehrten-„ und der „Volkssprache" hilfreich sein[16]. Als Ergebnis darf man sich vorstellen, die „kanzleimäßigen" von den vom Empfänger stammenden Schichten innerhalb einzelner Urkunden voneinander klar unterscheiden zu können[17].

Die inneren Merkmale der Urkunde bilden ein für Kanzleistudien höchst bedeutendes Ganzes – das Formular. Eben dieses ist in Bezug auf die serbischen Urkunden noch nicht systematisch erforscht worden[18]. Die etwaige Wiederholung des Formulars oder dessen einzelner Bestandteile, die bei einem Aussteller auf die „Kanzleimäßigkeit" hinweisen dürfte, wäre innerhalb der Datenbank zuverlässig überprüfbar. Es besteht auch die Möglichkeit, Urkundenteile mit steigenden Ziffern zu bezeichnen und somit größere Gruppen von Dokumenten schnell vergleichend untersuchen zu können (z. B. 1 – Invocatio, 2 – Intitulatio, 3 – Inscriptio, 4 – Salutatio, 5 – Arenga usw), wobei jede einzelne Urkunde durch diese Schema, die ihre Bestandteile und deren Reihenfolge einfach veranschaulicht, dargestellt werden kann.

Bei den serbischen Arengen, die sich als in der Regel frei gestalteten Texte der Formalisierung oft entziehen, würde sich das MWS-Verfahren lohnen, um Spuren von Wiederholungen schnell feststellen zu können. In diesem Zusammenhang wären insbesondere Kombinationen von Anfangswörtern, Motiven, Bibelzitaten und bestimmten Wortsequenzen in Betracht zu ziehen[19]. So erhält man die erheblich verbesserte Übersichtlichkeit, die der bisherigen Forschung bei der nicht immer treffenden und manchmal willkürlichen Erschließung vor allem der politisch-ideologischen Bedeutung der Arengen bestimmter Aussteller fehlte. Ähnliches gilt für die anderen Urkundenteile, bei denen die auf charakteristische Formeln, Wendungen oder Verben bezogene oben genannte Textsuche verwendet werden kann. Beispielsweise wäre in der serbischen Intitulatio insbesondere der vom Herrscher geführte Titelname (Stefan oder Stefan Uroš) zu beachten, genauso wie die angegebenen geogra-

---

[16] Ähnliches gilt für die byzantinischen Urkunden: DÖLGER/KARAYANNOPULOS, Urkundenlehre 1, S. 47f; N. OIKONOMIDÈS, La Chancellerie impériale de Byzance du 13ᵉ au 15ᵉ siècle, in: Revue des études byzantines 43 (1985) S. 176f.

[17] Vgl. die Methode bei H.-H. KORTÜM (s. Anm. 2), die jedoch noch ohne elektronische/digitale Hilfsmittel durchgeführt worden ist.

[18] Vgl. LJ. MAKSIMOVIĆ, Kanzleiwesen, 35–37.

[19] Material gibt es genug, da eine neuere systematische Untersuchung 216 Urkunden mit 116 mehr oder weniger stark voneinander abweichenden Arengen nachzuweisen vermochte: Ž. VUJOŠEVIĆ, Stari zavet u arengama srednjovekovnih srpskih i bugarskih povelja (das Manuskript der Magisterarbeit, 2007).

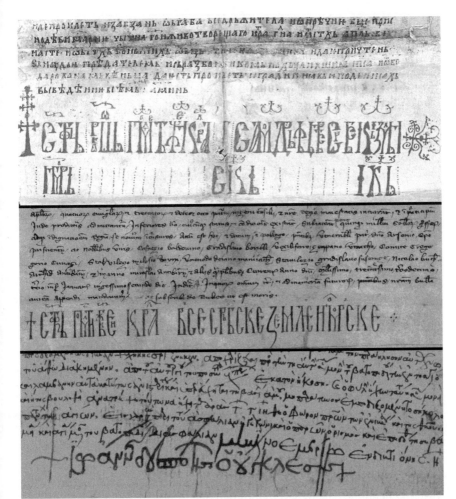

Abb. 6: Mehrsprachigkeit (von oben nach unten): Urkunde des Königs Stefan Dečanski von 1324–31 (Serbisch; Foto: Arhiv Srbije, Belgrad); Urkunde des Königs Stefan Dušan vom 22. Januar 1333 (Latein, Unterschrift Serbisch; Foto: Državni arhiv Dubrovnik); Urkunde des Despoten Jovan Uglješa vom November 1369 (Griechisch; Foto: Arhiv Srpske akademije nauka i umetnosti, Belgrad).

fischen Begriffe[20]. Das MWS-Verfahren empfiehlt sich ausdrücklich bei der geistlichen Pönformel der Sanctio, die in der Regel eine Liste der „himmlischen Rächer" (Christus, Maria, Apostel, andere Heiligen) an den Zuwider-

---

[20] So hat die schon länger bekannte Nennung der „griechischen Länder" im Titel des Königs Stefan Dušan zwischen 1343 und 1345 bei chronologischer Einordnung einiger undatierter Urkunden geholfen: M. BLAGOJEVIĆ, Kada je kralj Dušan potvrdio Dečansku hrisovulju, in: Istorijski časopis 16–17 (1970) 80–82.

handelnden ist[21]. Die Wiederholung oder hohe Frequenz solcher Elemente
bei bestimmten Ausstellern könnte als Indiz für ein fixiertes Formular verstanden werden, wie andererseits die Anführung anderer Persönlichkeiten
(etwa heilige Erzbischöfe oder Äbte in manchen Klösterurkunden) auf ein
„kanzleifremdes" Diktat hinweisen könnte[22].

Schließlich sei noch die Datierung erwähnt, die in den serbischen Urkunden übrigens nicht die Regel war – eine bezeichnende Tatsache für die Untersuchung eines „Kanzleibrauchs" in Serbien[23]. Dabei sind unterschiedliche
chronologische Systeme vertreten, indem neben byzantinischer und christli-
cher Ära auch weitere Elemente, vor allen die Indiktion, erscheinen. Insbesondere das Verhältnis zwischen den nebeneinander stehenden Jahres- und
Indiktionsangaben, in dem oft Fehler auftreten, ist mit der genannten Methode systematisch zu analysieren, da in der Forschung gegensätzliche Mei-
nungen über höherer Zuverlässigkeit der einen oder anderen Angabe geäu-
ßert worden sind. Die Frequenz der genannten Fehler ist auch als signifikant
für eine (nicht-)institutionelle Mitarbeit bei der Formulierung von Dokumenten zu betrachten.

Die dargestellte Datenbank bietet sowohl eine „gelenkte" Erforschung der
Bestände durch die aufgrund der diplomatischen Relevanz definierten und
hervorgehobenen Kategorien als auch eine „freie" Untersuchung der Urkundentexte durch das Stichwortregister und „multiple word search" an. Während das erste technische Konzept, den Vorstellungen der „klassischen"
Diplomatik entsprechend, im Kontext der Bedürfnissen der serbischen Kanzleiforschung als Zweck voll anzunehmen ist, muß das zweite offen für andere
Lösungen bleiben, die eine umfangreichere und vollkommenere digitale Bearbeitung ermöglichen. In diesem Zusammenhang empfiehlt sich in einer weiteren Phase die XML-Kodierung der Urkundentexte, die bekanntlich mehrere Vorteile für weitere Verarbeitung mit sich bringt[24]. Dies bedeutet die
Textauszeichung gemäß den Richtlinien der „Charters Encoding Initiative"
(CEI)[25]. Somit können auch der Kanzleianalyse neue Wege eröffnet werden,
indem man in den Transkriptionen die Formularteile oder verschiedene charakteristische Elemente des Urkundentextes (Abkürzungen, gefärbte Teile,

---

[21] Über die Sanctio in den serbischen Urkunden Lj. MAKSIMOVIĆ, Kanzleiwesen
S. 39.

[22] Vgl. Ž. VUJOŠEVIĆ, Povelja kralja Stefana Dušana o crkvi Svetog Nikole u
Dobrušti, in: Stari srpski arhiv 4 (2005) S. 55, 63.

[23] Zur Datierung der serbischen Urkunden Lj. MAKSIMOVIĆ, Kanzleiwesen S. 39–40.

[24] P. SAHLE, Urkunden-Editionen im Internet. Einführung und Überblick, in: AfD
52 (2006) S. 443.

[25] Siehe <http://www.cei.lmu.de>. Eine gewisse (und ständig zu steigende) Zahl der
von XML-kodierten serbischen Urkunden liegt bereits auf <http://www.monaste-
rium.net> vor.

Sonderzeichen) markiert, die als kanzlei(un)typische Gemeinsamkeiten erkannt werden könnten. Hinsichtlich der Besonderheiten des serbischen Urkundenmaterials ist in diesem Zusammenhang auch an einige Ergänzungen zu den CEI-Attributen (z. B. Logos-Formel – ein Element von der byzantinischen Kaiserkanzlei übernommen) sowie des Unicode-Standards (die immer noch fehlenden altslawischen Buchstaben Ш – „st" und ꙗ – „ja") zu denken.

Zusammenfassend seien am Ende die Vorteile einer zu schaffenden digitalen Datenbank der serbischen mittelalterlichen Urkunden noch einmal betont. Der Nutzen für die allgemeinen Belangen der serbischen Diplomatik liegt auf der Hand. Vor allem würde er von der ersten einheitlichen und vollständigen Edition der betreffenden Urkunden ausgehen. Weiterhin würde die Datenbank die neuen relevanten Urkundenausgaben sowie ihre Analyse nach unterschiedlichsten Aspekten innerhalb des ganzen Korpus oder der frei definierbaren Teilkorpora anbieten. Somit ist sie als das Grundwerk für die beiden miteinander eng verbundenen Hauptanliegen der serbischen Diplomatik zu betrachten: erstens, die Entwicklung der Kriterien, echte von unechten Urkunden unterscheiden zu können; zweitens, die Durchführung von neuen und die Überprüfung von früheren Untersuchungen, die das serbische Kanzleiwesen betreffen. Die oben dargestellte große Vielfältigkeit des nicht allzu umfangreichen Bestandes wäre deutlich übersichtlicher als bisher. Gerade diese Übersichtlichkeit samt anderen bekannten Vorteilen digitaler Medien sollte endlich zeigen, inwiefern die Vielfalt eine Folge der „ungeordneten Kanzlei" oder der uneinheitlichen Überlieferungsformen oder eines größeren Anteils an Empfängerausfertigungen als bislang vermutet ist. Die Bereitstellung dieses mächtigen Werkzeugs für die zuverlässigere und effektivere Erschließung der wahrscheinlich wichtigsten Quellengruppe für die serbische mittelalterliche Geschichte hätte auch eine breitere Bedeutung, da es, soweit den Verfassern bekannt, das erste Beispiel eines digital vollständig verarbeiteten „nationalen" Bestands sein könnte – mit allen positiven Nachwirkungen für die diplomatische Forschung.

Some approaches to the semantic publication
of charter corpora
The case of the diplomatic edition
of Old Russian charters

ALEKSANDRS IVANOVS, ALEKSEY VARFOLOMEYEV

Nowadays, the term "semantic publication" is generally accepted. In the modern Web environment, this term is widely used due to the progress of Semantic Web technologies[1]. It denotes an electronic text publication that is equipped with additional information layers, which display the sense of the text, as well as the knowledge about the text in a formalised way suitable for automatic processing.

On the Web, semantic publications are represented first and foremost by research papers that are included in digital libraries and electronic journals[2]. Specialists in information technologies have already studied such publications. For instance, on the basis of a certain article which deals with the problems of computational biology, David Shotton has made a comprehensive analysis of the so-called "semantic enhancements", such as tables that contain initial data obtained through the research, interactive diagrams and graphs drawn using those data (it should be noted that in semantic publications diagrams can be transformed on a reader's request), references to terminological vocabularies, etc.[3]. Obviously, in this case, "semantics" denotes a defined complex of tools that promotes the perception of an article by a human reader.

---

[1] T. BERNERS-LEE/J. HENDLER/O. LASSILA, The Semantic Web, in: Scientific American 284,5 (2001) p. 34–43.

[2] A. BARUZZO et al., Toward Semantic Digital Libraries. Exploiting Web2.0 and Semantic Services in Cultural Heritage, in: Journal of Digital Information 10,6 (2009) <http://journals.tdl.org/jodi/article/viewArticle/688/576>; D. SHOTTON, Semantic Publishing. The Coming Revolution in Scientific Journal Publishing, in: Learned Publishing 22 (2009) p. 85–94.

[3] D. SHOTTON et al., Adventures in Semantic Publishing. Exemplar Semantic Enhancements of a Research Article, in: PLoS Computational Biology 5,4 (2009) e1000361 <http://dx.doi.org/10.1371/journal.pcbi.1000361>.

Anita de Waard has made a further step in the development of the idea of semantic publications. She thoroughly categorises three semantic layers that can be added to traditional electronic publications of research papers[4]. The first layer embraces the terms and concepts that are marked out in the texts. The terms and concepts are linked with terminological vocabularies – thesauri and ontologies. Within the second layer, there are different facts related to the texts, in other words, the meta-information that is represented in the form of triplets (subject-predicate-object), since such triplets are the universal mode of data capturing on the Semantic Web. The third layer represents the so-called scholarly discourse, e.g., statement of questions and problems in research papers, advancement of hypotheses, description of experiments, argumentation and discussion. The above-mentioned semantic layers can be perceived and understood not only by a human reader, but also by a computer.

There is a number of other scholarly publications that substantiate original conceptual and methodic approaches to semantic description and semantic annotation of research papers[5]. Sometimes, semantic description patterns encompass both the results and the initial data of a definite research[6]. However, up to now only a limited set of problems related to semantic publishing has been comprehensively represented in scholarly works[7].

---

[4] A. DE WAARD, From Proteins to Fairytales. Directions in Semantic Publishing, in: IEEE Intelligent Systems 25,2 (2010) p. 83–88.

[5] T. GROZA et. al., SALT – Semantically Annotated LaTeX for Scientific Publications, in: The Semantic Web. Research and Applications. Lecture Notes in Computer Science 4519, ed. E. FRANCONI/M. KIFER/W. MAY (2007) p. 518–532; C. H. MARCONDES, A Semantic Model for Scholarly Electronic Publishing, in: Proceedings of the First Workshop on Semantic Publishing (SePublica 2011), co-located with the 8th Extended Semantic Web Conference. Hersonissos, Crete, Greece, May 30, 2011, ed. A. DE WAARD et al. (2011) p. 47–58 <http://ceur-ws.org/Vol-721/paper-06.pdf>; L. J. GARCÍA-CASTRO/O. GIRALDO/A. GARCÍA, Using Annotations to Model Discourse. An Extension to the Annotation Ontology, in: Proceedings of the 2nd Workshop on Semantic Publishing (SePublica 2012). 9th Extended Semantic Web Conference. Hersonissos, Crete, Greece, May 28, 2012, ed. F. VAN HARMELEN et al. (2012) p. 13–22 <http://ceur-ws.org/Vol-903/paper-02.pdf>.

[6] For example, historical census data, see A. MEROÑO-PEÑUELA et al., Linked Humanities Data: The Next Frontier? A Case-study in Historical Census Data, in: LISC–2012. Proceedings of the Second International Workshop on Linked Science 2012 – Tackling Big Data. Boston, MA, USA, November 12, 2012, ed. T. KAUPPINEN/L. C. POUCHARD/C. KESSLER (2012) <http://ceur-ws.org/Vol-951/paper3.pdf>.

[7] An overview of recent publications is provided in the monograph published by the authors of the paper, see A. VARFOLOMEEV/A. IVANOVS, Komp'iuternoe istochnik-ovedenie. Semanticheskoe sviazyvanie informatsii v reprezentatsii i kritike is-toricheskikh istochnikov [Computer-based Source Studies. Semantic Linkage of Information in Representation and Criticism of Historical Records] (2013) p. 126–161.

Nevertheless, the advantages of semantic publications are rather obvious[8]. Firstly, semantic editions provide better facilities for information search, because such publications draw together search algorithms used by both humans and computers. For instance, if in ontology a specific term is linked to its synonym, the search for the term and its synonym can be performed simultaneously; and it is not necessary to mention the synonym in the request. Secondly, since formalised knowledge can generate new knowledge, semantic publications can be used as knowledge bases in advancing research hypotheses by means of automatic inference. Thirdly, the semantic layers in semantic publications (and especially in those of historical records) reflect researchers' interpretations, which can be verified by means of formalised, computer-based procedures.

This paper demonstrates how the basic principles of semantic publications can be applied to electronic scholarly editing of charter corpora. The authors' focus is on the different approaches to the creation of additional semantic layers in the diplomatic publications of medieval documentary records. It is desirable that semantics represented within the above-mentioned layers should be suitable for computational processing; however, in any case, the creation of the semantic layers per se can contribute to a better understanding of information provided by medieval charters.

Some principal theses advanced in the present paper have already been tested in the articles recently published by the authors[9]. In order to reveal the usefulness of semantic documentary editions for the diplomatic and historical research of medieval charters, this paper presents a multifunctional prototype of a semantic publication of a complex of Old Russian charters. This complex emerged in the 13th century; it forms a constituent part of the vast collection

---

[8] E. AHONEN/E. HYVÖNEN, Publishing Historical Texts on the Semantic Web – A Case Study, in: Proceedings of the Third IEEE International Conference on Semantic Computing (ICSC 2009) (2009) p. 167–173; V. MIRZAEE/L. IVERSON/B. HAMIDZADEH, Computational Representation of Semantics in Historical Documents, in: Humanities, Computers and Cultural Heritage. Proceedings of the XVI International Conference of the Association for History and Computing (2005) p. 199–206.

[9] See e.g. A. VARFOLOMEYEV/A. IVANOVS, Knowledge-Based Scholarly Environment Project for Regional Historical Studies, in: Interactive Systems and Technologies. The Problem of Human-Computer Interaction 3. Collection of Scientific Papers (2009) p. 273–276; A. VARFOLOMEYEV/A. IVANOVS, Semanticheskie publikatsii kompleksov istoricheskikh istochnikov [Semantic Publications of the Complexes of Historical Records], in: El'Manuscript–10. Infromatsionnye tekhnologii i pis'mennoe nasledie [El'Manuscript–10. IT and Written Heritage], ed. V. BARANOV (2010) p. 42–46; A. VARFOLOMEYEV/A. IVANOVS, Modeli struktury i soderzhaniia istoricheskikh istochnikov [Structural and Semantic Models of Historical Records], in: Informatsionnyi biulleten' Assotsiatsii "Istoriia i komp'iuter" 37. Spetsial'nyi vypusk [Bulletin of the Association for History and Computing 37. Special Issue] (2011) p. 25–31, etc.

(corpus) of medieval and early modern records "Moscowitica–Ruthenica"[10] kept in the Latvian State Historical Archives (Riga, Latvia)[11]. The historical name of this collection was mentioned for the first time in the archival inventories drawn up in the 1630s[12]. The core of this collection was compiled from the documents that had been initially kept in the department "Moscowitica–Ruthenica" of the former External Archives of Riga City Council[13]. Another part of the collection was created from the documents preserved in the former Internal Archives of Riga City Council[14], as well as from the documents from the former Archives of the Knighthood of Livland[15]. This collection of documents provides researchers with firsthand information concerning the relations of Old Russian and Byelorussian lands and towns (Smolensk, Novgorod, Pskov, Polotsk, etc.), as well as Lithuania (later – Poland-Lithuania) with Riga, Livonia, Gothland, Hanseatic League, and some German towns in the late 12th – early 17th centuries. Since the beginning of the 19th century, these documents have always been in the focus of attention of historians, philologists, and linguists; therefore, many of them have been published in collections of historical records[16].

It is rather obvious that semantic publications should be based on "natural" (historical) complexes of interconnected documentary records. Actually,

---

[10] See in detail A. Ivanovs, Moscowitica–Ruthenica v Latviiskom gosudarstvennom istoricheskom arkhive [Moscowitica–Ruthenica in the Latvian State Historical Archives], in: Drevniaia Rus'. Voprosy medievistiki [Ancient Russia. The Questions of Medievistics] (2004) 3 p. 47–54, 4 p. 94–106; A. Ivanovs/A. Varfolomeyev, Editing and Exploratory Analysis of Medieval Documents by Means of XML Technologies. The Case of the Documentary Source Complex Moscowitica–Ruthenica, in: Humanities, Computers and Cultural Heritage (2005) p. 156.

[11] In 2011, according to the Archives Law of the Republic of Latvia the former state archival system of Latvia was reorganized within one body – the National Archives of Latvia <http://www.arhivi.lv/index.php?&371>. The Latvians State Historical Archives has become a structural unit of the National Archives of Latvia; however, it has preserved its former name <http://www.arhivi.lv/index.php?&110>.

[12] Latvian State Historical Archives (Latvijas Nacionālā arhīva Latvijas Valsts vēstures arhīvs, hereafter – LVVA) 673 (record group), 1 (inventory), Nr. 1482 (Capsule R IV[tio], 1228–1615, "Ruthenica"); Nr. 1483 (Capsule M III[tio], 1558–1663, "Moscowitica").

[13] LVVA 673, 4, K. 18, Nr. 1–268; K. 19, Nr. 1–269; K. 20, Nr. 1–227.

[14] LVVA 8, 3, Capsule A, Nr. 14–18, 41, 72; Capsule B, Nr. 42; Capsule C, Nr. 1–11, 23, 27, 34, 43; LVVA 8, 4, Nr. 6–58.

[15] LVVA 214, 6, Nr. 114–116, 140.

[16] The most comprehensive and vast publications were prepared in the 19th century – beginning of the 20th century: Russisch-livländische Urkunden, ed. K. E. Napiersky (1868); Liv-, Esth- und Curländisches Urkundenbuch nebst Regesten Abt. I. Bd. 1–12 (1853–1910), Abt. II. Bd. 1–3 (1900–1914).

such complexes represent integral parts of definite systems that documents form in the course of performing their initial functions[17]. The main features of a natural complex of historical records are as follows: first, common origin (provenance) of the documents that belong to a complex. As a rule, the common origin of historical records means that they are connected either with a concrete institution, or with a system of institutions, as well as with the thread of life of a person. Hence, any complex of documents comes into existence spontaneously; and researchers can only reconstruct such historical complexes. Second, there are close historical interconnections between the components within a natural complex of documents. The links between the documents can be, on the one hand, direct ones, e.g., one document refers to another document and vice versa. On the other hand, there can be implicit links, too. For instance, historical records of different origin, which provide information about the same fact, represent the single complex of historical records. It is noteworthy that hierarchical disposition within a system is a characteristic feature of any historical complex of documents. This hierarchy reveals the relative significance of the documents in the course of their circulation.

Taking into account the above-mentioned considerations, in the prototype of the semantic publication, we used five interconnected charters, which reflect the course of relations between Riga and Smolensk in the 13th century[18]. Most of these charters were published in the 19th – 20th centuries[19]; however, these publications do not meet the present-day requirements of the diplomatic edition of medieval documents. Therefore, a new diplomatic edition of the charters has been produced[20].

In the centre of the semantic network represented in the prototype there is the missive of Archbishop of Riga Johann II (1285–1297) to Fedor Rostislavich, Prince of Smolensk (1279–1297); it blames the inhabitants of Vitebsk for

---

[17] A. IVANOVS, Vēstures avotu kompleksa rekonstrukcijas problēma [Complex of Historical Records – Problems of Reconstruction], in: Proceedings of the 14th International Scientific Readings of the Faculty of Humanities. History VIII, ed. V. ŠALDA (2004) p. 49–57.

[18] Actually, there should be mentioned twelve charters, however, this article has its limits therefore the basis of the prototype has been reduced.

[19] See e.g. Smolenskie gramoty XIII–XIV vekov [Smolensk Charters of the 13th–14th Centuries], comp. T. SUMNIKOVA/V. LOPATIN (1963).

[20] A. IVANOVS/A. KUZNETSOV, Smolensko-rizhskie akty, XIII v. – pervaia polovina XIV v. Dokumenty kompleksa Moscowitica–Ruthenica ob otnosheniiakh Smolenska i Rigi [Charters of Smolensk and Riga, 13th – First Half of the 14th Century. Documents of the Complex Moscowitica–Ruthenica about Relations between Smolensk and Riga] (2009).

the unjustified complaint against Rigans (Figure 1)[21]. Conventionally, in the prototype, this charter bears number 6 in accordance with the numeration of the documents accepted in the latest paper edition[22]. This document bears no date; the issuer's name is not mentioned.

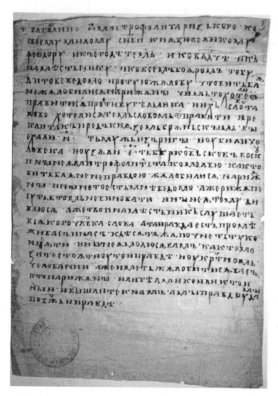

Figure 1: Missive of Archbishop of Riga Johann II (?) to Fedor Rostislavich, Prince of Smolensk. Riga, [1284-1297, presumably 1285–1287]. Draft document. Parchment, 16.7 × 23.5 cm. LVVA, 673, 4, K. 18, Nr. 8, p. 3 recto.

Another document included in the prototype is the missive of Fedor, Prince of Smolensk, to the authorities of Riga. The prince granted the German merchants free passage to Russian lands and confirmed the treaty between Riga, Gothland, German towns, and Smolensk in 1229 (Charter no. 4)[23]. There is no doubt that both documents are closely interconnected: some clauses in the missive of Archbishop Johann II indirectly refer to the clauses of the missive of Prince Fedor; furthermore, some persons mentioned in Charter no. 6 are

---

[21] Riga, [1284–1297, presumably 1285–1287]. Draft document (?). Parchment, 16.7 × 23.5 cm. LVVA, 673, 4, K. 18, Nr. 8, p. 3 recto.

[22] The other charters are also numbered according to the same edition: IVANOVS/ KUZNETSOV, Smolensko-rizhskie akty.

[23] Smolensk, [May 18] 1284. Original. Parchment, 20.0 × 24.5 cm. Golden seal. LVVA, 8, 3, Capsule A, Nr. 72, p. 1.

also mentioned in Charter no. 4. In another missive of Prince Fedor, which describes the legal proceedings concerning a counterfeit weight (Charter no. 5) [24], the recipient of the missive of Archbishop of Riga – Governor of Smolensk – is probably mentioned. At the same time, Charter no. 6 has more definite links with the so-called Smolensk Provisions for Negotiations with Riga and Gothland, which took place in 1228–1229 (Charter no. 1) [25], as well as with the Trade and Peace Treaty concluded by Mstislav Davidovich, Prince of Smolensk (1228–1230), with Riga, Gothland, and German towns in 1229, Gothland Redaction, Version A (Charter no. 3a) [26]. The above-mentioned documents formed a legal basis for mutual relations between Riga and Smolensk in the 13th – first half of the 14th century. Therefore, Charter no. 6 reproduces one of the principal clauses of the treaty of 1229 in a shorter way.

The prototype of the semantic publication is designed as a comprehensive diplomatic edition of Old Russian charters that represents paleographic features of the documents. Diplomatic transcriptions of the texts are based on the well developed TEI and CEI markup schemes and elements [27]: for instance, such tags as <lb> (line break) and <sup> (superscript material) are widely used. The first element marks the end of a line and the start of a new line in the original, the second one marks superscript letters and words that were very common in Old Russian manuscripts (Figure 2).

There are also other elements that can be used to reproduce the paleographic features of the manuscripts: e.g., <del> – to indicate deleted fragments; <add> – to indicate inserted letters and fragments; <damage> – to mark out damaged areas in the texts; the combination of <del> and <add> – to mark corrections made by the scribes, etc. At the same time, the diplomatic transcription of the charters written in Old Russian poses a number of problems. For example, with some exceptions, Old Russian letters and special symbols can be reproduced using Unicode symbols; however, sometimes it

---

[24] Smolensk, 1284. Original. Parchment, 13.0 × 18.3 cm. Silver seal. LVVA, 673, 4, K. 18, Nr. 6, p. 3.

[25] [Smolensk], [1219–1228/9]. Original. Parchment, 25.05 × 53.30 cm. Silver seal (has been lost). LVVA, 8, 3, Capsule A, Nr. 16, p. 1.

[26] Nowadays, in the Latvian State Historical Archives, there are five versions of this treaty. In historiographic tradition, exactly Version A is considered to be the original of the treaty of 1229, that is why this document is used in the prototype: [Gothland], [1229]. Original. Parchment, 53.4 × 77.8 cm. 2 silver seals (one of them has been lost). LVVA, 8, 3, Capsule A, Nr. 14, p. 1. However, diplomatic analysis proves that this document obviously might be a draft copy (Konzept) of the treaty. In the second half of the 13th century, in the course of relations between Riga and Smolensk Version A was used as an original of the treaty of 1229, therefore it bears a seal.

[27] Text Encoding Initiative <http://www.tei-c.org>; Charters Encoding Initiative <http://www.cei.lmu.de>.

can come into conflict with the present-day conventional pronunciation and, consequently, the meaning of Cyrillic letters. For instance, in the 12th – 13th centuries, the graphic form of Cyrillic letter 'и'('i') was similar to the graphic form of the modern Cyrillic letter 'н'('n'); Old Russian letter 'н'('n') usually resembled Latin 'N', etc. (see Figure 2). This mode of representation of Old Russian letters can hinder analytical computer-based operations of semantic linkage of the documentary records, as well as searching for information.

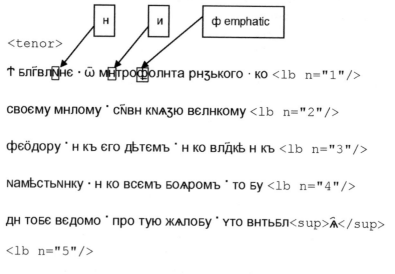

Figure 2: Diplomatic transcription of Charter no. 6 (fragment)

All in all there are two modes of representation of outdated symbols (letters). Firstly, an original text is transcribed in a phonetic way. If it is necessary, displaying the text on the monitor, the phonetic transcription can be substituted for paleographically precise representation of the letters. Secondly, the transcription preserves the paleographic particularities of initial texts. It is understood that the principal aim of a publication predetermines the mode of representation of the symbols. Since semantic publications of Old Russian charters can be useful for their dating and attribution based on an in-depth analysis of paleographic features of the documents, the original graphic forms of the letters should be precisely reproduced. This transcription might be conditionally called a "paleographic" transcription. In its turn, the phonetic transcription of the outdated symbols can be represented in an additional information layer.

In TEI, there are special elements – glyphs (<glyph>), which are used to describe letters that have peculiar, non-typical graphic forms. These elements should be supplemented with another element <g> in order to insert a letter into the text. Such mapping actually transforms the outdated (non-typical) graphic forms of Old Russian letters into the modern (typical) forms (Markup example 1).

```
<charDecl>
  <glyph xml:id="n1">
    <glyphName>SMALL CAPITAL CYRILLIC N LIKE LATIN N</glyphName>
    <mapping type="standardized">н</mapping>
  </glyph>
</charDecl>

...........

<g ref="#n1">N</g>
```

Markup example 1: Representation of non-typical (outdated) graphic forms of Old Russian letters

However, the same operations can be performed by means of Web-programming languages such as PHP, JavaScript, etc. Thus, the substitution of letters can be made simultaneously in two directions in order to achieve different aims. On the one hand, the non-standard letters are substituted for standard ones in order to perform searching operations within a digital publication of the charters. On the other hand, standard letters can be replaced by non-standard ones in order to show them on the monitor as integral parts of the palaeographically transcribed texts. Finally yet importantly, specialized Web-fonts can be developed on the basis of SVG (Scalable Vector Graphics) technologies[28] in order to fulfill the requirements of a definite editing project.

It is understood that comprehensive diplomatic transcriptions of the texts is a prerequisite for the production of any qualitative publication of medieval documents including a semantic one. However, the advantages of the semantic publications mentioned before are determined by the possibility to capture, link, and aggregate historical information, which is provided by different documentary records that are included into a definite semantic publication. Therefore, paramount importance should be attached to the semantic layer that contains the information about persons, place-names, and other historical objects – institutions, terms, events (historical facts), docu-

---

[28] Scalable Vector Graphics (SVG) 1.1 (Second Edition). W3C Recommendation 16 August 2011. Part 20. Fonts <http://www.w3.org/TR/SVG11/fonts.html>.

ments (references to documents), etc.[29], which are directly or indirectly mentioned in the texts. Many of the above-mentioned objects are marked up using CEI markup scheme, which has been supplemented with some additional elements (Markup example 2). For example, the element <refToDoc> that means "reference to another document" has been introduced, since in CEI markup scheme the element <ref> defines a reference to another location in the current document. It should be noted that sometimes such markup of the charters is based on a researcher's interpretation of the tenor (e.g. identification of some persons, determination of references to other documents, fixing of interpolations, etc.). In the diplomatic editions, this semantic markup can be supplemented with the structural markup of the texts, which forms a basis for further pattern analysis (some elements of the structural markup of Charter no. 6[30] are also shown in Markup example 2). In contrast to the markup scheme that is focused on historical objects and realities, the structural markup is not expressed by means of knowledge representation languages; it provides formal models of the charters that can be automatically processed including such operations as classification, comparison, and visualization of the structures of the charters. It means that the traditional, in-depth pattern analysis of medieval charters can be performed by means of computer-based technologies[31]. However, the structural markup of the charters is not confronted with the semantic markup, since the pattern analysis reveals not only the internal form (structure) of documentary records, but also, to a certain extent[32], the sense of their structural parts. In order to represent this sense exhaustively, the information about structural parts (clauses) should be represented in controlled natural languages that are used for knowledge representation, as shown further in this paper.

---

[29] See A. VARFOLOMEYEV/H. SOMS/A. IVANOVS, Knowledge-Based Information Systems in Research of Regional History, in: Digital Humanities 2008. Conference Abstracts, ed. L. L. OPAS-HÄNNINEN et al. (2008) p. 210–211.

[30] The text of this charter has been translated from Old Russian into English; it seems that English is the most appropriate language for semantic representation of the information of documentary records.

[31] IVANOVS/VARFOLOMEYEV, Editing and Exploratory Analysis p. 157–159.

[32] VARFOLOMEYEV/IVANOVS, Modeli struktury p. 27, 29.

<charter id="6">
<chDesc> ... </chDesc>
<tenor>
<protocol>
<invocatio> † </invocatio> <intitulatio> <issuer> <roleName id="Archbishop">
Metropolitan's </roleName> of **Riga** </issuer> </intitulatio> <salutatio> **benedic-
tion over** </salutatio> <lb n="1"/> <inscriptio> **our beloved son,** <addressee>
<persName id="Fedor Rostislavich Prince of Smolensk"> <roleName id="Grand
Prince"> **Grand Prince** </roleName> <lb n="2"/> **Fedor** </persName> </addres-
see>, **and over his children, and over Bishop** <supplied> **of Smolensk** </supplied>,
and over <lb n="3"/> <recipient> <roleName id="governor of Smolensk"> **Governor** </roleName> <supplied> **of Smolensk** </supplied> </recipient>, **and over all
boyars.** </inscriptio>
</protocol>
<context>
You <lb n="4"/> **should know about that complaint, which the inhabitants of**
<placeName> **Vitebsk** </placeName> <lb n="5"/> **lodged against Rigans in order**
<lb n="6"/> **to set themselves right with** <persName id="Helmich merchant from
Munster"> **Helmich** </persName>. **And their words were as follows –** <lb n="7"/>
they wanted to justify themselves with those words – and <supplied> **they** </sup-
plied> **said** <lb n="8"/> **to** <roleName id="Prince of Briansk"> **Prince of**
<placeName>**Briansk** </placeName> </roleName> **that** <lb n="9"/> **50 men had
ridden out of** <placeName> **Riga** </placeName>, **and killed a man,** <lb n="10"/>
and taken 10 <term id="unit of weight"> **berkovets** </term> **of wax.** <lb n="11"/>
And now I, <roleName id="Archbishop"> **Metropolitan** </roleName>, **say that
those** <lb n="12"/> **inhabitants of** <placeName> **Vitebsk** </placeName> **unjustly
complained on Rigans.** <lb n="13"/> **And now I know that Rigans** <lb n="14"/>
are not guilty of that. And now I am surprised <lb n="15"/> **that Governor listens
to** <lb n="16"/> **anyone. But there is** <refToDoc> **an agreement** <lb n="17"/> **between you and us: if a controversy arises, it should be settled** <supplied> **between
you and us** </supplied> </refToDoc>. <lb n="18"/> **And now I pray that you
would** <lb n="19"/> **observe** <refToDoc> **that agreement and oath:** </refToDoc>
<lb n="20"/> **if anyone complains to you** <lb n="21"/> **about Rigans, or** <pers-
Name id="Helmich merchant from Munster"> **Helmich**</persName>, **or somebody
else,** <lb n="22"/> **you should send** <supplied> **a missive** </supplied> **to us, but we
will render justice** <lb n="23"/> **in accordance with God's justice.** <lb n="24"/>
</context>
</tenor>
</charter>

Markup example 2: Markup of Charter no. 6 on the basis of CEI markup scheme

In the semantic publication, marked out objects should be linked either with analogous objects marked out in other documents, or with the corresponding data, which are represented in different specialized (historical) ontologies. In this regard, the ontology CIDOC CRM (Comité International pour la Documentation – Conceptual Reference Model)[33] can be useful. It has been specially created for the description of different cultural heritage objects, e.g., museum artifacts, works of art, monuments, archival collections, etc. This ontology contains classes and relations that can be used in describing historical persons, sites, and entire historical events, which are related to the abovementioned objects. CIDOC CRM has served as a basis for the elaboration of a number of specialized ontologies for the purposes of description of diverse historical aspects. Thus, we can mention the ontologies created within Pearl Harbor Project in the USA[34] or CultureSampo Project in Finland.[35] It should be also noted that CIDOC CRM ontology can be combined with TEI markup scheme that makes it possible to use this ontology for the description of medieval charters[36]. However, it seems that the basic principles of CIDOC CRM do not fully correspond to the aims of the semantic publishing of charter corpora. In particular, according to the event-oriented approach accepted in the abovementioned ontologies, "[d]ocumentation is an interpretation of cultural materials in relation to a historical context, which can be described in terms of events and processes"; the historical context, in its turn, "can be abstracted as things, people and ideas meeting in space-time"[37]. In our opinion, it is desirable that the links between the charters are described directly (apart from other historical events) in order to reflect the course of their circulation.

To solve this problem, the ontology specially designed for the semantic publication of the corpus "Moscowitica–Ruthenica" can be created. In con-

---

[33] The CIDOC Conceptual Reference Model <http://www.cidoc-crm.org>; see also M. DOERR, The CIDOC CRM. An Ontological Approach to Semantic Interoperability of Metadata, in: AI Magazine 24,3 (2003) p. 75–92.

[34] N. IDE/D. WOOLNER, Historical Ontologies, in: Words and Intelligence 2. Essays in Honor of Yorick Wilks, ed. K. AHMAD/C. BREWSTER/M. STEVENSON (2007) p. 137–152.

[35] AHONEN/HYVÖNEN, Publishing Historical Texts.

[36] Ø. EIDE/C.-E. ORE, TEI, CIDOC-CRM and a Possible Interface between the Two, in: Digital Humanities 2006. The First ADHO International Conference. Conference Abstracts (2006) p. 62–65; C.-E. ORE/Ø. EIDE, TEI and Cultural Heritage Ontologies: Exchange of Information?, in: Literary and Linguistic Computing 24 (2009) p. 161–172; C.-E. ORE, New Digital Assets – How to Integrate Them?, in: Digitale Diplomatik. Neue Technologien in der historischen Arbeit mit Urkunden , ed. G. VOGELER (AfD Beiheft 12, 2009) p. 238–254.

[37] M. DOERR/A. KRITSOTAKI, Documenting Events in Metadata, in: The 7th International Symposium on Virtual Reality, Archaeology and Cultural Heritage VAST, ed. M. IOANNIDES et. al. (2006) [p. 1] <http://www.cidoc-crm.org/docs/fin-paper_cyprus.pdf>.

trast to the event-oriented approach, the authors of the paper propose a doc-
ument-oriented approach to representation of historical data and description
of different historical objects – documentary records, persons, place names,
historical events, etc. This ontology reflects two kinds of semantic links,
which are constituted in the semantic publication. First, there are the links
between historically and thematically interconnected charters. These interconnections emerged when the charters were drawn up, as well as during
their circulation – when they were used for documenting relations between
Smolensk and Riga in the 13th century. Second, there are the links to other
historical records, which do not belong to the complex of charters represented in the semantic publication. In this case, the "internal" information
extracted from the charters is linked with the "external" information, provided either directly by other historical records (e.g., Livonian charters dating
back to 1274, 1279, and 1286[38]), or indirectly by research papers, specialized
ontologies, etc. The above-mentioned links create a definite semantic network that represents the knowledge about the charters. Actually, this semantic network provides a model for capturing extensive information related to
this complex of charters; therefore, it can form a solid basis for the production of the semantic publication of the documentary records.

Figure 3 shows a segment of the semantic network that has been created
on the basis of the complex of Old Russian charters within the corpus "Moscowitica–Ruthenica". In the center of this segment, there is Charter no. 6,
which is related to other documents (Charters nos. 4, 5, 3a, and 1). The links
between these documents are constituted in accordance with the interpretation of the internal information provided by the semantic publication of the
charters. The external information has been used to identify the persons mentioned in the documents, as well as to give comprehensive descriptions of
other historical objects. Within the semantic network, the semantic relations
between its objects are described using such triplets as "charter written by
person", "charter sent to person", etc. As it is commonly done in different
ontologies, inverse relations can also be introduced, e.g., "charter mentions
person" – "person is mentioned in charter". This semantic network is partly
based on hypothetical data; the hypothetic nature of some relations is reflected using either symbols (question mark – "?") or combinations of words
("probably refers to" instead of "refers to"). In this regard, it should be noted
that the representation of uncertain information in ontologies poses a number

---

[38] See e.g. Gramoty, kasaiushchiesia do snoshenii severo-zapadnoi Rossii s Rigoiu i
ganzeiskimi gorodami v XII, XIII i XIV veke [Charters Related to Relations between
North-West Russia with Hanseatic Towns in the 12th, 13th, and 14th Centuries], ed.
K. E. Napiersky (1857) Nr. III, etc.

of serious problems, which are discussed in scholarly publications[39]; however, in this paper the possibilities of logic inference from uncertain data are not discussed. The hypothetic nature of some relations is only stated.

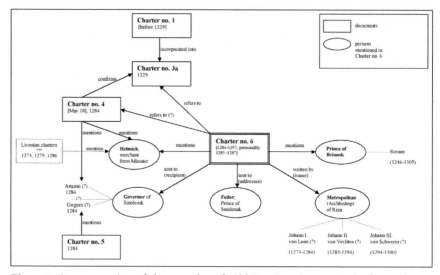

Figure 3: Representation of the complex of Old Russian charters in the form of a semantic network (fragment)

To create the ontology for the description of the above-mentioned semantic network, widely used technologies – RDF and OWL – can be applied. However, the production of semantic publications based on the ontologies, which are directly recorded using RDF or OWL, is time-consuming. It seems that the tools provided by semantic Wiki-systems can facilitate this process. Therefore, the authors of the paper propose an alternative modification of the prototype of the semantic publication of the complex of Old Russian charters, which reveals the advantages and opportunities afforded by Wiki-systems in production of the semantic publications of documentary records.

---

[39] See e.g. T. LUKASIEWICZ/U. STRACCIA, Managing Uncertainty and Vagueness in Description Logics for the Semantic Web, in: Web Semantics: Science, Services and Agents on the World Wide Web 6 (2008) p. 291–308, doi:10.1016/j.websem.2008.04.001; D. REYNOLDS, Uncertainty Reasoning for Linked Data, in: Uncertainty Reasoning for the Semantic Web 5. Proceedings of the Fifth International Workshop on Uncertainty Reasoning for the Semantic Web (URSW 2009), collocated with the 8th International Semantic Web Conference (ISWC–2009), Washington DC, USA, October 26, 2009 (2009) p. 85–88 <http://ceur-ws.org/Vol-527/pospaper3.pdf>. Unfortunately, a generally accepted solution has not been found yet.

Nowadays, Wiki-systems are often used as the specific editors of ontologies, which are created by Web communities of researchers[40]. One of the semantic Wiki-systems is Semantic MediaWiki[41]; it offers special, rather simple markup tools, which can be used to indicate different objects in the texts of the charters and to supply the texts with meta-information[42].

The principle feature of this system is the use of typified hyperlinks between pages. These hyperlinks are marked in double square brackets and usually composed of three parts: (1) the type of relation ("written by", "sent to", "refers to", "probably refers to", etc.); (2) the name of an object, i.e. the name of the page indicated by a hyperlink ("archbishop of Riga" "Helmich", etc.); (3) the text of a document related to the object (e.g. "Metropolitan's of Riga"). The pages containing the texts of the charters supplied with the hyperlinks constitute the main objects of the semantic network (see Markup example 3); the hyperlinks, in their turn, denote relations between the objects.

[[written_by::Archbishop of Riga|Metropolitan's of Riga]] benediction over our beloved sun, [[sent_to::Fedor Rostislavich, Prince of Smolensk|Grand Prince Fedor]], and over his children, and over [[sent_to::Bishop of Smolensk]], and over [[sent_to::Governor of Smolensk]], and over all boyars. You should know about that complaint, which the inhabitants of Vitebsk lodged against Rigans in order to set themselves right with [[mentions::Helmich]]. And their words were as follows – they wanted to justify themselves with those words – and they said to [[mentions::Prince of Briansk]] that 50 men had ridden out of Riga, and killed a man, and taken 10 berkovets of wax. And now I, Metropolitan, say that those inhabitants of Vitebsk unjustly complained on Rigans. And now I know that Rigans are not guilty of that. And now I am surprised that Governor listens to anyone. But there is [[refers_to::Charter 3|an agreement between you and us]]: if a controversy arises, it should be settled between you and us. And now I pray that you would observe [[probably_refers_to::Charter 4|that agreement and oath]]: if anyone complains to you about Rigans, or [[Helmich]], or somebody else, you should send a missive to us, but we will render justice in accordance with God's justice.

Markup example 3: Semantic MediaWiki markup of Charter no. 6

Due to the hyperlinks, certain fragments of the text can be linked with other pages, which contain the texts of the documents, as well as the data related to

---

[40] A. Souzis, Building a Semantic Wiki, in: IEEE Intelligent Systems 20,5 (2005) p. 87–91; S. Auer/S. Dietzold/T. Riechert, OntoWiki – A Tool for Social, Semantic Collaboration, in: The Semantic Web – ISWC 2006. Lecture Notes in Computer Science 4273 (2006) p. 736–749.

[41] Semantic MediaWiki (SWM) <http://www.semantic-mediawiki.org>.

[42] M. Krötzsch et al., Semantic Wikipedia, in: Journal of Web Semantics 5,4 (2007) p. 251–261.

historical persons, places, events, etc.[43] Semantic MediaWiki tools make it possible to visualize the hyperlinks to the pages within the semantic network. These hyperlinks automatically generate the set of the facts related to the text of Charter no. 6: "Charter 6 mentions Helmich", "Charter 6 probably refers to Charter 4", "Charter 6 refers to Charter 3a", "Charter 6 is written by Archbishop of Riga", etc. The above-mentioned facts are linked with the text of Charter no. 6; in some cases, this linkage is based on the interpretation of the definite fragments of the tenor.

Other pages of the semantic network including those containing historical data are designed according to the same pattern. The information concerning persons, places, and events is usually represented as chains of triplets. For instance, in Semantic MediaWiki markup the text "Helmich is a merchant from Münster. He is mentioned in Charter 6 and Charter 4" is represented as follows:

Helmich is a [[is_a::merchant]] from
[[is_from::Münster]]. He is mentioned in
[[is_mentioned_in::Charter 6]] and [[is_mentioned_in::Charter 4]].

It is obvious, that within the semantic network the information about the objects, which are recorded by means of Semantic MediaWiki tools, can be automatically transformed into the RDF triplets. It means that Wiki-systems can be used for the production of the semantic publications of medieval charters and other documents. At the same time, some shortcomings of Wiki-systems should be mentioned. For example, non-standard fonts cannot be used in the transcriptions of the texts; the texts of the charters cannot be linked with raster images of the documents; the texts cannot be marked up on the basis of XML markup standard in accordance with TEI or CEI markup schemes. Therefore, to produce a comprehensive publication of the charters, it is necessary to develop a specialized Wiki-system.

Unfortunately, the semantic layers that embrace different objects marked out in the texts and, to a certain extent, also the meta-information about the texts do not represent the tenor of the charter clauses. It seems that in the semantic publication the contents of the clauses can be represented comprehensively by means of one of the so-called "controlled natural languages"[44]. The texts recorded in such languages can be understood not only by a human reader, but also by a computer.

---

[43] See publication of Charter no. 6 and corresponding data on the Web: Historical Documents Semantic Publishing <http://histdocs.referata.com>.

[44] Controlled Natural Language. Workshop on Controlled Natural Language, CNL 2009, Marettimo Island, Italy, June 8–10, 2009. Revised Papers. Lecture Notes in Computer Science 5972 (2010).

Nowadays, controlled natural languages for knowledge representation develop intensively. The features of these languages are simplified syntax and restricted semantics. The following controlled natural languages may be mentioned: Controlled English to Logic Translation (CELT)[45], Processable English (PENG)[46], Computer-Processable Language (CPL)[47],and Attempto Controlled English (ACE), which is being developed at the University of Zurich by Norbert Fuchs and his colleagues[48]. In order to represent the sense (meaning) of the charters, Attempto Controlled English has been chosen since it is one of the most expressive and widely spread controlled natural languages.

ACE texts can be translated into the so-called Discourse Representation Structures (DRS)[49]. It is clear that ordinary languages cannot be translated into logic formulas due to ambiguities of any discourse; therefore, the sense can be revealed only within a definite context. On the contrary, Discourse Representation Structures provide an unambiguous subset of a natural language. Therefore, DRS can be translated into formal languages that are based on first order logic and are used for knowledge representation (e.g. OWL, Rule Markup Language, Semantic Web Rule Language, etc.). Thus, ACE may seem to be completely natural, but it is actually a formal language; more precisely, it is a first-order logic language with English syntax. This language is human and machine understandable. Nowadays, Attempto Controlled English is supported by a number of tools[50]: the parser (Attempto Parsing Engine, APE) that translates ACE texts into Discourse Representation Structures; the reasoner (Attempto Reasoner RACE) that makes logical inference from the statements represented in ACE; the editor for the correction of ACE texts, etc. It is very important that when processing ACE texts it is possible to use different domain-specific lexicons. Furthermore, the texts in ACE can be

---

[45] A. Pease/W. Murray, An English to Logic Translator for Ontology-Based Knowledge Representation Languages, in: Proceedings of the 2003 IEEE International Conference on Natural Language Processing and Knowledge Engineering, Beijing (2003) p. 777–783.

[46] R. Schwitter, Processing Coordinated Structures in PENG Light, in: AI 2011. Advances in Artificial Intelligence. Lecture Notes in Computer Science 7106 (2011) p. 658–667.

[47] P. Clark et al., Acquiring and Using World Knowledge Using a Restricted Subset of English, in: The 18th International FLAIRS Conference FLAIRS'05 (2005) <http://www.cs.utexas.edu/users/pclark/papers/flairs.pdf>.

[48] J. L. de Coi et al., Controlled English for Reasoning on the Semantic Web, in: Semantic Techniques for the Web. Lecture Notes in Computer Science 5500 (2009) p. 276–308.

[49] H. Kamp/U. Reyle, From Discourse to Logic. Introduction to Modeltheoretic Semantics of Natural Language, Formal Logic and Discourse Representation Theory (1993).

[50] Attempto Project Tools <http://attempto.ifi.uzh.ch/site/tools/>.

processed using the reasoner, which can generate new hypotheses on the basis of the facts revealed by a researcher. Therefore, this language is quite appropriate for the purposes of the semantic publication of medieval charters.

ACE construction rules are rather simple. For example, these rules require that each noun should be introduced by a determiner (a, every, no, some, etc.), with the exception of proper names, which are written with capital letters; anaphoric references can be used (He = Metropolitan), however, in other cases they are forbidden ("Rigans are not guilty of that"), etc. Although this language puts some substantial restrictions on text rendering (e.g., the verbs can be used in the Present Indefinite Tense only), nevertheless, it seems that ACE construction rules can be applied to the texts of medieval charters (see Table 1). Unfortunately, the translation of these texts into ACE comprises, to a certain extent, researchers' interpretations of the tenor of the documents.

Text of Charter no. 6 (fragments)	Translation into ACE
You should know about that complaint, which the inhabitants of Vitebsk lodged against Rigans in order to set themselves right with Helmich.	The metropolitan of Riga demands that the prince of Smolensk knows about a complaint that is lodged against some inhabitants of Riga by some inhabitants of Vitebsk. The metropolitan of Riga supposes that the inhabitants of Vitebsk want to justify their actions to Helmich.
And now I, Metropolitan, say that those inhabitants of Vitebsk unjustly complained on Rigans.	The metropolitan of Riga says that the inhabitants of Vitebsk complain on the inhabitants of Riga unjustly.
And now I know that Rigans are not guilty of that.	The metropolitan of Riga knows that the inhabitants of Riga are not guilty.
And now I am surprised that Governor listens to anyone.	The metropolitan of Riga is surprised by the credulity of the governor of Smolensk.
But there is an agreement between you and us: if a controversy arises, it should be settled [between you and us].	There is an agreement that is concluded by Riga and Smolensk. The agreement states that if a controversy arises then it must be settled by Riga and Smolensk.

Table 1. Translation of the text of Charter no. 6 into ACE

It is important that different facts (information) related to the documents can be also translated into ACE: "The charter_6 is written by the archbishop of Riga"; "The charter_6 probably refers to the charter_4"; "The charter_6 mentions Helmich and the prince of Briansk", etc. Furthermore, ACE makes it possible to record axioms and inference rules, e.g., "if something X is written by someone Y, then Y is the author of X". As a result, large amounts of facts related to the texts, which should be entered and processed manually in the course of the production of semantic publications on the basis of Semantic

MediaWiki, can be entered and processed automatically due to the opportunities offered by ACE. At the same time, new knowledge about the charters, namely, new facts and hypotheses may be acquired by means of automatic inference. Therefore, ACE might prove to be a very promising tool for the purposes of the semantic publication of the charter corpora.

* * *

In conclusion, it should be emphasized that the prototype of the semantic publication discussed in this paper develops a specific mode of representation of historical data retrieved from documentary records. In fact, this representation is determined by the links between the charters that form a historical ("natural") complex of interconnected documents. It means that the data extracted from the documents imply the initial links between these documents as such. As a result, historical events (facts) may be reconstructed as systems of relations between different objects, which are described or mentioned in documentary records, as well as in research papers, terminological vocabularies, etc. It is obvious that semantic publications should reveal these relations in order to provide researchers with appropriate tools of historical source criticism. Although the creation of the prototype of the semantic publication of Old Russian charters is still in progress, the principal approaches presented in the paper can be used as a pattern for the representation of other charter corpora on the Semantic Web. Semantic publications of this kind will provide a solid basis for specific Web information systems that incorporate texts, research tools, and research results into knowledge-based systems, which are created for a network community.

III. Digital diplomatics in the work of the historian

Diplomata Belgica
Analysing medieval charter texts (dictamen)
through a quantitative approach
The case of Flanders and Hainaut (1191–1244)[1]

ELS DE PAERMENTIER[2]

Studying the editorial customs and dictamen of a territorial chancery[3] in the Central Middle Ages first entails distinguishing those charters drawn up within the chancery of the public authority it serves from those which were produced outside of the chancery by their recipients, and afterwards approved and sealed by the author[4]. Until recently, analysis of a charter dictamen to determine the place of production was mainly based on *Stilvergleichung*, a methodology developed by Léopold Delisle and Theodor von Sickel at the end of the 19th century[5]. However, this method of comparing editorial

---

[1] This contribution is a summarised and translated version of a French article that will shortly appear in the Bibliothèque de l'École des chartes (BECh), E. DE PAERMENTIER, Le dictamen de la chancellerie comtale de Flandre et de Hainaut (1191–1244). Méthode d'analyse assistée par ordinateur, résultats et opportunités, in: BECh 169 (2011, 2) (in press).

[2] The research presented in this article was facilitated by funding from the Flemish Hercules Foundation (Project: *Sources from the Medieval Low Countries* (SMLC)). I would like to thank Thérèse de Hemptinne and Shennan Hutton for their suggestions and comments on this article.

[3] For this type of 'institution', Edmond Reusens introduced the term 'chancellerie inférieure', meaning a chancery in the service of a local territorial secular or ecclesiastical ruler (a count or bishop), in contrast to a 'chancellerie supérieure' belonging to sovereign rulers, such as the pope, the French king or the German emperor. E. REUSENS, Les chancelleries inférieures en Belgique depuis leur origine jusqu'au commencement du XIIIe siècle, in: Analectes pour servir à l'histoire ecclésiastique de la Belgique 26 (1896) p. 20–207, p. 20–21.

[4] B.-M. TOCK, Auteur ou impétrant? Réflexions sur les chartes des évêques d'Arras au XIIe siècle, in: BECh 149 (1991, 2) p. 215–248, p. 216, 224–229.

[5] L. DELISLE, Catalogue des actes de Philippe Auguste. Avec une introduction sur les sources, les caractères et l'importance historique de ces documents (1856); TH. VON SICKEL, Beiträge zur Diplomatik (Sitzungsberichte der philosophisch-historische

styles was limited to protocol formulas, for practical reasons[6]. After all, in the pre-digital world of diplomatics, researchers had to collect the charter texts one at a time and perform the stylistic comparisons manually[7].

Fortunately, the process of digitalisation has not bypassed the auxiliary science of diplomatics. In the last few decades, many edited charter collections from all kinds of secular and ecclesiastical authorities have been made

---

Classe der Kaiserlichen Akademien, 1861–1882) 8 vols. Voir aussi H. Bresslau, Handbuch der Urkundenlehre für Deutschland und Italien (1889).

[6] For Flanders, see, among others, F. Vercauteren, Actes des comtes de Flandre, 1071–1128 (1938) p. LIX-LXII; W. Prevenier, De oorkonden der graven van Vlaanderen (1191–aanvang 1206) I. Diplomatisch paleografische inleiding, II. Uitgave, III. Documentatie en indices (1964–1966); Th. de Hemptinne, De oorkonden der graven van Vlaanderen (juli 1128–sept 1191), I: Peiling naar de oorkondingsaktiviteit van de grafelijke kanselarij in de periode 1128–1191, op grond van een diplomatisch en paleografisch onderzoek (unpublished volume of the doctoral thesis, 1978). For the county of Holland: J. Kruisheer, De oorkonden en de kanselarij van de graven van Holland tot 1299 (1971). For the county of Namur: M. Walraet, Actes de Philippe I, dit le Noble, comte et marquis de Namur (1196–1212) (1949). For the county of Hainaut: V. Van Camp, De Oorkonden en kanselarij van de graven van Henegouwen, Holland en Zeeland. Vorstelijke communicatie tijdens een personele unie: Henegouwen, 1280–1345 (2011). For the duchy of Brabant: the present doctoral study of David Guilardian, see: A. Dierkens and D. Guilardian, Actes princiers et naissance des principautés territoriales: du duché de Basse-Lotharingie au duché de Brabant (XI-XIIIᵉ siècles), in: Chancelleries princières et Scriptoria dans les anciens Pays-Bas Xᵉ–XVᵉ siècles. Vorstelijke kanselarijen en Scriptoria in de Lage Landen 10ᵉ –15ᵉ eeuw, ed. Th. de Hemptinne and J.-M. Duvosquel (2011) p. 245–260, p. 246, note 4. See also G. Croenen, Latin and the vernaculars in the charters of the Low Countries: the case of Brabant, in: The Dawn of the Written Vernacular in Western Europe, ed. M. Goyens and W. Verbeke (Mediaevalia Lovanensia Series 1, Studia 33, 2003) p. 107–125; by the same author: the introduction in De oorkonden van de familie Berthout: 1212–1425 (2006) pp. i-lxxxii, and L'entourage des ducs de Brabant au XIIIᵉ siècle. Nobles, chevaliers et clercs dans les chartes ducales (1235–1267), in: À l'ombre du pouvoir. Les entourages princiers au moyen âge, ed. A. Marchandisse and J.-L. Kupper (2003) p. 277–293. For the ecclesiastical chanceries, see, among others, B.-M. Tock, Une chancellerie épiscopale au XIIᵉ siècle. Le cas d'Arras (Publications de l'Institut d'Études Médiévales, 1991); E. Van Mingroot, Kanzlei, Jurisdiktion und Verwaltung im Bistum Kammerich (Cambrai 1057–1130), in: Recht en instellingen in de oude Nederlanden tijdens de middeleeuwen en de nieuwe tijd: Liber amicorum Jan Buntinx, ed. G. Asaert e.a. (1981) p. 1–26 and C. Vleeschouwers, De oorkonden van de Sint-Baafsabdij te Gent (819–1321) (1990) I: Inleiding. See also the contributions of B.-M. Tock (Thérouanne), of J.-L. Kupper (Liège), of Nathalie Barré (Cambrai) and of J. Burgers (Utrecht) in: Chancelleries princières et Scriptoria, ed. Th. de Hemptinne and J.-M. Duvosquel.

[7] W. Prevenier, La chancellerie des comtes de Flandre dans le cadre européen à la fin du XIIᵉ siècle, in: BECh 125 (1967) p. 34–94, 43–44.

available online or published on CD Rom[8]. This talk focuses on the useful application of the digital database *Diplomata Belgica*[9] in my recently completed doctoral research on the charters and chancery of the counts of Flanders and Hainaut during the late-twelfth and early-thirteenth century (between 1191 and 1244). The period covers the successive reigns of Count Baldwin V/VIII (1191–1194/5), double-numbered in this way because he was the fifth count of Hainaut and the ninth count of Flanders to bear the name Baldwin; his eldest son, Count Baldwin VI/IX (1194/5–1206)[10]; Philip of Namur, regent during the minority of Joan of Constantinople, the eldest daughter of Baldwin VI/IX (1206–1212); and finally of Joan of Constantinople herself, who became countess of both territories in 1212, at the age of twelve (1212–1244) [11]. In this study, I applied a combined methodo-

---

[8] For a general overview on the utility of digitized editions of medieval charters, see G. VOGELER, Vom Nutz und Frommen digitaler Urkundeneditionen, in: Archiv für Diplomatik, Schriftgeschichte, Siegel- und Wappenkunde 52 (2006) p. 449–466.

[9] See below in this article.

[10] For the reigns of Baldwin V/VIII and Baldwin VI/IX, I only examined the comital charters destined for Hainaut, since those destined for Flanders had already been studied by Walter Prevenier (for the period 1191–1206) (see note 6).

[11] On the life and government of Count Baldwin V/VIII, see: PREVENIER, De Oorkonden II p. lviii-lxi. See also J. J. DE SMET, Baudouin V (VIII) le Courageux, comte de Flandre et de Hainaut (?–1195), in: Biographie Nationale 1 (1866) col. 810–813, and TH. DE HEMPTINNE, Vlaanderen en Henegouwen onder de erfgenamen van de Boudewijns (1070–1244), in: Algemene Geschiedenis der Nederlanden, ed. D. BLOK, W. PREVENIER and D. J. ROORDA (1977–1983) p. 372–402, 392–395. On Count Baldwin VI/IX: W. PREVENIER, Boudewijn VI/IX, in: Nationaal Biografisch Woordenboek 1 (1964) col. 224–237; ID., De Oorkonden II p. lxi-lxv, R. L. WOLFF, Baldwin of Flanders and Hainaut, First Latin Emperor of Constantinople: His Life, Death, and Resurrection, 1172–1225, in: Speculum 27 (1952, 3) p. 281–322, and J. J. DE SMET, Baudouin IX (VI), comte de Flandre et de Hainaut, empereur de Constantinople (1171–1205/1206), in: Biographie Nationale I (1866) col. 804–807. On the regent Philip of Namur, see B. HENDRICKX, Het regentschap over Vlaanderen en Henegouwen na het vertrek van Boudewijn VI/IX op kruisvaart (1202–1211), in: Revue Belge de Philologie et d'Histoire 48 (1970, 2) p. 377–393, 380–381 and WALRAET, Actes de Philippe I p. 17–20. On Countess Joan of Constantinople, the most complete work is that of T. LUYKX, Johanna van Constantinopel, gravin van Vlaanderen en Henegouwen. Haar leven (1199/1200–1244), haar regering (1205–1244), vooral in Vlaanderen (1946). See also G. LECUPPRE, Jeanne de Flandre, traîtresse et parricide. Thèmes radicaux d'une opposition politique, in: Reines et princesses au moyen âge. Actes du cinquième colloque international de Montpellier, Montpellier, 1999 (Ass. CRISIMA 2001) 1 p. 63–74. On the policies of this countess towards the religious institutions in her comital domains, see E. JORDAN, Women, Power and Religious Patronage in the Middle Ages (2006).

logy[12] of diplomatics, palaeography and prosopography in order to determine the membership of the counts' administration, as well as ascertaining which charters were drawn up and written down within the comital chancery, and which ones were not[13]. Subsequently, on the basis of the charters identified as editorial products of the chancery, I analysed the extent to which these documents reveal a proper 'chancery tradition', the ways that the comital chancery tended to differentiate itself from other secular or ecclesiastical editorial centres during the period 1191–1244, and the influence that some important chancery clerks had on the organisation and editorial customs within the administrative entourage of the counts. In what follows, however, I shall mainly focus on the diplomatic analysis of the comital charters, because it is particularly for this research that the digital source collection *Diplomata Belgica* was an invaluable support.

Diplomata Belgica

Diplomata Belgica is a source recovery project, set up initially in the 1970s by order of the Royal Historical Commission. Its mission was to collect digital copies of all pre-1350 charters issued by or destined for any secular or ecclesiastical persons or institutions situated within the area of present-day Belgium[14]. In 1997, a first version was published by Brepols Publishers as a CD

---

[12] In order to investigate questions on the further development of the comital chancery during the first half of the 13th century, the comital acts of this period were analysed through three methodological approaches: a diplomatic analysis of the charter text or dictamen, a palaeographical study of the charters preserved in the original and a prosopographical study of the chancery employees. This contribution will mainly focus on the methodology and the results of the diplomatic study. The doctoral dissertation, defended in November 2010, will be published by the end of this year. E. DE PAERMENTIER, *In cuius rei testimonium et firmitatem*. Oorkonden en kanselarijwerking in de entourage van de graven en gravinnen van Vlaanderen en Henegouwen (1191–1244). Een diplomatische en paleografische studie (Ghent University 2010, will appear in 2014 (Hilversum: Verloren). All references in this article refer to the pages of the manuscript.

[13] PREVENIER, La chancellerie p. 40. Both Benoît-Michel Tock and Walter Prevenier also consider another possibility, namely a 'mixed' dictamen that shows editorial influences from the entourages of both the issuer and the recipient of the charter. TOCK, Auteur ou impétrant pp. 216–217; PREVENIER, De Oorkonden I p. 3.

[14] A. WAUTERS, Table chronologique des chartes et diplômes concernant l'histoire de Belgique, continué par Stanislas Bormans, Joseph Halkin, e.a. (1866–1971) 16 vols. See also G. DECLERCQ, P. DEMONTY, K. NAESSENS and G. TRIFIN, L'informatisation de la 'Table chronologique' d'A. Wauters. Méthodologie du nouveau répertoire des documents diplomatiques belges antérieurs à 1200, in: Bulletin de la Commission Royale

Rom called *Thesaurus Diplomaticus*, and contained about 13,000 records of charters up to the year 1200[15]. In more than half of these records the Latin charter text was recorded, and for about 2,400 original charters the picture was available. Now the database *Diplomata Belgica* is being incorporated into a larger project, the 'Sources from the Medieval Low Countries (SMLC)', supported by the Hercules Foundation and the Belgian Royal Historical Commission[16]. The plan is to launch the database online in the near future.

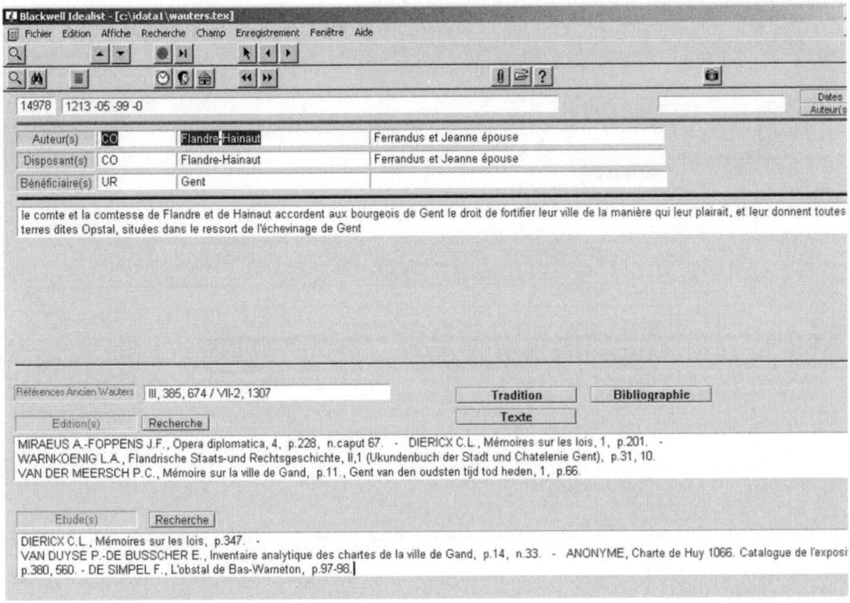

Fig. 1

d'Histoire 153 (1987) p. 223–302. For the user's guide to this CD Rom, see P. TOMBEUR, PH. DEMONTY and M.-P. LAVIOLETTE, *Thesaurus Diplomaticus*. Guide de l'utilisateur. CD-Rom (1997) (Commission Royale d'Histoire, Comité national du Latin médiéval, Cetedoc).

[15] P. TOMBEUR, PH. DEMONTY, W. PREVENIER and M.-P. LAVIOLETTE, *Thesaurus Diplomaticus* (1997) (CD Rom).

[16] <http://www.narrative-sources.be>. In 2009, the Hercules Foundation, an agency of the Flemish Community responsible for funding infrastructure for fundamental scientific research, approved the project 'Sources from the Medieval Low Countries (SMLC). A Multiple Database System for the Launch of *Diplomata Belgica* and for a Completely Updated Version of Narrative Sources' (director: prof. dr. Jeroen Deploige, Ghent University). For more information on this project, see <http://www. herculesstichting.be>. See also J. DEPLOIGE, B. CALLENS, PH. DEMONTY and G. DE TRÉ, Remedying the Obsolescense of Digitised Surveys of Medieval Sources. Narrative Sources and Diplomata Belgica, in: Bulletin de la Commission Royale d'Histoire 176 (2010, 1) p. 1–14.

Currently this corpus not only houses the digital texts of more than 30,000 charters promulgated by secular and religious authorities from the area of present-day Belgium and northern France up to the year 1250, it also contains digital photographs of about 5,000 original acts.

Let me give a short introduction to the different search engines of this database. On top of this record, you have the fields for the promulgation date of the charter, the name and function of its author (promulgator), and the names of the issuer and recipient of the document.

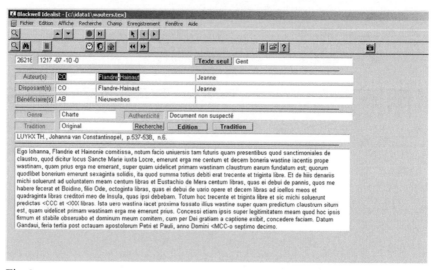

Fig. 2

Below is a summary (regesta) of the act, as well as the bibliographical references to edition(s) or publications which cite the charter. The 'Text' button opens up the complete Latin text of the charter, while the 'Tradition' button indicates where the original document is archived. On the research screen – this is the most important tool for digital diplomatic analysis – it is possible to query several data choices within each of these white fields. By clicking on the binoculars, you obtain a results list of charters for a single query, or a combination of queries.

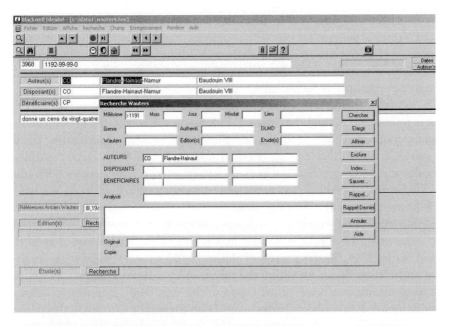

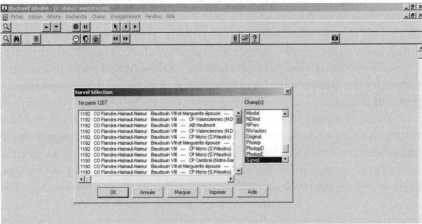

Fig. 3

Advantages for diplomatic research

The structure of this digital instrument offers many advantages for diplomatic research on territorial chanceries, such as that of the counts of Flanders and Hainaut.

First of all, the enormous saving of research time (heuristics) gave me the opportunity to organise the dispositive text parts into charter dictamen analysis for the first time, and to examine them from a much more comparative and 'creative' perspective – as will be demonstrated. Since the dispositive sections of charter texts are significantly more diverse than protocol formulas, using the dispositive text adds indicators or 'tell tale signs' that help to reveal who was responsible for the editorial draft of the charter.

Secondly, thanks to the multiple search engines of the *Diplomata Belgica*, it is possible to extend the existing diplomatic method of the manual comparison of text styles to a whole new dimension, i.e. into a quantitative word approach, or 'word statistics'.[17] Furthermore it is possible to search the entire collection of almost 20,000 digitised charter texts issued between 1191 and 1244 by assorted secular and ecclesiastical authorities. For example, we want to know how many times the pious formula, *divini amoris intuitu*, occurs within the area of present-day Belgium and northern France during the given period. First, we select the charter texts registered in the database after 1191 and before 1244. We get a result of almost 20,000 charters issued by a variety of authorities. Next, we refine the selection by querying the words *divini amoris intuitu* as a single word group in the 'text field'. From the previous selection of thousands of charters only twelve remain that contain this pious expression. Eight of them were issued by the count of Flanders and Hainaut, but the other four charters were issued by other secular and ecclesiastical authors. This example shows how the dispositive text part of the charter, in addition to the protocol text, becomes a 'treasury' of elements. When their frequency is measured, these elements help locate the editorial origin of a charter, and show the chronological and geographic dispersion of an expression or protocol formula.

A third advantage of measuring 'word frequency' relates to the political situation of the personal union of Flanders and Hainaut, and its impact on the administrative organisation within these two counties, which were now joined by a common ruler. Since all queries for the frequency of word groups, expressions, or protocol formula are rather 'neutral', the system does not make geographical distinctions between recipients in Flanders or Hainaut. Several queries thus revealed interesting patterns in the editorial customs of both counties and in the organisation of the comital chancery[18].

---

[17] B.-M. Tock, L'apport des bases de données de chartes pour la recherche des mots et des formules, in: Digitale Diplomatik. Neue Technologien in der historischen Arbeit mit Urkunden, ed. G. Vogeler (AfD Beiheft 12, 2009) p. 283–293.

[18] De Paermentier, Oorkonden en kanselarijwerking I p. 322–325 and ead., La chancellerie comtale en Flandre et en Hainaut sous Baudouin VI/IX (1195–1206) et pendant la régence de Philippe de Namur (1206–1212), in: Bulletin de la Commission Royale d'Histoire 176 (2010, 2) p. 247–286.

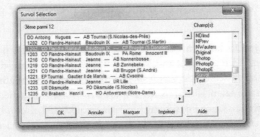

Fig. 4

Methodology and procedure of determination

In order to determine which charters issued by the counts of Flanders and Hainaut were actually edited by a chancery clerk, I developed a 'three-step action plan'. According to the traditional method of *Stilvergleichung*[19], a group of charters issued by the same author, bestowed on different recipients, and sharing the same stylistic elements ('protocol formulas'), can be considered documents edited in the area of their common author – in this case, the comital chancery. A group of charters issued by different authors, bestowed on the same recipient, and sharing the same stylistic elements, can be considered texts that are produced in the area of the recipient. The availability of *Diplomata Belgica* enabled me to adapt this method to new standards and criteria. Here is the procedure I followed[20]:

FIRST PHASE: search for significant frequencies

In the first phase, I searched for word groups, expressions or distinctive protocol formulas that either dominated in the charters issued by the counts of Flanders and Hainaut, or dominated in the charters addressed to a certain recipient during the period from 1191 to 1244. I sought inspiration for the queries from the texts of approximately 700 charters issued by or destined for the counts of Flanders and Hainaut, or issued by people from the counts' familial or administrative entourage.

    Overall, I wanted to detect the *ars dictaminis* of the comital chancery within these two counties. Using trial and error, I entered about 5,500 queries into the database – that is, between five and ten 'new' words, expressions, or protocol formulas per charter text[21]. Not all of these results were useful. Many of the results lists showed that certain expressions or protocols were

---

[19] PREVENIER, De Oorkonden I p. 7–159 and ID., La chancellerie p. 39–41. See also TH. DE HEMPTINNE, W. PREVENIER and M. VANDERMAESEN, La chancellerie des comtes de Flandre (XIIᵉ-XIVᵉ siècle), in: Landesherrliche Kanzleien im Spätmittelalter. Referate zum 6.internationalen Kongreß für Diplomatik 1983 (Münchener Beiträge zur Mediävistik und Renaissance Forschung 35, 1984) p. 433–454, 435–436.

[20] For a more detailed explanation of the three methodological phases, see DE PAERMENTIER, Oorkonden en kanselarijwerking I pp. 48–67 and in EAD., Le dictamen.

[21] These selections or queries could be very diverse: a word, a word group, an expression, a part of a protocol formula. Often the query ended with an asterisk in order to include all conjugations or declensions. Examples: *mand** (verb *mandare*) *et vol** (verb *velle*), *werpi** (verb *werpire*) *et effestuc** (verb *effestucare*), *illust** (*illuster*) *et karissim** (*karissimus*) *domin** (*dominus*), *sigill** (*-o, -is*) *nostr** (*-o, -is*) *roborari decrev** (*-i, -imus*). DE PAERMENTIER, Oorkonden en kanselarijwerking I p. 54–55.

commonly known and used in many secular and ecclesiastical areas, without being typical of any one of them. In order to determine the editorial origin of the comital charters, I was particularly interested in expressions and protocol formulas that occurred most frequently in the charters of the counts of Flanders and Hainaut within my time span[22]. I called them 'characteristic dictamen elements'. As a selection criterion to define this linguistic construction, the characteristic dictamen element had to appear within the same results list in at least three comital charters for three different recipients[23].

For example, in one of the comital charters I found the *expression (absolvere) ab omni servitio (...) feodali*, and I wanted to know if this word group was typical for the administrative entourage of the counts of Flanders and Hainaut between 1191 and 1244. First, I queried the word group *ab omni servitio*, and selected a promulgation date after 1190. Then, I refined the results by selecting charters issued before 1245, and by requesting in the 'text field' the charters in which the words *servitio* and *feodali* occur at a maximum distance of five words. The results list revealed that within our time frame, and particularly after the 1230s, this expression appears in 13 charters, of which eight were issued by the counts of Flanders and Hainaut, and to at least three different recipients. Consequently, I classified this word group as a 'characteristic dictamen element'. An even more interesting example shows the opposite result. In another comital charter I read the passive verb *adheredari* (to be put in possession of). This passive verb construction appears exclusively in charters bestowed on the chapter of Ste-Waudru in Mons (Hainaut), and should thus be considered a typical editorial custom of this scriptorium. When such a 'suspicious' element appears in comital charters, it may also reveal an editorial draft in the area of the recipient, in this case, the chapter of Ste-Waudru.

---

[22] Sometimes in a results list, a text formula appeared twelve times within a group of acts issued by different abbots or local seigneurs, and 'only' eight times in charters issued by the count(esse)s of Flanders and Hainaut. In such a case, the cluster of comital acts was still considered 'the most homogenous group', since they were all issued by a same comital entourage, whereas the 'abbey group' or 'seigneur group' was often comprised of acts each issued by a different institution or person. In doing so, a results list could reveal at the same time an enormous diversity in the dispersion of a certain expression or protocol formula, and yet, the cluster of comital charters of Flanders and Hainaut were the largest single users of the expression or formula, even though they only comprised a third or fourth of all the charters on the results list. In other words, there was no larger homogeneous group of acts issued by a same author, or destined for a same recipient than those issued by the count(esse)s of Flanders and Hainaut. DE PAERMENTIER, *Oorkonden en kanselarijwerking* I p. 58–59.

[23] It concerns the same 'principle of diversity' that is applied in the basic reasoning of Prevenier's method. See note 19.

SECOND PHASE: some quantitative conditions

It would naturally be premature to determine the origin of a charter text on the basis of a single characteristic dictamen component. Since linguistic elements could not be monopolised, a local clerk might notice an element in a charter edited elsewhere, pick it up temporarily, and apply it in his own work in the count's service[24]. To 'solve' this problem, I imposed quantitative conditions to ensure that a comital charter had actually been drawn up by a chancery clerk[25]. Benoît-Michel Tock developed a similar system of quantitative conditions in his study of the episcopal chancery of Arras[26]. However, the standards he applied depended on the occurrence of text elements that showed up exclusively in episcopal circles, making them too rigid for the case of Flanders and Hainaut. Therefore, I had to adapt his conditions.

In my study, I considered a charter to be an editorial chancery product if:

- the text contained at least four characteristic dictamen elements, either within the dispositive or protocol text parts[27], if at least two appeared in the dispositio; or
- the charter text contained at least three characteristic dictamen elements, if at least one appeared exclusively within the charters of the counts of Flanders and Hainaut[28]; or
- when the charter was a mandate, which in the case of Flanders often did not total more than fifty words[29]: if the charter text had at least one characteristic dictamen element; or

---

[24] DE HEMPTINNE, PREVENIER and VANDERMAESEN, La Chancellerie comtale p. 435 and PREVENIER, De Oorkonden I p. 567.

[25] DE PAERMENTIER, Oorkonden en kanselarijwerking I p. 60–62.

[26] TOCK, Une chancellerie épiscopale p. 24–25.

[27] Namely: invocatio, intitulatio, notificatio, address, salutatio, corroboratio and datatio. Because no other protocol formula was as diverse as a corroboratio, and in order to facilitate the comparison of different text parts of this formula, the corroboratio was considered as two separate parts: first, as the introductory formula expressing the desire for the firmness of the juridical action (for example: *In cuius rei testimonium et munimen*), and second, as the announcement of the validation signs (for example: *presentes litteras feci scribi et sigilli mei feci roborari*). On the 'compound' content of the corroboratio formula, see O. GUYOTJEANNIN, J. PYCKE and B.-M. TOCK, Diplomatique médiévale p. 84 (L'Atelier du Médiéviste 2, 1993).

[28] A text element was considered both 'characteristic and exclusive' if it appeared exclusively in at least two charters issued by the count(esse)s of Flanders and Hainaut that were destined for two different recipients. DE PAERMENTIER, Oorkonden en kanselarijwerking I p. 62.

[29] Moreover, because it was a direct order from the lord to one of his officials, a mandate provides 'external' evidence in favour of an editorial origin from within the chancery. DE HEMPTINNE, PREVENIER and VANDERMAESEN, La Chancellerie comtale p. 452.

– when it was a long legislative charter or keure: if the dispositio of the charter text had at least six characteristic dictamen elements[30].

THIRD PHASE: final determination

Once a charter text met all the quantitative requirements and lacked 'suspicious' elements that might suggest an editing process in the area of the recipient, I made the final determination that it was an editorial chancery product[31]. None of these 'chancery charters' contained any 'suspicious' elements. In fact, most of them contained more than the four 'characteristic dictamen elements' initially required. In some cases, this number rose up to eight or more expressions or protocol formulas that dominated in the charters of the counts of Flanders and Hainaut within the studied period[32].

Results[33]

To conclude, and to emphasise the usefulness of quantitative approaches to medieval charter texts, I will briefly share the main conclusions from the quantitative analysis, more specifically, from the many queries that led to the identification of characteristic wording for the charters of the counts of Flanders and Hainaut.

---

[30] At that time, in Flanders most of the legislative charters were only composed of an invocatio, a dispositio and a datatio. DE PAERMENTIER, Oorkonden en kanselarijwerking I p. 62, 358–360.

[31] In fact, before concluding the identification as 'editorial chancery product', both the charter text and the results lists of the queries of all word groups, expressions and protocol formulas that occurred in this text were put through some additional controls and tests a contrario, such as for the presence of 'suspicious' text elements that were rather typical for the entourage of a destinary (for example a local abbey) (proof contra chancery origin), the presence of charters issued by chancery clerks in a results list (proof pro chancery origin), the presence of comital acts destined for Flanders that already were identified as chancery products by Walter Prevenier (Flanders, 1191–1206) (proof pro chancery origin). See DE PAERMENTIER, Le dictamen ('Contrôles et contre-épreuves') and EAD., Oorkonden en kanselarijwerking I p. 63–66.

[32] EAD., Oorkonden en kanselarijwerking I p. 65.

[33] This contribution only covers a selected portion of the general conclusions of my diplomatic study. The detailed overview of all results includes a discussion of the increased editorial chancery production within the framework of the fluctuating political situation in Flanders and Hainaut during the first half of the 13th century and in the context of the growing literacy at that time. The longer study also treats the relationship between the production of evidentiary and dispositive charters, the language of

On the basis of the preceding methodology, I identified approximately 400 out of the 700[34] analysed charters as 'definite' or 'most probable' editorial chancery products[35]. Although most were comital charters, 25 revealed that not only the count and countess, but also their relatives[36], court officials such as the constable or the butler, and even people from the count's own administration[37] appealed to the editorial service of the chancery for their own personal charters[38]. This is quite logical, because while the count participated in the judicial action in the first group of acts, the second group of charters concerned people who were honoured with an 'informal' authority deriving from comital power, either by their office and associated skills, or by their personal family relationship to the count[39]. The chronological and geographi-

---

chancery charters and the consequences and implications of the personal union between the counties of Flanders and Hainaut for the organisation of the comital chancery. See DE PAERMENTIER, Oorkonden en kanselarijwerking I p. 311–367; EAD., Le dictamen and EAD., La chancellerie comtale.

[34] This number totals 608 comital charters from the period from 1191 to 1244, for which the full text is available in *Diplomata Belgica* (the 302 comital charters issued by count Baldwin VI/IX and destined for Flanders, already studied by Walter Prevenier, are not included), together with approximately 100 acts issued by other people but destined for the count(ess) of Flanders and Hainaut, and acts issued by people from the familial or administrative entourage of the count(ess), among which were the *protonotarius* and court officials, such as the butler or the senechal. DE PAERMENTIER, Oorkonden en kanselarijwerking I p. 37. By way of comparison: in his study, Walter Prevenier identified 176 out of 302 comital charters as editorial chancery products. However, one should consider that his methodology was only based on the comparison of protocol formulas. PREVENIER, De Oorkonden I p. 157–159.

[35] DE PAERMENTIER, Oorkonden en kanselarijwerking I p. 311–312; PREVENIER, La chancellerie comtale pp. 41–42.

[36] For example, Marguerite of Constantinople, the younger sister of Countess Joan, or William of Thy-le-Château, natural son of Baldwin IV and great-uncle of Countess Joan. D. DERECK, Guillaume l'Oncle (ca. 1150–novembre 1219). Rôle politique, fortune et descendance d'un fils naturel du comte de Hainaut Baudouin IV, in: Annales du cercle archéologique de Mons 78 (1999) p. 43–135.

[37] Among them were the chancellor and the two successive 'leading' chancery clerks, Walter of Kortrijk and Gilles of Bredene.

[38] In total it concerns 16 charters dated between 1197 and 1243. For a chronological list of all the approximately 400 charters that were identified as 'certain' (312 acts) or 'most probable' (81 acts) editorial chancery documents, see DE PAERMENTIER, Oorkonden en kanselarijwerking II p. 13–51 (Appendix 6.2).

[39] In the first case, one speaks of *positional* and *expert* power; in the second case, one speaks of *referent* power. Doede KEUNING and Jan EPPINK, Management en Organisatie. Theorie en toepassing (2008) p. 572–573.This theoretical model is based on that of J. FRENCH and B. RAVEN, The bases of social power, in: Studies in Social Power, ed. D. CARTWRIGHT (1959) p. 150–167.

cal overview of the chancery acts also points to the relative continuity of the chancery production, though this was more obvious in Flanders than in Hainaut. However, in periods that were politically unstable, such as the long captivity of Count Ferrand after the defeat of Bouvines in 1214, editorial chancery activities tended to decrease[40].

During the first half of the thirteenth century, the dictamen of the chancery charters consisted of many phrases and protocol formulas that were widespread and commonly used in many areas. However, within the group of approximately 400 identified chancery texts, there were also around 250 unique 'characteristic' word groups, expressions[41], and protocol formulas[42] that occurred predominantly, or even exclusively[43], in the charters of the counts of Flanders and Hainaut at that time[44]. Yet, this does not mean that the results of all the other thousands of queries, that in the end were not 'characteristic', were useless – on the contrary. Those results lists showing the chronological and geographical dispersion of those word groups are highly important for comparative argument. For example, the expression, 'late', *bone memorie*, used to indicate a deceased person, was well known within the area

---

[40] DE PAERMENTIER, *Oorkonden en kanselarijwerking* I p. 313–316. See also EAD., Le dictamen.

[41] Examples of 'characteristic' word groups and expressions that occurred most frequently in charters issued by the count(esse)s of Flanders and Hainaut between 1191 and 1244: from the theme, 'donations and granting possession': *dare in perpetuam elemosinam*; from the theme, 'the feudal contract and renunciation of a fief': *in manus (meas, nostras) resignare* (or *werpire*) and *(de, a) (me, nobis) teneba(n)t in feodum*; from the theme, 'penalty clauses': *reputare (...) factum*; from the theme, 'combinations of verbs in mandates': *mandamus et volumus*, or *mando et precipio*. DE PAERMENTIER, Oorkonden en kanselarijwerking II appendices 6.1 and 6.5.

[42] Examples of 'characteristic' protocol formulas (period 1191–1244): the salutatio, *salutem et dilectionem*, or *salutem et amorem*; the address formula, *omnibus presentes litteras inspecturis*; the corroboratio formula, *Ut (hec, hoc) ratum et stabile permaneat*, or *(presentem) paginam (...) contuli(mus) sigilli mei appensione (...) munitam*. DE PAERMENTIER, Oorkonden en kanselarijwerking II appendices 6.1 and 6.6.

[43] Examples of dispositive formulas that occurred *exclusively* in the charters issued by the count(esse)s of Flanders and Hainaut (1191–1244): from the theme 'renunciation of a fief (court procedure)', *audito (...) iudicio*, the count's address of the countess as *dilecta consors mea*, the word group in which the comital power is described as *in plena et libera potestate*. Examples of 'exclusive' protocol formulas: the salutatio formula, *salutem et sinceri amoris affectum*, the corroboratio formula (introductory part), *quod ut perpetui roboris obtineat firmitatem*, the combination of the address-notificatio formulas, *omnibus notum faci(-o, -mus) tam presentibus quam futuris*. Ibid., II appendices 6.5 et 6.6.

[44] From more than 5,500 'trial-and-error' queries, 199 dispositive formulas and 44 protocol formulas could be considered 'characteristic' and/or 'exclusive' for the comital charters studied. DE PAERMENTIER, Oorkonden en kanselarijwerking I p. 318–319, 362.

of present-day Belgium and northern France between 1191 and 1244, whereas the adapted alternative *bone recordationis* was typical for the charters of the counts of Flanders and Hainaut. Another example would be the following: the commonly used expression *libere et absolute possidendum*, used commonly throughout the region, contrasts with the 'characteristic comital' variant *libere et pacifice possidendum*. In the field of protocol formulas the same tendency occurred: the combination of the salutation formula *salutem* and *salutem in Domino* were customary wordings, whereas *salutem et dilectionem*, or *salutem et sinceri amoris affectum* were dominantly, if not exclusively, used by clerks of the comital chancery. These and many other examples reveal that, by slightly adapting and combining commonly known expressions, the chancery clerks tended to differentiate themselves from other secular and ecclesiastical editing centres, and shaped an individual 'identity' if not 'image' for the count and his chancery[45]. Furthermore, the results lists of 'characteristic dictamen elements' also reveal that until the early 1220s, the editorial traditions that were predominant in the chancery dated from around 1200[46], the time of count Baldwin VI/IX and his chancellor Gerard of Alsace[47]. After 1225, many new 'editorial innovations' found acceptance in the chancery, and were consistently applied in the comital charter texts from that time onwards[48]. At this moment, there was also a more consistent use of the *salutatio* formula, as well as a change in the sequence of some protocol formulas[49]. Finally, several queries revealed that some expressions only occurred within a very specific time span in comital charters, or only in the count's

---

[45] Ibid. I p. 362–364.

[46] Ibid. I p. 320–322. See also DE PAERMENTIER, Le dictamen.

[47] DE PAERMENTIER, Oorkonden en kanselarijwerking I p. 365–366. On Gerard of Alsace (chancellor between 1183 and 1206), see A. VERHULST and Th. DE HEMPTINNE, Le chancelier de Flandre sous les comtes de la Maison d'Alsace (1128–1191), in: *Bulletin de la Commission Royale d'Histoire* 141 (1975) pp. 267–311, 303–308; REUSENS, Les chancelleries inférieures p. 82–90; PREVENIER, La chancellerie p. 53–59 and ID., De Oorkonden I p. 307–313.

[48] Examples from the theme, 'donations and putting into possession of': the expression *in perpetuum pacifice (...) possidendum*; from the theme, 'the feudal contract and renunciation of a fief': the expression, *werpire et effestucare*; from the theme, 'exemption of feudal service': the expression, *pro nobis et successoribus nostris (...) quitare*; from the theme, 'penalty clauses (renunciation clause)': *nichil de cetero (...) posse (...) reclamare*; from the theme, 'piety formulas': *divine pietatis intuitu*. DE PAERMENTIER, Oorkonden en kanselarijwerking II pp. 57–66.

[49] After 1225, the most prevalent structure of chancery charters was intitulatio-address-salutatio-notificatio (INT-ADR-SAL-NOT), instead of intitulatio-notificatio + address (INT-NOT-ADR). For reconstruction of the 'chancery formulary' of protocol formulas used until 1220 and the 'chancery formulary' that predominated after 1227–1228, see ibid. I p. 358–359.

charters destined for Flanders rather than Hainaut, or vice versa. Consequently, we can link these editorial traditions to the careers of certain leading chancery clerks and representatives of chancellors, and estimate their personal influence on editorial chancery customs[50].

Since there is not sufficient time to clarify all of the conclusions from my quantitative diplomatic analysis, I do hope that the ones demonstrated today may illustrate the great value of digital source collections, such as *Diplomata Belgica*, and the many opportunities these offer for more comparative and creative diplomatic research on medieval charters and chancery activities.

---

[50] Like Gilbert of Mons (Hainaut, 1195–1206), Walter of Kortrijk (until 1225) and Egidius of Bredene (from 1227 onwards). DE PAERMENTIER, Le dictamen (section: 'L'influence des cadres sur le dictamen de la chancellerie') and EAD., Oorkonden en kanselarijwerking I pp. 495–500, 512–517 and 527–530. See also DE PAERMENTIER, La chancellerie comtale pp. 247–286 for more detailed argumentation on the role of Gilbert of Mons, former chancellor of Count Baldwin V/VIII, in the local bureau of the comital chancery in Hainaut between 1195 and 1206.

De l'accumulation à l'exploitation? Expériences et propositions pour l'indexation et l'utilisation des bases de données diplomatiques[1]

NICOLAS PERREAUX

«Indépendamment même de toute éventualité d'application à la conduite, l'histoire n'aura donc le droit de revendiquer sa place parmi les connaissances vraiment dignes d'effort, seulement dans la mesure où, au lieu d'une simple énumération, sans liens et quasiment sans limites, elle nous promettra un classement rationnel et une progressive intelligibilité.»
MARC BLOCH, *Apologie pour l'histoire ou métier d'historien* (1943)

Depuis maintenant plusieurs décennies, les diplomatistes disposent de bases de données numérisées remarquables, dont le contenu est désormais propre à révolutionner nos connaissances concernant le Moyen Âge et ceci à plus ou moins court terme. Ainsi, sans même évoquer Google Books et ses milliers d'éditions d'actes diplomatiques numérisés, les médiévistes sont de plus en plus nombreux à connaître l'existence de sites tels que celui des *Chartes originales* de l'Artem[2],

---

[1] De nombreuses pistes et réflexions proposées dans cet article doivent beaucoup à des échanges avec Alain Guerreau: qu'il en soit tout d'abord chaleureusement remercié. Nous tenions aussi à remercier ceux qui ont contribué à sa structuration, soit par une relecture et des conseils circonstanciés – Eliana Magnani, notre directrice de thèse avec Daniel Russo, Marie-José Gasse-Grandjean et Sébastien Barret –, soit par des discussions, à la suite de notre intervention à Naples – Georg Vogeler, Michael Gervers, Benoît-Michel Tock, Dominique Stutzmann, Olivier Canteaut et Frédéric Glorieux.

[2] B.-M. TOCK (dir.)/M. COURTOIS/M.-J. GASSE-GRANDJEAN/P. DEMONTY, La diplomatique française du Haut Moyen Âge: inventaire des chartes originales antérieures à 1121 conservées en France, (1) «Introduction générale, album diplomatique, table chronologique, table des auteurs», (2) «Table des destinataires, table des genres diplomatiques, table des états de la tradition manuscrite, table des sceaux, table des chirographes, table des cotes d'archives ou de bibliothèques» (2001). En dernier lieu, pour une présentation globale du *corpus*, voir l'article introductif de B.-M. TOCK, La diplomatique française du Haut Moyen Âge vue à travers les originaux, ibid. p. 1–37. Depuis 2011, en dehors des reproductions photographiques, le *corpus* est désormais entièrement consultable en ligne: <http://www.cn-telma.fr/originaux/colophon/>.

Monasterium[3], le *Deeds Project*[4], les *Chartae Burgundiae Medii Aevii*[5], le

---

[3] Monasterium.net est sans aucun doute l'un des sites hébergeant des documents diplomatiques qui génère le plus de réflexions abstraites, méthodologiques, mais aussi techniques. Voir entre autres: TH. AIGNER, MOnasteriuM –Die mittelalterlichen Urkunden der Klöster des Landes Niederösterreich (A) im Internet (www.mom.archiv.net), in: Archivpflege in Westfalen und Lippe 58 (2003) p. 43–44; ID., Digitale Bereitstellung historischer Quellen aus Ordenstiftsarchiven, in: Der Archivar 8 (2003) p. 295–306; K. HEINZ, Monasterium.Net – Das virtuelle Urkundenarchiv niederösterreichischer Klöster, in: Österreich in Geschichte und Literatur 49 (2005) p. 48–49; ID., Monasterium. net – Auf dem Weg zu einem europäischen Urkundenportal, in: Regionale Urkundenbücher. Die Vorträge der 12. Tagung der Commission Internationale de Diplomatique [Sankt Pölten, 2009], éd. T. KÖLZER/W. RÖSENER/R. ZEHETMAYER (2010) p. 139–145; A. KRAH, Monasterium.net – das virtuelle Urkundenarchiv Europas. Möglichkeiten der Bereitstellung und Erschliesung von Urkundenbeständen, in: Archivalische Zeitschrift 91 (2009) p. 221–246; ID., Monasterium.net: Auf dem Weg zu einem mitteleuropäischen Urkundenportal, in: Digitale Diplomatik. Neue Technologien in der historischen Arbeit mit Urkunden, dir. G. VOGELER (AfD Beiheft 12, 2009) p. 70–77. Le site est disponible à l'adresse suivante: <http://www.monasterium.net/>

[4] L'origine du projet remonte à 1975 et la base actuelle contient environ 10 000 documents. Présentation du site et expériences dans: M. GERVERS, The DEEDS Project and the Development of a Computerized Methodology for Dating Undated English Private Charters of the Twelfth and Thirteenth Centuries, in: Dating Undated Medieval Charters, éd. M. GERVERS (2000) p. 13–36; ID., The dating of medieval English private charters of the twelfth and thirteenth centuries, in: A Distinct Voice. Medieval Studies in Honour of Leonard E. Boyle, O. P., dir. J. BROWN/ W. P. STONEMAN (1997) p. 455–505; M. GERVERS/M. MARGOLIN, Managing Meta-data in a Research Collection of Medieval Latin Charters, in: Digitale Diplomatik. Neue Technologien p. 271–282. En ligne: <http://deeds.library.utoronto.ca/>

[5] La base des CBMA est sans doute celle qui propose, à l'heure actuelle et avec la base des originaux, le plus d'expériences/d'études concrètes. Voir en particulier I. ROSÉ, À propos des *Chartæ Burgundiæ Medii Ævii* (CBMA). Éléments de réflexion à partir d'une enquête sur la dîme en Bourgogne au Moyen Âge, in: Bulletin du Centre d'études médiévales d'Auxerre (Collection CBMA. Les cartulaires, Études, 2008), version en ligne <http://cem.revues.org/index8412.html>; E. MAGNANI, L'échange dans la documentation diplomatique bourguignonne: autour d'un champ sémantique, in: L'acte d'échange, du VIIIe au XIIe siècle/Tauschgeschäft und Tauschurkunde vom 8. bis zum 12. Jh., Limoges 11–13 mars 2010, dir. PH. DEPREUX/I. FEES (AfD Beiheft 13, 2013), p. 403–426); EAD., Les moines et la mise en registre des transferts. Formules textuelles, formules visuelles, in: Cluny, le monachisme et la société au premier âge féodal (880–1050), éd. D. IOGNA-PRAT et al. (2013) p. 199–214; N. PERREAUX, L'eau, l'écrit et la société (IXe-XIIe siècle). Étude statistique sur les champs sémantiques dans les bases de données [CBMA et autres], in: Bulletin du Centre d'études médiévales d'Auxerre 15 (2011) p. 439–449, version en ligne: <http://cem.revues.org/index12062.html>; ID., La production de l'écrit diplomatique en Bourgogne. Hypothèses sur les dynamiques sociales inégales et les aires de scripturalité (IXe-XIIIe siècle) au regard des bases des données, in: Productions, remplois, mises en registre: la pratique sociale de l'écrit à travers

Codice Diplomatico della Lombardia medievale[6],

la documentation médiévale bourguignonne Auxerre, Abbaye Saint-Germain, 24 et 25 septembre 2009, dir. E. MAGNANI, à paraître en 2013; ID., Dynamique sociale et écriture documentaire (Cluny, X[e]-XIIe siècle). Observations statistiques sur le champ sémantique de l'eau, in: Cluny, le monachisme et la société, p. 111–127. Présentation de la base en elle-même (plus de 11 000 documents), in: E. MAGNANI/M.-J. GASSE-GRANDJEAN, *Chartae Burgundiae Medii Aevi* (CBMA), in: Bulletin du Centre d'études médiévales d'Auxerre 9 (2005), p. 179–181; EAED., CBMA – *Chartae Burgundiae Medii Aevi*.1. Les fonds diplomatiques bourguignons, in: ibid. 11 (2007) p. 163–169; EAED., CBMA. – *Chartae Burgundiae Medii Aevi*. 2. Cartulaires, éditions, base de données, in: ibid. 12 (2008) p. 237–244; EAED., CBMA – *Chartae Burgundiae Medii Aevi*. 3. Systèmes d'interrogation et recherches sur les fonds diplomatiques bourguignons, in: ibid. 13 (2009) p. 245–251; EAED., CBMA. – *Chartae Burgundiae Medii Aevi*. 4. Études, éditions, historiographie, in: ibid. 14 (2010) p. 197–209; EAED., CBMA. – *Chartae Burgundiae Medii Aevi*. 5. Actes cisterciens et prémontrés, in: ibid. 14 (2010) p. 273–275, version en ligne <http://www.artehis-cnrs.fr/CBMA-Chartae-Burgundiae-Medii-Aevi,964> et <http://www.artehis-cbma.eu/> pour le site de la base de données. Pour le corpus des originaux de l'Artem, une liste d'expériences concrètes avait déjà été donnée par B.-M. TOCK, L'apport des bases de données de chartes pour la recherche des mots et des formules, in: Digitale Diplomatik. Neue Technologien, p. 283–293, à la p. 284. Quelques jalons importants: M. PARISSE, À propos du traitement automatique des chartes: chronologie du vocabulaire et repérage des actes suspects, in: La lexicographie du latin médiéval et ses rapports avec les recherches actuelles sur la civilisation du Moyen Âge (Actes du colloque de Paris, 1978) (1981) p. 241–249; ID., Premiers résultats d'un traitement automatique des chartes, in: Le Moyen Âge 2 (1978) p. 337–343; ID., Remarques sur les chirographes et les chartes-parties antérieurs à 1120 et conservés en France, in: AfD 32 (1986) p. 546–568; ID., Croix autographes et souscriptions dans l'Ouest de la France au XIe siècle, in: Graphische Symbole in mittelalterlichen Urkunden. Beiträge zur diplomatischen Semiotik, éd. P. RÜCK (Historische Hilfswissenschaften 3, 1996) p. 143–155; ID., Écriture et réécriture des chartes: les pancartes aux XIe et XIIe siècles, in: Pratiques de l'écrit documentaire au XIe siècle, éd. O. GUYOTJEANNIN/ L. MORELLE/M. PARISSE (in: BECh 155 [1997] p. 5–347]) p. 247–265; ID., Les pancartes. Étude d'un type diplomatique, in: Pancartes monastiques des XIe et XIIe siècles, éd. M. PARISSE/P. PÉGEOT/B.-M. TOCK (1998) p. 11–62; B.-M. TOCK, La diplomatique sans pancarte. L'exemple du diocèse d'Arras et de Thérouanne, 1000–1120, in: Pancartes monastiques p. 131–157; ID., *Altare* dans les chartes françaises antérieures à 1121, in: Roma, Magistra Mundi. Itineraria culturae medievalis. Mélanges offerts au Père L. E. Boyle à l'occasion de son 75e anniversaire (2), éd. J. HAMESSE (1998) p. 901–926; ID., L'étude du vocabulaire et la datation des actes: l'apport des bases de données informatisées, in: Dating Undated Medieval Charters p. 81–96; ID. Scribes, souscripteurs et témoins dans les actes privés en France (VIIe-début du XIIe siècle) (ARTEM 9, 2005) (ne porte pas exclusivement sur la base de l'Artem); ID., Les actes entre particuliers en Bourgogne méridionale (IXe-XIe siècles), in: Die Privaturkunden der Karolingerzeit, éd. P. ERHART/K. HEIDECKER/B. ZELLER (2009) p. 121–134.

[6] La base actuelle contient environ 5 000 documents. Présentation complète du projet à l'adresse suivante: <http://cdlm.unipv.it/progetto/>. Voir aussi M. ANSANI, Il

les dMGH[7], ou encore les *Cartulaires numérisés d'Île de France*[8], etc. Des corpus remarquables, dont le dénominateur commun est d'avoir choisi l'option du libre accès: un point essentiel sur lequel il est parfois encore nécessaire d'insister[9].

Pourtant, malgré cette profusion, ainsi que le faisait encore récemment remarquer Benoît-Michel Tock[10], force est de constater que l'exploitation de ces vastes corpus – ou plutôt devrions-nous dire de *ce* vaste corpus – reste encore largement à faire, les entreprises dans le domaine restant pour le moment embryonnaires, ceci malgré la bonne volonté et l'intérêt notable (mais aussi, il faut bien l'admettre, ponctuel) des médiévistes pour les nouvelles technologies. Souvent rebutés par la difficile gestion d'une telle masse documentaire, les chercheurs qui tentent l'expérience des bases de données retournent souvent à des méthodes plus traditionnelles, employant certes, en parallèle, ces corpus, mais presque toujours comme de simples carrières de données. Il ne s'agit pas d'un phénomène nouveau: le *Thesaurus Diplomaticus* aura en effet bientôt 15 ans et les résultats de son exploitation systématique sont pour le moment largement en deçà de ce que nous aurions pu attendre d'un tel «trésor»[11]. Le constat est donc simple: il existe un décalage important entre la

---

Codice diplomatico digitale della Lombardia medievale, in: Comuni e memoria storica: alle origini del comune di Genova; atti del Convegno di studi, Genova, 24–26 settembre 2001, dir. D. Puncuh (2002) p. 23–49; M. Ansani/V. Leoni, Experiment einer digitalen Edition urkundlicher Quellen. Der «Codice diplomatico della Lombardia medievale» (8.–12. Jahrhundert), in: QUFIAB 86 (2006) p. 538–561; V. Leoni, Der Codice diplomatico della Lombardia medievale, in: Editionswissenschaftliche Kolloquien 2005/2007: Methodik – Amtsbücher, digitale Edition – Projekte, dir. M. Thumser (2008) p. 219–228. Site en ligne: <http://cdlm.unipv.it/>.

[7] C. Radl, Die Urkundeneditionen innerhalb der dMGH, in: Digitale Diplomatik. Neue Technologien p. 101–115. En ligne: <http://www.dmgh.de/>.

[8] Site en ligne: <http://elec.enc.sorbonne.fr/cartulaires/>.

[9] A. Guerreau, Textes anciens en série. Outils informatiques d'organisation et de manipulation de bases de données textuelles, in: Bulletin du Centre d'études médiévales d'Auxerre (Collection CBMA, 2012), version en ligne <http://cem.revues.org/index12177.html>; id., Pour un corpus de textes latins en ligne, in: ibid. (Collection CBMA, 2011), version en ligne <http://cem.revues.org/index11787.html>.

[10] «Mais curieusement, celles [les bases de données de textes diplomatiques] qui existent ne sont pas encore très utilisées. Disons-le franchement: elles sont sous-utilisées, et n'ont pas, ou pas encore, révolutionné la diplomatique comme elles auraient dû le faire», in: B.-M. Tock, L'apport des bases de données p. 283.

[11] C'était ce même exemple qu'avait déjà choisi B.-M. Tock dans son article pour les actes du colloque Digital Diplomatics (ibid.) Sur CD-ROM: *Thesaurus Diplomaticus,* version 1.0, 1997 (environ 6000 textes en mode texte); G. Declercq/P. Demonty, L'informatisation de la Table chronologique d'A. Wauters. Méthodologie du nouveau répertoire des documents diplomatiques belges antérieurs à 1200, in: Bulletin de la Commission royale d'Histoire 153 (1987) p. 223–302; P. Demonty, Le *Thesaurus*

création de bases de données – activité en quoi les médiévistes excellent, et c'est une bonne chose – et l'exploitation de celles-ci. Dans cet article, on propose l'hypothèse que cette situation relève d'une inadaptation de la méthode historique traditionnelle à ce nouveau matériau[12], inadaptation qui ne pourra être dépassée que par une mise en ordre globale – aussi bien technique qu'historique – du matériau diplomatique, à l'échelle européenne. De fait, ainsi que le faisait remarquer à juste titre Alain Guerreau en 2001[13], si les médiévistes disposent d'une méthode solide afin de gérer quelques dizaines/centaines d'occurrences de *molendinum*, force est d'admettre qu'une difficulté, non pas seulement différente au plan quantitatif mais d'abord et avant tout au plan qualitatif, émerge lorsqu'il s'agit de donner du sens à plusieurs milliers ou plusieurs dizaines de milliers d'occurrences d'un même vocable. Pourtant, il fait pour nous peu de doutes que seule une approche globale de cette documentation pourrait aider à avancer radicalement dans la compréhension des phénomènes sociaux consignés dans les chartes[14]. Ainsi, nous faisons nôtre la logique systématique d'une partie de l'École des Annales, exprimée par Lucien Febvre en 1933: «Pas une concession à l'esprit de spécialité, qui est l'es-

---

Diplomaticus, un instrument de travail pour une nouvelle approche en diplomatique médiévale, in: La diplomatique urbaine en Europe au Moyen Âge, éd. W. PREVENIER/ TH. DE HEMPTINNE (2000) p. 123–132. Lors du colloque de Naples, plusieurs communications en rapport avec cette base ont cependant été présentées, montrant que sa grande richesse attire toujours beaucoup les chercheurs; voir la contribution d'Els De Paermentier au présent volume.

[12] Une enquête sur les convergences et divergences entre ce «nouveau» matériel et les textes marquants de l'historiographie traditionnelle serait sans doute des plus instructives. On pense en particulier à J. G. DROYSEN, Grundriss der Historik (1875); C. SEIGNOBOS, Introduction aux études historiques (1898); A. COMTE, Discours sur l'esprit positif (1842); M. BLOCH, Apologie pour l'histoire ou métier d'historien (1943). Dans le domaine diplomatique aussi, une telle confrontation épistémologique serait, sans doute, tout aussi intéressante (en considérant les textes classiques de Mabillon, Giry, Bresslau, etc.).

[13] A. GUERREAU, L'avenir d'un passé incertain. Quelle histoire du Moyen Âge au XXIe siècle? (2001).

[14] Par là, nous n'entendons évidemment pas dénigrer les études visant à exploiter un *corpus* géographiquement circonscrit, par ailleurs tout à fait indispensables; on pense en particulier à H. FICHTENAU, Das Urkundenwesen in Österreich vom 8. bis zum frühen 13. Jahrhundert (1971). Simplement, nous pensons que la compréhension du phénomène «charte», dans son unité, ne peut venir que d'études prenant en compte l'échelle de cette production: *a minima* l'échelle européenne. La réflexion sur cette question de l'échelle, conjointe avec celle de seuil, nous semble être une étape essentielle pour voir naître une histoire médiévale renouvelée. Voir J. LE GOFF, la civilisation de l'Occident médiéval (1964); ID., L'Europe est-elle née au Moyen Âge? (2003); A. BORST, Lebensformen im Mittelalter (1973); M. MITTERAUER, Warum Europa? Mittelalterliche Grundlagen eines Sonderwegs (2003).

prit de mort dans l'état actuel du travail humain»[15]. Le but de cet article est ainsi de montrer que cette mise en ordre est non seulement possible, mais aussi nécessaire, afin d'exploiter les bases de données diplomatiques, et ceci même si elle soulève d'importants problèmes aussi bien au niveau épistémologique que technique. Tenter de comprendre comment s'agencent ces textes à l'échelle européenne, tant au plan typologique que chronologique ou géographique, nous semble en effet être un préalable afin de pouvoir réaliser des études lexicales comparées[16] réellement fondées. Sur l'ensemble de cet espace, les différences dans la production textuelle sont en effet telles que tout rapprochement semble parfois audacieux. Ici, nous ne prétendons pas donner une solution générale au problème, mais simplement le mettre en lumière, tout en proposant quelques pistes techniques envisageables pour le dépasser. Notre hypothèse, encore une fois, est qu'il faudra nécessairement traverser cette «étape de masse» pour passer à une exploitation raisonnée des corpus diplomatiques numériques, autrement dit de l'accumulation à l'exploitation.

Au moins depuis l'important livre de Thomas Kuhn, *La structure des révolutions scientifiques*, en 1962[17], nous savons en effet que le progrès en science ne s'effectue pas d'une manière linéaire, mais à travers une série de ruptures, au sein desquelles l'apparition de nouveaux paradigmes – souvent

---

[15] L. FEBVRE, Contre l'esprit de spécialité. Une lettre de 1933, in: Combats pour l'Histoire (1953) p. 104–106. Voir aussi A. GUERREAU, Fief, féodalité, féodalisme. Enjeux sociaux et réflexion historienne, in: Annales ESC 1 (1990) p. 137–166, en part. p. 137–138.

[16] «Certains aussi concevaient qu'au-delà de l'étude des chancelleries particulières devait naître, ou plutôt renaître, une diplomatique comparative, condition de nouveaux développements de secteurs entiers des sciences historiques», R.-H. BAUTIER, La Commission internationale de diplomatique. Sa genèse. Son organisation. Son programme de travail, in: BECh 129 (1971) p. 421–425, ici p. 421.

[17] T. S. KUHN, La structure des révolutions scientifiques (1983) (trad. de: The structure of Scientific Revolutions (1962). Sur la question, très débattue, du lien entre production du savoir scientifique, paradigmes scientifiques et structures sociales, on renvoie aux travaux clés de G. BACHELARD, La formation de l'esprit scientifique. Contribution à une psychanalyse de la connaissance objective (1947); P. BOURDIEU, Science de la science et réflexivité (2001). Dans le domaine de l'histoire médiévale, sur ce même problème, voir L. KUCHENBUCH, Zwischen Lupe und Fernblick: Berichtspunkte und Anfragen zur Mediävistik als historischer Anthropologie, in: Mediävistik im 21. Jahrhundert. Stand und Perspektiven der internationalen und interdisziplinären Mittelalterforschung, dir. H. W. GOETZ/J. JARNUT (2003) p. 269–293; GUERREAU, L'avenir d'un passé incertain; J. MORSEL, L'histoire (du Moyen Âge) est un sport de combat ...: réflexions sur les finalités de l'histoire du Moyen Âge destinées à une société dans laquelle même les étudiants d'histoire s'interrogent (2007); J. DEMADE, Pourquoi étudier l'histoire (médiévale) au XXIe siècle?, version en ligne <http://lamop.univ-paris1.fr/IMG/pdf/Demade_1.pdf>; ID., Produire un fait scientifique. La méthodologie de l'histoire des prix entre structures académiques et enjeux intellectuels (milieu XIXe-milieu XXe), version en ligne <http://lamop.univ-paris1.fr/IMG/pdf/Demade_2-2.pdf>.

concomitante à l'apparition de nouveaux outils – joue un rôle fondamental. La situation de blocage face à ces bases de données, même si tous ne s'accordent pas sur ce sujet, la situation que vivent actuellement les médiévistes lorsqu'il s'agit de reconstruire la logique globale du système de l'Occident médiéval (d'abord, nous l'admettons, par désintérêt de cette perspective globale) – deux phénomènes dont le parallélisme est plus que troublant –, constituent, à en croire Kuhn, une situation typique de la science en crise. Est-ce l'accumulation qui apportera une solution à ces difficultés? Il est possible d'en douter[18]... Ainsi, si à première vue, ces bases de données diplomatiques ne font que numériser et compiler des séries de documents déjà abordables, soit sous la forme de parchemins, soit sur papier, elles proposent probablement bien plus que cela. Elles ne sont pas uniquement un changement d'échelle, une vitesse supplémentaire lors des recherches, elles ne proposent pas seulement un changement d'objet mais bien davantage: la numérisation des données textuelles du Moyen Âge occidental invite à notre sens à une double rupture, d'ordre méthodologique et conceptuelle. En d'autres termes, il s'agit d'inventer un questionnaire scientifique et un dispositif technique – certes, ce n'est pas chose facile –, en s'appuyant sur des outils qui n'ont peu ou pas retenu l'attention des médiévistes jusqu'ici: dans le cadre du présent exposé, nous pensons en particulier au data/text mining[19]. Cependant, la mise en place de tels outils nécessite une restructuration des données textuelles livrées par le Moyen Âge, et ceci à grande échelle. Cette formalisation est essentielle, puisque c'est d'elle dont dépend l'ensemble du travail d'exploitation

[18] «La même recherche historique qui met en lumière combien il est difficile d'isoler les inventions et découvertes individuelles nous amène à douter profondément du processus cumulatif par lequel, pensait-on, ces contribution individuelles s'étaient combinées pour constituer la science», in: Kuhn, La structure des révolutions scientifiques p. 19.

[19] Les exceptions sont récentes et montrent, dans ce domaine précis, un certain retard non seulement par rapport aux sciences dites «dures», mais aussi en regard des autres sciences sociales (psychologie, sociologie, etc.). La bibliographie du data/text mining est devenue, en quelques années seulement, à proprement parler gigantesque. Mentionnons simplement quelques ouvrages considérés comme canoniques ou relativement simples d'accès pour un non-mathématicien: C. D. Manning/H. Schütze, Foundations of Statistical Natural Language Processing (1999); I. H. Witten/E. Frank/M. A. Hall, Data Mining. Practical Machine Learning Tools and Techniques (³2011); C. D. Manning/H. Schütze/P. Raghavan, An Introduction to Information Retrieval (2008); R. Feldman/J. Sanger, The Text Mining Handbook. Advanced Approaches in Analyzing Unstructured Data (2007); H. A. Do Prado/E. Ferneda, Emerging Technologies of Text Mining: Techniques and Applications (2008); L. Torgo, Data Mining with R. Learning with Case Studies (2011); R. Bilisoly, Practical Text Mining with Perl (2008); The Handbook of Computational Linguistics and Natural Language Processing, éd. A. Clark/C. Fox/S. Lappin (2010).

qui devrait découler de ces bases de données. Il apparaît donc que cette mise en forme, autant technologique qu'abstraite, est une étape cruciale et non une banalité formelle, afin de passer de l'accumulation documentaire brute à l'exploitation des documents[20]. Au plan historique, celle-ci passe par une mise en ordre typologique, géographique et chronologique du matériau disponible. Afin de nous insérer dans cette discussion, nous aimerions présenter une série d'outils et d'expériences, réalisée dans le cadre d'une thèse en cours à l'Université de Bourgogne, sous la direction d'Eliana Magnani et de Daniel Russo, menée avec l'aide d'Alain Guerreau. Cette thèse vise à exploiter systématiquement une base de données de documents diplomatiques, en réalisant plusieurs investigations statistiques sur les champs sémantiques, en particulier ceux dits de l'«environnement» ou, mieux, de l'espace[21] (*aqua, terra, mundus, silva, arbore, campus, villa*, etc.), ceci afin de faire ressortir les inégalités régionales, dans le domaine de la scripturalité tout d'abord, et, par là, s'interroger sur la dynamique de l'Occident médiéval. Concrètement, on présentera deux expériences visant à montrer qu'un dispositif technique global et adapté permettrait de mieux mettre en ordre la documentation numérisée, ceci afin de rendre accessible une information pour le moment seulement disponible *en puissance*.

---

[20] Cela implique aussi que la mise en forme des données dépend, au moins dans une certaine mesure, du questionnaire que l'on souhaite leur appliquer. Concrètement, cela exclut toute prétention à un formatage définitif de la documentation.

[21] En histoire médiévale, les investigations portant sur les champs sémantiques restent, pour le moment, relativement rares. Première approche de la question dans les textes d'un des fondateurs du concept: J. TRIER, Über Wort- und Begriffsfelder (1931), in: Wortfeldforschung. Zur Geschichte und Theorie des Sprachlichen Feldes, éd. L. SCHMIDT (1973) p. 1–38; ID., Das sprachliche Feld. Eine Auseinandersetzung (1934), in: Wortfeldforschung p. 129–161; ID., Der heilige Jodocus, sein Leben und seine Verehrung, zugleich ein Beitrag zur deutschen Namengebung (1924); plus récemment: A. GUERREAU, Le champ sémantique de l'espace dans la *vita* de saint Maïeul (Cluny, début du XIe siècle), in: Journal des Savants 1997:2 (1997) p. 363–419; A. GUERREAU-JALABERT/B. BON, *Pietas*: réflexions sur l'analyse sémantique et le traitement lexicographique d'un vocable médiéval, in: Médiévales 42 (2002) p. 73–88; IID., Le trésor au Moyen Âge: étude lexicale, in: Le trésor au Moyen Âge: discours, pratiques et objets, dir. L. BURKART/P. CORDEZ/P.-A. MARIAUX (2010) p. 11–32; L. KUCHENBUCH/U. KLEIN, 'Textus' im Mittelalter: Erträge, Nachträge, Hypothesen, in: 'Textus' im Mittelalter: Komponenten und Situationen des Wortgebrauchs im schriftsemantischen Feld, éd. L. KUCHENBUCH/U. KLEIN (2006) p. 416–453. Sur la question, seulement évoquée ici, du lien entre structure sociale, langage et milieu: C. LÉVI-STRAUSS, La pensée sauvage (1962); M. GODELIER, L'idéel et le matériel – Pensée, économies, sociétés (1986); P. DESCOLA, Par-delà nature et culture (2005).

Typologie(s), data mining et catégorisation
(AI::Categorizer; Text-to-CSV)

Notre présente réflexion s'appuie sur une base de données en cours de réalisation, base de données dans laquelle une majeure partie du matériau diplomatique numérisé disponible en ligne a été collecté, puis entièrement reformaté afin de devenir une méta-source à part entière. Nous avons fait le choix de réencoder l'ensemble des chartes ainsi obtenues, principalement en employant des séries de scripts Perl *ad hoc*[22], en un format XML-«TEI light», acceptable par le seul logiciel actuellement capable de gérer efficacement autant de documents: Philologic[23]. Ce dernier est en effet à notre connaissance l'unique solution, en dehors de l'austère (mais puissant) CQP/CWB[24], capable d'absorber une telle masse de textes: 64 000 unités, soit à l'origine 64 000 chartes. Grâce à une série d'échanges avec son créateur Mark Olsen, nous avons pu modifier cette limite et amener le logiciel à gérer non plus seulement 64 000 documents, mais 64 000 volumes d'éditions. De fait, notre collecte, basée avant tout sur les bases déjà disponibles, mais aussi sur des numérisations personnelles[25], aidée par de nombreux chercheurs, a abouti à une base de données contenant près de 150 000 chartes en mode texte, soit

---

[22] Le langage Perl s'impose, avec Python, comme l'une des voies possibles pour les médiévistes souhaitant traiter des corpus. Créé par Larry Wall en 1987, celui-ci est simple d'apprentissage, tout en étant particulièrement adapté au traitement de fichiers textuels. Surtout, sa gestion puissante mais aussi très souple des *regex* (expression régulière) permet d'écrire des scripts de conversion et de manipulation de textes avec une grande facilité.

[23] Logiciel développé par Mark Olsen et son équipe à l'Université de Chicago, disponible en ligne: <http://sites.google.com/site/philologic3/> (version 3.2). Il s'agit du choix initialement fait par l'équipe du projet CBMA.

[24] Disponible en ligne, <http://cwb.sourceforge.net/>.

[25] Relues ou non. Quelques exemples: Chartes et documents concernant l'abbaye de Cîteaux: 1098–1182, éd. J. MARILIER (1961); Le livre des serfs de l'abbaye de Marmoutier suivi de chartes sur le même sujet et précédé d'un essai sur le servage en Touraine, par Ch.-L. de Grandmaison (*Liber de servis majoris monasterii*), éd. A. SALMON (1865); Cartulaire de Brioude. *Liber de honoribus Sancto Juliano collatis*, éd. H. DONIOL (1863); Codex diplomaticus Fuldensis, éd. E. DRONKE (1850); etc. Ces numérisations ont été réalisées en fonction des «vides» géographiques laissés par les bases de données actuellement disponibles. D'autre part, on a ajouté à ce noyau initial une série d'autres fichiers pour lesquels la relecture n'avait pas été systématique. Ces fichiers en «dirty-OCR» permettent d'ajouter plusieurs dizaines de milliers de chartes à cette collection, sans grand effort de relecture, et offrent des possibilités de comparaisons accrues. Pour les comptages fiables, il suffit alors de réaliser deux versions de la base: l'une comprenant les fichiers en dirty-OCR, l'autre les excluant. Rappelons au passage que l'exhaustivité documentaire est une chimère et que c'est plutôt un souci d'homogénéité (très relative, en l'occurrence) qui a guidé notre démarche.

plus de 570 éditions, pour une période allant du VIIe siècle au début du XIVe siècle, et ceci pour une large part de l'Europe chrétienne. D'une manière générale cependant, la base a aussi été générée dans d'autres formats, en particulier celui employé par le logiciel Textométrie[26]: cette flexibilité voulue, aux antipodes d'un modèle fixiste, nous semble être une considération centrale dans un domaine où la réactualisation technologique est constante et difficilement prévisible.

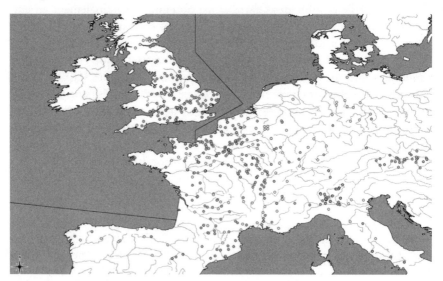

Fig. 1: Carte des corpus présents dans notre base. Légende: en gris, les corpus relus; en blanc: les corpus en dirty-OCR. (Carte générée grâce à Q-GIS).

---

[26] Le projet Textométrie, développé à Lyon par l'équipe de Serge Heiden et qui vient tout juste de sortir dans sa version 0.6 (6 avril 2012), semble être une alternative importante à Philologic: tout d'abord parce que le logiciel gère la lemmatisation des textes (formes / lemmes / POS). Le logiciel est en outre basé sur le moteur de CQP, ce qui est un gage de sa solidité. Il fonctionne sur trois systèmes d'exploitation (Linux/Windows/Mac), ce qui le rend accessible au plus grand nombre. Enfin, *last but not least*, le logiciel possède une interface – encore en travail – le liant au logiciel de statistique R. À l'heure actuelle, Textométrie apparaît donc comme un challenger de premier ordre, même s'il connaît encore quelques difficultés face aux plus larges corpus. Voir S. Heiden/J.-P. Magué/B. Pincemin, TXM: Une plateforme logicielle opensource pour la textométrie – conception et développement, in: Proc. of 10th International Conference on the Statistical Analysis of Textual Data – JADT 2010, éd. I. C. Sergio Bolasco (2010) p. 1021–1032 (2); S. Heiden, The TXM Platform: Building Open-Source Textual Analysis Software Compatible with the TEI Encoding Scheme, in: 24th Pacific Asia Conference on Language, Information and Computation – PACLIC24, éd. K. I. Ryo Otoguro (2010) p. 389–398. Logiciel disponible en ligne: <http://textometrie.ens-lyon.fr/>.

Rapidement cependant s'est imposée la question de l'indexation de cette masse: un critère déterminant pour passer de l'accumulation à une exploitation globale, en particulier statistique. C'est aussi, évidemment, une opération qu'il est improbable de réaliser en considérant les actes un à un. Or, nous savons tous, en effet, qu'il est important de distinguer les catégories diplomatiques, afin de ne pas tomber dans des effets de corpus redoutables[27]. Le text mining offre une série d'algorithmes d'intelligence artificielle, largement utilisés dans d'autres disciplines, permettant d'attribuer automatiquement – moyennant un entraînement –, des catégories typologiques ou même chronologiques à un ensemble documentaire. Une de nos problématiques visait donc à établir un programme non seulement capable de reconnaître, dans une masse de documents, les bulles, les diplômes, les actes épiscopaux, de distinguer les chartes des notices, mais surtout à même de réinjecter par la suite ces catégories dans un formatage XML lisible et indexable par Philologic (et, par extension, par d'autres logiciels). Les obstacles sont cependant nombreux: outre la sensibilité de ces algorithmes au bruit (difficulté technique), certaines catégories diplomatiques possèdent des contours flous (difficulté disciplinaire/historiographique)[28].

La stratégie retenue ici consiste à déterminer, dans un premier temps et de manière globale, sur un échantillon documentaire aléatoire, les typologies/ catégories diplomatiques les plus distinctes les unes des autres. Pour ce faire, nous avons employé un second logiciel développé dans le cadre de cette thèse, intitulé Text-to-CSV, et qui permet de transformer une série de textes en matrices afin d'en évaluer la proximité. Cette estimation de la distance d'un texte à un autre est obtenue grâce à une comparaison d'une partie (sélectionnée de manière non a priori) ou de la totalité du lexique de ceux-ci. Pour cela, on

---

[27] La base des CBMA offre plusieurs bons exemples de biais liés à des corpus factices: on pense en particulier à l'édition du Cartulaire général de l'Yonne. Sur ce point, voir le très pertinent article de I. ROSÉ, À propos des Chartæ Burgundiæ Medii Ævii. Sur cette thématique de la production documentaire et de la gestion/interprétation des biais/ effets structuraux dans les corpus diplomatiques numérisés, on se permet de renvoyer à: N. PERREAUX, La production de l'écrit diplomatique en Bourgogne.

[28] Beaucoup de clarifications utiles dans O. GUYOTJEANNIN/J. PYCKE/B.-M. TOCK, Diplomatique médiévale (³2006), en particulier le chapitre 4: «Brève typologie des actes médiévaux», p. 103–222. On est bien conscient que, pour prendre un exemple, la totalité des «actes des papes ne sont pas, loin s'en faut, des bulles». Néanmoins, la majorité des actes papaux dans les recueils d'actes diplomatiques le sont: c'est ce qui compte dans le cadre de notre démarche. L'algorithme n'a donc pas pour but d'effectuer un classement «parfait», qui, s'il est louable comme objectif, n'est pas réalisable par un tri automatique. Les «niveaux de confiance», décrits plus bas, servent à palier – mais seulement en partie – cette difficulté. La machine ne remplace donc pas le diplomatiste/l'historien, elle aide à construire un dispositif, avec ses limites, propre à l'exploitation de questionnaires renouvelés.

applique différents traitements à la matrice, d'abord en la transformant – pour réduire sa taille, à travers un échantillonnage, et le «bruit» qu'elle contient – (par exemple *via* des coefficients tels que le TF-IDF[29], ou encore *via* des AFC/ACP[30]), puis en tentant de donner une modélisation graphique ou un résumé de l'information qu'elle renferme (AFC / Clustering)[31]. Or, si l'on applique ce logiciel à un échantillon de textes provenant de toutes les catégories diplomatiques («auteurs» et typologies) à la fois, et que nous réalisons ensuite une analyse factorielle[32] sur le tableau obtenu, ceci afin de visualiser la distance entre les différents textes considérés, nous voyons que le bruit de fond est extrêmement fort. Autrement dit, il sera impossible, dans une telle configuration et avec un test unique, d'obtenir une classification automatique valable. Dans ces conditions, seuls les diplômes seront, dans presque tous les cas de figure, facilement identifiés par les algorithmes (fig. I, voyez les planches en couleur, pages 321–322). En revanche, lors d'une seconde phase de nos expériences, on a pu observer que la discrimination entre un nombre réduit de catégories était beaucoup plus efficace. Prenons un exemple: si une analyse considérant en même temps les bulles, les documents épiscopaux et les diplômes semble vouée à se fourvoyer très fréquemment (fig. II)[33], une analyse sur un nombre de catégories plus réduit, par exemple considérant d'une part les bulles et les documents épiscopaux et, d'autre part, les diplômes, a une probabilité nettement plus faible de se tromper (fig. III).

---

[29] Pour Term Frequency-Inverse Document Frequency. Cette méthode a pour but d'évaluer le poids relatif d'un terme ou d'un ensemble de termes dans un document, par rapport à un ensemble documentaire. Schématiquement, l'indice TF-IDF d'un terme augmente proportionnellement avec le nombre d'occurrences de celui-ci dans le document considéré, mais diminue si le mot se trouve aussi dans les autres documents du corpus. On peut ainsi distinguer les termes qui caractérisent le mieux un document donné au sein d'un ensemble documentaire.

[30] AFC: Analyse factorielle des correspondances; ACP: Analyse en composantes principales.

[31] Littérature en français sur la question: A. SALEM/P. LAFON, L'inventaire des segments répétés d'un texte, in: Mots 6 (1983) p. 161–177; A. SALEM, Segments répétés et analyse statistique des données textuelles, Histoire & Mesure 1 (1986) p. 5–28; E. BRUNET, Peut-on mesurer la distance entre deux textes?, in: Corpus 2 (2003), version en ligne: <http://corpus.revues.org/index30.html>; L. LEBART/A. SALEM, Statistique textuelle (1994).

[32] Sur cette méthode devenue standard dans de nombreuses sciences sociales, un classique et une introduction: J.-P. BENZÉCRI, L'analyse des données, 3 vol. (1984); P. CIBOIS, L'analyse factorielle: analyse en composantes principales et analyse des correspondances (2000).

[33] Dans la figure II, on note en effet un fort recouvrement entre les catégories «bulles» et «actes d'évêques», ce qui était prévisible. Il s'agit donc d'éviter ce recouvrement, afin de faciliter la tâche de l'algorithme de reconnaissance.

Construction du schéma de catégorisation

Partant d'une série d'observations de ce type, on a pu construire un schéma, puis un programme permettant de tester les actes de notre base un à un, pour enfin «réinjecter» le résultat de la catégorisation dans un fichier XML Philologic. Pour créer la bibliothèque d'entraînement nécessaire au logiciel pour l'apprentissage des catégories diplomatiques, nous sommes partis de deux bases: les CBMA et les originaux de l'Artem, auxquelles nous avons adjoint des diplômes carolingiens et ottoniens des MGH. Ces deux premières bases possèdent en effet un nombre conséquent de champs d'ores et déjà renseignés (auteur, bénéficiaire, genre ou typologie, fiabilité de l'acte, etc.), et existent toutes deux dans des formats relativement simples à manipuler *via* des scripts Perl ou XSLT (pour *Extensible Stylesheet Language Transformations*). Une fois ce corpus d'entraînement organisé, il s'agit de trouver un logiciel dédié ou adapté à la catégorisation textuelle. Dans ce domaine en pleine émergence, les possibilités de qualité, gratuites voire libres/open sources, ne manquent pas: Weka[34], le logiciel de statistique R avec une myriade de *packages* adaptés[35], RapidMiner[36], Tanagra[37], Knime[38], etc. Pour notre part, tout en continuant de travailler avec ces différents logiciels, nous avons retenu, pour cette expérience, la bibliothèque Perl AI::Categorizer, développée par Ken Williams[39]. Celle-ci inclut la plupart des algorithmes utiles à la classification textuelle et dispose d'une interface pour envoyer et recevoir des informations vers/depuis Weka[40]. D'autre part, étant une bibliothèque Perl, elle convenait parfaitement

---

[34] M. Hall et al., The WEKA Data Mining Software: An Update, in: SIGKDD Explorations 11,1 (2009) p. 1–18. Le manuel de Witten, Frank et Hall, déjà mentionné, est basé sur Weka. En ligne: <http://www.cs.waikato.ac.nz/ml/weka/>.

[35] R, qui constitue le standard en matière de statistiques open source, ne se présente plus <http://www.r-project.org/>. Liste de packages dédiés au «machine learning» à cette adresse: <http://cran.r-project.org/web/views/MachineLearning.html>. A noter que R communique facilement avec Weka, via le package *RWeka*.

[36] <http://rapid-i.com/content/view/181/190/>.

[37] <http://eric.univ-lyon2.fr/~ricco/tanagra/fr/tanagra.html>.

[38] <http://www.knime.org/>.

[39] Le package et ses algorithmes font l'objet de la thèse de l'auteur: K. Williams, A Framework for Text Categorization (2003), version en ligne: <http://search.cpan. org/~kwilliams/AI-Categorizer-0.09/>.

[40] Naive Bayes, SVM, k-Nearest-Neighbor, arbres de décisions, etc. La bibliographie, même de synthèse, sur les algorithmes de catégorisation/d'apprentissage supervisé est énorme et se développe à une vitesse surprenante. Voir, entres autres, Y. Yang/X. Liu, A re-examination of text categorization methods, in: SIGIR '99 Proceedings of the 22nd annual international ACM SIGIR conference on Research and development in information retrieval (1999) p. 42–49; F. Sebastiani, Machine Learning

à notre problématique qui était d'intégrer une catégorisation dans une série de traitements (extraction du texte, puis réinjection de celui-ci, accompagné des catégories, dans un nouveau fichier). Autre avantage, enfin: ce choix nous permettait de traiter facilement les résultats, de les comparer et de les manipuler, voire d'adjoindre au test un algorithme extérieur à la bibliothèque, tout cela sans interfaçage complexe, puisque l'ensemble des opérations se déroulent alors sous Perl. Après de nombreux essais, le principe du modèle retenu consiste à combiner un arbre de décision à une série de tests (cross-validation) qui interviennent à chaque nœud de l'arbre: le Support Vector Machine (Machine à vecteurs de support – SVM)[41], l'algorithme Naive Bayes (ou Classification naïve bayésienne – NB)[42], mais aussi un test développé pour l'occasion et qui se base sur une analyse des syntagmes ou morceaux de

---

in Automated Text Categorization, in: ACM Computing Surveys 34,1 (2002) p. 1–47; MANNING/SCHÜTZE/RAGHAVAN, An Introduction to Information Retrieval p. 234–320 (particulièrement intéressant sur ces points). En outre, la plupart des manuels récents concernant le data mining contiennent un chapitre sur l'apprentissage (supervisé / non supervisé) et la catégorisation: TORGO, Data Mining with R. Learning with Case Studies p. 185–186. Cf. plus bas pour plus de détails sur les algorithmes retenus.

[41] Méthode d'apprentissage supervisé, inspirée des travaux de Vladimir Vapnik et introduite en 1995; V. VAPNIK, The Nature of Statistical Learning Theory (1995). D'une grande efficacité mais assez lente, elle se base sur une séparation des données via une méthode à noyaux (Kernel). WITTEN/FRANK/HALL, Data Mining. Practical Machine Learning Tools and Techniques p. 192: «Support vector machines select a small number of critical boundary instances called support vectors from each class and build a linear discriminant function that separates them as widely as possible. This instance-based approach transcends the limitations of linear boundaries by making it practical to include extra nonlinear terms in the function, making it possible to form quadratic, cubic, and higher-order decision boundaries». D'une manière générale, le Wikipedia anglais propose des articles de grandes qualités en ce qui concerne les algorithmes de data mining. Voir aussi: V. KECMAN, Learning and Soft Computing – Support Vector Machines, Neural Networks, Fuzzy Logic Systems (2001); bonne synthèse dans: K. P. BENNET/C. CAMPBELL, Support Vector Machines: Hype or Hallelujah?, in: SIGKDD Explorations 2,2 (2000) p. 1–13; pour une application concrète sous R: A. KARATZOGLOU/D. MEYER, Support Vector Machines in R, in: Journal of Statistical Software 15,9 (2006), disponible en ligne <http://www.jstatsoft.org/v15/i09/paper>

[42] Les méthodes bayésiennes sont plus anciennes que le SVM: elles sont basées sur les théories du mathématicien et pasteur anglais, Thomas Bayes [1702–1761]. Souvent d'une bonne efficacité (cependant moindre que le SVM), en particulier dans le cas de données nombreuses ou complexes – ce qui est le cas avec les actes diplomatiques –, elles se montrent d'abord particulièrement rapide. Ces caractéristiques sont principalement dues à son algorithme qui suppose une indépendance des caractéristiques analysées pour une classe donnée. H. ZHANG, The Optimality of Naive Bayes, in: FLAIRS2004 (2004), disponible en ligne <http://courses.ischool.berkeley.edu/i290-dm/s11/SECURE/Optimality_of_Naive_Bayes.pdf>; D. J. HAND/Y. YU, Idiots

formules présents dans les actes[43]. L'avantage qu'il y a à combiner ces techniques est évident: s'il arrive fréquemment qu'un test attribue une mauvaise catégorie à un acte donné, il est en revanche peu probable que l'erreur se répète sur trois tests différents, d'abord car leur «sensibilité» porte sur des éléments statistiques différents[44]. Le second avantage de cette technique est qu'elle nous permet d'intégrer la probabilité d'erreur d'attribution dans notre logiciel de fouille textuelle. L'idée est la suivante: si les trois tests proposent une seule et même catégorie – disons par exemple une bulle –, non seulement celle-ci sera donnée au document, mais aussi le niveau «1», ce qui signifie une très forte probabilité d'attribution réussie. Ce sont les modules de décision, visibles sur le schéma ci-dessous, qui se chargent de cette tâche visant à attribuer jusqu'à 3 niveaux de confiance. L'intérêt est évident: le chercheur peut ainsi sélectionner un échantillon plus ou moins large d'un type donné, et espérer travailler soit un échantillon très représentatif (en prenant seulement les documents classés en niveau 1), soit un échantillon plus large mais contenant plus de bruit (en retenant aussi les documents de niveau 2 ou 3).

Bayes – not so stupid after all?, in: International Statistical Review 69 (2001) p. 385–389; G. I. WEBB/J. R. BOUGHTON/Z. WANG, Not So Naive Bayes: Aggregating One-Dependence Estimators, in: Machine Learning 58,1 (2005) p. 5–25.

[43] Cet algorithme, codé en Perl par nos soins, est rudimentaire. Il s'agit, à partir de corpus déjà indexés (par exemples les CBMA ou l'Artem), d'extraire les termes ou groupes de termes qui ne se rencontrent que dans une catégorie diplomatique donnée. On obtient ainsi une liste d'environ 34 500 éléments, qui contient à la fois des formes, des bi-formes, et des tri-formes. Lorsque le document est examiné par l'algorithme, celui-ci attribue des points en fonction des groupes de termes rencontrés: *imperio atque pro*, ajoutera, par exemple, 4 points à la variable \$count_dip (pour les diplômes donc), car c'est un indice qui pousse fortement à penser qu'il s'agit d'un acte de souverain. Au terme de l'examen de l'ensemble des mots et syntagmes du document, on compare les scores obtenus pour des différentes variables (\$count_dip; \$count_bul; \$count_cha; etc.), après les avoir pondérés. Une pondération en effet nécessaire car le nombre de termes typiques n'est pas équivalent en fonction des «genres» documentaires. Le score pondéré permet enfin d'attribuer le document à une catégorie.

[44] Cette affirmation est avant tout un résultat empirique: c'est à la suite de tests successifs et avec des séries de comparaisons que nous sommes arrivés à cette conclusion. L'examen des algorithmes tend par ailleurs à confirmer théoriquement ce que montrent les expériences. Ces différentes méthodes sont en effet toutes fondées sur le calcul puis la comparaison de distances, directes ou indirectes, entre les éléments à analyser. Mais ces distances ne sont pas calculées de la même manière, d'où l'instabilité fondamentale des résultats, qui sont en fait complémentaires: pour le dire autrement, en utilisant différents algorithmes, on ne regarde pas l'objet (i.e. les chartes, ou plutôt le tableau de mots qui en résulte) sous le même angle. C'est la combinaison comparative des visions obtenues depuis ces différents plans qui donne une tendance générale.

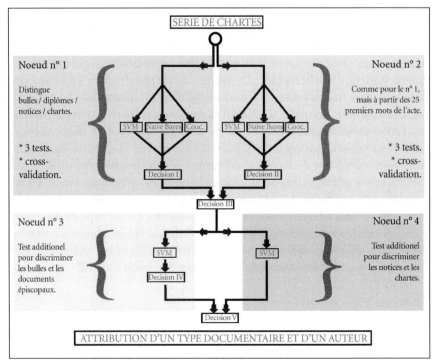

Fig. 2: Schéma du «*classifier*», combinant arbre de décision et, à chaque nœud, un ou plusieurs algorithmes (SVM, NB, Cooc).

Validité de la méthode et possibilités d'extensions

Qu'en est-il maintenant des résultats obtenus grâce à ce schéma? Afin de tester la qualité de cette classification automatique, nous avons opté pour des matrices de confusion[45], outil standard en apprentissage supervisé et qui permet d'évaluer non seulement le taux d'erreurs positives mais aussi le taux d'erreurs négatives (autrement dit ce que notre modèle n'a pas réussi à identi-

---

[45] J.-P. Benzécri, Sur l'analyse des matrices de confusion, in: Revue de statistique appliquée 18,3 (1970) p. 5–63. D'une manière générale, on peut résumer la matrice de confusion pour une classe donnée – ici, pour l'exemple, les bulles – aux cases suivantes: a: vrais positifs (bulles correctement catégorisées comme telles) / b: faux positifs (autres documents catégorisés comme bulles) / c: faux négatifs (bulles catégorisées comme autre chose qu'une bulle) / d: vrais négatifs (tous les documents «non-bulles» correctement catégorisés comme tels). On possède ensuite différents indices pour calculer la précision (= ((a+d)/(a+b+c+d)), le rappel (=a/(c+a)), le taux de faux positifs (=b/(d+b)), le taux de vrais négatifs (=d/(d+b)), le taux de faux négatifs (=c/(c+a)) et enfin l'exactitude de la classification (=a/(b+a)).

fier). Pour ce faire, il faut tester la validité du modèle obtenu sur des documents non renseignés mais dont on connaît la typologie, et, surtout, qui n'ont pas été inclus dans la base d'entraînement. Ce dernier point est fondamental, car réaliser un test de validité sur des textes déjà contenus dans la base d'entrainement fausse totalement les résultats, donnant des scores largement favorables au modèle. En comparant les résultats obtenus aux résultats attendus (encore une fois: il faut partir de documents dont on connaît la typologie, mais qui n'ont pas été inclus dans le lot destiné à l'apprentissage du logiciel), on peut connaître la précision de son modèle et savoir s'il est plutôt précis ou plutôt fautif. Dans ce cas, il s'agit d'examiner aussi bien les résultats obtenus pour les vrais positifs, que pour les faux positifs, les faux négatifs ou encore les vrais négatifs[46]: on connait ainsi le taux de reconnaissance, mais aussi de rejet, pour chaque catégorie. C'est à partir de ces résultats de tests que nous avons progressivement et empiriquement amélioré notre modèle, par exemple en ajoutant des coefficients de pondération pour le troisième algorithme, décrit plus haut. Néanmoins, il est très probable que si l'expérience devait être réitérée, il faudrait chercher d'autres combinaisons d'algorithmes et de méthodes, car il nous semble qu'il en existe, après examen, de plus puissantes, offrant des résultats plus stables. Dans cette optique, les classifications hiérarchiques ascendantes (type arbre de décision), réalisées sur les coordonnées obtenues suite à une analyse factorielle des correspondances, elle-même effectuée sur une matrice de groupes de formes, sont connues pour donner des résultats robustes[47] et semblent fournir, dans le cas des chartes, des scores prometteurs. À l'heure actuelle, sans entrer dans des détails superflus, le modèle élaboré permet de reconnaître correctement environ 95 % des bulles, environ 95 % de diplômes – ces deux éléments constituant notre objectif initial, étant donné qu'il s'agissait du point le plus crucial pour une exploitation efficace de notre base de données –, plus de 85 % des documents épiscopaux, et une large majorité des chartes et des notices. Pour arriver à ces taux de reconnaissance, il nous a bien entendu fallu tester toute une série de modèles et créer une longue liste de fichiers d'entraînement pour chaque nœud, le programme final ne comptant pas moins de 42 000 documents indexés, ajoutés par itérations successives[48].

---

[46] Voir note précédente.

[47] Cf. plus haut les travaux déjà mentionnés de J.-P. BENZÉCRI.

[48] Un point clé pour une évaluation correcte du modèle consiste à réaliser ces tests sur des documents choisis aléatoirement et non inclus dans les fichiers d'entraînement. Si ce dernier point n'est pas respecté, on obtient, en toute logique, des résultats très supérieurs à l'efficacité réelle du schéma.

En outre, il ne faut pas concevoir cette expérience de statistique linguistique[49] – puisqu'après tout, c'est bien de ça qu'il s'agit avec le text mining – comme un simple outil de classification typologique. Une telle méthode est bien entendu extensible à une vaste série de problématiques, en premier lieu à l'épineuse question de la datation des actes[50]. Dans cette optique, il s'agirait de constituer une autre base d'entraînement, contenant cette fois des actes dont la chronologie est assurée, et qui deviendraient alors des références pour les documents à la datation floue ou inconnue.

Régionalisation et géographie des pratiques de l'écrit (Text-to-CSV)

Cependant, il nous a aussi semblé que ces questions de mise en ordre et de classification ne pourraient progresser qu'en créant des corpus d'entraînement régionaux. De fait, on peut supposer que les spécificités locales des actes diplomatiques soient telles que les résultats du classement dépendraient aussi, pour une large mesure, du rapport géographique entre documents à classer et groupe d'entraînement. Existe-t-il des particularités régionales, plus ou moins fixes dans le temps, en ce qui concerne l'écriture documentaire? C'est là le cœur de notre problématique: les spécificités des pratiques de l'écrit et la dynamique de l'Occident médiéval. Sans en venir à la question des champs sémantiques, qui nécessiterait des développements beaucoup plus longs, il est fort probable que de «simples» études de lexicographie statistique pourraient apporter des éléments favorisant notre compréhension de l'Occident médiéval. Un peu plus haut, nous avons évoqué un programme développé lors de cette première année de thèse, programme nommé provisoirement

---

[49] C'est un point à ne jamais oublier: les textes et les mots possèdent des spécificités statistiques qui les rendent très complexes à étudier et à manipuler: «Similarly, the parameters of many models for word frequency distribution are highly dependent on the sample size. This property sets lexical statistics apart from most other areas in statistics [...]», in: H. BAAYEN, Word Frequency Distributions (2001) p. 1. Les distributions lexicales suivent en effet un modèle que ce dernier auteur à nommé, à juste titre, LNRE (Large Number of Rare Events). Quelques autres ouvrages clés sur ce sujet: MANNING/ SCHÜTZE, Foundations of Statistical Natural Language Processing; S. EVERT, The statistics of word cooccurrences: Word pairs and collocations (2004); B. MANDELBROT, Les objets fractales. Forme, hasard et dimension. Troisième édition, révisée par l'auteur et augmentée d'un «Survol du langage fractal» (³1990); ID., Fractales, hasard et finance (1997); dans le domaine historique, une exception de par son contenu avancé: A. GUERREAU, Statistique pour historiens, cours professé à l'École des chartes (2003–2004) (2004), disponible en ligne <http://elec.enc.sorbonne.fr/statistiques/stat2004.pdf>.

[50] Outre les travaux de M. GERVERS déjà mentionnés plus haut, on renvoie à son article donné dans le présent volume.

Text-to-CSV, et qui permet de convertir une série de textes en tableau. Aucun programme en effet ne proposait une conversion de ce type en dehors de tout logiciel tiers, à la fois flexible, transparente, nous offrant un contrôle total et clair sur toutes les étapes de la procédure. Le logiciel développé pour l'occasion gère donc la tokenization des fichiers[51], le traitement des mots isolés mais aussi des syntagmes (bi/tri/quadri et penta-formes), le clustering en interne (algorithme Fuzzy C-means/FCM, par Mizuki Fujisawa[52]), plusieurs types de pruning, et différents traitements sur les tableaux tels que le coefficient TF-IDF[53], la binarisation, le traitement par rangs, etc. Ces sorties sont directement utilisables sous R, mais aussi sous Weka, qui accepte les formats CSV «classiques».

Afin de prendre un exemple concret, nous avons ainsi passé en tableau une série de corpus à notre disposition, pour la période allant de 900 à 1050. Cette première approche sur à peine plus d'un siècle nous a semblé intéressante, car

---

[51] Cette étape est essentielle afin de normaliser des traditions d'éditions divergentes. Écrite en Perl, cette routine permet de résoudre les ligatures (œ/æ), en séparant les lettres (oe/ae), de convertir des j en i et les v en u, de retirer certaines ponctuations ou éléments propres aux choix éditoriaux. En procédant ainsi, on perd sans doute une part d'information, mais l'étape est inévitable pour ne pas confondre groupes de textes et groupes d'éditeurs. Dans la dernière version du programme, nous avons intégré certaines parties du script de tokenisation réalisé par Renaud Alexandre et Alain Guerreau dans le cadre de l'ANR OMNIA (IRHT/École nationale des Chartes/UMR 6298 Artehis; Alain Guerreau, Anita Guerreau-Jalabert, Eliana Magnani, Marie-José Gasse-Grandjean, Bruno Bon, Renaud Alexandre, Olivier Canteaut, Frédéric Glorieux et nous-même). Ce programme, aussi écrit en Perl, est disponible en ligne, sur le site de l'ANR: <http://www.glossaria.eu/>.

[52] Il s'agit d'un autre package Perl, et par là-même, très facile à implémenter dans notre script; disponible en ligne, <http://search.cpan.org/~fujisawa/Algorithm-FuzzyCmeans-0.02/>. À l'origine, le Fuzzy C-means est une méthode de «soft clustering»: c'est-à-dire que les points/données ne sont pas associés à un cluster de manière binaire (oui/non), mais par un certain degré (une variable). Par rapport à un K-means classique, cet algorithme permet de jouer sur les seuils afin d'observer les liens multiples qu'entretient un document/corpus avec un cluster. Sur cette «nouvelle» tendance en clustering, voir: R. NOCK/F. NIELSEN, On Weighting Clustering, in: IEEE Transaction on Pattern Analysis and Machine Intelligence 28 (2006) p. 1–13.

[53] Pour Term Frequency-Inverse Document Frequency. Cette méthode a pour but d'évaluer le poids relatif d'un terme ou d'un ensemble de termes dans un document, par rapport à un ensemble documentaire. Schématiquement, l'indice TF-IDF d'un terme augmente proportionnellement avec le nombre d'occurrences de celui-ci dans le document considéré, mais diminue si le mot se trouve aussi dans les autres documents du corpus. Le but est de distinguer le groupe de mots qui caractérise le mieux un document donné au sein d'un ensemble documentaire.

cette fourchette est souvent considérée comme relativement homogène. Le but était évidemment de détecter des différences et des similitudes entre nos corpus, sans faire de choix a priori sur le vocabulaire étudié[54]. Une fois le tableau obtenu, passé en codage logique, on réalise une série d'analyses factorielles afin d'observer comment se distribuent les corpus explorés. Au passage, on rappelle que l'analyse factorielle des correspondances n'est pas une technique nouvelle, mais, découverte par Jean-Paul Benzécri dans les années 1970, elle est désormais intégrée au corpus des outils du data mining, dont, *a posteriori*, elle fait indubitablement partie. Dans le cas présent, outre ses capacités heuristiques liées à ses propriétés graphiques, cette technique possède l'insigne l'avantage de ne pas (ou peu) être soumise aux effets de corpus[55].

---

[54] Voir A. SALEM/P. LAFON, L'inventaire des segments répétés d'un texte, in: Mots 6 (1983) p. 161–177; A. SALEM, Segments répétés et analyse statistique des données textuelles, in: Histoire & Mesure 1 (1986) p. 5–28.

[55] Or, ces effets sont une difficulté structurelle lorsqu'on examine des corpus. Par «structurelle», on entend ici que ces effets sont en fait le résultat de structures historiques: en particulier les différences de quantité de production documentaire d'un établissement à un autre. Il ne s'agit donc pas de les effacer, ce qui est par ailleurs impossible, mais de les contourner. Or, depuis les travaux de Zipf/Mandelbrot, mais plus encore ceux d'Harald Baayen (cités plus haut), nous savons que les distributions lexicales n'ont rien de commun avec les distributions normales. Les difficultés liées à l'inégale production documentaire sont ainsi multipliées par la nature complexe et évolutive des distributions lexicales, car les distributions de mots sont sensibles à la taille de l'échantillon. Quand les corpus n'ont pas la même taille – ce qui est, en fait, la situation standard –, les proportions relatives des mots au sein de ces ensembles ne sont pas les mêmes. L'analyse factorielle ne solutionne pas totalement ce lourd problème, loin s'en faut, car elle se base elle aussi sur des calculs à partir d'écarts. Mais parce qu'elle considère plus ou moins indépendamment les lignes et les colonnes du tableau, elle «isole», en quelque sorte, chaque profil/élément du corpus et le rend comparable avec les autres. C'est pour cela qu'un traitement du tableau est nécessaire, car il renforce cette propriété de l'AFC, en l'éloignant d'une analyse basée sur des concepts mathématiques tels que la moyenne, le pourcentage, la variance, l'écart-type, tous parfaitement impropres dans le cas de distributions lexicales. Sur les effets de corpus, voir: I. ROSÉ, À propos des *Chartæ Burgundiæ Medii Ævi* (C.B.M.A.). Éléments de réflexion à partir d'une enquête sur la dîme en Bourgogne au Moyen Âge, in: Bulletin du Centre d'études médiévales d'Auxerre 12 (2008), disponible en ligne: <http://cem.revues.org/document6822.html>; EAD., Enquête sur le vocabulaire et les formulaires relatifs à la dîme dans les chartes bourguignonnes (IXᵉ-XIIᵉ siècle), in: La dîme, l'Église et la société féodale, éd. M. LAUWERS (2012) p. 191–234; nous nous permettons de citer l'article que nous avons presque essentiellement consacré à cette question: N. PERREAUX, La production de l'écrit diplomatique en Bourgogne.

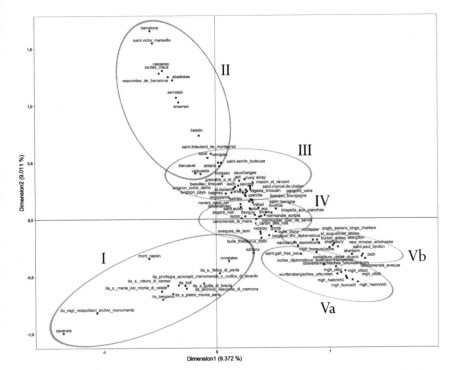

Fig. 3: Analyse factorielle (axe 1–2) du tableau généré par Text-to-CSV, à partir d'une sélection de corpus présents de notre base (900–1050).

Ainsi, sur cette analyse automatique du vocabulaire des actes, nous voyons plusieurs groupes se former. Tout d'abord en bas à gauche, on peut remarquer que l'ensemble des documents provenant de la péninsule italique se sont regroupés: actes de la Trinité de Cava[56], chartes lombardes du Codice Diplomatico della Lombardia Medievale[57], de Naples[58], ou encore du Mont-Cassin[59] (groupe I). À l'opposé, en haut sur l'axe 2, mais toujours à gauche sur l'axe 1, émerge un groupe formé les documents catalans: Cathédrale de Barcelone[60],

---

[56] Codex diplomaticus Cavensis, éd. M. Morcaldi/M. Schianni/S. De Stephano (1873–1970).

[57] Il s'agit de documents issus du CDLM (voir note 6).

[58] Monumenta regii Neapolitani archivi edita ac illustra (1845–1861).

[59] Documents inédits ou peu connus des archives du Mont-Cassin, éd. E. Cuozzo/J.-M. Martin, in: Mélanges de l'École française de Rome – Moyen Âge 103 (1991) p. 115–210; Les premiers contrats agraires du Mont-Cassin. Les *livelli* de l'abbé Aligerne dans les Abruzzes (948–985), éd. L. Feller, in: Histoire et sociétés rurales (2004) p. 133–185.

[60] Diplomatari de l'Arxiu Capitular de la Catedral de Barcelona – Segle XI, éd. J. Baucells i Reig et al. (2006).

San Pere de Casseres[61], Serrateix[62]... mais aussi Saint-Victor de Marseille[63] (groupe II). Cet ensemble est d'ailleurs contigu à un autre, un peu plus en bas à droite, et qui contient cette fois les documents de la France du sud-ouest (Montauriol[64], Aniane[65], Saint-Sernin de Toulouse[66], Moissac[67]), mais aussi, plus loin, du centre (Sauxillanges[68], Cluny[69], Mâcon[70], Savigny[71], ainsi que Baignes[72], Angoulême[73]) (groupe III). Le paquet central dérive ensuite encore un peu plus vers le nord, et nous voyons ainsi se regrouper automatiquement Saint-Aubin d'Angers[74], le Cartulaire noir de la cathédrale d'Angers[75], Marmoutier[76], Le Mans[77], etc., ainsi que des régions telles que la Normandie (groupe IV). Enfin, à l'opposé des deux premiers groupes sur l'axe 1, apparaît un dernier ensemble qui en contient, en définitive, deux autres: d'une part les documents impériaux ainsi que ceux qui proviennent, d'une manière plus générale, de l'Empire[78] (groupe Va). D'autre part, les documents anglo-saxons:

---

[61] Col·lecció diplomàtica de Sant Pere de Casserres, éd. I. Llop (2009).

[62] Diplomatari del monestir de Santa Maria de Serrateix (segles X-XV), éd. J. Bolòs i Masclans (2006).

[63] Cartulaire de l'abbaye de Saint-Victor de Marseille, éd. B. Guérard (1857).

[64] Cartulaire de Saint-Théodard de Montauriol, éd. D. Panfili. Nous remercions chaleureusement l'auteur de nous avoir confié une copie de son travail.

[65] Cartulaires des abbayes d'Aniane et de Gellone: publiés d'après les manuscrits originaux, éd. L. Cassan/E. Meynial (1900).

[66] Cartulaire de l'abbaye de Saint-Sernin de Toulouse (844–1200), éd. C. Douais (1887).

[67] Recueil des actes de l'abbaye de Moissac [680]–1175, éd. R. La Haye (2001).

[68] Cartulaire de Sauxillanges, éd. H. Doniol (1864).

[69] Recueil des chartes de l'abbaye de Cluny, éd. A. Bernard/A. Bruel (1876–1903).

[70] Cartulaire de Saint-Vincent de Mâcon: connu sous le nom de Livre enchaîné, éd. M.-C. Ragut (1864).

[71] Cartulaire de l'Abbaye de Savigny suivi du petit cartulaire de l'Abbaye d'Ainay, éd. A. Bernard (1853).

[72] Cartulaire de l'abbaye de St.-Étienne de Baigne, (en Saintonge), éd. P. F. Cholet (1868).

[73] Cartulaire de l'église d'Angoulême, éd. J. Nanglard (1900).

[74] Cartulaire de l'Abbaye de Saint-Aubin d'Angers, éd. A. Bertrand de Broussilon (1903).

[75] Cartulaire noir de la Cathédrale d'Angers, éd. C. Urseau (1908).

[76] Le livre des serfs de l'abbaye de Marmoutier (1865).

[77] Cartulaire de l'abbaye de Saint-Vincent du Mans (Ordre de Saint-Benoît), Premier cartulaire, 572–1188, éd. C. Charles (1886).

[78] Codex chronologico-diplomaticus episcopatus Ratisbonensis, éd. T. Ried (1816); Württembergisches Urkundenbuch (1849–1913), version en ligne: <www.wubonline. de>; documents du site Monasterium.net et des dMGH, etc.

Rochester[79], Christ Church de Canterbury[80], Saint-Paul de Londres[81], etc. (groupe Vb). Cette expérience tout à fait grossière, très facilement perfectible, fait donc immédiatement ressortir la géographie des corpus et indique, par là même, que leurs spécificités lexico-sémantiques se répartissent plus ou moins géographiquement. Schématiquement, on voit s'opposer une Europe du sud, et une Europe du nord, même si, à une échelle plus fine, il y a fort à parier que des ruptures beaucoup plus complexes et nuancées, des gradients inattendus, des isolats aussi, apparaissent. Précisons au passage, sans pouvoir pour autant développer ce point clé, que ce n'est pas, dans notre expérience, le vocabulaire toponymique ou anthroponymique qui «classe» les documents en ensembles géographiques, mais bien des parties de formules, des termes médiolatins endémiques, ou encore du lexique à forte consonance vernaculaire[82].

---

[79] Charters of Rochester, éd. A. CAMPBELL (1973).

[80] Charters of Christ Church, Canterbury, éd. N. P. BROOKS/S. E. KELLY (2010).

[81] Charters of St Paul's, London, éd. S. E. KELLY (2004).

[82] Notre thèse en cours, intitulé *l'Ecriture du monde. Dynamique du féodalisme et perception du* mundus*: essais statistiques sur les champs sémantiques* (aqua/terra) *dans les bases de données (750–1350)*, reviendra très largement sur cette question. Par ailleurs, nous avons co-organisé, avec Coraline REY, dans le cadre des journées du programme CBMA, une journée d'étude consacrée au «Vocabulaire courant en diplomatique» (CBMA 7). Au cours de celle-ci, nous sommes largement revenus sur cette question de l'ancrage géographique des textes diplomatiques, à partir du vocabulaire dit «courant» donc. On a alors pu formuler les trois hypothèses suivantes: a) Le stock de vocabulaire très courant – dans le cas où le qualificatif est entendu au sens d'une omniprésence spatiale –, est relativement réduit. b) Dans ce domaine, il existe bel et bien des emplois régionaux. c) Ce sont les associations entre les termes courants qui jouent un rôle dans la formation des entités géographiques. D'autres analyses, portant sur des termes courants à l'échelle d'une période précise, dans les chartes de Cluny (par exemple *increpitus*), mais presque totalement absents du reste de la production diplomatique, ont permis de montrer qu'une partie du lexique ne se rencontre que dans certaines zones: en s'inspirant de la biogéographie, nous avons proposé de les qualifier d'«endémiques». En définitive, l'examen des zones ainsi révélées nous mène à une interrogation sur le lien entre la fréquence d'un terme et sa sémantique, cette dernière émergeant d'abord d'une pratique d'écriture (donc d'une pratique sociale) régionale. Nous nous permettons de renvoyer à l'annonce et au compte-rendu détaillé de cette journée: N. PERREAUX/C. REY, CBMA. – *Chartae Burgundiae Medii Aevi. 7. Le «vocabulaire courant» en diplomatique: techniques et approches comparées*, in: Bulletin du Centre d'études médiévales d'Auxerre 16 (2012), disponible en ligne: < http://cem.revues.org/12513>; IID., CBMA – *Chartae Burgundiae Medii Aevi. 7. «Le "vocabulaire courant" en diplomatique: techniques et approches comparées»*, in: ibid. 17 (2013), à paraître en ligne.

Une meilleure formalisation est nécessaire pour passer de l'éclatement à une exploitation concrète

Cette étude sommaire – et, encore une fois, aisément perfectible –, portant sur une large part du vocabulaire contenu dans ces corpus pour la période 900–1050, semble montrer que les spécificités lexicales sont avant tout régionales, c'est-à-dire liées à des zones géographiques. Les zones observées ici, même si elles restent très largement à déterminer, pourraient être relativement vastes. Surtout, à une échelle plus fine, il y a fort à parier que de nouvelles oppositions apparaissent. Schématiquement, on voit s'opposer une Europe du sud, – contenant elle-même des groupes foncièrement différents, la Péninsule Ibérique s'opposant par exemple à la Péninsule Italique –, et une Europe du nord, toutes deux très différentes. Bien entendu, nous ne pouvons en rester à cette exploitation sommaire. Il s'agirait maintenant d'affiner ces remarques très rapides, mais aussi de comprendre ce qui oppose sémantiquement ces différentes zones, dans une perspective d'histoire sociale. C'est ce second point qui nous ferait entrer dans une étude beaucoup plus poussée au plan historique. On reprendrait alors les classements réalisés dans notre seconde partie, afin d'en tirer des résultats. Reste que, pour nous, ces deux expériences, sur la typologie documentaire et sur sa régionalisation, forment en fait un tout. Il s'agit en effet de mieux saisir comment se structure la production documentaire, typologiquement, chronologiquement, spatialement. C'est à notre sens une étape préalable si l'on souhaite construire une diplomatique numérique solide: de l'accumulation à l'indexation, puis enfin à l'exploitation, il faut penser la totalité des étapes comme un dispositif technique et méthodologique englobant. Ainsi, les études sur les champs sémantiques, les études recourant à la linguistique de corpus, si elles semblent extrêmement prometteuses, ne pourront être réalisées qu'à partir d'ensembles de chartes plus ou moins homogènes, au plan chronologico-spatial. Il s'agirait donc, dans un premier temps, de mieux saisir la structuration interne de la documentation médiévale conservée, et surtout de considérer cette étape comme un préalable indispensable qui ne peut se résumer à une présentation des «sources» disponibles. Dans l'optique de l'exploitation maintenant, bien qu'ils soient d'ores et déjà capables de nous rendre d'importants services, il y fort à parier que les logiciels disponibles ne pourront suffire aux besoins, plutôt spécifiques, des historiens. Notre jeune expérience de la *digital diplomatics* montre que le médiéviste doit bien souvent s'armer de courage et modifier/programmer lui-même ses outils propres s'il souhaite exploiter la masse documentaire numérisée d'une manière plus efficace.

Statistical methods for applying chronology to undated English medieval documents

GELILA TILAHUN, MICHAEL GERVERS,
ANDREY FEUERVERGER

Introduction

In this paper we will describe two computer intensive statistical learning methods for estimating missing features of a text. The example that we take (and the original motivation for the development of these methods) is the Documents of Early England Data Set or DEEDS documents. These documents are medieval charters describing rights and obligations pertaining to properties. Unfortunately, very few charters from 1066 (the Norman Conquest) to 1307 (the beginning of the reign of Edward II) bear dates. The current data set contains over 10,000 such documents, but for the first century (1066–1154) the number of internally dated documents is extremely sparse. From the end of the first decade of the fourteenth century, virtually all documents of this type bear dates. One of the main tasks of the DEEDS project has been to develop methods to estimate (in a computer automated manner), the dates of these undated charters[1]. We will describe two such methods, the Distance Based method and the Maximum Prevalence method, and also show possible approaches for identifying charters composed by the same authors (or religious houses) and charters originating from the same geographic location.

The corpus of 10,000 documents is in machine readable format. Each document in the corpus either bears an internal date or has been accurately dated by historians. The dating method we have developed therefore assumes that these dates are in fact the true dates of these documents. We thus use the DEEDS database as a „training set" for the dating algorithms.

---

[1] For a previous attempt to date medieval English deeds based on the appearance of individual names, with a sample size of 314 documents, see F. D. NEIMAN/N. W. ALCOCK, Archeological Seriation by Correspondence Analysis: An Application to Historical Documents, in: History and Computing 7,1 (1995) p. 1–21.

The data analysis of this work was done on 3353 of the DEEDS documents (prior to the full set of 10,000 documents becoming available)[2]. In order to carry out our study, we divided the set of documents into three parts – the *training set*, the *validation set* and the *test set*. The training set is the largest of the three parts (approximately eighty per cent of the documents). It is used to „teach“ or „train“ the dating algorithm, and all the data-related information is derived from it. The validation set is used to estimate certain parameters of the model, and the test set is used, in the end, to evaluate how well the method works – that is, to estimate the date of the documents from the test set and then compare how close these estimates are to the true dates. The validation and test sets each contain about ten per cent of the documents in the corpus. Since the Distance Based method uniquely determines the necessary optimal parameters for each document, the documents from the validation and the test sets were combined to form one large test set. As a result, the test set used in the Distance Based method is larger than the one based on the Maximum Prevalence method – 745 test documents were used for the former and 326 test documents were used for the latter. The training documents used in both the Distance Based method and the Maximum Prevalence method, however, are the same.

Distance Based Method

One of the methods used for the dating of documents, which we call the Distance Based method, is based on a simple idea[3]. For example, if we wish to date a given document, we will start by denoting it as D. If we had an appropriate method to measure similarity between D and the training documents, then the date of document *D* should be closer to the dates of those documents

---

[2] We have evaluated the dating methodology on 9911 documents based on the second method (the Maximum Prevalence method). Results are presented in section 3.1. For the purpose of comparison to the first method (the distance based method) our discussions are based on the smaller 3353 documents.

[3] Measuring distance, and smoothing, among medieval manuscripts and pages of the World Wide Web, online version by A. FEUERVERGER/P. HALL/G. TILAHUN/M. GERVERS, 2004 <http://dx.doi.org/10.1198/106186005X47291>, follow the supplemental materials link; ID., Distance measures and smoothing methodology for imputing features of documents, in: Journal of Computational and Graphical Statistics 14 (2005) p. 255–262 (*short title:* FEUERVERGER et al., Distance measures); ID., Using statistical smoothing to date medieval manuscripts, in: Beyond Parametrics in Interdisciplinary Research: Festschrift in Honour of P. K. Sen, ed. N. BALAKRISHNAN/E. PENA/M. J. SILVAPULLE (IMS Collections 1, 2008) p. 321–331 (*short title:* FEUERVERGER et al., Using statistical smoothing).

in the training data set which were most similar to it (recall that all the documents in the training set bear dates). This assumes that language use tends to evolve in a continuous way through time, so that the more similar two documents are, the more likely it is that they were produced at approximately the same time.

In order to apply statistical methodologies to this idea, we must be able to determine a quantitative notion of similarity between two documents. In fact, we define an intuitive notion of „distance" between documents, and then say that two documents are relatively similar when the distance between them is small. Note that the notion of distance between documents is in common use in day-to-day life – for example, we measure distances between two documents every time we search a query on a search engine, such as Google or databases for journal articles. The results returned by these algorithms are ranked in order of similarity to our query – the smaller the distance between our query and a document in the database, the closer that document will be ranked to number one. The exact means by which the ranking is accomplished in Google or any other search engine is of course very complicated – the number of links between websites, the frequency of hits to a website, the time of day in which a website is accessed, geographic location of the user, the length of time one spends on a website, advertisements, among other considerations, affect the rank of a retrieved document. As an illustration, consider the following as an example of how to measure distances between two documents. Let D_1 and D_2 be two documents[4] :

$D_1 = \{a\ rose\ is\ a\ rose\ is\ a\ rose\}$ and $D_2 = \{a\ rose\ is\ a\ rose\ is\ a\ flower\}$.

Define a vector such that the values of the coordinate points in order correspond to the frequency of the distinct words „a", „rose", „is", „flower". In this way, we construct a vector representation of the document D_1 which we denote by V_1:

$$V_1 = (3, 3, 2, 0).$$

(The first and the second coordinate points have the value 3 because „a" and „rose" each occurred three times in document D_1. Similarly, the third and the fourth coordinate points have the values 2 and 0, respectively, since „is" oc-

---

[4] These two documents are examples taken from an article by A. Z. BRODER, On the resemblance and containment of documents, in: International Conference on Compression and Complexity of Sequences (SEQUENCES '97), June 11–13 1997, Positano, Italy (1998) p. 21–29. In the article, Broder studies document retrieval methods in search engines.

curred twice and „flower" did not occur in D_1.) Similarly, the vector representation V_1 of the document D_2 is given by

$$V_2 = (3, 2, 2, 1).$$

We note here that in place of individual words, we could use the sequences of consecutive words that make up a given document. For example, the sequence of two consecutive words that make up the document D_2, which we call 2-shingle or shingle order 2, is given as

{a rose, rose is, is a, a rose, rose is, is a, a flower}.

The vector representation of the 2-shingle sequence would then be (2, 2, 2, 1) – values of the coordinate points one, two and three correspond to the frequency of the word patterns „a rose", „rose is" and „is a", respectively, and each one of these word patterns occurred exactly twice. The value of the fourth coordinate point is 1 since the word pattern „a flower" occurred only once. We also note here that the coordinate values of the vectors representing documents need not necessarily be frequencies of word patterns. They can, for instance, be some function of the frequency of a word, the number of documents containing the word and the total number of documents in the corpus. This form of vector representation is typically used by those working in the field of information retrieval.

We can now define *similarity* between the documents D_1 and D_2 to be the cosine of the angle between the vectors V_1 and V_2, and 1 minus this value can be defined to be the *distance* between the documents D_1 and D_2. There are many measures of distances between documents[5], however, the cosine based distance measure is the one that is most widely used. In the analysis of the DEEDS documents, we used a distance measure similar to the cosine distance measure, with the only difference being in the normalisation factor[6]. One advantage of this type of distance measure is that it preserves the so-called „triangle inequality", which means that from a mathematical perspective it is a valid way of measuring distance, whereas the cosine distance measure is not. Furthermore, this distance measure is more conservative than the one based on the cosine distance measure, in the sense that the distance measure between two documents would register to be smaller under the cosine distance measure than the one based on the newer distance measure.

---

[5] M. McGill/M. Koll/T. Noreault, An evaluation of factors affecting document ranking by information retrieval systems. Technical Report (1979).

[6] Feuerverger et al., Distance measures; id., Using statistical smoothing.

As mentioned earlier, the idea behind this approach is that the smaller the distance between two documents, the higher the probability that the documents' dates are close[7]. Suppose the undated document we wish to date is denoted by D. The date estimate of document D is a weighted average of the date of the documents from the training data. The weight associated with the date of a document from the training data depends on how close the corresponding training document is to D – the smaller the distance to D, the larger the assigned weight. Therefore, to describe the method fully it only remains to specify how the weights are determined. Before doing this, we note that there are many possibilities here – for example, one simple approach would be to take the date of the document whose distance from the undated document is smallest amongst all documents in the training set. How these weights are determined will now be described.

We first define a non-negative, non-increasing function on the positive half line (i.e. the first quadrant on the Cartesian graph). An exponential function of the form $f(x) = \exp(-x^2/h) \times 1/h$, for a fixed number $h>0$, which we also call a kernel function, serves as an example of such a function. This function defines a bell-shaped curve with maximum value at $x=0$. By varying the value of h, called a „bandwidth", the speed at which the curve decreases as x moves away from zero can be controlled. For very small values of h, the decrease is very quick and for large values of h the decrease is slower. Let us assume for the moment that the bandwidth h is fixed to be a particular „optimal" value. How we determine this optimal value of h will be discussed shortly. Since the date of every document in the training data is known, the weight assigned to the date of a given document from the training data is the value of this exponential function where the argument is the distance between D and the training document. We note here that the function is at its maximum at 0, and therefore, a maximal weight is attained when the distance between D and the training document is equal to 0[8]. We then multiply the dates of each of the documents from the training set by its corresponding weight, add them together and normalise the sum (i.e. divide it by the sum of the weights). The value that we obtain is then taken to be the date estimate of document D.

The manner by which we choose the optimal value of the bandwidth parameter is as follows: given a document D that we wish to date, we first begin

---

[7] In the case of the inspeximus, in which an earlier document is „inspected" and confirmed at a later time, the earlier and later texts are separated and entered in the database under the same document number as „A" and „B", each with a distinct date. To be consistent with the underlying notion of the methodology, two documents otherwise similar in content and word order in the database will thus retain a similar chronology.

[8] If the distance between D and the training document is equal to zero for shingle order 2 or larger, then D and the training document are exact copies.

by assembling a given number, say *m* of documents from the training set closest to document D. We will call these documents the *neighbours* of document D. For a given, fixed bandwidth value *h*, we perform the dating procedure on each of the neighbouring documents (assuming that we do not know their dates), and measure the average error which was made in these estimations. This gives us an average error as a function of *h*, and the value of *h* which minimises this error, the optimal *h* value, is used to date the undated document.

There is one last detail to consider. We recall that different shingle orders of a document give rise to different vector representations of the same document, and hence the distance between two documents will be different depending on the shingle order used. By multiplying the kernel functions that correspond to each of the shingle orders (we multiply in order to preserve the necessary mathematical properties of the resulting kernel function), we combine all the distances that arise from considering the different shingle orders. Each of the optimal bandwidths corresponding to the kernels of the various shingle orders are then computed as described in the previous paragraph.

The method for dating an undated document presented above can be readily extended to estimate other attributes of a document. One such example would be the problem of classifying the geographical location of a document's origin. In this situation, the attribute, instead of the date of a document, would be a vector of two coordinate points where one coordinate point corresponds to the longitudinal and the other coordinate point corresponds to the latitudinal cartographic coordinates of a geographic location. If the document attribute on the other hand is not ordinal, such as the type of religious house that drafted the documents, then we can represent the different houses geometrically: if we have *n* different variates for an attribute, we represent each one as the vertices of an (n-1)-simplex. For example, if the variate of the attribute „religious houses" are Franciscan, Benedictine and Carmelite, then the vertices of an isosceles triangle on a 2-dimensional graph, (0, 0), (0, 1) and (1/2, $\sqrt{3}$ /2) would, respectively, represent the three religious houses. Prior notions of closeness between, for example, document writing styles of the different religious houses can be represented by contorting the length of the edges of the triangle and by drawing certain vertices more closely. Following the same procedure for computing the date of an undated document, where in this case we would replace the date of a training document with the vector point representing the religious house which wrote the training document, the estimated vector point in the simplex would be rendered discrete by shrinking it to the nearest vertex. This nearest vertex is the estimated variate of the document we wish to categorise.

The Distance Based method has yet to be implemented on the full data set of the DEEDS corpus.

Results of the Distance Based Method

Having experimented with a combination of different shingle orders and *m* values, we found that the shingle order 1&2 performed the best where $m=100$. The mean absolute error was 12 years and the median absolute error was 6 years. If the mean year was used as the date estimate, then the mean absolute error would be 37 years and the median absolute error would be 24 years. In Figure 1, we see the plot of estimated document dates to actual document dates for 745 documents from the test set (since there were no extraneous parameters to estimate, the 419 validation documents and the 326 test documents together form this new test set of 745 documents. The number of training documents equals 2608). As can be seen, there is some edge bias on the left side (i.e. those documents with actual date of approximately 1100 to 1175 systemically have higher estimated dates, because there is an insufficient number of dated documents from a previous period upon which to calculate estimations). It is possible to overcome this problem by applying adjustment weights to the dates of the training documents when estimating the dates of documents from the test set.

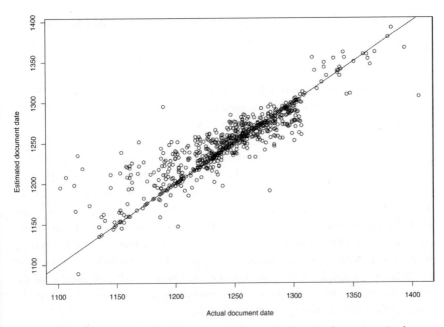

Figure 1: True document date versus date estimates for the 745 documents in the test set based on a combination of shingle order 1 and 2, and m=100. Solid line indicates the „X=Y" axis.

Maximum Prevalence Method

The Maximum Prevalence Method estimates the date of an undated document by computing the probability of occurrence of the document at different time values. The time value that maximises the probability is the date estimate for the document. Since words are the fundamental elements of documents, to date a given document, we first begin by modelling the probability of occurrence of each shingle (a shingle is a consecutive sequence of words, see section 2 for an example) of the document as it varies through time. This estimation is based on the frequency of occurrence of these same shingles in documents with known dates. Assuming the occurrences of the shingles to be „independent" of one another (this is a statistical term which intuitively means that the occurrence of one particular shingle does not influence whether or not any other shingle occurs in a document), we multiply the probability of occurrences of these shingles together for various fixed time values. We interpret the resulting value to be the probability of occurrence of the undated document at various time points. The date at which this function achieves its maximum value is then assumed to be the most likely date at which this undated document was written.

In order to make this method more explicit, we will describe how we estimate the *probability of occurrence* of a shingle as a function of time. Given a shingle from an undated document D, we first compute the proportion of times the shingle occurs among the training documents for each date where training documents are available (recall that the date of every training document is known). As an example, consider Figure 2a. In this plot, the „*" indicates the proportion of time the shingle *ibidem Deo seruientibus/Deo ibidem seruientibus* occurs at each date for which there are training documents. The „*" points drawn on the horizontal line below the value zero are artificial in the sense that it is arbitrary and chosen only to illustrate graphically that there is zero occurrence of the shingle corresponding to the dates, even though there are training documents at these dates. The dashed curve is the most significant indicator. This curve is the estimate of the probability of occurrence of the shingle as a function of time (date). Under certain modelling assumptions, which we will discuss in the optional section below, this curve is the best fitting single curve through the data points. We note here that the curve mainly lies below the data points since there are many documents in the training data that do not contain the shingle.

As another example, we illustrate in Figure 2b the proportion of times the shingle *testimonium huic* occurs among the training documents for each date where training documents are available. The data from the training documents indicate that this shingle is more likely to occur from the middle of the 1200s to the middle of the 1300s. The curve estimate clearly tracks this trend.

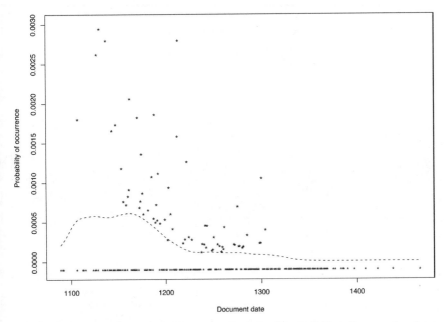

Figure 2: (a) Fitted probability of occurrence of the shingle *ibidem Deo seruientibus/ Deo ibidem seruientibus* as a function of time.

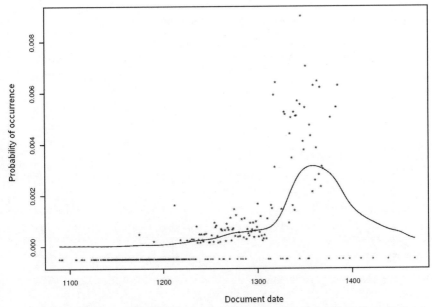

Figure 2: (b) Fitted probability of occurrence of the shingle *testimonium huic* as a function of time (adapted from Tilahun *et al.*, 2012).

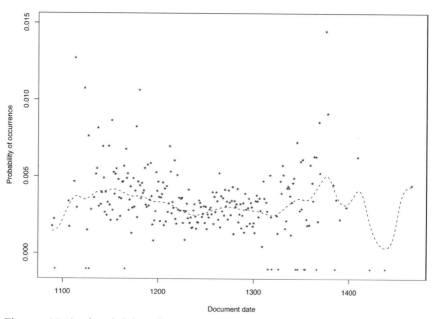

Figure 2: (c) Fitted probability of occurrence of the shingle *omnibus* as a function of time. The asterisks indicate the proportion of time a shingle occurs at a date for which training documents are present. Asterisks plotted below the point 0 indicate that the shingle was not observed even though training documents were present at the given document date.

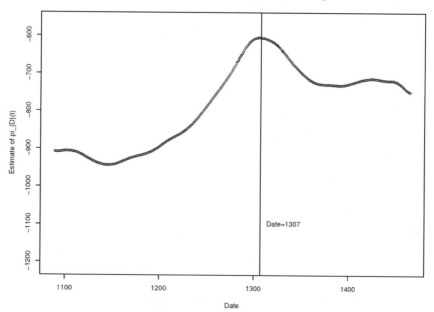

Figure 3: The plot is that of the function IID(t). The actual date for the document is 1299 and the estimated date is 1307 (vertical line).} (Adapted from Tilahun *et al.*, 2012)

We can think of this curve, which is a function of time, as an input-output machine. Input any date, not necessarily one for which we have a training document, and the value corresponding to the vertical line tells us the probability of observing the shingle *testimonium huic* at the date of interest. As mentioned above, the „*" points drawn on the horizontal line below the value zero are artificial.

We will now describe the statistical model we used to estimate the probability of occurrence of a shingle. Let $S(D)$ be the set that contains all (not necessarily distinct) shingles constructed from document D. Let $n_s(D)$ be the number of times the shingle s occurs in document D, and let $N(D)$ denote the total number of elements in $S(D)$. Let t_i denote the date in which document D_i was written. We estimate the probability of the occurrence of the shingle s as a function of time, $\Pi_s(t)$, to be

$$\Pi_s(t) = \Sigma_{i \in T} \, n_s(D_i) K_h(t_i - t) \, / \, \Sigma_{i \in T} N(D_i) K_h(t_i - t) \quad \text{(equation 1)}$$

where K_h is a weighted kernel function of the form $K_h(x) = \exp(-x^2/h \times 1/h)$, and the summation is over the training data denoted by T. This function is akin to a weighted average of the observed shingle proportions, with the particular weights being used in the average for a given point t in time being determined by the relative distances in time between t and the dates of each contributing observation. We refer the reader to Tilahun *et al.* for the technical derivation of the above formula[9].

To estimate the date of the undated document D (under the assumption of the independence of the occurrences of the shingles in $S(D)$[10]), for every shingle s in $S(D)$, we first compute the $\Pi_s(t)$s and multiply them together. Suppose we have $s_1, s_2, ..., s_n$ shingles in $S(D)$, (the shingles are not necessarily distinct, i.e., some shingles could be repeated). We compute the function $\Pi_D(t)$ given by

$$\Pi_D(t) = \Pi_{s1}(t) \times \Pi_{s2}(t) \times \cdots \times \Pi_{sn}(t) \quad \text{(equation 2)}$$

which we interpret as being the probability of occurrence of document D as a function of time. The value on the time axis for which this function attains its maximum is taken to be the date estimate of the document D. An example of such a function can be seen in Figure 3. The peak of the curve (the highest

---

[9] G. TILAHUN/A. FEUERVERGER/M. GERVERS, Dating Medieval English Charters, in: Annals of Applied Statistics 6 (2012) p. 1615–1640 (see Section 5, equation 5.5).

[10] The independence assumption states that if we were to pick two shingles, say, s_1 and s_2, from $S(D)$, then the probability of the occurrence of s_1 is not changed by the presence or absence of s_2. This is a gross assumption, but one we nevertheless need to make in order to simplify the mathematical theoretical framework.

point of this probability curve) is attained in the year 1307, the estimated date at which this document was written. This year is indicated by the vertical line. The actual date of this document is 1299.

In passing, we note that the Maximum Prevalence method automatically scales down the contribution of uninformative or insignificant shingles – these are shingles that do not provide any indication as to the date they were most likely to have been used. An example of such a shingle would be the word *omnibus* which occurs often with about the same frequency at different time values. As shown in Figure 2c, the fitted curve for *omnibus* is close to a horizontal line, and therefore the contribution of $\Pi_{(omnibus)}(t)$ to the evaluation of $\Pi_D(t)$ is minimal.

As in the Distance Based method, the Maximum Prevalence method can be extended to accommodate other types of document attributes. If we wish, for example, to categorise the geographical location where a document ori-gi-nates, we would estimate the probability of occurrence of the shingles of the document over cartographic coordinate points (we are assuming here that the geographic location where the training documents originate is known). Equations (1) and (2) would in this case be functions of vectors with two coordinate points – one for the longitudinal and the other for the latitudinal cartographic coordinate points. If the attributes of the documents are categorical, such as the religious house which wrote the documents, then we could estimate the probability of occurrence of a shingle of one such document by considering the frequency with which the shingle occurs within documents of each given attribute. We then compute the probability of occurrence of the document for each attribute via equation (2) (here, the probability function ranges over the attributes). The attribute that attains the maximum probability is the one under which we would categorise the document.

The document dating method described above is currently in use at the DEEDS project. We invite the reader to date a medieval English Latin charter by referring to the web address at http://deeds.library.utoronto.ca.

Results of the Maximum Prevalence Method

Having experimented with the above dating methodology on shingle orders 1,2,3 and 4 singly, we found that shingle orders 2 and 3 performed the best (perhaps because, given the data size, matches based on shingle orders larger than 3 were more rare, and those based on shingle order 1 only were not sufficiently discriminative.) On a test set containing 326 documents, the mean absolute error based on shingle order 2 and 3 was found to be 9 years and the median absolute error was 6 years. The mean absolute error on this same test set based on shingle orders 1 and 4 was 12.5, and the median absolute error was 8 years and 7 years, respectively. Figure 4 shows the date estimate versus the true dates for 326 documents of the test set based on shingle order 2. The „X" axis is the true date of the documents and the „Y" axis is the date estimate. The solid line indicates the X=Y axis. If the date estimates were to match up perfectly with the actual document dates, then the points would all fall on the X=Y axis. In this analysis, we used 2608 training documents (the same training documents used for the Distance Based method), 326 test documents and 419 validation documents.

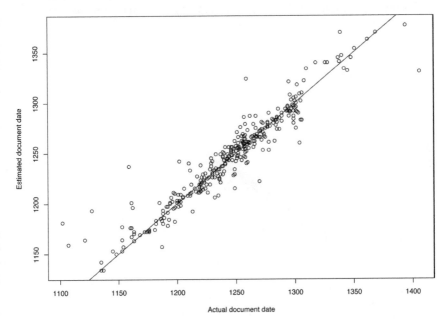

Figure 4: Estimated versus actual document date for 326 documents in the test set based on shingle order 2. The solid line is the „X=Y" axis.} (Adapted from Tilahun *et al.*, 2012)

Again, having experimented with the dating methodology on 9911 DEEDS documents (7709 in the training documents, 1238 in the validation set and 964 in the test set) we found that, based on shingle order 2, the mean absolute error on the test set was 9.5 years and the median absolute error was 5 years. Figure 5 shows the date estimates versus the true dates for the 964 documents of the test set based on shingle order 2. As in the previous plot, the „X" axis is the true date of the documents and the „Y" axis is the date estimate. The solid line indicates the X=Y axis.

Regarding the problem of predicting the geographic location of a document's origin, we are currently in the process of testing the necessary computer programmes. The problem is computationally intensive since we are dealing with a multidimensional issue – we need to take into account how word/shingle usage varies through both time and geographic locations.

The methodology presented here, and the results generated, provide the diplomatist with an innovative guideline for determining a chronological value for an undated document, and is especially useful for acts which have no historical context other than the words contained in them. This methodology also allows one to trace the usage of words and phrases through the passage of time. It can naturally be extended to other fields of historical research including topography, authorship and the identification of institutional affiliation.

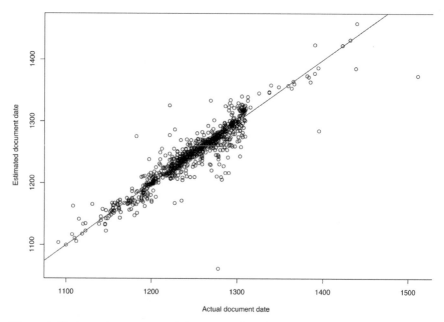

Figure 5: Estimated versus actual document date for 964 documents in the test set based on shingle order 2. The solid line is the „X=Y" axis.

Neue Perspektiven für die Memorialforschung

Die datenbankgestützte Erschließung digitaler Urkundencorpora am Beispiel der Bestände von Aldersbach und Fürstenzell im 14. Jahrhundert

MICHAEL HÄNCHEN

1.) Einleitung

Die analytische Aufarbeitung von Urkunden erfährt durch die Möglichkeiten der modernen Informationstechnologie einen signifikanten Wandel. Mit der Urkundendigitalisierung scheint in besonderem Maße eine Forderung Otto Posses erfüllt, der bereits gegen Ende des 19. Jahrhunderts die weitreichenden Möglichkeiten der damals noch jungen Fotografie für die paläographisch-diplomatische Forschung erkannte. Der Dresdner Archivar formulierte im Jahr 1887, dass „einzig und allein die Photographie in richtiger Verwendung das zutreffende Mittel ist, um flache Objekte, also etwa Substrate mit Schriftzügen, Zeichnungen, Siegel u.s.w. in unbestechlicher Richtigkeit zu faksimilieren", und dass sie auch „für Zwecke der Erhaltung der Urkunden [...] von grossem Vortheil" [1] ist.

Mit dem Internet und der digitalen Fotografie ist es der Forschung nun möglich, jederzeit ortsunabhängig auf diese ubiquitären Textzeugnissen des Mittelalters mittels hochauflösender Digitalisate zuzugreifen. Virtuelle Forschungsumgebungen wie beispielsweise das Virtuelle deutsche Urkundennetzwerk (<http://www.vdu.uni-koeln.de>[2]), das durch ICARUS (Interna-

---

[1] O. Posse, Die Lehre von den Privaturkunden (1887) S. 5f., 7.

[2] Das Verbundunternehmen Virtuelles deutsches Urkundennetzwerk, an dem die Generaldirektion der staatlichen Archive Bayerns, das Landesarchiv Baden-Württemberg und die Landesarchivverwaltung Rheinland-Pfalz kooperativ ebenso beteiligt sind wie die Abteilung Historisch-kulturwissenschaftliche Informationsverarbeitung (HKI) der Universität Köln, das Institut für Geschichtliche Landeskunde (IGL) Mainz sowie die Professur für Historische Grundwissenschaften und Historische Medienkunde an der LMU München, schafft für die Quellengruppe der Urkunden eine dokumentarische Plattform, indem sie Digitalisate (Faksimiles) der Urkunden für hilfswissenschaftliche und historische Studien bereitstellt und damit alle Vorteile moderner Informationstechnologie wie orts- und zeitunabhängige Zugriffsmöglichkeiten bietet.

tional Centre for Archival Research) betriebene Portal Monasterium (<http://
www.monasterium.net>) oder das Marburger Lichbildarchiv für Originalurkunden (<http://lba.hist.uni-marburg.de/lba/pages/>) stellen digitalisierte
Urkunden in großer Stückzahl bereit und ermöglichen die diplomatische Arbeit jederzeit und ohne kostenaufwendige Archivreisen, welche vonnöten
wären, um vergleichend große Urkundencorpora zu erforschen. Erst vor wenigen Jahren hob Georg VOGELER hervor, dass die Nutzung digitaler Urkundencorpora in erheblichem Maße völlig neue Ansatzpunkte in der Urkundenforschung ermöglicht. Er betonte, dass deren Verwendung „aus der
Evolution diplomatischer Arbeit durch digitale Editionen vielleicht doch
noch eine Revolution machen wird."[3] Tatsächlich erlauben Regestenwerke
und Urkundeneditionen nicht in vollem Umfang eine detaillierte Repräsentation von Urkunden, denn sie benachteiligen visuelle Eigenschaften des Origi-
naldokuments mit all seinen Besonderheiten.

Ziel der vorliegenden Studie ist es nun, die Möglichkeiten der Auswertbarkeit
digitalisierter Urkundenbestände über den rein diplomatisch-paläographischen
oder bestandserhaltenden Aspekt hinaus auch für die historische Memorialforschung aufzuzeigen. Es wird darum zunächst kurz ein Projekt vorgestellt, welches auf den oben genannten digitalen Urkundencorpora fußt und seit September 2010 an der Forschungsstelle für Vergleichende Ordensgeschichte (FOVOG)
der TU Dresden durchgeführt wird[4]. Sodann wird auf die Methode der Erschließung und Formalisierung mittels einer Datenbank eingegangen, um abschließend
anhand zweier Beispiele das einer solchen Datenbank inhärente Analysepotential
zum Nutzen der Geschichtswissenschaft aufzuzeigen. Als Untersuchungsgegenstand für das oben genannte Projekt wurden Memorialstiftungen[5], also Dotationen

---

[3] G. VOGELER, Vom Nutz und Frommen digitaler Urkundeneditionen, in: AfD 52
(2006) S. 449–466, hier S. 464.
[4] Titel des Projektes: „Klösterliche Memorialstiftungen von Adel und Bürgertum im
Spiegel der Urkundenüberlieferung des 14. Jahrhunderts am Beispiel des Bistums Passau".
[5] Zum sehr weiten Feld der Memorialforschung hier nur ein kleiner Ausschnitt: A.
ANGENENDT, Missa specialis. Zugleich ein Beitrag zur Entstehung der Privatmessen,
in: FMSt 17 (1983) S. 153–221; Memoria als Kultur, hg. von O. G. OEXLE (Veröffentlichungen des Max-Planck-Instituts für Geschichte 121, 1995); „Memoria". Der geschichtliche Zeugniswert des liturgischen Gedenkens im Mittelalter, hg. von K.
SCHMID/J. WOLLASCH (Münstersche Mittelalter-Schriften 48, 1984); Gedächtnis, das
Gemeinschaft stiftet, hg. von K. SCHMID (1985); Materielle Kultur und religiöse Stiftung im Spätmittelalter. Internationales Round-Table Gespräch Krems an der Donau
26. September 1988, hg. von G. JARITZ (SB Wien, 554 / Veröffentlichungen des Instituts für Mittelalterliche Realienkunde Österreichs 12, 1990); R. BARTSCH, Seelgerätstiftungen im 14. Jahrhundert. Ein Beitrag zur Geschichte des Testaments in Österreich,
in: Festschrift Karl Amira (1908, Neudruck 1979) S. 1–58. Nicht zuletzt die durch M.
BORGOLTE ins Leben gerufene Reihe „Stiftungsgeschichten", welche seit dem Jahr
2000 in bisher zehn Bänden erschienen ist.

für das Seelenheil[6] durch Adel und Bürgertum, im Spiegel der Urkundenüberlieferung des 14. Jahrhunderts im Donaubistum Passau gewählt. Obwohl die zahlreich vorhandenen Stiftungsurkunden für das Seelenheil bisher wegen ihrer prosopographischen Informationen geschätzt oder für Studien des klösterlichen Wirkungsbereiches herangezogen worden, wurden sie in diesem Zusammenhang bisher wenig in das Blickfeld genommen. Es besteht also eine Forschungslücke über die Funktion von Stiftungen in der Urkundenüberlieferung[7]. Dass diese Lücke bis heute nicht geschlossen worden ist, kann mit der räumlichen Verstreutheit der Quellen begründet werden. Der Untersuchungsraum des Projekts, das Bistum Passau[8], war mit weit über 70 geistlichen Institutionen, davon 51 projekt-

---

[6] „Es ist eine bekannte Tatsache, daß Klöster und Stifte ihren Grundbesitz den Stiftungen großer und kleiner Grundherren verdankten, die sich durch diese Gaben Heil für ihre Seele erwarteten, Anspruch auf Teilhabe an den ‚Werken' des liturgischen Gebetes erwarben." H. Dienst, Regionalgeschichte und Gesellschaft im Hochmittelalter am Beispiel Österreichs (MIÖG, Ergänzungsband 27, 1990) S. 213.

[7] Vgl. M. Borgolte, Gedenkstiftungen in St. Galler Urkunden, in: „Memoria", hg. von Schmid/Wollasch, S. 578–602, hier S. 579. Dies unterstreicht nochmals D. Geuenich, Von der Adelsforschung zur Memoriaforschung, in: Pro remedio et salute anime peregamus. Totengedenken am Frauenstift Essen im Mittelalter, hg. von T. Schilp (Essener Forschungen zum Frauenstift 6, 2008) S. 9–18, hier S. 13. Und 2001 resümierte Joachim Wild, es sei „eine eigene Studie wert, die Beurkundung von Jahrtagsstiftungen näher zu untersuchen." J. Wild, Das Aufkommen der Siegelurkunde bei den bayerischen Klöstern, in: Auxilia historica. Festschrift für Peter Acht zum 90. Geburtstag, hg. von W. Koch (Schriftreihe der Bayerischen Landesgeschichte 132, 2001) S. 461–477, hier S. 473. Zum prosopographischen Wert der Stiftungsurkunden und Einzugsbereich vgl. K. Schmid/J. Wollasch, Societas et Fraternitas. Begründung eines kommentierten Quellenwerkes zur Erforschung der Personen und Personengruppen des Mittelalters (Frühmittelalterliche Studien 9, 1975) S. 1–48, hier S. 4; F. Freise, Studien zum Einzugsbereich der Klostergemeinschaft von Fulda, in: Die Klostergemeinschaft von Fulda im früheren Mittelalter 2,3: Untersuchungen, hg. von K. Schmid, bearb. von G. Althoff (Münstersche Mittelalter-Schriften 8, 1978) S. 1003–1269.

[8] Die Geschichte des Bistums ist bereits Untersuchungsgegenstand verschiedener Studien zur Kirchenentwicklung und zu politischen Prozessen vor allem vom 10. bis zum 14. Jahrhundert gewesen, so dass die historischen Hintergründe gut aufbereitet sind. Auch hier nur ein kleiner Auszug wichtiger Forschungsliteratur: E. Boshof, Stadt und Hochstift Passau um 1300: Der Pontifikat Wernhards von Prambach (1285–1313), in: ZBLG 74 (2011) S. 45–79; F.-R. Erkens, Das Niederkirchenwesen im Bistum Passau, in: MIÖG 102 (1994) S. 53–97; J. Lenzenweger, Das Bistum Passau und die Kirche in Österreich, in: OG 22 (1980) S. 129–136; R. Zinnhobler, Bistum Passau, in: Die Zeit der frühen Habsburger. Dome und Klöster 1279–1379. Niederösterreichische Landesausstellung. Wiener Neustadt 12. Mai bis 28. Oktober 1979 (Katalog des Niederösterreichischen Landesmuseums / N.F. 85, 1979) S. 182–187; 1250 Jahre Bistum Passau 739–1989. Symposion des Instituts für Ostbairische Heimatforschung der Universität Passau, hg. von A. Leidl (Neue Veröffentlichungen des Instituts für Ost-

relevanten Häusern neun verschiedener Orden und Kongregationen klösterlich dicht besiedelt. Die Urkunden dieser Klöster sind von der Digitalisierung nun vollständig erfasst worden[9]. 14.500 Urkunden sind allein für das zu untersuchende 14. Jahrhundert überliefert, was eine ausgezeichnete Basis darstellt. Die Intention des hier vorgestellten Projektes ist die datenbankgestützte[10] Untersuchung der Stiftungsmentalität bestimmter sozialer Gruppen des Passauer Bistums – gemeint sind hoher und niederer Adel, Stadtbürgertum und Geistliche – im Kontext genau jener Urkundenüberlieferung. Dabei stehen zwei Fragen im Vordergrund: Zum einen wird der Fokus auf die Form der Verschriftlichung von Recht (Formalkriterien) in der Urkundenüberlieferung gelegt. Lassen sich etwa Wandlungsprozesse im Kontext der historischen Ereignisse feststellen? Gibt es regionale oder soziale Unterschiede und lassen sich Veränderungen in den äußeren und inneren Merkmalen von Stiftungsurkunden nachweisen? Zum anderen wird der Fokus auf inhaltliche Kriterien gelegt. Lassen sich Wandlungen bei der Stiftungsanzahl, dem materiellen Aspekt der Stiftung, der spirituellen Gegenleistung, den sozialen Gruppen und Personen oder dem Empfänger dieser Stiftungen erkennen?

Ferner soll unter vergleichender Perspektive den Fragen nachgegangen werden, ob und wenn ja, welche Relationen zwischen den religiösen, rechtlichen und wirtschaftlichen Faktoren des Gedenkwesens im 14. Jahrhundert bestehen. Man denke zum Beispiel an die Bevorzugung bestimmter Orden oder Klöster durch gewisse soziale Gruppen. Welche Stiftungsakte und -ma-

---

bairische Heimatforschung der Universität Passau 46, 1989); H. W. WURSTER, Das Bistum Passau unter Bischof Herzog Albert von Sachsen-Wittenberg, 1320–1342, in: Aus Bayerns Geschichte. Forschungen als Festgabe zum 70. Geburtstag von Andreas Kraus, hg. von E. J. GREIPL/A. SCHMID/W. ZIEGLER (1992) S. 179–207; A. A. STRNAD, Das Bistum Passau in der Kirchenpolitik König Friedrichs des Schönen (1313–1320), in: Dynast und Kirche. Studien zum Verhältnis von Kirche und Staat im späteren Mittelalter und in der Neuzeit, hg. von J. GELMI/H. GRITSCH/C. BALDEMAIR (Innsbrucker historische Studien 18–19, 1997) S. 51–90; Alte Klöster in Passau und Umgebung. Geschichtliche und Kunstgeschichtliche Aufsätze, hg. von J. OSWALD ([2]1954).

[9] So fand vom 16.–17. September 2010 in Passau eine internationale Tagung aus dem Anlass statt, dass „die vollständige online-Bereitstellung der geistlichen Urkundenbestände des vormaligen Donaubistums Passau im europäischen Urkundenportal www.monasterium.net" abgeschlossen war. Vgl. das Resümee zur Tagung von A. KRAH/H. W. WURSTER, Die virtuelle Urkundenlandschaft der Diözese Passau, 16.–17. September 2010 / Passau, <http://www.monasterium.net/pdf/Tagung_Passau_resuemee_Krah_Wurster.pdf>, S. 1.

[10] Für das Projekt wird das Datenbanksystem askSam (<http://www.asksam.de/>) verwendet, welches ebenfalls in Göttingen bei dem Projekt „FemMoData – Femal Monasticism" verwendet wird. Vgl. K. BODARWÉ, FeMo-Data – Female Monasticism's Database. Von einem internen Hilfsmittel zum internationalen Internetprojekt, in: Datenbanken in den Geisteswissenschaften, hg. von I. JONAS (2007) S. 49–61.

terien sind etwa in den Urkunden festgehalten und wie präsentiert sich die wirtschaftliche Potenz der Stifter und Bestifteten?

Denn thesenhaft formuliert geht das der vorliegende Studie zugrunde liegende Projekt davon aus, dass sich, beeinflusst durch die erheblichen Katastrophen des 14. Jahrhunderts, die formalen wie inhaltlichen Aspekte der Urkunden des „totalen sozialen Phänomens"[11] Memorialstiftung, also etwa auch der materielle Einsatz durch die Stifter und die geforderten spirituellen Gegenleistungen durch die Konvente, gewandelt haben müssen.

Im 14. Jahrhundert, einem von angstvoller Endzeiterwartung geprägten „Krisenjahrhundert", gekennzeichnet zum Beispiel durch Hungersnöte, Viehseuchen, wirtschaftlichen Niedergang und Wüstungsprozesse, Attraktivitätsverlust traditioneller Orden, Pestepidemien, das Avignonesische Papsttum und schließlich das Große Schisma[12], haben einschneidende kirchliche, wirtschaftliche und überhaupt sozio-kulturelle Wandlungsprozesse stattgefunden, weshalb sich das 14. Jahrhundert für eine komparative Untersuchung zum Stiftungsverhalten besonders anbietet. Denn bei der vergleichenden Untersuchung von Stiftungen aus der Pestzeit sollte – mit Joachim Wollasch gesprochen – „die Frage nicht vergessen werden, ob sich die Stiftungen von früheren unterschieden, und wenn ja, worin"[13].

---

[11] M. MAUSS, Die Gabe. Form und Funktion des Austauschs in archaischen Gesellschaften (Suhrkamp Taschenbuch Wissenschaften 743, 1968, Nachdr. 2007) S. 17, 90, 176. Vgl. dazu auch M. BORGOLTE, „Totale Geschichte" des Mittelalters? Das Beispiel der Stiftungen (Öffentliche Vorlesungen der Humboldt-Universität zu Berlin 4, 1993) S. 1–5; O. G. OEXLE, Soziale Gruppen und Deutungsschemata der sozialen Wirklichkeit in der Memorialüberlieferung, in: Prosopographie als Sozialgeschichte? Methoden personengeschichtlicher Erforschung des Mittelalters. [Sektionsbeiträge zum 32. Deutschen Historikertag Hamburg 1978 mit einem Bericht über das kommentierte Quellenwerk zur Erforschung der Personen und Personengruppen des Mittelalters Societas et fraternitas] (1978) S. 33–38, hier S. 35f.

[12] „In ganz besonderem Maß ist die Epoche vom 14. Jahrhundert bis weit ins 16. Jahrhundert in ganz Europa von einer angstvollen ‚Endzeiterwartung' bedrückt [...]." P.-J. SCHULER, Das Anniversar. Zu Mentalität und Familienbewußtsein im Spätmittelalter, in: Die Familie als historischer und sozialer Verband. Untersuchungen zum Spätmittelalter und zur frühen Neuzeit, hg. von DEMS. (1987) S. 67–117, hier S. 92. Vgl. allgemeiner B. W. TUCHMAN, Der ferne Spiegel, das dramatische 14. Jahrhundert (Spiegel Edition 32, 2007); Europa 1400. Die Krise des Spätmittelalters, hg. von F. SEIBT/W. EBERHARD (1984); F. GRAUS, Pest – Geissler – Judenmorde: das 14. Jahrhundert als Krisenzeit (Veröffentlichungen des Max-Planck-Instituts für Geschichte 86, 1994); G. FOUQUET/G. ZEILINGER, Katastrophen im Spätmittelalter (2011).

[13] J. WOLLASCH, Hoffnungen der Menschen in der Zeit der Pest, in: HJb 110 (1990) S. 23–51, hier S. 37.

2.) Die Erschließung und Formalisierung digitaler Urkundencorpora mittels einer Datenbank

Schon jetzt sind die digitalisierten Urkundenfaksimiles in einer solchen großen Anzahl verfügbar, dass es sinnvoll ist, diese weiter nach den jeweiligen Erkenntnisperspektiven, beispielsweise einem bestimmten Raum, einer Institution oder dem rechtlichen Inhalt, zusammenzufassen, um sie für geschichtswissenschaftliche Fragestellungen fruchtbar zu machen. Das Projekt konzentriert sich auf original überlieferte Urkunden und schließt die Überlieferung in Kopialbüchern aus, da die Datenmenge schon genügend Material zur Auswertung bereitstellt. In einigen Fällen muss noch auf Editionen zurückgegriffen werden, da Monasterium.net nicht für alle Kommunitäten Digitalisate zur Verfügung stellt. Die Aufbereitung der digitalisierten Stiftungsurkunden geschieht mittels einer an Kriterien orientierten, typologisch strukturierten Datenbank, welche flexibel nach unterschiedlichen formellen und inhaltlichen Fragestellungen ausgewertet werden kann. Die Datenbank fungiert hierbei sowohl als erschließendes als auch thematisch fokussierendes Werkzeug, kann aber den Blick auf die Digitalisate der Originalurkunden bei der abschließenden Auswertung nicht obsolet machen.

Zielstellung ist es, Aufschlüsse über die Form der Verschriftlichung von Rechtsmaterien in der Urkundenüberlieferung durch eine komparative Gegenüberstellung sowie statistisch-analytische Auswertung der erfassten Bestände zu erhalten. Auf diese Weise können nicht nur quantitativ gestützte Entwicklungen und Tendenzen des Umgangs mit bestimmten Rechtsinhalten im Zusammenhang mit der jeweiligen Form der Verschriftlichung (Format, Schrift und Schriftspiegel, Beschreibstoff, Ausstattung, Besiegelung usw.) in einem umfangreichen zeitlichen, historischen, geographischen und politischen Kontext korreliert werden, sondern es kann auch eine Typologie der Dispositionen selbst erstellt werden, die anderen historischen Teildisziplinen, beispielsweise Wirtschafts-, Kultur- und Sozialgeschichte, nutzbringend zur Verfügung stehen soll. Hierzu werden aus den Digitalisaten die Informationen anhand einer die relevanten Untersuchungsgegenstände ansprechenden Erfassungsmatrix in die Datenbank übertragen, wobei jede Urkunde einem Datensatz entspricht. Die Matrix ist in 11 Erfassungskategorien gegliedert und sie registriert diese formellen (I.–IV.) sowie inhaltlichen (V.–XI.) Aspekte der Digitalisate wie folgt:

– I.	Metadaten der Urkunde (z. B. Ausstellungsdatum, Ort, Regest, Archiv/Signatur u. a.)
– II.	Äußere Merkmale der Urkunde (z. B. Größe, Plica/Umbug, Siegelanzahl, Siegelanbringung, Beschreibstoff, besondere Ausstattung, Formatausrichtung, Schrift, Symbole, Sprache u. a.)

– III.	Innere Merkmale der Urkunde und Typologie (z. B. Geschäftsschriftgut, feierliches Diplom, Vorkommen von Arenga und ggf. Narratio, Unterfertigung, Zeugen u. a.)
– IV.	Beschreibung des geistlichen Stiftungsempfängers (z. B. Name des Klosters oder ggf. Pfarrei, Ort, Diözese, Männer-, Frauen- oder Doppelkloster, weltlicher Landesherr und Landesherrschaft, Orden, Mutterkloster, Vogteirechte u. a.)
– V.	Stiftungsart (Stiftung, Revers, Testament)
– VI.	Erfassung und Präzisierung des Stifters und des Stiftungszwecks (Stiftergeschlecht, Stifterfamilie / Dynastie, Stifter aus weltlicher oder geistlicher Landesherrschaft, Stiftung zu Eigen, Stiftung für Dritte, Stiftung für Lebende oder Verstorbene, soziale Gruppe wie Bischof, Abt, Konventsmitglied, König / Kaiser, Herzog, Graf, Stadtbürger etc.)
– VII.	Disposition / Stiftungsmaterie (bewegliches Gut, unbewegliches Gut, Rechte und Immunitäten)
– VIII.	Präzisierung der Disposition / Stiftungsmaterie (Lehenschaft, Nießbrauchrecht, Allodiale Rechte, Zuwendung [Geld, Naturalien, Einkünfte], bestimmte Liegenschaften, Bau- und Klosterausstattung etc.)
– IX.	Spirituelle Gegenleistung (Seelgerätstiftung ohne explizite Bestimmung, Jahrtag, Prozession, Messe, Beleuchtung, Almosen, Armenspeisung, Begräbnis u. a.)
– X.	Klauseln durch den Stifter gegenüber dem bestifteten Konvent (Stiftungsverlust bei Nichterfüllung, Rückkaufrecht, lebenslange Nutznießung u. a.)
– XI.	Klauseln des Klosters gegenüber dem Stifter (z. B. Zustimmung durch Erben, sonstige Besonderheiten u. a.)

Mithilfe dieser Erfassungsmatrix wird zugleich eine größtmögliche Formalisierung der Beschreibung angestrebt, um die Abfragen unter gleichen terminologischen Voraussetzungen zu ermöglichen. Zweck dabei ist es, sowohl die Urkunden diplomatisch zu beschreiben als auch die erheblichen Schreibvarianten von Namen und zentralen Begriffen sowohl innerhalb der Urkundenbestände (Original bzw. Volltext) wie in den Metadaten (Regest) auszugleichen. Die integrierten Suchfunktionen der virtuellen Forschungsumgebungen (Monasterium / VdU) können aufgrund der verschiedenen Schreibweisen in den Regesten bzw. Volltexten bei der Suche nach Übereinstimmungen von Namen und Sachbegriffen nur unvollständige Suchergebnisse liefern. Die Datenbank dient also als formalisierendes Werkzeug für die thematisch fokussierte und historische Studie, die auf der quantitativen Auswertung der digitalen Urkundencorpora beruht. Die systematische Aufbereitung der Urkunden in der Datenbank ermöglicht es, zu verallgemeinerbaren Ergebnissen zu gelangen.

Für alle Orte, Klöster und Herrschaftsräume werden so in der Datenbank, soweit bestimmbar, die modernen, landesüblichen und offiziellen Namensformen verwendet. Ebenso werden Personennamen, Geschlechternamen, Titel und Berufsbezeichnungen (z. B. *miles*/Ritter, *samnung*/Konvent), Stiftungsmaterie (z. B. *hube*/Hufe) und Beziehungs- und Verwandtschaftsbezeichnungen (z. B. *wirt*/Ehemann, *witib*/Witwe, *sun*/Sohn, *vorvadern*/Vorfahren) durch moderne Termini angegeben[14]. Gängige Abkürzungen werden gemäß dem Katalog des Lexikons für Theologie und Kirche (LThK) verwendet (z. B. Zisterzienser/OCist, Kartäuser/OCart, Augustinerchorherren/CanReg). Die Datierung nach Heiligen- und Festkalender wird nach Hermann Grotefend[15] ebenso formalisiert angegeben, wobei regionale Besonderheiten zu beachten sind. Das Augenmerk bei der Auswertung wird dabei weniger auf das Datum an sich als vielmehr auf den Heiligenbezug zum Stiftungszeitpunkt gelegt wird, welcher gerade dann interessant ist, wenn die Stiftungstätigkeit lange vor dem Tod vorgenommen wurde und es sich zum Beispiel nicht um Testamente handelt, die durch das mittelalterliche Stiftungswesen erheblich beeinflusst wurden[16].

Diese Formalisierung birgt schwierige Grenzfälle, derer man sich bewusst sein muss. Eine Formalisierung und Zuordnung in moderne Begriffe und Bezeichnungen kann nämlich nicht immer einwandfrei erfolgen. Für Zweifelsfälle bietet die Datenbank jedoch die Möglichkeit, Schreibvarianten und Zusatzinformationen aufzunehmen und diese jederzeit anhand neugewonnener Informationen zu aktualisieren. Um es noch einmal deutlich auf den Punkt zu bringen: Die eigene formalisierte Datenbank dient der Extraktion der Stiftungsurkunden aus der Gesamtheit, das Monasterium zur Verfügung stellt.

3.) Auswertungsmöglichkeiten digitaler Urkundencorpora mittels einer Datenbank am Beispiel der Zisterzienserklöster Aldersbach und Fürstenzell

Der Vorteil beim Umgang mit einer Datenbank liegt, wie bereits erwähnt, im schnellen Zugriff auf untersuchungsrelevante Kategorien und Kriterien. Wird beispielsweise nach dem Format, der Sprache oder Schrift einer Stiftungsur-

---

[14] Hierzu werden verwendet: Mittelhochdeutsches Wörterbuch, bearb. von G. F. BENECKE et al., 5 Bde. (1854–1866, Nachdruck 1990). Spezifischer für den Untersuchungsraum: Vom Abbrändler zum Zentgraf. Wörterbuch zur Landesgeschichte und Heimatforschung in Bayern, hg. von R. HEYDENREUTER/W. PLEDL/K. ACKERMANN (²2009); Das Deutsche Wörterbuch von Jacob und Wilhelm Grimm auf CD-Rom und im Internet: <http://woerterbuchnetz.de/DWB/>.

[15] H. GROTEFEND, Zeitrechnung des deutschen Mittelalters und der Neuzeit, 2 Bde., Hannover 1891–1898; DERS., Taschenbuch der Zeitrechnung des deutschen Mittelalters und der Neuzeit, bearb. von J. ASCH (¹³1991).

[16] Vgl. A. ANGENENDT, Geschichte der Religiosität im Mittelalter (⁴2009) S. 714.

kunde zu einem besonderen Zeitpunkt durch bestimmte Personen an gewisse Klöster oder Orden gesucht, kann die Datenbank schnell und zuverlässig die entsprechenden Urkunden liefern. Die Verlinkung innerhalb der Datenbank führt direkt zum Faksimile und ermöglicht weiterführende Analysen. Im Folgenden soll an zwei Beispielen die Auswertungsmöglichkeit an fünf Kategorien aufgezeigt werden. Herangezogen werden hierfür die Urkundenbestände des Zisterzienserklosters Aldersbach und seinem Filialkloster Fürstenzell[17], beide in ländlicher Region in der Umgebung der Stadt Passau gelegen. Diese Häuser bieten sich an, da ihre Urkundenbestände je eine Serie ohne erkennbare zeitliche Lücken bilden. Bei einer Gesamtzahl von 490 Urkunden Aldersbacher und 369 Urkunden Fürstenzeller Provenienz zwischen 1300–1400 entfallen auf das Kloster Aldersbach 77 und auf Fürstenzell 50 überlieferte Memorialstiftungen. Es wurden folgende fünf Kategorien zur weiteren Strukturierung gewählt:

(1) Formalkriterien der Stiftungsurkunden
(2) Stiftungsanzahl
(3) Bestimmungen zum liturgischen Gedenken
(4) Stiftungsmaterie unter der Kategorie Zuwendungen
(5) Tradenten der Zuwendungen

Bei der auf Aldersbach und Fürstenzell bezogenen exemplarischen Auswertung der **Formalkriterien (1)** dieser Memorialstiftungen zeigte sich, dass die Stiftungsurkunden des 14. Jahrhunderts erwartungsgemäß den vollständig ausgeprägten, subjektiv verfassten und besiegelten Urkunden des Spätmittelalters mit den fünf Formularteilen Intitulatio, Publicatio, Dispositio, Corroboratio und Datatio entsprechen. Die Texte sind überwiegend volkssprachlich. Es stehen 121 Urkunden in deutscher lediglich sechs Urkunden in lateinischer Sprache gegenüber – letztere ausnahmslos ausgestellt durch geistliche Personen. Drei volkssprachlich verfasste Urkunden geistlicher Aussteller verdeutlichen jedoch, dass die Volkssprache auch hier ihren Einzug in die Verschriftlichung von Recht fand. Dabei wird die vergleichende Untersuchung mit anderen Regionen, Klöstern und Orden Aufschlüsse über die geistig-kulturelle Durchdringung der Verschriftlichung von Recht mittels Volkssprache geben, die bei den Memorialstiftungen gegenüber beiden genannten Klöstern bereits das Lateinische nahezu vollständig aus den Stiftungsurkunden verdrängt hatte. Ein Zusammenhang zwischen der Sprache und den Schreiberhände könnte vertiefte Erkenntnisse liefern, lenkt aber doch von der zentralen Zielstellung – dem Stiftungs- und Memorialwesen – ab und wird daher im Projekt nicht weiter verfolgt.

---

[17] Vgl. zu diesen Klöstern: Alte Klöster in Passau, hg. von Oswald, hier zu Aldersbach (gegr. 1120) S. 249–264, zu Fürstenzell (gegr. 1274) S. 265–280.

Teilt man die Formate der Urkunden in Gruppen ein, die in etwa klassischen Buchformaten (Oktav, Quart, Folio …) entsprechen, so stellt sich die Statistik der Urkundengröße in den beiden Beispielbeständen wie folgt dar: Die Größe der ausschließlich verwendeten Pergamente ist mit 86 Exemplaren (67 %) zumeist dem modernen Oktavformat nah. 15 (etwa 12 %) der Urkunden sind im Format Quart, 18 Diplome (etwa 14 %) mischen beide Formate und 8 Stück (etwa 6 %) entsprechen Folio oder sind größer. Einen Zusammenhang von sozialer Stellung des Tradenten und dem Urkundenformat lässt sich derzeit noch nicht feststellen: Das Folio-Format wird zwar vorwiegend durch den Adel (Kaiser, Bischof, Graf) verwendet, doch in einem Falle auch durch einen Bürger der Stadt Passau, was vielleicht auf den wirtschaftlichen Aufstieg des aufstrebenden Stadtbürgertums hinweist[18]. Demgegenüber ließen allerdings auch Bischöfe, Könige, Herzöge und Grafen Stiftungen im oktavähnlichen Format ausfertigen. Sowohl das Eindringen der Volkssprache in die schriftlichen Textzeugnisse als auch die zumeist kleinformatigen Urkunden korrelieren mit einer intensivierten und zentralisierten Verwaltung in den Territorialfürstentümern, gefördert durch die Schwächung des Königtums seit dem 13. Jahrhundert. Die Ursachen hierfür sind selbstredend vielgestaltig und sollen hier noch nicht abschließend bewertet werden. Keines der untersuchten Stücke weist Illuminationen auf. Majuskelbuchstaben kommen regelmäßig in unterschiedlicher Größe und Ausfertigung vor. Weit weniger erscheinen ornamentartige Verzierungen auf den Stücken. Auch hier wird die komparative Heranziehung weiteren Urkundenmaterials aufzeigen können, ob es sich dabei um regionale, ordens-, oder klosterspezifische Entwicklungen im Passauer Raum handelt oder hier bereits verallgemeinerbare Tendenzen der Verschriftlichung von Recht im 14. Jahrhundert auszumachen sind.

Ein Schwerpunkt der Untersuchung liegt, wie oben bereits genannt, auf der Analyse von äußeren Einflüssen auf die Stiftungspraxis. Die Projektarbeit wird nicht nur zum allgemeinen Verständnis von Memoria im 14. Jahrhundert einen Beitrag leisten und zugleich die damit verbundenen materiellen Aspekte in den Blick nehmen, sondern auch generell zum Verständnis von Frömmigkeitspraxis und deren Wandel in Krisenzeiten beitragen. Haben sich krisenhafte Entwicklungen in den Stiftungen für das eigene Seelenheil und das der Verwandten niedergeschlagen? Im Folgenden soll dies am Beispiel der Pest sowie der Verbreitung der Fegefeuerlehre exemplarisch versucht werden. Folgende Forschungsergebnisse werden mit den Ergebnissen verglichen.

Zum einen vertritt der Medizinhistoriker Manfred VASOLD die These, dass wir die spekulativen Opferzahlen dieser Zeit drastisch nach unten korrigieren müssen, ohne jedoch einen endgültigen Beweis hierfür anführen zu können,

---

[18] „Zur Verbreitung der Stiftungen trugen im späten MA v.a. die Stadtbürger bei." M. BORGOLTE, Art. Stiftung, I. Abendländischer Westen, in: LexMA 8 (2003) Sp. 179.

da zuverlässige Untersuchungen „von vielen deutschen Städten und über die Landbevölkerung sowieso" fehlen würden und genauere Schätzungen daher „vorläufig nicht möglich" seien. Konträr dazu steht die pauschale Aussage, dass „durch den Schwarzen Tod, die erste spätmittelalterliche Pestpandemie, die Bevölkerung [...] um etwa ein Drittel reduziert wurde, [und dies] heute – als Ergebnis intensiver demographischer Forschung – zum Handbuchwissen [gehört]."[19] Doch, so Vasold, wird „man [...] die demographischen Verluste allenfalls im Umweg [...] erfassen können"[20] – beispielsweise, und hier vorläufig thesenhaft formuliert, durch die Häufigkeit der **Stiftungsanzahl**, da natürlich ein erheblicher Bevölkerungsrückgang zwangsläufig auch einen Rückgang der Stiftungen nach der ersten Pestwelle, die um 1349/50 den Passauer Raum erreichte, nach sich ziehen muss.

Zum anderen kann die Analyse der **Bestimmungen zum liturgischen Gedenken** als Weg gesehen werden, den Einfluss der Pest oder der sich seit dem 13. Jahrhundert ausbreitenden Fegefeuerlehre auf die Stiftungspraxis und -mentalität im Donaubistum besser einschätzen zu können. Hierbei werden die Stiftungsurkunden etwa dahingehend ausgewertet, ob sich die Pestzüge auch im Bistum Passau dergestalt ausgewirkt haben, dass die geforderte liturgische Gegenleistung sich hinsichtlich zeitlich begrenzter liturgischer Gegenleistungen (Messen) wandelte, wie es für Lübeck sowie für Avignon und das Comtat Venaissin nachgewiesen wurde. Diese Studien belegen nämlich ein signifikantes Ansteigen vor allem von explizit geforderten Messen im Zuge der Pest[21]. Die Analyse der Stiftungsurkunden erlaubt beispielsweise auch

---

[19] N. Bulst, Bevölkerung – Entvölkerung. Demographische Gegebenheiten, ihre Wahrnehmung, ihre Bewertung und ihre Steuerung im Mittelalter, in: Sozialer Wandel im Mittelalter. Wahrnehmungsformen, Erklärungsmuster, Regelungsmechanismen, hg. von J. Miethke/K. Schreiner (1994) S. 427–445, hier S. 427.

[20] M. Vasold, Die Ausbreitung des Schwarzen Todes in Deutschland nach 1348. Zugleich ein Beitrag zur deutschen Bevölkerungsgeschichte, in: HZ 277 (2003) S. 281–308, hier S. 302, 304; vgl. auch Ders., Die Pest: Ende eines Mythos (2003).

[21] Vgl. J. Chiffoleau, Sur l'usage obsessionnel de la messe pour les morts à la fin du Moyen Âge, in: Faire croire. Modalités de la diffusion et de la réception du message religieux du XIIᵉ au XVᵉ siècle. Table ronde organisé par l'École française de Rome (Rome, 22–23 juin, 1979), hg. von A. Vauchez (1981) S. 235–256, hier S. 254; A. v. Brandt, Mittelalterliche Bürgertestamente. Neuerschlossene Quellen zur Geschichte der materiellen und geistigen Kultur (SB Heidelberg 3, 1973), S. 14. Dies korrespondiert durchaus mit der seit dem 13. Jahrhundert etablierten Fegefeuerlehre. „Durch Fasten, Gebete, Almosen und vor allem durch die Stiftung von Messen." J. Le Goff, Die Geburt des Fegefeuers. Vom Wandel eines Weltbildes im Mittelalter (²1991) S. 356. „Im Mittelalter dachte man, vor allem vermittels von Seelenmessen die Toten aus ihrer schmerzlichen Lage [im Fegefeuer] befreien zu können." P. Dinzelbacher, Die Letzten Dinge: Himmel, Hölle, Fegefeuer im Mittelalter (Herder-Spektrum 4715, 1999) S. 89.

eine Überprüfung der These von Jean-Claude Schmitt, dass im Spätmittelalter unter dem Einfluss der Fegefeuerlehre die langfristige oder dauerhafte liturgische Memoria generell verdrängt wurde[22]. Es ist eine Zielstellung der gesamten Untersuchung, anhand der Urkundenüberlieferung klösterlicher Seelgerätstiftungen im Bistum Passau des 14. Jahrhunderts zu erheben, ob sich die Bestimmungen zum liturgischen Gedenken von dauerhaften und langfristig ausgelegten Ewigmessen, Ewiglichtern, ewigen Jahrtagen hin zu „kurzfristigen" Messeleistungen in einem knappen Zeitraum nach dem Tod – und eben auch auf die Verbreitung der Fegefeuerlehre bezogen – wandelten. Zur Vorstellung vom Purgatorium liegt für die Stadt Stralsund eine Studie vor, welche zeigt, dass den auf Dauer angelegten Stiftungen vom 14. bis zum beginnenden 16. Jahrhundert „ein[...] begrenzte[r], aber stabile[r] Platz in der Jenseitsvorsorge" bleibt, „wie auch an anderen Indizien zu erkennen ist, [dass sich] der Fegefeuerglaube in Stralsund weitaus später und weniger durchgreifend als in Südfrankreich ausgebreitet hat."[23]

Werten wir nun die Beobachtungen zu den beiden Zisterzen aus und beginnen mit dem Stiftungsaufkommen im Zusammenhang mit der Pest. Hier zeigt sich eine interessante Entwicklung betreffs der **Stiftungsanzahl (2)**: Ersichtlich ist in Abbildung 1, dass bereits um 1344, fünf Jahre vor der Pestwelle, ein signifikantes Abfallen der Stiftungsanzahl bei beiden Zisterzen erkennbar ist, die bis zum Ende des 14. Jahrhunderts keinen nennenswerten Anstieg mehr verzeichnete. Für diese Abnahme der Stiftungen zwischen 1344–1349 kann die Pestwelle mit ihren Folgen also ursächlich nicht in Frage kommen[24]. Hier dürften andere Faktoren wirksam gewesen sein, wie beispielsweise ein wirtschaftlicher Niedergang der Region, ein möglicher Attraktivi-

---

[22] Memoria wird hier, durchaus rational, als Trennungsarbeit der Menschen verstanden, welche erst durch das Wissen um deren Seelenheil vollzogen werden könne. Vgl. J.-C. Schmitt, Les revenants. Les vivants et les morts dans la société médiévale (1994) S. 18–22.

[23] R. Lusiardi, Die Lebenden und die Toten: Spätmittelalterliche Memoria zwischen Vergegenwärtigung und Vergessen, in: Annali dell'Istituto storico italo-germanico in Trento. Jahrbuch des italienisch-deutschen historischen Instituts in Trient 27 (2001) S. 671–690, hier S. 679; vgl. hierzu auch ders., Fegefeuer und Weltengericht: Stiftungsverhalten und Jenseitsvorstellungen im spätmittelalterlichen Stralsund, in: Stiftungen und Stiftungswirklichkeiten. Vom Mittelalter bis zur Gegenwart, hg. von M. Borgolte, bearb. von W. E. Wagner (Stiftungsgeschichten 1, 2000) S. 97–109; Siehe auch R. Lusiardi, Stiftung und städtische Gesellschaft. Religiöse und soziale Aspekte des Stiftungsverhaltens im spätmittelalterlichen Stralsund (2000).

[24] Dass auch die Pest als Ursache für den Niedergang der Zisterzienser in der Forschung angeführt wird, kann durch diese Ergebnisse folglich nicht verifiziert werden. Vgl. etwa B. Nagel, Norm und Wirklichkeit des Zisterzienserordens (Leipziger juristische Vorträge 15, 1996) S. 25–29; vgl. auch FN 21 des vorliegenden Beitrages.

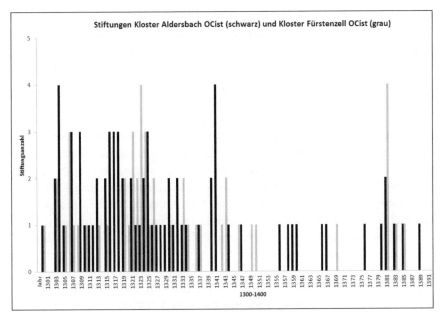

Abb. 1

tätsverlust der Zisterzienser[25] oder regionale politische Ereignisse. Gleichzeitig ist nicht von der Hand zu weisen, dass sich das Stiftungsaufkommen in der zweiten Hälfte des 14. Jahrhunderts bei beiden Klöstern nicht wieder erholte, was durchaus mit den demographischen Auswirkungen der Pest, aber eben auch mit einem bereits eingetretenen Attraktivitätsverlust des Ordens in einem Zusammenhang stehen könnte. Die Auswertung der Gesamtdatenbank wird hierüber detailliertere Auskunft geben können. Da der Wunsch nach liturgischem Gedenken für die Menschen im Mittelalter existentielle Bedeutung hatte, stellt sich also beispielsweise die Frage, ob dieses für die Zisterzen Aldersbach und Fürstenzell gewonnene Ergebnis bei allen Häusern des Ordens im Donaubistum auftrat, und zu welchen anderen Klöstern, Orden oder Institutionen der Region, evtl. Bettelorden, die Stiftungen ab 1344 gewissermaßen abwanderten.

Eine weitere Tendenz zeichnet sich bei den **Bestimmungen zum liturgischen Gedenken (3)** ab: Wäre nach den Erfahrungen der ersten Pestwelle durchaus eine Zunahme oder durch die Verbreitung des Fegefeuerglaubens ein

---

[25] Bei einer überregionalen Betrachtung konnte Dominique Stutzmann für die Abtei Fontenay einen signifikanten Einbruch der Urkundentätigkeit ab 1309 nachweisen, welche ebenfalls keinen Anstieg bis 1400 mehr verzeichnete. Hier kann durchaus ein leicht zeitversetzter Zusammenhang vermutet werden, welcher auf einen Attraktivitätsverlust der Zisterzienser hindeutet. Vgl. D. STUTZMANN, Écrire à Fontenay: esprit cistercien et pratiques de l'écrit en Bourgogne, XIIᵉ-XIIIᵉ siècles (2009) S. 152f. Die Untersuchung weiterer Zisterzen im Bistum Passau wird dies weiter erhellen.

kontinuierlicher Anstieg expliziter Bestimmungen zum liturgischen Gedenken in den Stiftungsurkunden (zum Beispiel Messe, Pitanz, Prozession, ewiges
Licht, Begräbnisort, Armenspeisung, Almosen, Aufnahme in die Bruderschaft
etc.) erwartbar, so zeigt sich hingegen, dass dies für die Klöster Aldersbach
und Fürstenzell nicht nachgewiesen werden kann. Auf das Auftreten der Pest
bezogen, verhalten sich solche Festlegungen in Relation zur Gesamtstiftungs-
anzahl gleich. Im Hinblick auf die Verbreitung der Fegefeuerlehre ist ebenfalls
keine überzeugende Veränderung festzustellen, da sich ihre Durchsetzung zumindest in einem sichtbaren Schwinden der Stiftungen ohne explizite Bestimmungen zum liturgischen Gedenken darstellen müsste, was aber nicht der Fall
ist. (Abb. 2a [Aldersbach], Abb. 2b [Fürstenzell]). Daraus lässt sich der Schluss
ziehen, dass der Fegefeuerglaube auch im Gebiet um die Stadt Passau bei wei-
tem nicht so stark verbreitet war, wie etwa in Südfrankreich nachgewiesen. Bei
der Pest ist ebenfalls keine direkte Auswirkung auf die geforderten liturgischen Gegenleistungen ersichtlich.

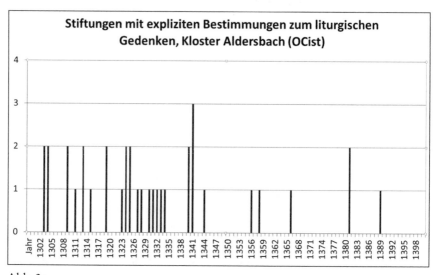

Abb. 2a

Ebenfalls markant ist, dass unter den 127 urkundlich überlieferten Memorialstiftungen für die Klöster Aldersbach und Fürstenzell bei der durch die Konvente geforderten Gegenleistung nur zwei die Vergabe von Almosen bzw. die
Armenspeisung beinhalten. Diese geringe Anzahl ist deshalb besonders interessant, da es sich ohne Zweifel um essentielle und bereits durch die Bibel be-
gründete Bestandteile zur Erlangung von Gnade durch Gott handelt, um von
den eigenen Sünden losgesprochen zu werden[26]. Möglicherweise deutet sich

---

[26] Vgl. ANGENENDT, Geschichte S. 337, 627f.

hier ein Wandel in der Stiftungsmentalität an. Diese Besonderheit wird durch die Ausweitung der Datenbank näher zu untersuchen sein.

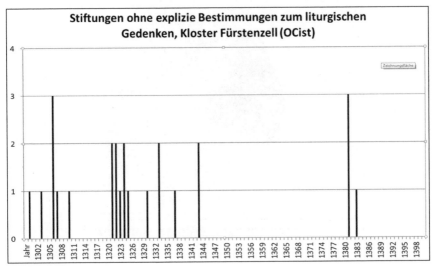

Abb. 2b

Abbildung 3 stellt die Stiftungsmaterie der Kategorie **Zuwendungen**[27] **(4)** dar. Auch wenn die hier untersuchten Mengen gering erscheinen, so sind sie im Vergleichskontext des Gesamtprojektes aussagefähig genug, um die spätere Auswertbarkeit des Gesamtbestandes der erfassten Urkunden[28] zu plausibilisieren. Die angegebenen Prozentzahlen sollen die Vergleichbarkeit erleichtern. Während Aldersbach (insgesamt 38 „Zuwendungen") in 25 Fällen (67 %) mit monetären Einkünften bedacht wurde, liegt der Wert bei Fürstenzell (insgesamt 22 Zuwendungen) bei 10 Stück (46 %). Dagegen erhielt letztgenanntes Kloster mit 6 Donationen (ca. 27 %) erheblich mehr Zehntrechte als das Mutterkloster mit einer Urkunde (3 %). Reine Geldstiftungen sind in Aldersbach mit 4 Stück (ca. 11 %) vertreten, während Fürstenzell keine Zuwendung dieser Art erfahren hat. Bei den Naturalienstiftungen kann von einem ausgeglichenen Verhältnis gesprochen werden (Aldersbach 7 Stück [19 %] / Für-

---

[27] Siehe Punkt VIII auf S. 5 des vorliegenden Beitrags. Gemeint sind hier also keine Stiftungen von Erlässen, Freiheiten, Menschen, bestimmte Liegenschaften, unbestimmte Liegenschaften, Bau- oder Klosterausstattung, sondern vor allem Einkünfte in Form von Geld (dauerhaft oder einmalig) sowie Naturalien (Getreide, Salz, Wachs, Wein usw.).

[28] Hochgerechnet von den bisher erfassten Stückzahlen, wird die Datenbank bei ihrer Fertigstellung ca. 2000 Stiftungsurkunden des Bistums Passau zur Auswertung bereithalten. Komparative Untersuchungen werden in Anbetracht solcher Quantitäten natürlich noch aussagekräftiger, als es die hier vorgestellten Beispiele andeuten können.

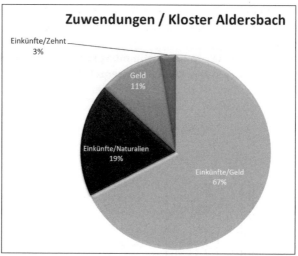

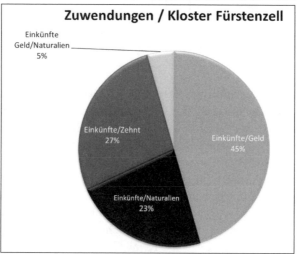

Abb. 3

stenzell 5 Stück [ca. 23 %]). Eine gemischte Zuwendung von Einkünften in
Form von Naturalien und Geld ist nur bei Fürstenzell mit 1 Urkunde (ca.
5 %) nachzuweisen. Dass beide Zisterzen etwa gleiche Zuwendungen an
Naturalien erhielten, darf als Hinweis auf ein klösterlich bedarfsbedingtes
Stiftungsverhalten gelten[29] und verdeutlicht den Vertragscharakter von Stiftungen für das Seelenheil, welcher den Austausch real-materieller Güter
gegen transzendent-spirituelle Leistungen beinhaltet.

---

[29] Vgl. dazu G. JARITZ, Seelgerätstiftungen als Indikator der Entwicklung materieller
Kultur, in: Materielle Kultur, hg. von DEMS., S. 13–36, hier S. 15–20.

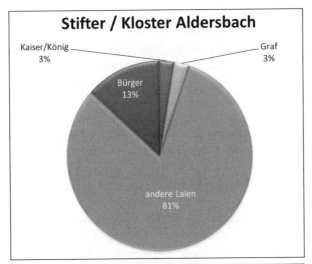

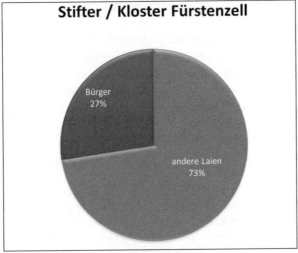

Abb. 4

Abbildung 4 zeigt die soziale Zugehörigkeit der **Stifter (5)** dieser Zuwendun-
gen: Aldersbach erhielt Zuwendungen von 31 (81 %) nichturbanen Laien
(Ritter, Edelfreie, u. a.), 5 (13 %) Stadtbürgern (Straubing, Passau, zweimal
Vilshofen, Krems im Hzm. Österreich), eine (3 %) gräfliche (Graf Heinrich
III. von Ortenburg, † 1345) und eine königliche Zuwendung (3 %) durch den
Habsburger Friedrich III. den Schönen († 1330). Fürstenzell dagegen ist mit
16 (73 %) Zuwendungen durch Laien bedacht worden und durch 6 (27 %)
Bürger aus Passau. Es wird ersichtlich, dass Fürstenzell neben dem Landadel
auch von Bürgern des näherliegenden Passau mit Zuwendungen bedacht
worden ist, jedoch keine Donationen durch den Hochadel erfuhr. Die ge-

nannten Zahlen zu den Stiftern lassen aufgrund der exemplarisch geringen
Quantität nur einige vorläufige Schlüsse zu.

Betrachten wir zuerst die Stiftung Friedrichs des Schönen im Zusammenhang mit seinen weiteren Stiftungen im Donaubistum, so kann eine Vorliebe
des Habsburgers für die Zisterzienser konstatiert werden. Von seinen 13 Donationen zwischen 1300 bis zu seinem Tod, waren sieben Häuser des Zisterzienserordens Empfänger umfangreicher königlicher Gaben. Daraus können
folgende Schlussfolgerungen gezogen werden: Zum einen war nicht die personale Bindung zwischen König Friedrich III. und der Zisterze Aldersbach
ausschlaggebend für seine Stiftung, wie sie beispielsweise durch Jürgen DEN-
DORFER als wichtiger Beweggrund stifterischen Handelns konstatiert wurde[30].
Auf der anderen Seite jedoch setzte er zugleich auf das Prinzip der Streuung,
wie es seitens der Forschung von Karl-Heinz SPIESS und Arnold ANGENENDT
hervorgehoben wird[31], indem er einen Teil seiner Stiftungen ebenso an weitere Orden vergab (Benediktiner, Dominikanerinnen, Kartäuser und Prä-
monstratenser[32]). Mit Graf Heinrich von Ortenburg stiftete der Inhaber des
Vogteirechts über Aldersbach an die Zisterzienserabtei. Hier wird die persönliche Bindung zum Kloster besonders deutlich. Blicken wir auch bei ihm über
den Rahmen der hier untersuchten Stiftungen hinaus, zeigt sich, dass Heinrich mit Fürstenzell die Filiation Aldersbachs und mit dem Prämonstra-
tenserkloster St. Salvator ein weiteres Kloster in seinem unmittelbaren gräfli-
chen Herrschaftsbereich bedachte. Folglich sind persönliche Verbindungen
zu den umliegenden Klöstern im Gesamtkontext seiner Stiftungspraxis eher
zu vermuten als der Wunsch nach einer möglichst breiten Streuung. Beim
Vergleich der beiden Zisterzen wird deutlich, dass Aldersbach eine deutlich

---

[30] Bezogen auf seine Fallstudie zum bayerischen Adel des 12. Jahrhunderts zeigt
DENDORFER, ausgehend von einer bereits in der Forschung angenommenen Streuung
für das späte Mittelalter, auf „daß aber personale Bindungen, sei es für die Versorgung
Angehöriger einzelner Geschlechter im jeweiligen Konvent oder für andere Adlige,
die dort ihre Memoria pflegten, eine wichtige Motivation für die Schenkungen waren."
DENDORFER, Verwandte S. 87. Für Dendorfer bleibt das die einleuchtendste Erklä-
rung. Vgl. ebd.

[31] „In der Verteilung der für das Totengedächtnis zur Verfügung stehenden Summe
an zahlreiche Institutionen ist unschwer das Verlangen zu erkennen, die Memoria an
möglichst vielen Orten von möglichst vielen Personen unterschiedlicher Lebensweise
zu sichern." K.-H. SPIESS, Liturgische Memoria und Herrschaftsrepräsentation im
nichtfürstlichen Hochadel des Spätmittelalters, in: Adlige und bürgerliche Erinne-
rungskulturen des Spätmittelalters und der Frühen Neuzeit, hg. v. W. RÖSENER (Formen der Erinnerung 8, 2000), S. 97–123, hier S. 109f. Diese Tendenzen erkannte A.
ANGENENDT bereits für das Frühmittelalter. Vgl. A. ANGENENDT, Theologie und Litur-
gie der mittelalterlichen Toten-Memoria, in: „Memoria", hg. von SCHMID/WOLLASCH,
S. 79–199, hier S. 191.

[32] So zumindest im Rahmen der noch erhaltenen Stiftungsurkunden.

größere Attraktivität auf alle sozialen Stifterkreise ausübte als Fürstenzell. Interessant ist die Stiftung eines Kremser Bürgers, denn auch hier ist aufgrund der Liegenschaften, die Aldersbach in der Region unterhielt[33], anzunehmen, dass diese Stiftung ebenfalls auf einer persönlichen Bindung zum Kloster beruht. Die zahlreichen Gaben landsässiger Laien untermauern den Forschungsstand, dass die Zisterzienser ein vom Landadel bevorzugter Orden gewesen sind und es auch im Donaubistum des 14. Jahrhunderts waren[34]. Jeweils etwa 3/4 der Stifter entstammen diesen sozialen Schichten. Im näheren Umfeld und in der Stadt Passau selbst existierten zahlreiche Klöster verschiedener Orden und Kongregationen. Die Stiftungen der Bürgerschaft an beide Zisterzen, vor allem an Fürstenzell, können ohne weitergehende Untersuchungen nicht näher bestimmt werden, doch ist es wegen der Anzahl an weiteren Stiftungsmöglichkeiten (mehr als) wahrscheinlich, dass sowohl Vorlieben für den Orden oder persönliche Bindungen zu den jeweiligen Konventen bestanden und die Praxis der Memorialstiftungen beeinflussten. Eine umfassendere Betrachtung der jeweiligen Personen und deren Stiftungspraxis kann darüber Auskunft geben, was die Auswahl der Klöster bestimmte. Zumindest ist festzuhalten, dass Aldersbach auch hier eine größere Anziehungskraft als die eigene Filiation ausübte, da – wie oben erwähnt – auch Bürger anderer Städte Stiftungen an das Kloster Aldersbach vollzogen.

---

[33] Dies wird durch weitere Urkunden im Bestand Aldersbachs belegt. Vgl. beispielsweise: BayHstA KU Aldersbach 146 (<http://www.mom-ca.uni-koeln.de/mom/DE-BayHStA/KUAldersbach/00146/charter>, Regest: Abt Heinrich und der Konvent zu Alderspach verleihen einen Weingarten beim langen Acker zu Wolfgraben an Frau Berhten von Golden zu rechtem Burgrecht gegen Abgabe von Guld, Wein und Zehnten und die Pflicht im Kloster pressen zu lassen. Bei Säumnis soll sie nach Chremser Burgrecht wandeln) oder: BayHstA KUAldersbach 211 (<http://www.mom-ca.uni-koeln.de/mom/DE-BayHStA/KUAldersbach/00211/charter>, Regest: Schuldbrief Pilgrims von Chrems über 13 Pfund Wiener Pfennig für das Kloster A. wegen eines Hauses, vordem dem Chuchenmeister gehörig, das Pilgrim vom Kloster zu Burgrecht innehat. Er verspricht jenes weder zu verkaufen, noch zu zertrümmern). Die Beispiele ließen sich zahlreich fortführen.

[34] „Während im Altreich und in Westeuropa der niedere Adel, insbesondere Edelfreie, manchmal sogar Ministeriale, in der Lage waren, neue Zisterzen zu gründen und sie auch auszustatten, so handelte es sich im Osten fast ausschließlich um nach Landesherrschaft strebende Geschlechter, denen daran gelegen war, die Zisterzienser in den Landesausbau mit einzubeziehen. Die aufstrebenden Landesherren stärkten so ihre politische Macht [...], wobei sie durchaus auch an bestehende Institutionen anknüpften." W. Ribbe, Politische Voraussetzungen und Motive der Ansiedlung von Zisterziensern in England und Deutschland, in: Zisterzienser. Norm, Kultur, Reform. 900 Jahre Zisterzienser, hg. von U. Knefelkamp (Schriftenreihe des Interdisziplinären Zentrums für Ethik an der Europa-Universität Viadrina Frankfurt/Oder, 2001) S. 13–36, hier S. 27.

4.) Schlussbetrachtung

Auch wenn hier noch keine verallgemeinerbaren Ergebnisse zum Untersuchungsgegenstand präsentiert werden konnten, sollte es aber sichtbar geworden sein, dass sich neue Perspektiven für die Memorialfoschung durch die
Nutzung einer typlogisch strukturierten Datenbank für die Analyse großer
Urkundencorpora eröffnen.

Folgende Ergebnisse lassen sich zu den eingangs benannten Fragen der
Studie zusammenfassen: Die Statistik der inneren und äußeren Merkmale der
Urkunde zeigt, dass die voll entwickelte, besiegelte Geschäftsurkunde, das
kleine Urkundenformat und die Volkssprache in den beiden ländlichen Zisterzen vorherrschen und kaum Abweichungen bei den äußeren Merkmalen
durch die soziale Stellung der Stifter nachweisbar sind. Inhaltlich lässt sich
feststellen, dass ein Abfallen der Stiftungsanzahl bereits vor der Pestwelle ein-
setzte, wobei die Zuwendungen an die Klöster, sowohl in der Kategorie „Art
der Zuwendung" als auch bei den „Tradenten", durchaus Unterschiede aufweisen. So wurde Aldersbach weitaus mehr mit dauerhaften und einmaligen
Geldeinkünften bedacht als Fürstenzell, welches dagegen deutlich mehr
Zehntrechte erhielt, hingegen keine einmalige monetäre Zuwendung erfuhr.
Weitgehend homogene Werte erscheinen in der Kategorie der reinen Naturalienstiftungen. Aldersbach wurde nicht nur vom niederen Adel sondern auch
vom Hochadel und fünf Stadtbürgern bestiftet und es scheint so, als besäße
die Filiation allgemein weniger Attraktivität für verschiedene soziale Schichten, als das Mutterkloster. Bei der Zisterze Fürstenzell zeigt sich, dass hier
neben dem landsässigen Adel auch sechs Bürger der Stadt Passau stifteten,
was auf die geographische Nähe zur Bischofsstadt zurückzuführen sein kann.
Eine Veränderung oder ein Ansteigen der in den Urkunden von den Tradenten geforderten „spirituellen Gegenleistungen" (Messen) nach den Pestwellen
konnte in den beiden Beispielbeständen nicht nachgewiesen werden.

Dabei darf freilich der Gesichtspunkt nicht aus den Augen verloren werden, dass in der vorliegenden Studie der Schwerpunkt vor allem auf die Methode und weniger auf die Ergebnisse gelegt wurde. Erst die Erschließung,
Auswertung und Einbeziehung narrativen Quellenmaterials sowie zusätzli-
cher Forschungsliteratur und -ansätze vermag es, die urkundliche Memorialstiftungen in einen größeren kulturgeschichtlichen und prosopographischen
Kontext einzuordnen und somit ein Fenster zu einem umfassenderen Verständnis von Memoria in der Urkundenüberlieferung zu öffnen. Die Verwendung und Auswertung einer typologischen Datenbank kann Tendenzen sowie
Entwicklungen unter bestimmten Fragestellungen aufzeigen, die angesichts
der Verstreutheit der Quellen bisher nicht quantitativ untersucht wurden.

Illuminierte Urkunden im digitalen Zeitalter
Maßregeln und Chancen*

MARTIN ROLAND

Am Beginn dieses Beitrages wird der Untersuchungsgegenstand anhand einiger charakteristischer Beispiele vorgestellt (1) und ein Beispiel exemplarisch etwas ausführlicher vorgestellt (1a). Anschließend wird eine Definition versucht (2). Dann folgen praktische Beobachtungen und Vorschläge (Maßregeln), wie man illuminierte Urkunden konkret in Projekte einbinden könnte und welche Perspektiven und Chancen sich ergeben könnten.

1) Beispiele illuminierter Urkunden

Von ottonischer Zeit an gibt es Beispiele, bei denen gemalter „Buch"-Schmuck Teil von Urkunden ist[1]. Nach derzeitigem Kenntnisstand stehen

---

* Die während des Vortrags in Neapel gezeigte englischsprachige PowerPoint-Präsentation, die naturgemäß über die hier abgedruckten Bildbeispiele hinausgeht, wird von der Ludwig-Maximilian-Universität in München unter der URL <http://www.cei.lmu.de/digdipl11/slides-rep/Roland/index.pdf> zur Verfügung gestellt.

[1] Das Phänomen ist den Diplomatikern seit langem durchaus bewußt. Bereits in der Revue archéologique 1847/48 veröffentlichte L. DOUET-D'ARCQ einen Beitrag unter dem Titel „Chartes à vignettes. Représentation de Charles V" (S. 749–756), der zwar nur französisches Material erwähnt, aber doch über die bekannten Beispiele aus der Regierungszeit von Karl V. (1364–80) hinausgreift. Einen profunden Überblick bietet A. GIRY in seinem erstmals 1871 erschienenen Manuel de diplomatique (vgl. S. 502–507 der Auflage von 1925 [diese digitalisiert auf gallica.bnf.fr]). W. WATTENBACH, Schriftwesen im Mittelalter (¹1871), weitet den Blick (erstmals?) über nationale Grenzen (vgl. die ganz kurzen Bemerkungen S. 221), die dritte Auflage (1896) enthält auf S. 383f. bereits eine ansehnliche Beispielfolge. Eine bemerkenswerte Initiative von Seiten der Archive stellt die Einrichtung und Publikation des Musée des Archives nationales. Documents originaux de l'histoire de France exposés dans l'Hôtel Soubise, introduction par A. MAURY (1872), dar, dem 1878 der Band Musée des Archives départementales folgte, der statt Nachstichen bereits photographische Abbildungen enthielt. Zur rezenteren Forschung siehe S. 261. An den Archives nationales wurde ein eigenes Selekt mit „chartes à vignettes" (illuminierten Urkunden) eingerichtet; vgl.

zwei Urkunden aus der Kanzlei der ottonischen Kaiser am Beginn der Entwicklung: das sogenannte Ottonianum für die römische Kirche von 962[2] und die berühmte Dotalurkunde für Theophanu, der byzantinischen Gemahlin Kaiser Ottos II., von 972, deren Oberfläche wie ein byzantinischer Seidenstoff gestaltet ist. Die Urkunde wurde in Rom anläßlich der Hochzeitsfeierlichkeiten ausgestellt und war offenbar ein zentrales Element der Selbstdarstellung des abendländischen Kaisertums gegenüber Byzanz[3].

Aus dem 11. Jahrhundert habe ich für diesen Überblick eine weitere „Hochzeitsurkunde" ausgewählt, die exemplarisch ausführlicher behandelt werden soll, um an einem ganz konkreten Beispiel das interdisziplinäre Potential aufzuzeigen, das das Studium illuminierter Urkunden birgt.

1a) Magister Mel und Alfarana

Die Theophanu-Urkunde enthält erstmals figürliche Elemente, deren Verbindung zum Rechtsinhalt freilich als eher indirekt zu klassifizieren ist. Bei der nun zu besprechenden Urkunde[4] sind die Darstellung – ein Hochzeitspaar – und das

---

Images du pouvoir royal. Les chartes décorées des Archives nationales XIIIe–XVe siècle, hg. von G. BRUNEL (2005) S. 36.

[2] 962 Februar 13, Rom; Rom, Archivio Segreto Vaticano, Arm. 1, Caps. III, nr. 1, = MGH D O.I. 235). – Die Theophanu-Urkunde wird im Folgenden als Teil eines performativen Geschehens interpretiert; die Hinterlegung des Ottonianums in der Peterskirche wird ebenfalls keine auf das Juridische beschränkte Handlung, sondern eine theatralische Inszenierung gewesen sein. Der Zusammenhang zwischen besonders gestalteter äußerer Form der Urkunde und der Gestaltung des „Events" ist sicherlich kein Zufall.

[3] 972 April 14, Rom; Wolfenbüttel, Niedersächsisches Staatsarchiv, 6 Urk. 11, = MGH D O.II. 21). Der Sachinhalt ist bedeutend aber durchaus nicht außergewöhnlich. Entsprechende Dotalurkunden gab es schon für Adelheid, die spätere Mutter Ottos II., die deren erster Mann Lothar von Italien zusammen mit seinem Vater Hugo 937 Dez. 12, Colombier, für sie ausgestellt hatte. – Die Form – Goldschrift und Purpurgrund – weist auf Staatspolitisches. Wurde im Ottonianum (siehe Anm. 2) das Verhältnis zur römischen Kirche bestimmt, thematisiert die Form der „Hochzeitsurkunde" das Verhältnis des westlichen Kaisertums zu Byzanz, indem selbstbewußt byzantinische Anregungen rezipiert und umgestaltet werden (Mustergrund mit Tierkampfmedaillons). Zum Verhältnis der beiden Urkunden zu byzantinischen Auslandschreiben vgl. die umfangreichen Angaben in: M. ROLAND/A. ZAJIC, Les chartes médiévales enluminées dans les pays de l'Europe centrale, in: BECh 169 (2011) [2013 erschienen] S. 151–253, bes. S. 153–158; vgl. Anm. 57.

[4] Bari, Archivio del Capitolo Metropolitano, Perg 14: G. NITTO DE ROSSI/F. NITTI DI VITO, Le pergamene del Duomo di Bari (Codice diplomatico Barese 1, 1897) S. 24 (Nr. 14); in der online verfügbaren Datenbank Pergamene di Puglia online <http://www.sapuglia.it/index.php?option=com_content&view=article&id=46&Itemid=66> ist unter <http://www.sapuglia.it/Schedatura/02_mostra_dati_front.php?id_perg=1153&pag=1> das Digitalisat des Eintrags im genannten Urkundenbuch und das

Rechtsgeschäft offenkundig und ganz unmittelbar aufeinander bezogen (**Abb. IV, Farbtafelteil**): Magister Mel *filius Natalis de civitate Vari* (Bari), Vorort der byzantinischen Verwaltung in Süditalien[5], heiratete im Dezember des Jahres 1028[6] Alfarana *filia Bisantii de predicta civitate*[7], und übergab ihr die bis heute

---

Digitalisat der Urkunde selbst verlinkt (Zugriff jeweils 5.9.2013). Grundlegend M. Cannataro, Un insolito documento privato Barese del secolo XI, in: Annali della Facoltà di lettere e filosofia 19–20 (1976/1977) S. 203–221; H. Belting, Studien zur beneventanischen Malerei (1968) S. 186f.; Alle sorgenti del Romanico, hg. von P. Belli d'Elia, Ausstellung Bari 1975, S. 112 (Kat.-Nr. 128: W. F. Volbach) und Tafel II. Neben der älteren Literatur, die im Katalog von 1975 erwähnt ist, vgl. Medioevo. La chiesa e il palazzo. Atti del Convegno internazionale di studi, Parma, 20–24 settembre 2005, hg. von A. C. Quintavalle (2007) S. 242, und A. Amati Canta/L. Sinisi, Il dono del mattino, in: 1087 i costumi della traslazione – donne, gioielli e promesse nuziali, hg. von L. Spezzacatene (2011) S. 57–68. Zu diesem Ausstellungsprojekt siehe auch Anm. 29.

[5] Zu den historischen Umständen vergleiche V. von Falkenhausen, Untersuchungen über die byzantinische Herrschaft in Süditalien vom 9. bis ins 11. Jahrhundert (1967).

[6] Die Datierung des Stückes ist problematisch: Es werden die Herrscherjahre Konstantins VIII. angegeben (nämlich das 69. Jahr), die Indiktion (nämlich 11) und der Monat (nämlich Dezember). Offenbar konsequent wurden bei allen Bareser Urkunden die Herrscherjahre ab 960 gezählt, dem Jahr in dem Basileios (der Bruder des genannten Konstantin) am 22. April Mitkaiser wurde. Oft wird der jüngere Bruder ebenfalls erwähnt, was jedoch (spätestens ab der Jahrtausendwende) nichts an der (gemeinsamen) Zählung ändert. Die Zählung blieb auch bestehen, nachdem Konstantin alleine herrschte, obwohl er erst zwei Jahre nach seinem älteren Bruder Mitkaiser geworden war (30. März 962). Bemerkenswert ist nun, daß die Relation zwischen Kaiserjahren und Indiktion, die dem griechischen Gebrauch folgend am 1. September wechseln sollte, egal in welchem Monat die Urkunde ausgestellt wurde, immer konstant bleibt. Der Wechsel scheint sich, wenn ich das Material aus der Regierungszeit der beiden Brüder richtig deute, jeweils am 1. Jänner vollzogen zu haben. Daraus ergibt sich für unsere illuminierte Urkunde, wie schon die Editoren des Jahres 1897 richtig erkannt hatten, eine Entstehung im Dezember 1028 und nicht (wie von Maria Cannataro [siehe Anm. 4] S. 203 behauptet) im Dezember 1027.

[7] Die Bezeichnung ‚Magister' für den Bräutigam deutet wohl auf eine angesehene handwerkliche Tätigkeit hin. Er tritt in zwei weiteren Urkunden (1030 bzw. 1031) auf und wird dort als *Mel ferrarius* bzw. als *Mel magister ferrarius* bezeichnet (CDB 1, wie Anm. 4, Nr. 16f.); der Name seines Vaters (*Natalis*) sichert die Identität des Mannes, der mit einem gleichnamigen Verwandten ein Grundstücksgeschäft abwickelt. So werden auch die verschiedenen Metalle verständlich, die bei der an sich formelhaften Aufzählung der Besitztümer vorkommen (*de auro vel argento, here vel ferro, stagno vel plumbo*). Alfarana entstammt einer angesehenen, mit der bzyantinischen Verwaltung eng verbundenen Familie; detailliert zu ihrer sozialen Stellung Cannataro, Documento (wie Anm. 4) S. 214–218. Daß auch die Darstellung selbst einen sozialen Unterschied deutlich macht (so Cannataro S. 218), kann ich bei bestem Willen nicht erkennen.

erhaltene Urkunde und ein Viertel seines Besitzes als *morgincaph*[8]. Die Zeremonie wurde *secundum ritus gentis nostre La(n)gobardorum* vollzogen und in dem über weite Strecken formelhaften Vertrag festgehalten[9]. Die Schriftformen der Urkunde des Notars Pandus[10] sind stark buchschriftlich geprägt[11],

---

[8] Zu den auf langobardischem Recht beruhenden eherechtlichen Bedingungen in Bari vgl. L. TRIA, La disciplina giuridica del matrimonio secundo le consuetudini di Terra di Bari, in: Iapiga 7 (1936) S. 392–419, bes. S. 409, 413–415, und 8 (1938) S. 19–62, bes. S. 24–32; A. AMATI CANTA, Meffium, morgincap, mundium. Consuetudini matrimoniali longobarde nella Bari medievale (2006; vgl. auch „Morgengabe" im Deutschen Rechtswörterbuch 2004ff, <http://drw-www.adw.uni-heidelberg.de/drw-cgi/zeige?db=drw&index=lemmata&term=Morgengabe&darstellung=%DC> (mit vielen Verweisen).

[9] Das hier besprochene Stück scheint der älteste Beleg für ein offensichtlich für Bari und einige Orte in dessen Umgebung (Conversano 1181, XII; Acquaviva 1373, V 11) charakteristisches Diktat zu sein, das – mit gewissen Varianten – bis ins 14. Jahrhundert verwendet wurde; vergleiche die Belege in der Datenbank Pergamene di Puglia online (wie Anm. 4), Stichwort „morgincap". Die für die Urkunde von 1028 so typische Aufzählung von Besitztümern (vgl. TRIA, disciplina [wie Anm. 8] 8 [1938] S. 26f.) findet sich (mit deutlichen Abweichungen) sonst nur in einer Urkunde von September 1060. Eine einzige der Urkunden (1202 XII 3, Bari, Protonotar Lupo) weist (nicht historisierten) Buchschmuck auf, nämlich Palmettenfleuronnée und zoomorphe Elemente (siehe Anm. 72); zu Palmettenfleuronnée auf Urkunden vgl. **Abb. IX** und den Abschnitt zu den Urkunden Kaiser Friedrichs II. auf S. 263 f. zu weiteren Notaren, die ihre Dokumente mit Buchschmuck ausstatteten siehe Anm. 73.

[10] Zum Notar CANNATARO, Documento (wie Anm. 4) S. 207 f. und F. MAGISTRALE, Notariato e documentazione in Terra di Bari. Ricerche su forme, rogatari, credibilità dei documenti latini nei secoli IX–XI (1984). Pandus ist auch aus anderen Urkunden bekannt (bis Oktober 1065), in keiner derselben verwendet er jedoch eine vergleichbar hoch stilisierte Schrift (CANNATARO Anm. 9). Sein unauffälliges Signet, wie üblich als Abschluß der letzten Textzeile, ist aus mehreren zu einem Konglomerat vereinten Spirallinien gebildet und (nur in dieser Urkunde) rot-violett und grün koloriert. Über den eigenhändigen Anteil des Notars, über die ihm zu Gebote stehenden Schriftgrade und die Frage, ob er vielleicht auch der Zeichner war (wie CANNATARO S. 207 glaubt), ist sicher noch nicht das letzte Wort gesprochen.

[11] Ausführlich zur Schrift und deren Verhältnis zu Buchschriften CANNATARO, Documento (wie Anm. 4) S. 208–213, die S. 209 unter anderem eine Urkunde von April 1024 nennt (CDB 1, wie Anm. 4, Nr. 12). Auf paläographische Verbindungen zwischen der Exultet-Rolle „Bari 1" (siehe Exultet. Rotoli liturgici del medioevo meridionale, hg. von G. CAVALLO [1994] S. 129–141, bes. S. 134) und zwei Bareser Urkunden weist Francesco Magistrale in seiner Beschreibung der genannten Rolle hin; er nennt die Urkunde von April 1024 und ein Stück von November 1028 (Bari, Archivio di S. Nicola, B7; CDB 4, Nr. 19 [hier 1029]). Beide weisen tatsächlich buchschriftlichen Charakter auf und ragen damit aus der Gesamtüberlieferung hervor. Unsere Urkunde könnte hier durchaus auch genannt werden, zeichnet sich jedoch zusätzlich durch die weiten Zeilenabstände aus.

als erster der fünf Zeugen unterfertigt Joannes (Proto-)Spatarios und Tur-
marca die Urkunde[12].

Während all dies dem zeitgenössischen Urkundenwesen durchaus entspricht, stellt die kolorierte Federzeichnung[13] in der Mitte des Urkundentextes eine, wie schon erwähnt, zumindest aus heutiger Sicht erstmalige, jedenfalls jedoch herausragende Leistung dar. Das Bildfeld wurde bereits vor der
Mundierung festgelegt, denn die Schrift nimmt auf den unregelmäßigen
Umriß der Darstellung Rücksicht[14]. Von einer Arkade mit zwei übergroßen
Vögeln umgeben tritt der Betrachterin / dem Betrachter das Brautpaar entge-
gen[15], das gemeinsam einen länglichen Gegenstand hält, der auf Grund der
Falten textil wirkt[16].

---

[12] Dieser hohe byzantinische Repräsentant und ein weiterer Zeuge verfügen über
geübte griechische Schriftformen, die drei weiteren Zeugen verwenden das lateinische
Alphabet. Ob es derselbe Amtsträger war, der bei der Festlegung der Grenzen des
Territoriums von Troia im Juni 1019 anwesend war (vgl. VON FALKENHAUSEN, Byzantinische Herrschaft [wie Anm. 5] S. 177–179 [Nr. 41]), müßte noch geklärt werden.

[13] Die Farben treten auch bei der Ausschmückung von Elementen der Schrift auf
und machen daher einen einheitlichen Entstehungsprozeß (nicht zwingend aber
Handgleichheit) wahrscheinlich. Bemerkenswert ist, daß auch das Notariatssignet des
Pandus koloriert wurde. Die grüne Farbe hat das Pergament stark angegriffen. Besonders deutlich wird dies bei den beiden Säulen der Arkade und dem Bodenstreifen,
der sich über die gesamte Breite der Urkunde erstreckt.

[14] Dies ist übrigens ein Phänomen, das Jahrhunderte später auch bei den Wappenbriefen der Reichskanzlei, deren Bildfeld ebenfalls inmitten der Schrift plaziert ist,
beobachtet werden kann.

[15] Ikonographisch gibt es aus so früher Zeit kaum Vergleichbares: Kaiserpaare wurden zwar häufiger dargestellt, sind jedoch nur sehr bedingt als Parallele zu betrachten.
Hinzuweisen ist auf das königliches Paar im karolingischen Stuttgarter Psalter (Stutt-
gart, Württembergische Landesbibliothek, Cod. bibl. 2° 23, fol. 57v [zu Ps. 45]; siehe
M. MÜLLER, Die Kleidung nach Quellen des frühen Mittelalters [2003] S. 104 und
Abb. 1), auf das Benedictionale des Erzbischofs Landolf von Benevent (Rom, Biblio-
teca Casanatense, Cas. 724/2, Sektion 5c [Hochzeit zu Kana; Exultet (wie Anm. 11)]
S. 95) und auf ein (nach 1087 zu datierendes) Fresko in der Grotta dei santi in Calvi,
das als Stifter ein Ehepaar zeigt (BELTING, Studien [wie Anm. 4] S. 105–111 und
Abb. 120). Während das karolingische Beispiel den Bräutigam in kurzer Tunika zeigt,
kleiden ihn die beiden späteren Darstellungen – so wie unsere Urkunde – in fußlange
Tuniken.

[16] Das Urkundenformular erwähnt ausdrücklich die Übergabe der Urkunde,
entsprechend wurde die Darstellung bisher auch durchgehend (und wohl auch zu
Recht) interpretiert. Freilich weisen weder die kompositorischen Mittel klar auf eine
Übergabe hin, noch ist das Objekt als Schriftrolle klar zu erkennen. Besonders das
zweite Argument wiegt schwer, weil in den Exultet-Rollen Bildformeln für Schriftrol-
len ganz geläufig sind. Sollte es sich jedoch tatsächlich um ein Textil handeln, wäre auf
(bis ins 20. Jahrhundert belegte) Bräuche hinzuweisen, die das blutige Leintuch der
Hochzeitsnacht zur Schau stellten.

Bemerkenswert ist die Darstellung der Kleidungsstücke, vor allem weil diese fest lokalisiert und datiert und zudem einer ganz spezifischen Handlung zuzuordnen ist. Dies ist umso spannender, weil in schriftlichen Quellen der Kleidung oft eine ethnische Gruppen unterscheidende Funktion zugeschrieben wird[17]. So thematisiert etwa die um 1100 entstandene *Gesta Roberti Wiscardi* des Wilhelm von Apulien (*Guilelmus Apuliensis*) die Wirkung von fremdartiger Kleidung erstaunlich prominent[18]: Kann man anhand realienkundlicher Vergleiche die Kleidung unseres Brautpaares einer der damals in Bari lebenden Gruppen zuordnen oder entlarvt die Darstellung entsprechende Texte als ideologische Konstrukte der Verfasser?

Mechthild Müller gibt einen Überblick über die Entwicklung der Kleidung im Westen, Maria Parani in Byzanz[19]. Keines der bei unserem Brautpaar zu sehenden Stücke ist nur mit byzantinischen Quellen zu belegen: weder die mit reichen Borten besetzten Tuniken an sich (**Abb. IVc**)[20], noch

---

[17] MÜLLER, Kleidung (wie Anm. 15) S. 65, 170–172 zitiert verschiedene Belege, die herrscherliche Kleidung ethnischen Gruppen (Franken, Griechen) zuordnen, wobei Zweiteres von den Autoren in der Regel negativ konnotiert wird. Grundsätzlich zum Verhältnis von ethnischer Zuordnung und Kleidung PH. VON RUMMEL, Gotisch, barbarisch oder römisch? Methodologische Überlegungen zur ethnischen Interpretation von Kleidung, in: Archaeolgy of Identity – Archäologie der Identität, hg. von W. POHL/M. MEHOFER (Forschungen zur Geschichte des Mittelalters 17, 2010) S. 51–77, bes. S. 64–74.

[18] Edition des Textes in: Guillaume de Pouille, La Geste de Robert Guiscard, hg. von M. MATHIEU (1961) Buch 1, Verse 13–16. Davor wird die Fremdheit der Sprache der neu ins Land kommenden Normannen thematisiert, dann, als erste Szene, begegnen die Normannen als Pilger auf dem Monte Gargano dem (langobardischen) Rebellen Mel, der sich gegen die byzantinische Herrschaft (erfolglos) erhoben hatte. Mel wäre, so der Autor, *more virum Graeco vestitum* gewesen.

[19] MÜLLER, Kleidung (wie Anm. 15); M. G. PARANI, Reconstructing the Reality of Images. Byzantine Material Culture and Religious Iconography (11th–15th Centuries) (2003) S. 11–100, bes. S. 54f. und 72f. (zur mittelbyzantinischen Tunika), S. 67f. (zu männlichen Kopfbedeckungen; mit Abb. 77) und S. 79f. (zu Ohrringen).

[20] Hier ist auf die ottonische Buchmalerei im allgemeinen (und deren Aufarbeitung durch MÜLLER, Kleidung [wie Anm. 15]) und im speziellen auf die westlichen Beispiele in den folgenden Anmerkungen und auf die in Benevent (also außerhalb des byzantinischen Einflußgebietes) in den 980er Jahren entstandene Exultet-Rolle im Vatikan (Biblioteca Apostolica Vaticana, Vat. lat. 9820) zu verweisen, wo ein Fürst und die mit ihm dargestellten Personen derartig ausgestattete (freilich nur knielange) Tuniken tragen (Exultet, wie Anm. 11, S. 111 und MÜLLER S. 172f.). Müller leitet die lange Herrschertunika aus Byzanz ab, betont aber wohl zu stark die Dominanz der kurzen Tunika, die sie für den Regelfall hält, während lange nur vom Herrscher getragen würden (z. B. S. 181). Unsere Darstellung ist ein klares Gegenbeispiel. – Ein entsprechendes Kleidungsstück, die sogenannte Tunika Kaiser Heinrichs II. (Domschatz Bamberg; vor 1127; **Abb. IVc** , MÜLLER S. 271 und K. KANIA, Kleidung im Mittelalter.

Details wie die Oberarmborte[21] am rechten Arm des Bräutigams, die untere Borte seiner Tunika mit dem vertikalen Teil in der Mitte[22] noch die Brautkrone[23] und die Ohrringe[24] der Alfarana. Ganz im Gegenteil, wollten wir der

Materialien – Konstruktion – Nähtechnik. Ein Handbuch [2010] S. 276), ist sogar erhalten geblieben.

[21] PARANI, Reconstructing (wie Anm. 19) S. 54 (mit diversen Bildbeispielen) kennzeichnet Oberarmborten als mittelbyzantinische Entwicklung. Entsprechende Darstellungen gibt es freilich auch (und wohl sogar früher) im Westen; z. B. die Darstellung der Roma im sogenannten Evangeliar Ottos III. (München, Bayerische Staatsbibliothek, Clm 4453, fol. 23v).

[22] Dabei könnte es sich um die etwas unklare Wiedergabe einer in Byzanz belegten Besonderheit des 11. Jahrhunderts handeln, nämlich eine kürzere, vorne zu öffnende Tunika über einer geschlossenen unteren zu tragen; vgl. PARANI, Reconstructing (wie Anm. 19) S. 54f. und Tafel 26; vergleiche auch entsprechende Figuren im Madrider Skylitzes (Madrid, Nationalbibliothek, Cod. Vitr. 26–2, z. B. foll. 23r, 164r [farblich der Urkunde vollkommen entsprechend], 222r), bei denen (wie bei der Urkunde) nicht mehr deutlich ist, ob es sich tatsächlich um zwei Kleidungsschichten oder bloß um eine besondere Führung der unteren Borte handelt. – Der reich illustrierte Codex der Synopsis Historion des Ioannes Skylitzes (verfaßt um 1070/80, über Ereignisse von 811–1057 berichtend) ist nach einem byzantinischen Vorbild des 4. Viertels des 11. Jahrhunderts im 3. Viertel des 12. Jahrhunderts in San Salvatore in Messina entstanden. Ausführlich behandelt in: M. ROLAND, Zeitgeschichte ins Bild gesetzt. Ein Versuch zur Materialsammlung bis ca. 1450 (noch unpubliziert).

[23] PH. DITCHFIELD, La culture matérielle médiévale. L'Italie méridionale byzantine et normande (2007) S. 455f. und 482, verwendet unsere Illustration, um die Brautmode zu beschreiben, und beschreibt die Kleidung der Braut (nicht aber jene des Mannes) als charakteristisch für die Zeremonie. Dies mag für die (Braut-)Krone mit Kreuz zutreffen (eine Krone ohne Kreuz in der Anm. 15 erwähnten Darstellung der Hochzeit von Kana), für die Kleidung selbst wäre dies jedoch erst mit entsprechenden Abweichungen zur üblichen weiblichen Kleidung zu belegen. Der Kronreifen im Kathedralschatz von Bari (13. Jh.?), den DITCHFIELD S. 482 nennt, hat keine erkennbare Beziehung zu Hochzeitszeremonien.
Die Krönung als Teil der Hochzeitszeremonien ist sowohl in der griechischen als auch in der lateinischen Kirche weit verbreitet. Weder ein von AMATI CANTA/SINISI, Dono del mattino (wie Anm. 4) S. 61 genanntes byzantinisches Beispiel (10. Jh.), bei dem die Verwendung ganz ungesichert ist, noch zwei westliche Brautkronen aus dem 15. Jahrhundert (der Hedwig von Polen [1475; Passau, Oberhausmuseum] und der Mechthild von Hessen [1489, Soest, Burghofmuseum]) weisen irgendwelche formalen Parallelen auf.

[24] Ohrringe aus dem byzantinischen Reich sind reichlich überliefert, sowohl original als auch in Bildquellen. Man vergleiche die vorbildliche Studie von A. BOSSELMANN-RUICKBIE, Byzantinischer Schmuck des 9. bis frühen 13. Jahrhunderts. Untersuchungen zum metallenen dekorativen Körperschmuck der mittelbyzantinischen Zeit anhand datierter Funde (2011), zum Ohrschmuck S. 98–111, 125 (Fundumstände weibliche Gräber), 128–131 (zu den Darstellungen). Zu den von Alfarana getragenen halbmondartig geformten Ohrringen vgl. BOSSELMANN-RUICKBIE S. 104–107, Abb. 96–128, S. 342–366 (vergleichbare Stücke im Objektkatalog, bes. S. 253, Kat. 68 [für

Chronologie Paranis folgen, dürfte es die weiten (von Müller als tütenförmig beschriebenen) Ärmel von Alfaranas Kleid erst ab der Mitte des 11. Jahrhunderts geben[25]. Tragfähige Hinweise auf eine Differenzierung von Kleidung nach (ethnischer) Gruppenzugehörigkeit kann die Realienkunde (zumindest in diesem Fall) nicht erbringen.

Abschließend ist noch nach stilistischen Vergleichen zu fragen[26]. Die Ableitung der Technik (kolorierte Federzeichnung) und die stilistischen Grundlagen sind mit den frühen liturgischen Rollen aus Benevent unbestritten[27]. Als sowohl örtlich wie chronologisch nächstliegender Vergleich bietet sich die Exultet-Rolle „Bari 1" an[28]. Wenn man etwa die einfachen, vom Gürtel

---

Kreta, jedenfalls vor 961], zu den Fundumständen vgl. 41–44). Bei den bildlichen Quellen ist nicht nur die schiere Menge sondern auch Objekte bemerkenswert, die das einseitig offene Tragen der halbmondartigen Ohrringe zeigen (S. 342, D1; S. 345f., D14, S. 348, D22). Die Überlieferungslage ist freilich auch in Süditalien ab der Spätantike breit; vgl. unmittelbar entsprechende Funde bei DITCHFIELD, Culture matérielle (wie Anm. 23) S. 496 und Abb. 69 und ausführlich und sehr ausgewogen C. D'ANGELA, Le oreficerie bizantine del museo nazionale di Taranto, in: Vetera Christianorum 21 (1984) S. 181–196, bes. S. 182 (Nr. 1), S. 183 (Nr. 5) und umfassend zum Typus S. 187–192. D'Angela bestätigt den unmittelbaren Einfluß aus Byzanz, will aber eine lokale Produktion trotz des hohen Qualitätsniveaus wegen der ganz einheitlichen Machart der diversen Stücke nicht ausschließen. Sehr ähnliche Ohrringe trägt auch die Braut der Hochzeit von Kana in der Anm. 15 erwähnten Darstellung. AMATI CANTA/SINISI, Dono del mattino (wie Anm. 4) 61 können belegen, daß Ohrringe in Bari auch als Hochzeitsgeschenke dienten.

[25] PARANI, Reconstructing (wie Anm. 19) S. 73 (mit Tafel 81–83). Da jedoch in der zeitgleichen Exultet-Rolle „Bari 1" (siehe Anm. 28) eindeutig erkennbare weite Ärmel vorkommen (Sektion 3a: Darstellung der Tellus; Exultet [wie Anm. 11] S. 137), ist die Chronologie nicht aufrecht zu erhalten (weitere frühe westliche Beispiele bei MÜLLER, Kleidung [wie Anm. 15] S. 185f., 188–190 und z.B. Abb. 57). – Dieser Befund wird auch nicht beeinflußt von der unklaren Darstellung der Kleidung der Alfarana: Statt weiter Ärmel könnte durchaus auch ein kurzer Mantel über einer Tunika dargestellt sein (vgl. dazu PARANI S. 84 und als Beispiel Abb. 80).

[26] Der grundlegende Aufsatz von Maria Cannataro widmet dieser Frage kaum Aufmerksamkeit. Die Autorin verweist auf eine augenscheinlich irrige Zuschreibung des Paläographen Armando Petrucci an den Zeichner der Exultet-Rolle „Bari 2": CANNATARO, Documento (wie Anm. 4) S. 205f.; Zur Exultet-Rolle (Bari, Archivio del Capitolo Metropolitano, Exultet 2) siehe Exultet (wie Anm. 11) S. 201–210 (F. MAGISTRALE; vollständig abgebildet).

[27] Diese wurden für bzw. in unmittelbarer Nachfolge des (Erz-)Bischofs Landolf von Benevent (Ernennung zum Erzbischof im Jahr 969) hergestellt; vgl. Exultet (wie Anm. 11) S. 75–118 sowie z.B. Alle sorgenti del Romanico (wie Anm. 4) S. 112 (Kat.-Nr. 128: F. VOLBACH).

[28] Bari, Archivio del Capitolo Metropolitano, Exultet 1; vgl. Exultet (wie Anm. 11) S. 129–141 (F. MAGISTRALE; vollständig abgebildet). Die Darstellung zweier byzantinischer Kaiser als weltliche Autorität (Sektion 7b) weist auf Basileios II. und seinen

ausgehenden Faltenlinien und die graphischen Gesichtsformeln in der Darstellung der liturgischen Szene (Sektion 3b) betrachtet, dann spricht einiges für die Nähe (sicher jedoch nicht für die Handgleichheit) der Ausführung.

Zusammenfassend ist – wie bei der Theophanu-Urkunde – auch bei dem Stück aus Bari, eine kulturelle (Byzanz, Westen) und (hier zusätzlich) eine soziale Gemengelage (Mel als Aufsteiger) zu konstatieren. Stilistisch und paläographisch kann das Stück von 1028 gut als Fixpunkt in die jeweiligen Entwicklungen eingebunden werden. Unsere Analyse hat die starke Interdisziplinarität gezeigt, die bei der Beschäftigung mit illuminierten Urkunden gefordert ist. Ein Ausstellungsprojekt des Jahres 2011 hat zudem belegt, daß auch die zeitgenössische Kunstszene von einem derartigen Objekte profitieren kann (**Abb. IVb**)[29].

Aus dem 12. Jahrhundert können eine Urkunde des schottischen Königs Malcolm IV. von 1159/60[30], ein französischer Chirograph von 1177[31] und eine Bruderschaftsurkunde von 1195 aus Saint-Martin de Canigou in den Pyrenäen[32] angefügt werden. Als Beispiele des 13. Jahrhunderts erwähne

---

jüngeren Bruder Konstantin VIII., die bis zum Tod des älteren 1025 nominell gemeinsam regierten. Zwar sind solche Darstellungen mitunter aus Vorlagen übernommen worden (wie Magistrale in Bezugnahme auf einen [in vielerlei Hinsicht nicht mehr grundlegenden] Aufsatz von Gerhard B. Ladner aus dem Jahre 1952 argumentiert), er selbst nennt jedoch gut nachvollziehbare paläographische Vergleiche, die in die (späteren) 1020er Jahre weisen. Eine Datierung um 1025 erscheint daher, gegen die übliche Spätdatierung auch wegen des Stilvergleichs mit unserer Urkunde am wahrscheinlichsten. Eine Spätdatierungen z. B. in: Medioevo, hg. von QUINTAVALLE (wie Anm. 4) S. 242 (als Vergleich eine Exultet-Rolle im Museo dell'Opera del Duomo in Pisa [Exultet 2]; siehe Exultet [wie Anm. 11] S. 151–174 [A. R. CALDERONI MASETI; vollständig abgebildet], wo die Rolle unter Vorbehalt nach Capua lokalisiert und um 1059–1071 datiert wird).

[29] Die Kostüme wurden im Rahmen eines bemerkenswerten künstlerischen Ausstellungsprojekts nachgeschneidert (**Abb. IVb**); vgl. den Ausstellungskatalog (siehe Anm. 4) und <http://www.1087.eu> (Link derzeit nicht verfügbar).

[30] E. DANBURY, Décoration et enluminure des chartes royales anglaises au Moyen Âge, in BECh 169 (2011) [2013 erschienen] S. 79–107.

[31] Chirograph des Mathieu III., Grafen von Beaumont und des Abtes Geoffrey von Saint-Martin in Pontoise, bei dem eine Federzeichnung des Gekreuzigten als Beglaubigungszeichen diente (1177; Paris, Archives nationales, J 168, Nr. 2: B. M. BEDOS-REZAK, Cutting Edge. The Economy of Mediality in Twelfth-Century Chirographic Writing, in: Das Mittelalter. Perspektiven mediävistischer Forschung 15 (2010) S. 134–161 (mit sicher viel zu weitreichender Interpretation); P. BUREAU, Couper le corps du Christ en deux. Un chirographe imagé du XIIᵉ siècle, in: Revue française d'héraldique et de sigillographie 71–72 (2001/02) S. 153f.

[32] ROLAND/ZAJIC, Chartes médiévales enluminées (wie Anm. 3) Anm. 33.

ich die Urkunde der Lupusbrüder in Köln von 1246[33] und eine englische Königsurkunde von 1291, deren Schmuck zwar keine menschlichen Figuren, aber mit den jagdbaren Tieren im unteren Bereich doch einen eindeutigen Bezug zum Inhalt der Urkunde zeigt[34]. So wie in England, wo seit dem späteren 13. Jahrhundert eine kontinuierliche Produktion illuminierter Urkunden zu beobachten ist[35], dominiert auch in Frankreich der König und sein Umfeld. Kunsthistorisch bemerkenswert sind Beispiele aus der Regierungszeit von Karl V. (1364–80)[36]. Dieses Portrait aus einer Urkunde von 1367 (**Abb. Va**)[37] steht dem berühmten Tafelbild (**Abb. Vb**) um nichts nach, es ist vielmehr fest datiert und der Dargestellte ist unzweifelhaft, zwei Eigenschaften, die die Urkunde dem Tafelbild sogar voraus hat[38].

---

[33] Ausführlich analysiert in ROLAND/ZAJIC, Chartes médiévales enluminées (wie Anm. 3) S. 9 f.

[34] A. H. ZAJIC/M. ROLAND, Eine spätmittelalterliche Urkundenfälschung aus dem Augustiner-Chorherrenstift Dürnstein in Niederösterreich, zugleich ein Beitrag zu illuminierten Urkunden des Mittelalters in: AfD 51 (2005) S. 331–432, hier S. 399 und Abb. 21 – der Beitrag ist auch online verfügbar: URL: <http://www.monasterium.net/ Zajic_Roland.pdf> und in Zukunft DANBURY, Enluminure (wie Anm. 30) S. 84.

[35] Für England ist vor allem auf die Forschungen und Publikationen von Elizabeth Danbury ; zuletzt DANBURY, Décoration (wie Anm. 30). Kurz zusammengefaßt in ZAJIC/ROLAND, Urkundenfälschung (wie Anm. 34) S. 406 f. mit Abb. 21–23, 26. – Die als Abb. 26 abgebildete Urkunde für Merton College (1380 X 5; Oxford, Merton College, MCR 370) wurde dort von der französischen Entwicklung abgeleitet, was sicherlich für den Stil zutrifft. Die ungewöhnliche Anordnung der Figuren – die Universitätsangehörigen knien links außerhalb der Initiale – könnte jedoch Vorbilder bei den illuminierten Avignoneser Bischofssammelindulgenzen haben; ein erstaunlich ähnliche Anordnung findet sich etwa in einem Beispiel vom 22. Jänner 1343 für ein Ölbergrelief an der Magdalenenkapelle bei St. Stephan in Wien (Wiener Diözesanarchiv, sub dato), bei dem die Apostel zu Christus im Binnenfeld aufblicken (siehe *monasterium.net* und ROLAND/ZAJIC, Chartes médiévales enluminées [wie Anm. 3] Anm. 86 und Abb. 18b).

[36] Dazu ausführlich BRUNEL, Image du pouvoir (wie Anm. 1) und kurz zusammengefaßt ZAJIC/ROLAND, Urkundenfälschung (wie Anm. 34) S. 402–405 mit Abb. 27–32.

[37] 1367 I, Paris (ohne Tagesdatum), Paris, Archives nationales, J. 458, Nr. 12: Karl V. und Philipp, Herzog von Orléans, beurkunden Modalitäten der Thronfolge und Bestimmungen die Apanage des Herzogs betreffend; siehe BRUNEL, Image du pouvoir (wie Anm. 1) S. 142–149, Kat.-Nr. 19; Zum Portrait in Büstenform vergleiche auch zwei Urkunden, die 1940 vernichtet wurden; ehem. Tournai, Archives, 1371 II 6, Paris (A. HOCQUET, Portraits de Charles V et de Jeanne de Bourbon sur une charte ornée [1371], in: Revue belge d'archéologie et d'histoire de l'art 3 [1933] S. 30–35, mit Abb.) mit unterschiedlichem Rechtsinhalt aber jeweils sehr ähnlicher Gestaltung.

[38] Die Identifizierung mit König Johann dem Guten ist wegen der zweifelhaften Originalität der Aufschrift unsicher. Die physiognomische Ähnlichkeit zwischen dem

Im 14. Jahrhundert ändert sich die Überlieferungslage grundlegend. Mit den Wappenbriefen (ab 1316) und den illuminierten Bischofssammelindulgenzen (mit figürlichem Schmuck zwischen 1323 und 1363) treten Urkundengattungen auf, von denen sich jeweils mehrere hundert Stücke erhalten haben[39]. Die Kurie wird im 15. Jahrhundert mit den Prunksuppliken und den Kardinalssammelindulgenzen zwei weitere Bestseller kreieren. Als **Abb. VIII** bilde ich eine Sola Signatura-Supplik für Altenburg, ein heute noch bestehendes Benediktinerkloster in Niederösterreich, ab[40]. Die Abbildungsvorlage

---

gut abgesicherten Aussehen Karls V. und dem Dargestellten des Tafelbildes hat u. a. Gerhard Schmidt dazu veranlaßt, auch in dem Tafelbild den Sohn König Johanns des Guten zu sehen: G. SCHMIDT, Rezension: Claire Richter Sherman, The Portraits of Charles V of France (1338–1380), New York University Press. New York 1969 (Monographs on Archaeology and the Fine Arts 20), in: Zeitschrift für Kunstgeschichte 34 (1971) S. 72–88, bes. S. 82–87; wiederabgedruckt in: DERS., Malerei der Gotik. Fixpunkte und Ausblicke, hg. von M. ROLAND, 2 Bde. (2005) hier Bd. 2, S. 311–328, bes. S. 320–326 und 328 (Nachtrag 2003). Der Vater, dessen Gesichtszüge deutlich abweichen, war 1356–60 in englischer Gefangenschaft und kehrte in diese 1364, dem Jahr seines Todes, zurück. Bei dem ungekrönten Dargestellten könnte es sich um Karl als Dauphin handeln. Dann wäre das Bild wohl während der Jahre 1360–64 entstanden, einer Phase der politischen Entspannung. Karl führte zwar nicht die Regierung (vielleicht daher ohne Krone) wie in den Jahren davor und danach, war aber trotzdem politisch und intellektuell führend. Viele Aspekte des Louvre-Portraits (auch jenen einer Spätdatierung, nicht jedoch den hier vorgeschlagenen) behandelt in: S. PERKINSON, The Likeness of the King. A Prehistory of Portraiture in Late Medieval France (2009) zum Bild bes. S. 1–9, 278–303; zur Urkunde von 1367 bes. S. 228–231, 290.

[39] Beide Gruppen werden ausführlich behandelt in ROLAND/ZAJIC, Chartes médiévales enluminées (wie Anm. 3); mit zahlreichen Abbildungen.

[40] Die (wie üblich undatierte) Supplik stammt aus dem Pontifikat Papst Eugens IV. (1431–47); vgl. dessen Familienwappen (Condulmaro) und die Tiara in der Initiale. Die Genehmigung der Supplik durch Kardinal Christoph von Rimini schränkt die Zeitspanne auf 1435–44 ein (F. FABIAN, Prunkbittschriften an den Papst [1931] S. 113, Nr. 2). Das durch die Archivsignatur implizierte Datum, nämlich 1300, ist offensichtlich irrig. Die Daten und eine kunsthistorische Beschreibung stehen bei *monasterium. net* zur Verfügung. – Die durch Tiara und Papstwappen historisierte Deckfarbeninitiale mit Blattgold verfügt über eine Bordüre entlang des linken Randes des Schriftspiegels und der Hälfte des oberen Randes; die vergleichsweise lockeren Fadenranken gehen von Akanthusblättern aus, die sich aus dem Buchstabenkörper entwickeln, und sind mit vor allem kleinen Blättern und gestrichelten Goldscheiben besetzt; als Abschlußmotive auch einfache Blüten. Derartige Fadenranken sind auch in der Buchmalerei durchaus üblich (allgemein verwandt z. B. Rom, Biblioteca Casanatense, Ms. 101, Initiale auf fol. 1r; vgl. den Online-Katalog der Bibliothek mit Abb.). Weitere so frühe Stücke bzw. solche mit unmittelbarer stilistischer Nähe sind mir derzeit unbekannt. Ob sich unter den anderen Prunksuppliken Eugens vergleichbarer Dekor befindet, konnte wegen dem ungenügenden Zugang zu Abbildungen bisher noch nicht geprüft werden.

stammt aus dem Projekt *monasterium.net*, das über 250.000 Urkunden kostenfrei online zur Verfügung stellt.

Als Aussteller illuminierter Urkunden begegnen uns Herrscher – vgl. die Angaben zur englischen und französischen Königsurkunde – aber auch „Private", diese vor allem im deutschsprachigen Gebiet und angrenzenden Regionen Mitteleuropas aber auch in Italien. Daß diese Privaturkunden höchsten Ansprüchen genügen konnten, zeigt exemplarisch eine Urkunde des niederösterreichischen Aufsteigers Caspar von Roggendorf, der „seine" Pfarrkirche Pöggstall bestiftet (**Abb. VII**)[41].

Die behandelten Rechtsgeschäfte reichen von Eheverträgen – neben den beiden bereits erwähnten sei auf eine Ketubba von 1391/92 aus Krems in der Nähe von Wien hingewiesen[42] – über Dokumente zu Gründungsvorgängen – herausragendes Stück ist der Stiftbrief von Dürnstein ganz in der Nähe von Krems aus dem Jahr 1410[43] – bis zu politisch hochbedeutenden Stücken: Dieser Kategorie gehören der „Zweite geschworene Brief" der Stadt Zürich von 1373[44], der die Zunftverfassung festschrieb und eine überaus modisch gekleidete Frau mit kühnem Decolleté zeigt, sowie die Veräußerung von Herrschaftsgebieten durch den Bischof von Basel an die Stadt im Jahr 1400 an[45], entscheidender Rechtsakt für die Entstehung des heutigen Halbkantons Basel-Land. Daß die beiden zuletzt genannten Stücke aus der Schweiz stammen, eine gewisse erotische Komponente zeigen und jeweils der Zusammenhang von Bild und Rechtsinhalt ungeklärt ist, ist erstaunlich aber wohl Zufall.

2) Definition des Untersuchungsgegenstandes

Im Zusammenhang mit dem hier vorgestellten Forschungsfeld verstehe ich unter Urkunden original vorliegende Rechtsdokumente (Urkundenausfertigungen), die gewissen inhaltlichen und formalen Kriterien gehorchen.

---

[41] 1494 XI 11, Wien; St. Pölten, Diözesanarchiv, Pergamenturkunde sub dato; ausführlich behandelt in ROLAND/ZAJIC, Chartes médiévales enluminées (wie Anm. 3) S. 74.

[42] Das Stück in der Nationalbibliothek in Wien (Cod. Hebr. 218) stellt das einzige illuminierte Beispiel für einen derartigen ganz formelhaften hebräisch abgefaßten Ehevertrag dar; vgl. ROLAND/ZAJIC, Chartes médiévales enluminées (wie Anm. 3) S. 66. mit Abb. und der entsprechenden Literatur.

[43] Grundlegend ZAJIC/ROLAND, Urkundenfälschung (wie Anm. 34), bes. S. 331–389 (mit Edition und zahlreichen Abbildungen).

[44] ROLAND/ZAJIC, Chartes médiévales enluminées (wie Anm. 3) S. 65.

[45] ROLAND/ZAJIC, Chartes médiévales enluminées (wie Anm. 3) S. 67 mit Abb.

Kopialbücher, die ihrerseits oft bedeutenden Buchschmuck aufweisen, sind daher hier nicht in unserem Fokus[46].

Illuminiert ist ein Begriff der Kunstgeschichte, genauer der Buchmalereiforschung. Er bezeichnet künstlerisch ausgestattete Handschriften und differenziert weder nach Qualität noch nach Umfang der Ausstattung. Neben Prunkhandschriften mit vielfältigem und immer historisiertem Buchschmuck[47] steht als unteres Ende rein graphischer Dekor ohne inhaltliche Verbindung zum überlieferten Text. Dieser Dekor kann in Bezug auf Umfang und Qualität sehr unterschiedlich sein, von höchster graphischer Finesse bis zu dilettantischem Gekritzel[48]. Daß gerade auch im unfigürlichen Bereich bemerkenswerte Vergleiche möglich sind, belegen die folgenden Abbildungen, deren Fleuronnée augenscheinlich aus derselben, in Köln beheimateten Werkstatt stammt: Die bischöfliche Ablaßurkunde aus dem Jahr 1307

---

[46] Es gibt einige Fälle, bei denen Kopialbücher auch äußere Merkmale der Originalurkunden mit überliefern. Dies bezieht sich jedoch in der Regel auf graphische Beglaubigungszeichen, am häufigsten Rotae und Monogramme. Einen seltenen Fall, bei dem Original und Kopie überliefert sind, behandelt L. MORELLE, De l'original à la copie: remarques sur l'évaluation des transcriptions dans les cartulaires médiévaux, in: Les cartulaires, hg. von O. GUYOTJEANNIN [u. a.] (1993) S. 91–102, bes. Abb. 1–2. Mir ist bisher kein Fall aus dem Mittelalter (sehr wohl aber solche aus dem Barock; vgl. **Abb. IXb**) bekannt, bei dem Elemente des Dekors illuminierter Originale übernommen wurden.

[47] Dem höchsten Niveau gehört etwa – um ein Beispiel aus meinem unmittelbaren Forschungsschwerpunkt der mitteleuropäischen Buchmalerei der Gotik zu wählen – das um 1400 in Wien entstandene Rationale Duranti der österreichischen Herzöge an: Wien, Österreichische Nationalbibliothek, Cod. 2765; grundlegend: Mitteleuropäische Schulen II (ca. 1350–1410). Österreich, Deutschland, Schweiz (Österreichische Akademie der Wissenschaften. Veröffentlichungen der Kommission für Schrift- und Buchwesen des Mittelalters I: Die illuminierten Handschriften und Inkunabeln der Österreichischen Nationalbibliothek 11), bearb. von A. FINGERNAGEL, K. HRANITZKY, V. PIRKER-AURENHAMMER, M. ROLAND UND F. SIMADER (2002) S. 149–178 (Kat.-Nr. 31: A. FINGERNAGEL) mit Farbabb. 19–26, Abb. 139–167 und Fig. 43–49. Die letzte Ausstattungsstufe des Rationale und der oben erwähnte Dürnsteiner Stiftbrief gehören derselben Stilstufe der Wiener Buchmalerei an.

[48] Dieser graphische Dekor wird – falls er gewissen Prinzipien gehorcht – als Fleuronnée bezeichnet. Dieser Dekorationsstil entwickelt sich im späteren 12. Jahrhundert im nordfranzösischen-flämischen Bereich und wird – mit zahlreichen für die Einordnung wichtigen sowohl lokalen als auch zeitlichen Wandlungen – bis ins beginnende 16. Jahrhundert angewendet. Grundlegend dazu: W. AUGUSTYN, CH. JAKOBI-MIRWALD, M. ROLAND, CH. SAUER, Fleuronné, in: Reallexikon zur Deutschen Kunstgeschichte 9 (Lieferung 105/106, 1996/97) Sp. 1113–1196 (Online verfügbar unter: <http://rdk. zikg.net/gsdl/cgi-bin/library.exe>, Artikelsuche „Fleuronné"); zur Beschreibung konkreter Beispiele ist auf CH. JAKOBI-MIRWALD, Buchmalerei. Terminologie in der Kunstgeschichte. Dritte, überarbeitete und erweiterte Auflage unter Mitarbeit von M. ROLAND (2008) S. 65–70 hinzuweisen.

(Abb. VIa)[49] dokumentiert eine wichtige Stufe auf dem Weg hin zu den figürlich illuminierten Sammelablässen aus Avignon[50]. Die Vergleichshandschrift,
das Wettinger Graduale (Abb. VIb)[51], wird mit guten Gründen nach 1334 datiert[52]. Wie mit den jeweils sehr zuverlässigen aber weit auseinanderliegenden
Datierungen umzugehen ist, bedarf noch weiterer Überlegungen.

---

[49] 1307 XII 28, Köln (Firenze, Archivio di Stato, Diplomatico, S. Pier Maggiore, sub
dato). Der Kölner Erzbischof Heinrich II. von Virneburg erteilt den Besuchern jener
Kirche, in der Reliquien (zwei Ursulabüsten) Aufstellung finden werden, an genannten
Festtagen 40 Tage Ablaß; als Vermittler wird ein Florentiner Bankier genannt (weitere
Details in ROLAND/ZAJIC, Chartes médiévales enluminées [wie Anm. 3] S. 14 f.) – Die
Vorlage zu **Abb. VIa** wurde der digitalen Sammlung des Archivs entnommen (<http://
www.archiviodistato.firenze.it/pergasfi/index.php?opadmin=0&op=fetch&type=per
gamena&id=839819>). Das Archivio di Stato di Firenze stellt mehr als 85.000 digitalisierte Urkunden mit über 240.000 Bildern ohne Zugangsbeschränkung im Netz zur
Verfügung. Die erweiterte Suche bietet den Begriff „miniatura" an. Klickt man dieses
Feld an, werden 490 Treffer angezeigt (trotz der vorhandenen Digitalisate leider bisher
ohne Thumbnails). Alle versuchsweise aufgerufenen Treffer bezogen sich auf Wap-
pendarstellungen, die verso offenbar zu Ordnungszwecken angebracht wurden. Die
erwähnte Urkunde mit üppigem Fleuronnée ist – grundsätzlich zu Recht – nicht mit
dem Begriff „miniatura" indiziert. Weiters werden Monogramme, Rotae und andere
graphische Beglaubigungszeichen indiziert (nicht jedoch die häufigen Notariatssignete).

[50] Diese Entwicklung ausführlich behandelt und reich illustriert in ROLAND/ZAJIC,
Chartes médiévales enluminées (wie Anm. 3) S. 14–21.

[51] Aarau, Aarauer Kantonsbibliothek, MsWettFm 1–3. Die drei heute noch erhaltenen Bände wurden für einen Konvent der Augustinereremiten angelegt; die reiche
Deckfarben- und Fleuronnée-Ausstattung stammt von einer Kölner Werkstatt, der
auch der 1334 datierte Kasseler Willehalm zuzuordnen ist (Kassel, Landesbibliothek,
2°Ms. poet. et roman. 1) und gelangten erst spät in das heute namengebende Schweizer
Kloster. – Die Vorlage zu **Abb. VIb** wurde der Datenbank e-codices.ch entnommen
(<http://www.e-codices.unifr.ch/de/description/kba/WettFm0001>), einem vorbild-
haften Unternehmen, das sich zum Ziel gesetzt hat, das in Schweizer Bibliotheken
bewahrte Handschriftenerbe elektronisch verfügbar zu machen. Grundlage der Metadaten bildet (wie vorbildlich angegeben): CH. BRETSCHER-GISIGER/R. GAMPER, Katalog
der mittelalterlichen Handschriften des Klosters Wettingen. Katalog der mittelalterlichen Handschriften in Aarau, Laufenburg, Lenzburg, Rheinfelden und Zofingen
(2009) S. 156–162.

[52] Das Officium de tempore des Graduales enthält das Dreifaltigkeitsfest am
Sonntag nach Pfingsten, das erst 1334 von Papst Johannes XXII. für die Gesamtkirche
eingeführt wurde; M. MOLLWO, Das Wettinger Graduale. Eine geistliche Bilderfolge
vom Meister des Kasseler Willehalmcodex und seinem Nachfolger (1944) bes. S. 5,
74 f. und passim. Der Werkstattzusammenhang mit dem Kasseler Willehalm (siehe
oben) sichert die Datierung zusätzlich ab.

Definition 1
Illuminierte Urkunden im <u>weitesten</u> Sinn sind Urkunden mit graphischen oder gemalten Elementen, die nicht der Kontextschrift zuzuordnen sind.

Damit ist jegliche Form dekorativer Ausgestaltung Teil des Untersuchungsgegenstandes eingeschlossen, auch aufwendige Auszeichnungsschriften und graphische Zeichen und Symbole wie Chrismon, Monogramme oder Notarssignete.

Da eine so weit gefaßte Definition eine nicht handhabbare Fülle an Material generiert, erscheint eine enger gefaßte Definition, die vor allem kunsthistorisch relevante Stücke herausfiltert, sinnvoll:

Definition 2
Illuminierte Urkunden im <u>engeren</u> Sinn sind Urkunden mit figürlicher (gegenständlicher) Ausstattung, die historisiert ist, also auf Inhalt, Aussteller, Empfänger oder Rezipienten Bezug nimmt. Weiters alle Urkunden, die Farbe(n) prominent in ihr Gestaltungskonzept einbeziehen.

Der erste Teil der Definition schließt rein dekorative figürliche (vor allem auch zoomorphe) Elemente aus, die vielfach zum Standardrepertoire gehören und keine besondere Hervorhebung darstellen. Der zweite Teil der Definition berücksichtigt, daß neben dem Figürlichen zusätzliche Farben das zweite entscheidende Element sind, das illuminierte Urkunden aus der Masse der Überlieferung hervorhebt.

Die Urkunde mit der Gautier, Abt von Chaalis, eine Meßstiftung des französischen Königs Karl V. bestätigt **(Abb. XII)**[53], zeigt die außerordentliche Wirkung, die Farben und Goldgrund in der sonst farblosen Welt des Urkundenblattes ausüben obwohl der Dekor unfigürlich ist.

Die Erfahrungen bei der Durchsicht von Beständen (siehe unten) haben uns gelehrt, daß eine so restriktive Definition an den praktischen Anforderungen vorbeizugehen droht. Ich schlage daher eine pragmatische Formulierung vor, die bewußt den für Definitionen üblichen Absolutheitsanspruch ein Stück weit verläßt:

---

[53] 1379 IV 2, Chaalis; Paris, Archives nationales, J 466, n° 52: BRUNEL, Images du pouvoir (wie Anm. 1) Abb. S. 35 und Text S. 50 sowie G. BRUNEL, Trésor des chartes des rois de France. La lettre et l'image de Saint Louis à Charles VII (2007) S. 93, Kat.-Nr. 103.

Definition 3
Illuminierte Urkunden sind Urkunden mit graphischen oder
gemalten Elementen, die entweder über das allgemein Übliche der Zeit
hinausgehen oder einen speziellen Kanzleigebrauch dokumentieren.
Besonderes Augenmerk ist auf Urkunden mit figürlicher
(gegenständlicher) Ausstattung, die historisiert ist, und auf die
Verwendung von Farben zu legen. Weiters sind Urkunden mit graphisch
aufwendiger gestalteten Beglaubigungszeichen eingeschlossen.

Gegenüber der weitesten Definition ist die Erfassung von graphischem Dekor
nicht absolut definiert, sondern bestimmt sich aus den Gegebenheiten der
Entstehungszeit und des Entstehungsorts. Die ist schon deshalb unumgänglich, weil graphisch mitunter exuberant verzierte Urkunden ab dem 15. Jahrhundert vielerorts zum Standard gehören und daher eine vollständige Erfassung dieses Materials als ‚illuminierte Urkunde‘ sinnlos erscheint.
Andererseits ist es aber zweifelsohne sinnvoll, graphischen (in der Regel gezeichneten, in der Neuzeit vereinzelt auch gedruckten) oder gemalten tinten-
farbigem Dekor beispielhaft zu dokumentieren (aber eben nicht flächendek-
kend zu erfassen); vgl. **Abb. IX.**

Der folgende Satz der Definition ist – strenggenommen – redundant, da
die angesprochenen Phänomene schon vom ersten Teil abgedeckt sind. Er ist
aber bedeutsam, weil hier jenes Material benannt wird, das im Zentrum des
Interesses steht.

Graphische Beglaubigungszeichen (vor allem Chrismon, Monogramme,
Rota, Rekognitionszeichen, Notarssignete) sind für das Medium ‚Urkunde‘
typisch und stehen im Schnittpunkt von Rechtssicherung, auf die sie keines-
wegs reduziert werden dürfen, und angestrebter Wirkung auf den Betrachter,
die illuminierte Urkunden grundsätzlich auszeichnet[54]. Der Zusatz „graphisch aufwendiger gestaltet“ ist notwendig, um die Fülle ganz einfacher Zeichen, die die südeuropäische Notariatsurkunde prägen und deren flächendek-
kende Erfassung in unserem Zusammenhang unrealistisch ist, ausklammern
zu können.

3) Wie finde ich illuminierte Urkunden?

Nachdem wir unseren Gegenstand zuerst an Beispielen kennengelernt und
dann definiert haben, können wir uns der Praxis zuwenden. Die Tatsache,
daß es bisher keine Versuche einer umfassenden Darstellung der Materie gibt,

---

[54] Ein kanzleitypisches Beispiel ist Anm. 69 erwähnt, kunsthistorisch interessante
Beispiele zeigen **Abb. X** und **Abb. XIII.**

weist auf ein Kernproblem hin, nämlich die Frage, wie man illuminierte Urkunden überhaupt findet. Außer der in Anm. 1 genannten älteren Literatur und zahlreichen Einzelstudien gibt es kaum zusammenfassende Literatur. Einen systematischen Zugang verfolgten Dénes Radocay, der die ungarischen Wappenbriefe katalogmäßig aufarbeitete[55], und Homburger und von Steiger, die an Hand eines Avignoneser Ablaßbriefes, diese Großgruppe vorstellten[56]. Ebenfalls an Hand einer Einzelstudie zu dem bereits erwähnten Dürnsteiner Stiftbrief haben Andreas Zajic und ich 2005 versucht einen ersten Überblick zu geben, der bis vor kurzem den umfassendsten Einstieg in die Materie darstellte[57].

Eine logische Vorgangsweise zur Vervollständigung der Materialbasis wäre es, Urkundenbücher und Archivbehelfe auf illuminierte Beispiele durchzusehen[58]. Die Ergebnisse sind freilich dürftig, da der Schmuck entweder gar nicht erwähnt wird, oder wenn doch, dann in einer erstaunlich unsystematischen Form, jedenfalls wird er nicht registermäßig erfaßt.

Daß die Digitalisierung von umfangreichen Urkundenbeständen ganz neue Möglichkeiten bietet, ist offensichtlich. Tatsache ist freilich, daß die Metadaten, die online verfügbare Sammlungen erschließen, in fast allen Fällen auf älteren Vorarbeiten aufbauen und daher für unsere Fragestellung kaum wesentlich hilfreicher sind als der Zugang über Urkundenbücher und Archivbehelfe.

---

[55] D. RADOCSAY, Gotische Wappenbilder auf ungarischen Adelsbriefen, in: Acta historiae artium Academiae Scientiarum Hungaricae 5 (1958) S. 317–358 (zu den Jahren 1405–1489); DERS., Renaissance letters patent granting armorial bearings in Hungary, in: Acta Historiae Artium Academiae Scientiarum Hungaricae 11 (1965) S. 241–264 (Text) und 12 (1966) S. 71–92 (Katalog zu 1490–1540).

[56] O. HOMBURGER, CH. VON STEIGER, Zwei illuminierte Ablassbriefe in Bern, in: Zeitschrift für schweizerische Archäologie und Kunstgeschichte 17 (1957) S. 134–158 mit Taf. 39–50.

[57] ZAJIC/ROLAND, Urkundenfälschung (wie Anm. 34). – Aufgrund dieses Artikels wurden wir zu einer Journée d'études (Moyen Âge en images. Les chartes ornées dans l'Europe romane et gothique) nach Paris eingeladen (2007), veranstaltet anläßlich einer Ausstellung an den Archives nationales, die die illuminierten französischen Königsurkunden opulent behandelte: vgl. den bereits 2005 erschienenen Band: BRUNEL, Images du pouvoir (wie Anm. 1) und das Begleitheft zur Ausstellung: BRUNEL, Trésor des chartes (wie Anm. 53). Die Vorträge erschienen 2013 in einem Sonderband der Bibliothèque de l'École des chartes. Eine ungekürzte Fassung erschien zeitgleich unter dem Titel „Illuminierte Urkunden des Mittelalters in Mitteleuropa" im AfD 59 (2013) S. 241–432.

[58] Auch hier ist das Internet und die Digitalisierung von großer Hilfe: vgl. G. VOGELER, Digitale Urkundenbücher. Eine Bestandsaufnahme, in: AfD 56 (2010) S. 363–392.

Wenn ich etwa in *monasterium.net* den Suchbegriff „Initiale" eingebe, erhalte ich 1475 Treffer (davon 911 mit Digitalisaten), also etwas unter 0,59 % (0,36 %) des Gesamtbestandes von 251.367 digital verfügbaren Urkunden (Stand 20. Jänner 2012). Wären die Ergebnisse in der angezeigten Liste nicht auf ihre Textbotschaft reduziert, sondern von einem Thumbnail des Digitalisats begleitet, könnte man die Treffer effizient durchsehen[59].

Das Problem ist jedoch nicht die Form der Anzeige, sondern daß nur wenige Treffer den von uns genannten Kriterien entsprechen. Angezeigt werden Freiflächen, in denen die Initialen fehlen, einfache bloß vergrößerte Anfangsbuchstaben, Initialen mit graphischem Dekor und mitunter auch Dinge, die zum Kern unseres Interesses gehören. Auch das wäre irgendwie zu bewältigen, aber die Tatsache, daß Dinge, die zweifelsfrei als illuminiert einzustufen sind[60], eben nicht erfaßt werden, entwertet die Ergebnisse. Von zwei Bischofsammelindulgenzen aus dem Jahr 1337 ist bei einer die Suche nach dem Begriff „Initiale" erfolgreich[61], die andere fehlt in den Ergebnissen[62].

---

[59] Entsprechende Adaptierungen sind bereits angedacht und werden die ersten Früchte einer sehr interessanten Zusammenarbeit mit den Kollegen von *monasterium. net* sein. Vergleiche auch **Abb. XIV** für ein Beispiel gelungener Präsentation.

[60] Ich nenne hier ein Notariatsinstrument über einen Kardinalssammelablaß für das niederösterreichische Prämonstratenserstift Geras von 1514 X 16 (Geras, Stiftsarchiv). Wie das Digitalisat zeigt, ist das Stück mit abwechselnd roten und blauen Capitalis-Buchstaben in der ersten Zeile, einer rot/blau gespaltenen historisierten Initiale mit Halbfiguren der Apostelfürsten Petrus und Paulus, einem Wappen und einer Darstellung der Sudariums mit Vera Ikon, diese drei in Deckfarbenmalerei, ausgestattet.

[61] 1337 VIII 3, Avignon, Bischofssammelindulgenz für die Margarethenkapelle in Göttweig; Göttweig Stiftsarchiv, sub dato: Die Metadaten in *monasterium.net* stammen aus: A. FUCHS, Urkunden und Regesten zur Geschichte des Benedictinerstiftes Göttweig 1: 1058–1400 (Fontes rerum Austriacarum II/51, 1901) S. 373f. (Nr. 397). Fuchs erwähnt die Initiale folgendermaßen: „Die Urkunde beginnt mit der Initiale U, in welcher ein Miniaturbild ausgeführt ist. Dieses stellt die heil. Maria mit dem Jesukinde dar, vor welcher ein Mönch mit erhobenen Händen betend kniet. Hinter ihr ist eine andere Frauengestalt stehend dargestellt." Wiedergegeben ist offenbar die hl. Margaretha, für deren Altar der Ablaß ausgestellt wurde.

[62] 1337 V 15, Avignon, Bischofssammelindulgenz für Pauluskapelle im Wiener Schottenstift; Wien, Schottenstift, Archiv, sub dato (alt Scr. 66, Nr. 13). Die Metadaten in *monsaterium.net* stammen aus E. HAUSWIRTH, Urkunden der Benediktiner-Abtei Unserer Lieben Frau zu den Schotten in Wien vom Jahre 1158 bis 1418 (Fontes rerum Austriacarum II/18, 1859) S. 212 f. (Nr. 186). Hauswirth bietet zwar den vollen Text und erwähnt die 14 Siegelreste, die farbig gemalte Initiale mit dem stehenden Christus und den beiden knienden Mönchen ist ihm jedoch nicht bemerkenswert.

4) Ein Testlauf

Es führt also kein Weg daran vorbei, die digitalisierten Bilder selbst und nicht nur die Metadaten durchzusehen. Und genau das habe ich mit Hilfe von *monasterium.net* probiert. Dabei wurde bald klar, daß der Anteil jener Stücke, die kunsthistorisch vor allem interessant sind, verschwindend klein ist[63]. Selbst in einem Bestand wie dem Stiftsarchiv Herzogenburg – insgesamt etwa 2300 Urkunden – fanden sich außer den vier mit dem Dürnsteiner Stiftbrief verbundenen, bereits bekannten Stücken nur drei weitere Beispiele der Kerngruppe: eine Bischofssammelindulgenz von 1341 und zwei neuzeitliche Wappenbriefe. Von den sieben Treffern waren vier bereits bekannt, von den drei Neufunden stammt nur einer aus dem Mittelalter.

Mir schien der Aufwand, den die Probedurchsicht mit sich brachte, für einen so geringen Ertrag zu groß. Andererseits begegneten mir viele graphisch interessante Stücke, die entweder für die jeweilige Kanzlei oder für die Zeit aussagekräftige Dokumente darstellen. Ich entschloß mich daher, nicht nur Material zu erfassen, das der engeren Definition entspricht (so war der ursprüngliche Plan), sondern auch die erwähnten graphisch reicheren (aber weder figürlichen noch farbigen) Stücke und solche mit Beglaubigungszeichen mit einzubeziehen.

Zu beiden Gruppen möchte ich nun Beispiele vorstellen, um deren Relevanz für unsere Fragestellung zu verdeutlichen:

Für die erste Gruppe steht eine Urkunde Kaiser Friedrichs II. für Göttweig aus dem Jahre 1237, mit der er das niederösterreichische Benediktinerstift unter seinen Schutz stellte (**Abb. IXa**)[64]. Die FR-Ligatur und andere Lombarden sind mit Palmettenfleuronnée versehen, und stellen damit einerseits eine für das 13. Jahrhundert vergleichsweise reiche graphische Ausstattung von Urkunden dar[65] und sie sind andererseits typisch für den Kanzlei-

---

[63] Durchgesehen wurden Bestände aus Niederösterreich bzw. Wien: Aggsbach, Altenburg, Ardagger, Baden, Dürnstein (Chorherren und Klarissin), Geras, Göttweig, Heiligenkreuz, Herzogenburg, Lilienfeld, Seitenstetten, St. Pölten (Chorherren bzw. Diözesanarchiv), Traismauer, Waidhofen an der Ybbs, Wien, Deutschordensarchiv, Wien, Schottenstift, Wien, Wiener Stadt- und Landesarchiv, Wiener Neustadt, Neukloster, und Ybbsitz.

[64] 1237 I, Wien (ohne Tagesangabe), Göttweig, Stiftsarchiv, Urk. 118; vgl. *monasterium.net*.

[65] Ein vertiefender Untersuchungsansatz wäre, ob die Tendenz Urkunden graphisch reicher auszustatten nicht auf päpstliche Urkunden mit durchaus vergleichbarem Dekor reagiert. Erfahrungen mit anderen illuminierten Urkunden haben nämlich gezeigt, daß sehr häufig politische Konflikte zu besonderen Gestaltungen und zu Übernahmen von der Gegenpartei geführt haben. Zu nennen ist hier vor allem die Urkundenpraxis der Kurie und Kaiser Ludwigs des Bayern.

gebrauch[66]. Sucht man nämlich in *monasterium.net* nach weiteren Urkunden Friedrichs II. wird man feststellen, daß derartiges Fleuronnée vor allem bei Privilegienbestätigungen für österreichische und bayerische Stifte aus dem Jahr 1237 immer wieder anzutreffen ist (**Abb. IXa, c–e**)[67]. Neben der Göttweiger Urkunde steht die barocke Kopie (**Abb. IXb**), die der Göttweiger Archivar Hartmann Dückelmann für seine Materialsammlung angefertigt hat[68].

Für die zweite Gruppe, die graphischen Beglaubigungszeichen, nenne ich einige Beispiele, die die Breite der Möglichkeiten illustrieren sollen: Zuerst

---

[66] Zum Kanzleigebrauch bei Friedrich II. vgl. S. GLEIXNER, Sprachrohr kaiserlichen Willens. Die Kanzlei Kaiser Friedrichs II. (1226–1236) (AfD Beiheft 11, 2006). Gleixner bezieht den graphischen Schmuck als integralen Bestandteil in seine Arbeit ein, der Terminologie und manchen Beurteilungen merkt man freilich an, daß der Autor mit den kunsthistorischen Aspekten der Materie nicht so vertraut ist wie mit den paläographischen. Die hier vorgestellte Gruppe von Fleuronnée-Initialen (ein Terminus den Gleixner nicht verwendet und der die hier auftretenden Formen im Buchwesen bezeichnet) bildet offenkundig einen Neuansatz, denn – trotz der vergleichsweise hohen Konstanz der „Schreiber des graphischen Schmucks" (so Gleixner) treten die in **Abb. IX** auftretenden Formen in Gleixners Untersuchung, die bis 1236 reicht, nicht auf. Ob vielleicht üppigere Fleuronnée-Formen, die Gleixner dem Kontextschreiber Cc zuordnet (S. 276f., vor allem Abb. 511f.) vielleicht schon von dem Florator von 1237 stammen, ist aufgrund der Abbildungsqualität bei Gleixner derzeit nicht zu entscheiden.

[67] Neben dem Göttweiger Diplom (**Abb. IXa**) und seiner barocken Kopie (**Abb. IXb** – siehe folgende Anm.) eine Privilegienbestätigung für das Benediktinerinnenstift Erla in Niederösterreich (**Abb. IXc** – Wien, Haus-, Hof- und Staatsarchiv, AUR, sub dato [1237 I, Wien]), eine Unterschutzstellung für das Benediktinerstift Lambach in Oberösterreich (**Abb. IXd** – Stiftsarchiv, sub dato [1237 I, Wien]) und Mautfreiheiten für die Zisterze Raitenhaslach in Bayern (**Abb. IXe** – 1237 III, Wien, München, Bayerisches Hauptstaatsarchiv, KU Reitenhaslach KS 48a). Vergleichbaren Dekor findet sich auf einigen weiteren in Wien ausgestellten Urkunden des Kaisers aus den ersten vier Monaten des Jahres 1237 (Heiligenkreuz, St. Florian, Seitenstetten, Wien, Deutschordensarchiv, Wien, Schottenstift), ist aber offenkundig nicht auf den Ausstellungsort beschränkt. Zur Verwendung von „bildhaften" Zierelementen und einem Streben nach Ästhetik vgl. W. KOCH, Das staufische Diplom. Prolegomena zu einer Geschichte des Urkundenwesens Kaiser Friedrichs II., in: Civiltà del Mezzogiorno d'Italia. Libro, scrittura, documento in età normanno-sveva, hg. von F. D'ORIA (1994) S. 383–424, bes. S. 411/416. Hier wird auch der in Anm. 65 vermutete Zusammenhang mit der päpstlichen Kanzlei thematisiert.

[68] Göttweig, Stiftsbibliothek, Cod. 895 (rot), fol. 30r. Zu Dückelmann (1739–84) und seiner bebilderten Quellensammlung (Cod. 895, 896) vgl. A. ZAJIC, Die Inschriften des Politischen Bezirks Krems (Die Deutschen Inschriften 72 = Die Inschriften des Bundeslandes Niederösterreich 3, 2008) S. L–LI.

eine ganz kanzleigemäße Schenkung König Heinrichs II. an Stift St. Florian aus dem Jahr 1002 mit Chrismon und Monogramm[69]. Ein Vertreter der umfangmäßig größten Gruppe, der Notarssignete[70], ist jenes des in Wien tätigen *Nicolaus olim Conradi de Ysenaco* (**Abb. Xa–d**). Die Datierung innerhalb des Signets ist aus diplomatischer Sicht ziemlich ungewöhnlich, uns interessiert aber in erster Linie das (vor allem nördlich der Alpen anzutreffende) gegenständliche Beglaubigungszeichen, hier – wie besonders weitverbreitet – in Monstranzform[71]. Südlich der Alpen ist die Situation grundlegend verschieden: Einerseits ist die Überlieferung dort unvergleichlich umfangreicher, da ein Großteil des Urkundenmaterials von Notaren ausgestellt wurde, andererseits sind die Zeichen in der Regel sehr einfach. Bloß vereinzelte (jedoch sehr spannende) Ausnahmen bestätigen diese Regel: Das Archivio Metropolitano di Bari bewahrt z. B. eine Urkunde auf, auf der das Zeichen des um 1200 in Bari tätigen Protonotars Lupo sichtbar ist, nämlich einen durchaus naturnah gezeichneten Wolf[72]. Die Neapolitaner Notare Dionisio de Sarno und Ruggeriero Pappansogna statteten in den 1420er Jahren Dokumente sogar mit Farbe und figürlichen, mitunter sogar

---

[69] 1002 VII 20, Kirchberg; St. Florian, Stiftsarchiv, sub dato; vgl. MGH, D.H.II.7 und <http://www.hgw-online.net/abbildungsverzeichnis/dh-ii-7>; im von Irmgard Fees betreuten Abbildungsverzeichnis (<http://www.hgw-online.net/abbildungsverzeichnis>) sind alle Abbildungen zu europäischen Kaiser- und Königsurkunden aufgenommen. Die Urkunde ist in *monasterium.net* digital verfügbar (mit irrigem Datum: 1002 VII 18). – Daß die beiden hier vorgestellten Gruppen sich überschneiden können, zeigen einige besonders feierliche Urkunden Kaiser Friedrichs II. aus dem Jahr 1237, die von einem Chrismon mit Fleuronnée-Dekor der oben beschriebenen Hand eingeleitet werden.

[70] In diesem Zusammenhang ist auf großangelegte Studien zu Notarszeichen hinzuweisen, die durch derartige Online-Sammlungen kongenial ergänzt werden könnten und die Basis für den bisher fehlenden Gesamtüberblick bilden könnten: diverse Beiträge in Graphische Symbole in mittelalterlichen Urkunden. Beiträge zur diplomatischen Semiotik, hg. von P. Rück (Historische Hilfswissenschaften 3, 1996); P.-J. Schuler, Südwestdeutsche Notarszeichen. Mit einer Einleitung über die Geschichte des deutschen Notarszeichen (1976); E. Reckenzaun, Zur Kunstgeschichte des Notariatssignets in der Steiermark von 1344 bis zur Mitte des 16. Jahrhunderts, in: Mitteilungen des Steiermärkischen Landesarchivs 52–53 (2004) S. 119–155; E. Kern, Notare und Notariatssignete vom Mittelalter bis zum Jahre 1600 aus den Beständen der staatlichen Archive Bayerns (2008).

[71] Zu diesem Typus und der Frage der Gegenständlichkeit vergleiche eine kurze Bemerkung von P.-J. Schuler, Genese und Symbolik des nordeuropäischen Notarszeichen, in: Graphische Symbole, hg. von Rück (wie Anm. 70) S. 669–687, bes. 671f.

[72] Zur Datenbank siehe Anm. 4. Sechs Urkunden seiner Hand sind hier von 1189 bis 1216 nachweisbar. Eine davon zusätzlich mit gezeichnetem, teilweise zoomorphem Dekor (vgl. Anm. 9).

historisierten Elementen und Wappen aus; ihre Notarssignete, sind ebenfalls farbig und haben die oben erwähnte Monstranzform[73].

Zuletzt einen Sonderfall aus dem Königreich Leon: Die vom päpstlichen Kanzleigebrauch abgeleitete Rota (rueda; signum rodado) wird vom Siegeltier des Königreichs, dem Löwen, beherrscht **(Abb. XIII)**[74]. Unter Alfonso IX. (1188–1230) fallen mitunter die konzentrischen Kreise weg, der Löwe steht dann unvermittelt auf dem Pergament[75] und ist – obwohl weiterhin „heraldisch" geformt – von einer zoologischen Illustration optisch nicht zu unterscheiden. Das Beglaubigungszeichen nähert sich den Standards der Buchkunst an.

Als Resultat des Testlaufes kann man festhalten: Wenn man die eben umschriebenen Erweiterungen mitberücksichtigt und keine zeitliche Grenze in die Neuzeit festlegt, dann ergeben sich – bezogen auf den Bestand in Herzogenburg – 230 ausgewählte Stücke, ziemlich genau 10 % des digitalisierten Bestandes. Hochgerechnet auf den Gesamtbestand der von *monasterium.net* digitalisierten Urkunden ergäbe sich eine Sammlung von 25.000 Urkunden.

5) Perspektiven

a) Ganz schnell und ohne großen Aufwand könnten Thumbnails in die Datenbanken eingebaut werden. **Abb. XIV** zeigt eine leicht veränderte Ansicht, der Präsentation des Bestandes H 52 (Bemalte Urkunden) des Hauptstaatsarchivs Stuttgart, wo dies bereits vorbildlich gelöst ist[76].

b) Deutlich aufwendiger ist die Durchsicht der (digitalen) Bestände und das Zusammenstellen der gefundenen illuminierten Stücke zu Gruppen. Eine

---

[73] In der Datenbank *monasterium.net* sind sieben Beispiele nachweisbar; eine Fälschung auf das Jahr 1409 X 15, fünf Stücke aus dem Jahr 1423 und eines aus dem Jahr 1426; alle Stücke in der Biblioteca della Società Napoletana di Storia Patria in Neapel (9CCI–27 bis –33). Ich danke Antonella Ambrosio für die Gelegenheit die Stücke im Rahmen der Tagung in Neapel im Original studieren zu dürfen. Vgl. auch Gli inventari dei monasteri di San Pietro a Castello e di San Sebastiano rogati dai notai Dionisio de Sarno e Ruggiero Pappansogna (1423–1426), hg. von S. Severino (2010).

[74] Vgl. A. Martín Fuertes, El signum regis en el Reino de Léon (1157–1230). Notas sobre su simbolismo, in: Graphische Symbole, hg. von Rück (wie Anm. 70) S. 463–478.

[75] Martín Fuertes, Signum regis (wie Anm. 74) S. 473–478.

[76] Das Urkundenselekt wurde 1940 von Max Miller gebildet und in Folge erweitert. Die Online-Präsentation (https://www2.landesarchiv-bw.de/ofs21/olf/struktur.php?bestand=5147&klassi=&anzeigeKlassi=001) haben Axel Metz, Martin Schlemmer, Ulrich Schludi, Martin Spiller, Stefan Sudmann und Peter Rückert erarbeitet.

mögliche Vorgangsweise basierend auf den Beständen von *monasterium. net* wurde in Abschnitt 4 vorgestellt[77].

c) Über das Auffinden hinaus muß natürlich auch die Erschließung bedacht werden. Die ausgewählten Stücke müssen mit ganz wenigen Normbegriffen beschlagwortet werden, um so deren graphische bzw. malerische Ausstattung zu erschließen. Ich schlage folgende, einfach durch Ankreuzen auszufüllende Liste vor:

Illuminierte Urkunden im engeren Sinn (Niveau 1)
- ☐ Historisierter Dekor
  - ☐ Miniaturen ☐ Initialen
  - ☐ Randdekor ☐ Wappen
  - ☐ gezeichnet ☐ gemält
- ☐ Zusätzliche Farben

Graphisch bemerkenswerte weitere Stücke (Niveau 2)
- ☐ Gezeichnete Ausstattung (nicht historisiert)
  - ☐ Ornamentfelder ☐ Initialen ☐ Randdekor
- ☐ Gegenständliche Motive (nicht historisiert)
  - ☐ figürlich ☐ zoomorph ☐ andere
- ☐ Auszeichnungsschrift mit dekorativem Charakter

Graphische Beglaubigungszeichen (Niveau 3)
- ☐ Chrismon
- ☐ Monogramm
- ☐ Rota
- ☐ Signum recognitionis
- ☐ Signum notarile
- ☐ Andere Beglaubigungszeichen
- ☐ Anderer Dekor

Urkunden mit diesen Normbegriffen zu versehen, sollte auch kunsthistorischen Laien ohne große Schwierigkeiten möglich sein[78]. Die Supervision

---

[77] Zuletzt haben sich Kontakte zu Kollegen Björn Ommer in Freiburg ergeben, der sich mit Bilderkennung auseinandersetzt. Er geht davon aus, daß man mit beherrschbarem Aufwand diese Auswahl automatisieren könnte, daß also der Computer Urkunden mit Farben, Bildfeldern, graphischem Randschmuck, mit Chrismon, Monogramm, Rota oder Notarssignets erkennen könnte. Ob diese Verlagerung allerdings wünschenswert ist, muß genau überlegt werden, denn eine erneute Durchsicht wäre wohl kaum realistisch. Ein vergleichendes Pilotprojekt sollte aber Teil eines Projektantrages zur Identifizierung illuminierter Urkunden sein.

[78] Nach dem Vortrag in Neapel konnten die Teilnehmer der Tagung einen praktischen Versuch unternehmen. Sie erhielten Abbildungen von vier Urkunden und die obige Liste, wahlweise die in den Sprachen Deutsch, Italienisch, Englisch oder Fran-

und Beurteilung im Detail sowie das ikonographische Register müssen
aber natürlich dem ausgebildeten Kunsthistoriker vorbehalten bleiben, um
Einheitlichkeit und qualitativen Standard zu garantieren.

Nach Abschluß der Arbeiten steht eine grob in Gruppen geordnete Bil-
dersammlung zur Verfügung mit graphisch bemerkenswerten Beispielen
und Rekognitionszeichen, der in weiteren Schritten wissenschaftlich
strukturiert und ausgewertet werden kann.

d) Unabhängig von der Bestandsdurchsicht sollte man gezielt illuminierte
Urkunden im engeren Sinn sammeln. Dazu sind bereits erhebliche Vorarbeiten geleistet: Andreas Zajic und ich haben eine elektronische Materialsammlung aufgebaut, die über 400 Beispiele dokumentiert, wobei sich
durch die systematische Einarbeitung aller jener Stücke, die in der von uns
gesammelten Literatur erwähnt werden, der Bestand wohl zumindest ver-
doppeln ließe, freilich vor allem durch zusätzliche Bischofssammelindulgenzen und Wappenbriefe. Ich kann mir gut vorstellen, daß in absehbarer
Zeit vielleicht 1000 oder 1500 illuminierte Urkunden elektronisch verzeichnet sein werden, die einen Großteil der illuminierten Urkunden im
engeren Sinn bis ca. 1520 umfassen.

6) Wem nützt die Kenntnis illuminierter Urkunden?

Offensichtlich der Kunstgeschichte, denn sie erhält Zugang zu neuem, in
der Regel sowohl lokalisiertem als auch datiertem Material. Zu welch spannen-
den Fragen diese urkundenspezifischen Fakten führen können, habe ich oben
an einem Beispiel demonstriert (siehe S. 257 f. und **Abb. VIa** und **Abb. VIb**).

Die Katalogisierung illuminierter Urkunden nützt den Archiven, denn
ihnen steht ein wissenschaftlich aufgearbeiteter Bestand an optisch interes-
santem Material zur Verfügung, der z. B. für Ausstellungsanfragen genutzt
werden kann.

Die Diplomatik hat bisher vergleichsweise wenig Interesse an äußeren
Merkmalen der Urkunden gezeigt, zumal wenn diese nicht der Beglaubigung
dienen. Dabei sollte sie sich schon längst gefragt haben, warum manche
Stücke so prächtig ausgestattet wurden. Dies geschah wohl kaum als l'art
pour l'art. Kaiser Ludwig der Bayer dokumentierte ohne ein Wort seine her-
vorgehobene Stellung durch die Identifikation mit dem siegreichen Adler
(Abb. XV)[79]. Die Darstellung des Kirchenpatrons auf einem illuminierten

---

zösisch, und konnten ankreuzen; siehe <http://www.cei.lmu.de/digdipl11/slides-rep/
Roland/Bsp.pdf>

[79] Die grundlegende Studie zu den illuminierten Urkunden Kaiser Ludwigs stammt
von CH. WREDE, Leonhard von München, der Meister der Prunkurkunden Kaiser

Sammelablaß – offensichtlich für jeden Kirchenbesucher – hat die Freigiebigkeit des bußfertigen Besuchers, durch den Ablaß befreit von befürchteter Strafe, sicherlich erheblich gesteigert und hat so die zusätzlichen Herstellungskosten eines illuminieren Stückes gerechtfertigt. Der soziale Aufsteiger hat seine Kollegen (abends bei einem Glas Wein) mit einem schön gemalten und bunten Wappenbrief beeindruckt, ein neu gegründetes Kloster hat sich mit einem repräsentativen Stück ein Identifikationsobjekt – gleichsam als Ersatz für lange Tradition – zugelegt.

So modern das alles klingt, diese mediale, auf den Betrachter fokussierte Komponente kennt die Diplomatik schon lange: Freilich wurde dies – zumindest bei meinen Diplomatik- bzw. Paläographievorlesungen – an Hand der *litterae caelestes*[80] abgehandelt, also einer spätantiken (2.–5. Jh.) kaiserlichen Reservatschrift für Urkunden auf Papyrus.

7) Schlußwort

Illuminierte Urkunden wirkten auf Zeitgenossen, auf mittelalterliche Nachnutzer und sie wirken – wie der Erfolg bei Ausstellungen zeigt – auch auf heutige Betrachter. Diese Photomontage **(Abb. XI)** kombiniert einen Ferrari und einen Fiat Cinquecento mit dem noch ganz schmucklosen Wappenbrief des ungarischen Königs Ludwig des Großen für Kaschau/Kosice von 1369 und dessen Bestätigung durch Sigismund von 1423, jetzt eine Pracht, von einem führenden Buchmideratelier der Zeit ausgeführt[81]. Beide Urkunden besagen weitgehend dasselbe; auch mit beiden Fahrzeugen gelangt man von A nach B, bloß „WIE", das ist die entscheidende Frage.

Die Chancen, die sich durch die Erforschung illuminierter Urkunden bieten, liegen im kreativen Potential, das sich aus der impliziten Spannung zwischen dem Rechtsdokument *Urkunde* und dem *Bild* bzw. *Kunstwerk* mit dessen medienspezifischer Ausrichtung auf den Betrachter hin ergibt.

Wenn man also die beschriebenen Maßregeln befolgt, besteht die realistische Chance mit überschaubarem und kalkulierbarem Aufwand ein Material aufzubereiten, das in seiner gesamteuropäischen Dimension und durch seinen viele Teildisziplinen beschäftigenden Charakter der Mediävistik neue Impulse geben kann.

Ludwigs des Bayern (1980); diese Urkunde als Kat.-Nr. 17 behandelt.

[80] O. Kresten, Zur Frage der "Litterae caelestes", in: Jahrbuch der österreichischen byzantinischen Gesellschaft 14 (1965) S. 13–20; vgl. auch B. Bischoff, Paläographie des römischen Altertums und des abendländischen Mittelalters (1979) S. 83.

[81] Die beiden städtischen Wappenbriefen und die kunsthistorische Einordnung des Schmucks der Urkunde von 1423 ausführlich behandelt in Roland/Zajic, Chartes médiévales enluminées (wie Anm. 3).

Conjuger diplomatique, paléographie et édition électronique. Les mutations du XIIᵉ siècle et la datation des écritures par le profil scribal collectif

DOMINIQUE STUTZMANN

Paléographie et diplomatique, issues d'une commune origine, partagent des objectifs communs qui invitent aujourd'hui à retisser les liens qui les unissaient avant que ne se déchire la tunique sans couture[1]. De même que la diplomatique dépasse le *discrimen veri ac falsi* au sens étroit pour saisir la production documentaire dans son contexte ou le fonctionnement des chancelleries, réseaux et influences, la paléographie ne se limite pas à la lecture ou même à l'analyse stricte des formes, mais vise à une compréhension générale des processus évolutifs et sociaux de la scripturalité. Aujourd'hui, ces deux disciplines s'ouvrent en outre simultanément aux outils numériques. Pour appréhender plus finement les documents dans leur historicité, éventuellement en les datant et en les attribuant à une production identifiée, les deux disciplines ont beaucoup à partager et à échanger. La paléographie numérique permet en particulier une analyse nuancée d'évolutions imperceptibles à l'œil lors des transcription et édition et la mise en évidence des «profils scribaux collectifs» qui autorisent à leur tour à interroger les contextes, lieux et temps de la production écrite.

Une période s'impose pour étudier la production diplomatique selon cette méthodologie: le XIIᵉ siècle, époque de mutations graphiques entre caroline et gothique, où l'histoire des formes rend l'étude des systèmes graphiques particulièrement pertinente. Après une explication sur les techniques d'analyse, sera démontrée l'existence d'un «profil scribal collectif» (utilisation conjointe par plusieurs individus d'un même système graphique), ainsi que sa pertinence dans l'analyse historique pour la compréhension du matériau écrit.

---

[1] S. BARRET, Le diplomatiste et la paléographie, in: Gazette du livre médiéval 54 (2009) p. 1–9.

L'écriture des chartes au XIIe siècle

Dans les manuels de paléographie, le XIIe siècle est souvent traité rapidement, comme une période intermédiaire, ou plutôt comme la dernière étape d'une longue dérive par laquelle la Caroline aurait franchi un océan immense et plat pour aborder sur les rives escarpées de la Gothique. Un certain flou terminologique manifeste l'idée d'une «transition»[2], d'une évolution progressive et continue menant d'une écriture caroline à une écriture «gothicisante» puis à l'écriture «gothicisée» et enfin à l'écriture «gothique», selon le vocabulaire de Jacques Stiennon[3], qu'empruntent sans plus de précision d'autres auteurs («écriture gothique primitive», «Frühgotische Minuskel» etc.[4]). Une autre forme souligne son rôle dans une perception téléologique de cette évolution: *«littera praegothica»*[5]. Pourtant ce siècle, âge d'or de la production livresque dans les scriptoria monastiques et témoin de la résurgence du pouvoir royal, de la naissance des écoles urbaines et des premières copies de livres dans des ateliers laïcs en ville[6], est marqué dans le domaine scriptural par une inventivité formelle extrême, par la perméabilité entre écrits de types différents. En outre, la renaissance d'une écriture diplomatique au cours de ce siècle est l'un des phénomènes majeurs de l'histoire graphique de l'Occident médiéval après l'unification carolingienne. Le XIIe siècle est un carrefour, où les tendances graphiques qui, selon les lieux, finissent de converger ou commencent déjà de se séparer, provoquent d'importantes fluctuations. Un long processus s'achève en effet, par lequel l'écriture caroline s'est progressivement imposée à l'ensemble de la production écrite, y compris dans les écritures diplomatiques et pragmatiques, tandis qu'à l'opposé de ce processus d'unification se développent de nouvelles tendances. L'héritage carolin unifié se divise progressivement et donne naissance non seulement aux écritures *textualis* et *textualis formata*, mais aussi à des écritures moins formelles qui s'incarneront d'abord dans les écritures de la pratique et, avec retard, dans le

---

[2] A. DEROLEZ, The Palaeography of Gothic Manuscript Books from the Twelfth to the Early Sixteenth Century (Cambridge studies in palaeography and codicology 9, 2003) p. 56.

[3] J. STIENNON, Paléographie du Moyen Âge (1991) p. 125–126.

[4] B. BISCHOFF, La nomenclature des écritures livresques du IXe au XIIIe siècle, in: Nomenclatures des écritures livresques du IXe au XVIe siècle: premier colloque international de paléographie latine, Paris, 28–30 avril 1953, éd. B. BISCHOFF/G. I. LIEFTINCK/G. BATTELLI (Colloques internationaux du C.N.R.S. – Sciences humaines 4, 1954) p. 7–14; K. SCHNEIDER, Paläographie und Handschriftenkunde für Germanisten. Eine Einführung (Sammlung kurzer Grammatiken germanischer Dialekte, Ergänzungsreihe 8, 1999) pl. 6.

[5] DEROLEZ, Palaeography of Gothic Manuscript Books.

[6] P. STIRNEMANN, Quelques bibliothèques princières et la production hors scriptorium au XIIe s., in: Bulletin archéologique du C.T.H.S. 17–18/A (1981–1982) p. 7–38.

domaine livresque sous les formes des *cursiva* puis *hybrida*[7]. C'est ainsi, du reste, que l'on peut interpréter historiquement certains résultats de la classification automatisée des écritures livresques par analyse d'images obtenus dans le cadre du projet ANR Graphem[8]. Si l'on représente en deux dimensions la dispersion des écritures selon leur degré de similarité, il devient possible d'observer la division progressive de l'héritage carolingien, que nous mettons ici en évidence par des flèches qui permettent d'observer les dynamiques évolutives et le carrefour que constitue l'écriture du XIIe siècle (fig. XVI, voyez les planches en couleur, p. 333–336).

Au cœur du processus d'unification intervient une transformation majeure, qui modifie les rapports entre contextes de production écrite. Non seulement il se produit une fusion, soulignée en son temps par G. Cencetti[9], entre l'écriture usuelle, ou forme moyenne des signes alphabétiques effectivement tracés, et l'écriture normale, i.e. le canon graphique enseigné, mais surtout, il se produit une inversion des paradigmes. La quantité produite pour les livres surpasse celle des écritures de la pratique, ce qui engendre un fait nouveau: l'écriture usuelle ne se loge plus dans le champ du cursif ou du courant, mais dans celui du livresque.

Durant ce siècle, les rapports entre écritures livresques et diplomatiques sont particulièrement complexes. Du point de vue morphologique, en effet, l'unité créée par la caroline tardive peut faire supposer une fusion des deux courants graphiques cursif et livresque, les deux *modi scribendi* étudiés par E. Casamassima[10]. En reprenant sa terminologie, au XIIe siècle, l'avantage est à «l'archétype», c'est-à-dire à la morphologie et à la trace, sur l'écriture *recta via*, c'est-à-dire sur le mouvement, le *ductus* et le tracé. La main se ralentit et la forme prime sur le geste. Pour désigner certaines particularités des écritures diplomatiques italiennes, à savoir les formes isolées de la cursive antique conservées par delà les évolutions graphiques, le champ sémantique utilisé par E. Casamassima insiste sur l'incarnation dans une matière pesante de l'esprit qui guide la main: «cristallisé», «fossilisé», «pétrifié»[11]. En ces formes solidifiées, faussées par l'imitation d'un modèle *ex absentia*, il perçoit l'antithèse de l'écriture, qui est mouvement et mutabilité. Parmi les caractères externes les

[7] Sur cette nomenclature, voir Derolez, Palaeography of Gothic Manuscript Books.

[8] LIRIS, GRAPHEM: Projet ANR, s. d., <http://liris.cnrs.fr/graphem/>; D. Muzerelle, Graphem for Dummies (4 nov. 2009), en ligne: <http://www.uib.no/filearchive/graphemfords.pdf>.

[9] G. Cencetti, Paleografia latina, éd. P. Supino Martini (Guide allo studio della civiltà romana 10/3, 1978) p. 118.

[10] E. Casamassima, Tradizione corsiva e tradizione libraria nella scrittura latina del Medioevo (1988) p. 96–97, 129.

[11] Ibid., p. 36, 37, 59.

plus emblématiques de la diplomatique au XIIe siècle, certains relèvent du même processus de fossilisation, telles que les litterae elongatae[12].

Insister uniquement sur le ralentissement et la lourdeur serait cependant réducteur. E. Casamassima lui-même traite par ailleurs du renouvellement des écritures pragmatiques réalisées à main posée selon le modèle des écritures livresques[13]. Au sein même des composantes les plus conservatrices de l'écriture diplomatique, il faut noter la permanence d'une nécessaire structure de *distinction*[14], qui opère ici de façon double. La pétrification n'est pas seulement un facteur d'immobilisme, mais aussi une ouverture à une autre inventivité: non plus celle du bas, de l'évolution souterraine des formes par déformation progressive, mais celle du haut, de l'épigraphie et des écritures formelles, autorisant les gestes graphiques les plus artificieux et anti-naturels. Des formes qui ne trouvent pas leur place dans les écritures livresques pourront certes être introduites dans les écritures diplomatiques parce qu'elles reflètent des évolutions en cours dans des écritures moins formelles et non canonisées (par exemple, s long plongeant sous la ligne)[15], mais aussi parce que le rattachement typologique de l'écriture diplomatique à l'épigraphie, également artificielle et d'apparat, lui ouvre un espace de mutabilité et une perméabilité aux formes hors normes (par exemple, lettres enclavées ou hastes à treillis). Si la naissance de la «minuscule diplomatique», fondée morphologiquement sur la minuscule tardo-carolingienne, a pu être considérée comme une efflorescence d'une écriture moins formelle[16], c'est bien le double phénomène qu'il faut considérer. L'apparente unité formelle caroline ne crée pas réellement une unité systémique entre écriture de la pratique et écriture livresque, car les contextes de production sont distincts, mais surtout, il se produit un glissement où la partition livresque/cursive s'inverse et où les actes de la pratique (notamment ceux que l'on dit «privés», mais établis au nom d'autorités perçues comme «publiques» telles que les évêques) sont promus vers le haut, de

---

[12] Le même champ sémantique se retrouve chez B. Bischoff: «Cet ensemble harmonieux se décomposa. L'élan de l'écriture fut amorti et freiné», cf. B. Bischoff, Paléographie de l'Antiquité romaine et du Moyen Âge occidental, trad. H. Atsma/J. Vezin (1985) p. 134.

[13] Casamassima: Tradizione corsive e tradizione libraria p. 131–135.

[14] Cf. Cencetti, Paleografia latina p. 119.

[15] Pour l'antériorité des évolutions dans les écritures documentaires, voir aussi S. Zamponi, La scrittura del libro nel Duecento, in: Civiltà comunale. Libro, scrittura, documento. Atti del convengno, Genova 8–11 novembre 1988 (1989) p. 344.

[16] M. H. Smith, Les formes de l'alphabet latin, entre écriture et lecture (présenté à: Colloque de rentrée 2011: La vie des formes, Collège de France (Paris), 14 octobre 2011), part. 7'33–11'00, <http://www.college-de-france.fr/site/colloque-2011/symposium-2011-10-14-10h45.htm>.

sorte qu'il se retrouvent eux aussi dans un champ non-cursif et à un niveau de formalité supérieur et proche de l'épigraphie.

Souligner l'inventivité formelle des écritures d'apparat dans le domaine diplomatique – et ainsi rapprocher ces dernières des forces les plus créatives des domaines livresque et épigraphique[17] – permet de relire les observations d'E. Casamassima sur la disparition des écritures: il souligne en effet que les écritures canonisées sont artificielles et qu'en tant que telles, elles peuvent tomber en désuétude ou se voir remplacer de l'extérieur[18] – contrairement aux écritures *recta via*, issues d'un développement historique continu et reflétant la dynamique naturelle de la main. Le caractère arbitraire et artificiel du point de vue graphique des ornements diplomatiques du XIIe siècle nous semble les rapprocher des écritures canonisées et des traits fossilisés, et malgré l'inventivité des motifs issus de la pierre épigraphique, donc malgré leur vivacité, la facile disparition des *litterae elongatae*, capitales, lettres enclavées ou fusionnées, tildes ornés, hastes allongées nous semble être un exemple des «substitutions» historiques et confirme le changement de champ graphique et d'inspiration.

De cette nature construite des écritures aussi bien diplomatiques que livresques au XIIe siècle découle une nouvelle façon de dater et attribuer des productions de chartes élaborées par plusieurs scribes: étudier les effets d'écoles et les «profils scribaux collectifs», c'est-à-dire à l'emploi de formes et d'allographes selon des codifications propres à des groupes restreints.

Le «système graphique»

Les turbulences du XIIe siècle se traduisent en effet par la multiplication des formes variantes d'une même lettre («allographes»), ainsi que par leur étonnant usage concomitant et apparemment dénué de règles dans la production diplomatique. Au XIIe siècle, l'heure n'est plus où un ensemble d'allographes suffisait à distinguer un scriptorium ou ses différentes phases, comme à Corbie, où les lettres «ab» ou «eN» suffisent à indiquer une provenance[19]. Dans les chartes vernaculaires anglaises du XIe siècle, le principe est encore largement valable et la conjonction des allographes est perçue comme définissant

---

[17] P. Stirnemann/M. Smith, Forme et fonction des écritures d'apparat dans les manuscrits latins (VIIIe-XVe siècle), in: BECh 165 (2008) p. 67–100.

[18] Casamassima, Tradizione corsiva e tradizione libraria p. 35.

[19] En dernier lieu, voir D. Ganz, Corbie in the Carolingian Renaissance = Untersuchung zur monastischen Kultur der Karolingerzeit am Beispiel der Abtei Corbie (Beihefte der Francia 20, 1990), en ligne: <http://www.perspectivia.net/content/publikationen/bdf/ganz_corbie>; F. Gasparri, Le 'scriptorium' de Corbie, in: Scrittura e civiltà 15 (1991) p. 289–305.

la main d'un scribe[20]. Aux périodes ultérieures et notamment à la fin du Moyen Âge, les allographes multiples se retrouvent au contraire de main en main[21].

Pour le XIIᵉ siècle, deux exemples d'actes donnés presque à la même date pour l'abbaye bourguignonne de La Bussière suffiront à se convaincre que l'agencement des allographes est plus déterminant que leur forme (fig. XVII et XVIII). Dans la première charte, authentifiée par le chapitre de Beaune en 1197, la lettre s se présente sous cinq formes différentes:

- s long passant sous la ligne (forme très majoritaire en début et milieu de mot),
- s rond passant sous la ligne, ou «traînant»[22], en forme de *sigma* final (forme très majoritaire en fin de mot),
- s long sur la ligne (deux occurrences: l. 4, *promisit*; l. 6, *testes* dans ligature *st*; une forme dont seul un trait accessoire passe sous la ligne, l. 1, *ipsius*),
- s rond sur la ligne (une occurrence: l. 3, *libris*),
- s suscrit (une occurrence: l. 8, *impressione*)[23].

La seconde charte est donnée par le duc de Bourgogne en 1198 et présente également de multiples formes, notamment pour la lettre s, analogues à celles de l'exemple précédent (s long sur la ligne, l. 1, *futuris*, l. 2, *dedisse, concessisse, monachis*, l. 4, *eisdem, sue, predecessorum, suorum*, etc.; rond sur la ligne, l. 6, *querelis*, l. 9, *eis*; s long passant sous la ligne, l. 2–3, *eschangio*, l. 9, *pars, Li Crais*; suscrit, l. 4, *monachis*). Tandis que la charte de 1197 montre un système graphique très régulier, où le s en sigma est généralement utilisé en fin de mot et le s long plongeant en début et milieu de mot, la charte de 1198 reflète une situation plus variée

---

[20] D. Scragg et al., MANCASS C11 Database (Manchester Centre for Anglo-Saxon Studies, 1ᵉʳ avril 2010) <http://www.arts.manchester.ac.uk/mancass/C11database> (consulté le 12 avril 2012, entre-temps retiré des serveurs mais visibles aux adresses suivantes description de la base: <http://web.archive.org/web/20060621190544/ http://www.art.man.ac.uk/english/mancass/data/PalaeogIntro.pdf>, liste et caractéristique des scribes: <http://web.archive.org/web/20060528024512/http://www.art. man.ac.uk/english/mancass/data/scriptors.php>, catalogue des allographes: <http:// web.archive.org/web/20060528024512/http://www.art.man.ac.uk/english/mancass/ data/scriptors.php>. Cf. K. Powell, The MANCASS C11 Database: A tool for studying script and spelling in the eleventh century, in: Old English Newsletter, 38/1 (2004) p. 29–34. Des principes similaires sont utilisés par P. A. Stokes, Digital Resource for Palaeography (2011), en ligne: <http://digipal.eu/>.

[21] L. Mooney/S. Horobin/E. Stubbs, Late Medieval English Scribes (2012), en ligne: <http://www.medievalscribes.com/index.php?nav=off>.

[22] M. Careri/Ch. Ruby/I. Short, Livres et écritures en français et en occitan au XIIᵉ siècle: catalogue illustré (Scritture e libri del medioevo 8, 2011) p. 231.

[23] Les autres lettres présentent également des variantes (r sur la ligne ou plongeant, demi-r après o; jambages plongeants, notamment pour i et m en fin de mot, modifiant fortement la forme de m).

où trois formes de **s** alternent en fin de mot. Même si des différences morphologiques subsistent (les **s** ronds de l'acte de 1198 sont clairement tracés sur la ligne et les **s** traînants, en *sigma*, sont absents), il est ainsi impossible de désigner et caractériser l'une ou l'autre écriture uniquement par la présence de ses allographes.

Cette inconstance variable dans l'emploi des allographes s'avère plus révélatrice même que la présence de ces allographes, tous connus aux deux scribes qui en font néanmoins usage dans des proportions et mesures divergentes. Elle démontre en effet l'existence de systèmes graphiques différents, dont la rigueur ou la souplesse dans l'application des règles d'emploi est l'une des caractéristiques à observer. Le concept même de «système graphique» est connexe à celui de «profil scribal», développé par A. McIntosh dans les années 1970 et qui comprend deux parties: le profil linguistique et le profil graphique[24]. McIntosh soulignait déjà que les formes des lettres dépendent d'un contexte fait d'espaces multiples, graphiques et sémantiques. L'espace matériel du texte apparaît souvent le plus prégnant et joue autant sur la textualité (position de la lettre dans le mot ou dans la phrase) que sur la matérialité (début ou fin de ligne). L'espace sémantique joue de façon complexe: phrases ou parties diplomatiques, noms de lieux et de personnes, etc., et les différents champs s'entremêlent et interagissent: ainsi, l'on verra un scribe utiliser tel allographe dans les mots communs et tel autre dans les noms de personnes, ainsi que dans les mots abrégés[25]. Le système graphique est ainsi l'ensemble des règles mises en œuvre par un scribe et qui permettent de formaliser son profil graphique. L'emploi d'un système graphique n'est pas aléatoire et, en outre, il ne relève pas uniquement du scribe comme individu, mais s'insère dans un environnement et un contexte social.

Ainsi, par exemple, l'écriture de la chancellerie pontificale se distingue très tôt par un emploi constant et strict des allographes; de même, l'une des caractéristiques de la «mixte» développée à la chancellerie royale française vers 1300 consiste en des «allographes rigoureusement différenciés selon leur position dans le mot»[26];

---

[24] A. McIntosh, Scribal Profiles from Middle English Texts, in: Neuphilologische Mitteilungen 76 (1975) p. 218–235.

[25] Par ex.: Dijon, Archives départementales Côte d'Or, 15 H 190, pièce 7 (charte non datée, ca. 1154–1162) et 15 H 243 / 2 (charte de 1162), où le traitement diplomatique des hastes disparaît dans les listes de témoins; ibid., 15 H 291, pièce 1 (charte de 1199), où **s** en *sigma* et **s** rond finaux se répartissent selon le sens des mots et la présence d'abréviation dans la syllabe finale. Sur ce point voir aussi D. Stutzmann, Paléographie latine et vernaculaire (livres et documents), in: Annuaire de l'École pratique des hautes études (EPHE), Section des sciences historique et philologiques 144 (2013) p. 115–128, paragraphe «L'écriture des chartes comme système graphique complexe».

[26] M. H. Smith, L'écriture de la chancellerie de France au XIVe siècle. Observations sur ses origines et sa diffusion en Europe, in: Régionalisme et internationalisme. Problèmes de paléographie et de codicologie du Moyen Âge. Actes du XVe Colloque du

en revanche, la variabilité des autres écritures a jusqu'à présent découragé les études paléographiques et la notion même de système graphique est aujourd'hui plus commune en linguistique qu'en paléographie[27]. Or, les chancelleries pontificale et royale française ne sont assurément pas des exceptions isolées, et d'autres ateliers d'écriture forment des «écoles»: cela amène à parler de «profil scribal collectif» et autorise à exploiter celui-ci pour dater et localiser des écritures.

Éditer le texte pour dater et attribuer

La datation et la localisation d'une écriture est une opération difficile, à laquelle il faut se livrer avec prudence, mais elle n'en est pas moins cruciale. Dans l'espace français, la proportion de chartes non datées au XIIe siècle est considérable: dans le premier quart du siècle, elle s'élève à environ 40 %[28]; pour l'intervalle 1100–1199 dans l'espace couvert par le *Thesaurus diplomaticus*[29], ce sont encore plus de 30 % des actes qui sont dépourvue de date[30]. Dans le contexte documentaire d'une forte production par l'impétrant, tel que celui du scriptorium de l'abbaye de Fontenay, 57 % des actes antérieurs à 1195 ne

---

Comité International de Paléographie Latine [Vienne, 13–17 septembre 2005], éd. O. KRESTEN/F. LACKNER (Denkschriften / Österreichische Akademie der Wissenschaften, Philosophisch-historische Klasse 364, 2008) p. 283.

[27] S. BADDELEY/L. BIEDERMANN-PASQUES, Histoire des systèmes graphiques du français (IXe–XVe siècle): des traditions graphiques aux innovations du vernaculaire, in: La linguistique 39 (2003) p. 3–34; EAED., Histoire des systèmes graphiques du français à travers des manuscrits et des incunables (IXe–XVe siècle): segmentation graphique et faits de langue, in: Revue de linguistique romane 68 (2004) p. 181–201; N. CATACH, Que faut-il entendre par système graphique du français?, in: Langue française 20 (1973) p. 30–44; Systèmes graphiques de manuscrits médiévaux et incunables français: ponctuation, segmentation, graphies, actes de la journée d'étude de l'ENS LSH, 6 juin 2005, éd. A. LAVRENTIEV (Langages 3, 2007); P. MANEN, Variations graphiques en français médiéval (du 13e siècle au 15e siècle): étude du Roman de Troie et de ses réécritures et comparaisons avec l'écrit documentaire contemporain» (Thèse de doctorat, Université de la Sorbonne nouvelle [Paris], 2005); MCINTOSH, Scribal Profiles from Middle English Texts.

[28] B.-M. TOCK et al., La diplomatique française du Haut Moyen Âge: inventaire des chartes originales antérieures à 1121 conservées en France (2001). Il n'y a pas d'index des actes datés; notre estimation se fonde sur les tables chronologiques pour les années 1101–1125 (date ultime retenue pour tenir compte des actes non datés, avec *terminus ante quem* en 1125 mais probablement antérieurs à 1121), en comptant comme datés les actes pontificaux avec indication du jour, mais non de l'année.

[29] COMMISSION ROYALE D'HISTOIRE/CETEDOC/COMITÉ NATIONAL DU DICTIONNAIRE DU LATIN MÉDIÉVAL/Ph. DEMONTY, Thesaurus diplomaticus (1997).

[30] Sur l'ensemble du siècle, 3061 documents non suspectés comprennent la combinaison «[eschatocole]+anno» pour 4268 documents non suspectés en tout, soit 71,7 %, vérification faite de la pertinence de cette interrogation dans le corpus.

sont pas datés[31]. L'histoire de l'écriture de cette période est d'autant plus difficile à étudier que les XIe et XIIe siècles forment l'époque où les livres manuscrits portent proportionnellement le moins de mentions explicites de dates[32]. Outre l'absence de datation, les modes de production variés sont également source d'incertitude: notice impersonnelle ou charte subjective, rédaction par l'impétrant ou par la chancellerie, ou encore par un tiers, qu'il soit un familier de l'autorité sigillante ou un acteur de l'écrit inconnu par ailleurs. La reconnaissance de profils scribaux collectifs dans ce contexte d'incertitude peut offrir de nouveaux indices de datation et d'attribution.

Pour avancer dans cette direction et permettre des comparaisons à grande échelle, qui seules permettront d'identifier les systèmes graphiques et profils scribaux, il est évidemment nécessaire de disposer d'une base exploitable, contenant aussi bien le texte de l'édition que les informations paléographiques. C'est désormais possible dans le cadre des éditions électroniques, qui autorisent la dissociation du «texte» lui-même et de la «description» du texte édité, et une réconciliation des différentes traditions ecdotiques. L'édition imitative et, en particulier, le *record type* s'inscrivent désormais dans les productions électroniques pour des projets de recherche, où un texte normalisé (voire modernisé) et une édition imitative décrivant les caractéristiques (paléo)graphiques de l'original sont présentés en parallèle. L'utilité de l'édition imitative a certes été contestée en raison du lourd investissement en temps consacré aux manuscrits ainsi édités (généralement sous forme papier) et ne pouvant donner lieu qu'à l'étude autarcique d'un scribe unique[33]; mais aujourd'hui, en permettant d'ouvrir les questions et les corpus, l'édition électronique rend son intérêt historique et heuristique au modèle imitatif. Certaines éditions proposent ainsi trois versions, telles la *Base du Français Médiéval-Manuscrits* et la *Queste du Graal* (facsimilaire, diplomatique et

---

[31] D. STUTZMANN, Écrire à Fontenay. Esprit cistercien et pratiques de l'écrit en Bourgogne (XIIe-XIIIe siècles) (thèse de doctorat Histoire, Université Paris 1 Panthéon-Sorbonne, 2009) p. 411.

[32] D. MUZERELLE, Manuscrits datés des bibliothèques de France. I. Cambrai (2000) p. 306–307; MUZERELLE, Graphem for Dummies p. 3.

[33] M. CAVAGNA, Grégoire le Grand, Le Pastoralet. Traduction médiévale française de la *Regula Pastoralis*. Édition critique du manuscrit 868 de la Bibliothèque municipale de Lyon, édition en vis-à-vis du manuscrit Cotton Vitellius F VII de la British Library de Londres, publié par Martine Pagan, in: Cahiers de recherches médiévales et humanistes. Journal of medieval and humanistic studies (17 juillet 2008), en ligne: <http://crm.revues.org/7512>.

normalisée)[34] ou *Cantar de mio Cid* (normalisée dite «paléographique», modernisée dite «normalisée», vocalisée, et aussi traduite)[35].

Les informations graphiques intéressant l'histoire de l'écriture et la diplomatique demeurent cependant rares, souvent limitées à la mise en page, aux corrections et aux abréviations, tandis que les données allographétiques restent généralement omises et leur exploitation empêchée par un cloisonnement excessif. Du reste, les documents diplomatiques sont très faiblement représentés dans ces initiatives, alors même que leur unicité en fait de meilleurs candidats à une telle exploitation que l'univers livresque où, pourtant, les auteurs et œuvres prestigieux concentrent les efforts (Chaucer, Gower, Chrétien de Troyes, Christine de Pisan, Hugo von Montfort, Pétrarque et Dante)[36]. Dans le domaine diplomatique, le faible nombre d'éditions allographétiques est d'autant plus étonnant que l'action de l'éditeur dans la mise en forme est importante, ambiguë et signifiante, et qu'aucune des traditions éditoriales n'est pleinement satisfaisante: il faut renoncer soit à l'analyse fine, soit à la matérialité du texte. La tradition française, par exemple, impose de résoudre les abréviations, d'identifier les noms de personnes et de lieux en utilisant une majuscule pour l'initiale, de composer en italiques les mots en langue étrangère, de ponctuer, de restituer les lettres ramistes: toutes opérations qui accordent la prééminence au travail d'analyse intellectuelle et à la responsabilité scientifique de l'éditeur au détriment d'un accès à la matérialité du texte.

L'édition critique avec vue «facsimilaire» présenterait l'avantage d'obliger à une meilleure formalisation, tant dans la distinction entre ce qui relève de la source et de l'intervention de l'éditeur, d'une part, que dans la nature de ces interventions, d'autre part. Elle soulignerait notamment que la ponctuation et la résolution des abréviations sont précisément des choix critiques de l'éditeur. L'opération intellectuelle serait à la fois mieux valorisée et plus lisible si

---

[34] A. Lavrentev, BFM – Manuscrits, Base de Français Médiéval – Old French Corpus (22 juillet 2010), en ligne: <http://bfm.ens-lyon.fr/article.php3?id_article=177>; Ch. Marchello-Nizia, Queste del saint Graal (2011), en ligne: <http://portal.textometrie.org/txm/>.

[35] M. Bailey et al., Cantar de mio cid (2012), en ligne: <http://www.laits.utexas.edu/cid/main/info.php?v=nor>.

[36] Chrétien de Troyes: Le chevalier de la Charette (Lancelot): le «Projet Charette» et le renouvellement de la critique philologique des textes, éd. C. Pignatelli/M. C. Robinson (Œuvres et critiques 27/1, 2002); G. Chaucer, The general prologue, éd. E. Solopova, CD-ROM (2000); Mooney/Horobin/Stubbs, Late Medieval English Scribes; M. Aussems, Christine de Pizan and the scribal fingerprint: a quantitative approach to manuscript studies (thèse de doctorat, Université d'Utrecht, 2007), en ligne: <http://dspace.library.uu.nl/handle/1874/12537>; M. Aussems/A. Brink, Digital palaeography, in: Kodikologie und Paläographie im digitalen Zeitalter – Codicology and Palaeography in the Digital Age, éd. M. Rehbein/P. Sahle/T. Schassan Schriften des Instituts für Dokumentologie und Editorik 2, 2009) p. 293–308.

les choix étaient explicites: des points mis pour signaler une abréviation conservée ou séparer les parties du discours diplomatique ne sont pas de même nature, non plus que les italiques pour les mots étrangers ou les lettres restituées des abréviations[37]. De même, l'insertion de l'analyse grammaticale, traduite en ponctuation, serait-elle plus riche et intéressante que la restitution simple d'une ponctuation parfois ambiguë et masquant la ponctuation de l'original. La distinction des signes médiévaux et des interprétations sémantiques et syntaxiques actuelles est désormais possible et souhaitable.

Le verrou technique, du point de vue ecdotique, est une ergonomie parfaite qui permette une analyse sémantique aussi simple à indiquer que dans les modes interprétatifs actuels: par exemple, la désignation des incises, des noms et des mots étrangers doit être aussi aisée que l'insertion d'une virgule, d'une majuscule ou de l'italique. Avec un outil ergonomique, la restitution des abréviations et des lettres ramistes pourrait être favorisée par des outils intégrant lemmatiseur et dictionnaire, ainsi que des aides et alertes de désambigüisation, rares en latin, légèrement plus fréquentes en français (maieur/majeur, Evre/Eure, jeux/ieux)[38].

La conservation des allographes dans la transcription, au-delà des lettres ramistes, se heurte néanmoins à un obstacle supplémentaire: outre des enjeux d'ergonomie, il faut faire face à l'absence d'ontologie des formes. Celle-ci a pour conséquence la difficulté à choisir les allographes à conserver et le niveau de distinction souhaité. Cet obstacle explique que la plupart des projets linguistiques qui exploitent les divergences allographétiques pour étudier le système graphique se fonde sur les formes qui ont perduré via la longue tradition typographique ou dans d'autres alphabets (a, *a;* d, δ; e, ę; i, j; s, ſ, ſ, ß; u, v, w), alors que les formes sans postérité dans l'histoire de l'écriture n'ont généralement pas été retenues (on pense aux différentes formes de **a** sur lesquelles W. Oeser fonde ses classifications[39], mais aussi à la différence entre **s** long sur la ligne ou plongeant, ou bien entre **s** rond sur la ligne ou traînant en *sigma*). Les recherches en paléographie, même quand elles semblent aller dans cette direction, n'encouragent guère les linguistes à affronter cette diversité

---

[37] ÉCOLE NATIONALE DES CHARTES, Conseils pour l'édition de textes médiévaux (Fascicule I, Conseils généraux. Fascicule II, Actes et documents d'archives. Fascicule III, Textes littéraires) (2001) p. 63–67.

[38] Ibid. p. 23–27. Il faut ici rappeler que le refus de conserver le graphisme du texte pour **i,j** ou **u,v** tient au fait que l'attention à ces seules lettres est un anachronisme justifié par l'évolution et la spécialisation ultérieure des graphismes et le maintien de ces différentes formes dans le système graphique moderne, tandis que l'étude de la matérialité graphique doit aussi porter sur les phénomènes qui n'ont pas eu de postérité.

[39] W. OESER, Beobachtungen zur Strukturierung und Variantenbildung der Textura. Ein Beitrag zur Paläographie des Hoch- und Spätmittelalters, in: AfD 40 (1994) p. 359–439.

s'ils ne sont accompagnés par les paléographes: qu'il s'agisse de la constitution de vastes albums d'écritures datées ou datables, mais non analysées selon leur système graphique[40] (à l'exception notable des séries néerlandaises qui mettent en œuvre la classification de Lieftinck-Gumbert-Derolez[41], reposant sur une classification allographétique), ou bien de la mise en place de bases accumulant des milliers de formes sans hiérarchie[42]. Aussi le matériau exploitable par les linguistes pour l'étude des systèmes graphiques n'a-t-il pas été mis à profit par les paléographes, et, inversement, ceux-ci n'ont pas soutenu les efforts utiles aux linguistes, ni non plus œuvré pour une homogénéisation indispensable à la perception de la longue durée.

Outre l'absence d'ontologie, une autre difficulté, ergonomique, est d'importance cruciale. La capacité d'attention de l'esprit humain est en effet limitée, qui oblige, avec les moyens actuels, à séparer les tâches de transcription, de ponctuation, d'indexation et de distinction allographétique, car la concentration intellectuelle nécessaire à l'observation des formes engendre des fautes de compréhension et de transcription[43]. Aussi le processus de transcription allographétique comprend-il plusieurs phases. Certes, notre expérience dans ce domaine montre que ce travail d'enrichissement, s'il est effectué sur un texte déjà transcrit, voire disposant d'un alignement avec une image numérique, peut être rapide; il devient même envisageable pour des corpus de grande ampleur, tels que les archives virtuelles *Monasterium.net*, où l'application de la TEI permet déjà le marquage des lignes et des «glyphes» dans l'interface de transcription collaborative, et où de nouvelles fonctionnalités d'extraction d'image sont proposées depuis juillet 2011[44]. Pourtant, l'absence de système logiciel capable de pallier les insuffisances cognitives en cours de

---

[40] COMITÉ INTERNATIONAL DE PALÉOGRAPHIE LATINE/D. MUZERELLE, Manuscrits datés: État des publications, in: Palaeographia, s. d., en ligne: <http://www.palaeographia.org/cipl/cmd.htm>.

[41] DEROLEZ, Palaeography of Gothic Manuscript Books.

[42] SCRAGG et al., MANCASS C11 Database; MOONEY/HOROBIN/STUBBS, Late Medieval English Scribes.

[43] P. ROBINSON/E. SOLOPOVA, Guidelines for the transcription of the manuscripts of the Wife of Bath's Prologue, in: The Canterbury Tales Project Occasional Papers, éd. N. BLAKE (Office for Humanities Communication publications 5, 1993) p. 19–52, en ligne: <http://canterburytalesproject.com/pubs/op1-transguide.pdf>; D. STUTZMANN, Paléographie statistique pour décrire, identifier, dater ... Normaliser pour coopérer et aller plus loin?, in: Kodikologie und Paläographie im digitalen Zeitalter 2 – Codicology and Palaeography in the Digital Age 2, (Schriften des Instituts für Dokumentologie und Editorik 3, 2010) p. 247–277.

[44] ICARUS – INTERNATIONAL CENTRE FOR ARCHIVAL RESEARCH, Monasterium.net (2011), <http://www.mom-ca.uni-koeln.de/mom/home>. Documentation et historique du projet: Welcome to MOM-Wiki: Documenting the Development of MOM-CA (2008 sqq.), en ligne: <http://www.mom-wiki.uni-koeln.de/>.

transcription et de permettre la saisie, soit de toutes les informations à conserver en une seule fois, soit au moyen d'un système automatisant les tâches répétitives, nuit encore aux recherches dans cette direction.

S'il est peu envisageable avec les outils actuels d'éditer chaque forme de lettre lors d'une édition de texte diplomatique et d'en exploiter le résultat d'un point de vue historique ou linguistique, des outils permettent néanmoins déjà d'expliciter le travail intellectuel de l'éditeur et de favoriser un enrichissement des données utiles aux linguistes, aux paléographes, et aux diplomatistes.

C'est ainsi qu'au sein de deux projets d'édition électronique, couvrant les chartriers des abbayes cisterciennes de Fontenay et de La Bussière[45], nous procédons à l'enrichissement des éditions des chartes conservées en original par un encodage respectant la matérialité graphique des objets historiques. Un seul document permet des visualisations et des exploitations multiples: soit, en cours de travail, avec une CSS permettant une visualisation «record-type» et une autre permettant de voir les abréviations développées, les mots étrangers en italiques et les entrées d'index surlignées de différentes couleurs; soit avec une transformation XSLT permettant une édition normalisée (fig. 1).

Tout en fondant notre pratique sur la TEI et MUFI (Medieval Unicode Font Initiative)[46] et l'emploi d'une police associée telle qu'Andron Scriptor Web, Palemonas MUFI ou Junicode[47], nous utilisons un fichier d'entités HTML, qui déclare aussi bien les allographes que les abréviations. Un choix similaire a été fait pour les allographes par le laboratoire ICAR pour la *Base de Français Médiéval* et la publication de la *Queste du Graal*[48]. L'emploi d'entités pour les abréviations remplace avantageusement le traditionnel italique, car il permet de décrire les différentes abréviations du même mot ainsi que les multiples significations d'une même forme.

```
<!ENTITY s-long-sur-ligne "&#x017F;">
<!ENTITY s-long-plongeant "&#xF127;">
<!ENTITY s-rond-plongeant "&#xE476;">
```

Tabl. 1: Exemples de déclaration d'entités pour les allographes

---

[45] Les travaux sur les actes de La Bussière se fondent sur le travail préliminaire de Nicolas Perreaux et Mickaël Lauquin.

[46] MEDIEVAL UNICODE FONT INITIATIVE, MUFI character recommendations (2009), en ligne: <http://www.mufi.info/specs/>.

[47] <http://www.mufi.info/fonts/>.

[48] MARCHELLO-NIZIA, Queste del saint Graal. Le fichier XML publié renvoie pour les entités MUFI à <http://www.menota.org/menota-entities.txt> ainsi qu'à un fichier d'entités spécifique.

```
<!ENTITY que-q-point-virgule "<choice><expan>que</expan><abbr>&#xE8BF;</abbr></choice>">
<!ENTITY que-q-e-suscrit "<choice><expan>que</expan><abbr>q&#x0364;</abbr></choice>">
<!ENTITY que-q-tilde "<choice><expan>que</expan><abbr>q&#x0303;</abbr></choice>">
<!ENTITY que-q-r-rond "<choice><expan>que</expan><abbr>&#xE8B3;</abbr></choice>">
```

Tabl. 2: Exemples de déclaration d'entités pour les abréviations «que»

```
<!ENTITY que-q-r-rond "<choice><expan>que</expan><abbr>&#xE8B3;</abbr></choice>">
<!ENTITY quia "<choice><expan>quia</expan><abbr>&#xE8B3;</abbr></choice>">
```

Tabl. 3: Exemples de déclarations d'entités pour deux formes graphiques identiques à la signification différente

L'emploi d'un fichier d'entités est un choix délibéré qui place la visualisation et la vérifiabilité des données, ainsi que la commodité, au cœur des méthodes de travail: en un mot, nous faisons primer l'ergonomie[49], tout en préparant les conditions de l'interopérabilité puisque, par transformation et conversion, il est aisé d'obtenir un fichier répondant aux normes du module Gaiji et aux valeurs proposées par la gBank[50].

L'emploi de noms explicites et immédiatement compréhensibles, dans la langue de l'encodeur, tel que «s-long-sur-ligne» est à privilégier pour un travail quotidien commode et pour les formes plus rares[51].

Le premier exemple ci-dessus (Tabl. 1) met particulièrement en lumière combien la déclaration des entités pour les allographes peut présenter des risques pour l'interopérabilité, puisque les deux premières entités sont, sous un autre nom, l'équivalent des entités «slong» et «slongdes» de MUFI. Dans le cadre du travail quotidien, l'explicitation «s-long-sur-ligne» permet de toujours accorder suffisamment d'attention à l'éventualité d'une autre forme.

---

[49] Avec Oxygen, il est en effet aisé d'insérer une entité HTML déclarée dans un fichier séparé et, en un clic-droit, d'insérer une entité.

[50] Oxford University Computing Services, ENRICH gBank viewer – v.1.00 (2009), en ligne: <http://www.manuscriptorium.com/apps/gbank/gbank_table.php>; ENRICH Project, Gaiji Bank of non-standard characters and glyphs, in: Manuscriptorium. Building Virtual Research Environment for the Sphere of Historical Resources (2009), en ligne: <http://www.manuscriptorium.com/index.php?q=node/3>.

[51] De ce point de vue, les entités «&q2app;» ou «&q3app;» pour «latin small letter q ligated with r rotunda» et «latin small letter q ligated with final et» (c'est-à-dire avec un semi-colon en forme de 3 passant sous la ligne) paraissent mal nommées, voire mal décrites, même si nous avons repris l'idée de «r rond».

TESTIMONIU [1]Sollerti ꝑvidentia ſⸯcoꝛ patrū inſtitutū eſſe dinoſcīt ut quicꝗd [2]a
fidelib; ſꝯꝫ eccliꝫ tribuīt kartuliſ imꝑſſū memoriter teneatur [3] ne tēporiſ labente
curriculo oblitū alicujuſ violentia auferre [4]moliat. Horū igīt conſiliū ꝑ modulo nr̄o
imitanteſ oppido ap[5]ꝑbamuſ ac om̄ib; xꝑianiſ tā ꝑſentib; quā futuriſ notificare cu[6]
ramuſ quod donnᵒ burcardus prior virgiaci ex conſenſu tociuſ [7]capituli ſui totā terrā
quā habebat a villa *croalt* uſꝙ ad flumen [8]oſcre et a rupe quꝫ eſt juxta pontē *karral* uſ
ꝙ ad cumbā ray[9]bo abſꝙ prato molendinarii ſui abſꝙ ulla reclamatione don[10]no
Willermo abɓi valliſ ſꝯ mariꝫ cū ceteriſ ſ̄rib; ibi ꝺo mi[11]litantib; eoꝛꝙ ſucceſſorib;
libere donavit et ad uſuſ ꝑpos [12]nemora ſua circūadjacentia oſcrā in quantū ſui juriſ
eſt ad [13]piſcandū et ad molendinū conſtruendū ſi poterit fieri quoꝺ [14]ſuiſ non
nocea

TESTIMONIUm Sollerti providentia sanctorum patrum inſtitutum eſſe dinoſcitur
ut quicquid a fidelibus sanctꝫ eccleſiꝫ tribuitur kartulis impreſſum memoriter teneatur
ne temporiſ labente curriculo oblitum alicujuſ violentia auferre moliatur. Horum igit
ur conſilium pro modulo nostro imitanteſ oppido approbamuſ ac ommibus Christianiſ
tam preſentibus quam futuriſ notificare curamuſ quod donnus burcardus Prior virgiaci
ex conſenſu tociuſ capituli ſui totam terram quam habebat a villa *croalt* uſque ad
flumen oſcre et a rupe quꝫ eſt juxta pontem *karral* uſque ad cumbam raybo abſque
prato molendinarii ſui abſque ulla reclamatione donno Willermo abbati valliſ ſanctꝫ
mariꝫ cum ceteriſ fratribus ibi deo militantibus eorumque ſucceſſoribus libere donavit
et ad uſuſ proprios nemora ſua circumadjacentia oſcram in quantum ſui juriſ eſt ad
piſcandu

TESTIMONIUM
Sollerti providentia sanctorum patrum institutum esse dinoscitur ut quicquid
a fidelibus sancte ecclesie tribuitur kartulis impressum memoriter teneatur
ne temporis labente curriculo oblitum alicujus violentia auferre
moliatur. Horum igitur consiliumpro modulo nostro imitantes oppido ap-
probamus ac omnibus Christianis tam presentibus quam futuris notificare cu-
ramus quod donnus Burcardus priorVirgiaci ex consensu tocius
capituli sui totam terram quam habebat a Villa Croalt usque ad flumen
Oscre et a rupe que est juxta Pontem Karral usque ad Cumbam Raybo absque prato molendinarii sui absque ulla reclamatione donno Willermo abbati Vallis Sancte Marie cum ceteris fratribus ibi deo mi
litantibus eorumque successoribus libere donavit et ad usus proprios
nemora sua circumadjacentia oscram in quantum sui juris est ad
piscandum et ad molendinum construendum si poterit fieri quod

Fig. 1: Trois visualisations du même texte: «record type», abréviations
résolues, texte normalisé (pour les n° XVI–XXI voyez les planches en
couleur, aux pages 333–336).

Il est évident qu'au moment de la publication définitive des données, les entités devront être normalisées et rapprochées de celles qui existent.

Ensuite, l'entité «s-rond-plongeant», nécessaire à notre analyse et sans
correspondance dans MUFI, est associée ici à un code de caractère ressem-
blant, théoriquement utilisé pour un autre caractère (*latin small letter c with
ogonek*), mais sans emploi dans notre corpus. La voie de la normalisation et
de l'insertion dans les polices existantes est un processus lent et incrémental.

Comme nous l'avons souligné ailleurs, il reste encore beaucoup de chemin
à parcourir pour normaliser et faire interopérer des transcriptions allographétiques, tant sur les valeurs que sur la structuration des données (dont les abréviations) et la granularité descriptive[52]. La voie est pourtant prometteuse pour
les paléographes et les diplomatistes, historiens du fait graphique.

---

[52] Stutzmann, Paléographie statistique p. 261–268.

Exploiter le «profil scribal collectif» et les systèmes graphiques
de Fontenay et la Bussière

Avec les transcriptions allographétiques réalisées pour les chartriers des abbayes cisterciennes de Fontenay et La Bussière, en Bourgogne, réalisées ainsi
que décrit ci-dessus, il est possible d'obtenir des conclusions historiques
valides, qui légitiment l'analyse non seulement comme une enquête sur l'histoire de l'écriture, mais comme nouveau moyen heuristique pour la diplomatique.

L'on peut en effet appliquer les méthodes des statistiques descriptives aux
données paléographiques, en particulier procéder à des analyses en composantes principales comme cela se fait couramment en linguistique de corpus.
Pour visualiser les résultats, nous utilisons le logiciel Explorer3D, développé
par Matthieu Exbrayat et Lionel Martin[53].

À partir de fichiers avec encodage allographétique, le texte de chaque acte
peut être décrit avec différents attributs: par exemple, pourcentage de **d** onciaux ou de **s** long en début, milieu ou fin de mot; pourcentage de **d** onciaux
devant les voyelles **a, e, i, o** et **u**. La spécialisation des allographes peut également faire partie des attributs (différenciation des **s** longs sur la ligne ou passant sous la ligne, de même pour le **s** rond).

Une première observation permet de considérer l'analyse allographétique
comme un nouveau moyen de dater une production graphique dans un ensemble clos, identifié et homogène, et d'appréhender d'un point de vue paléographique et statistique le «système graphique» d'un scribe. Si l'on désire analyser l'emploi du **d** oncial dans les chartes produites par le scriptorium de
Fontenay, et vraisemblablement par un unique scribe, entre 1154 et la fin des
années 1170, l'on se trouve rapidement devant des séries de chiffres difficiles
à interpréter (fig. 2); l'analyse en composante principale (ACP) permet
d'identifier des évolutions et de décrire chronologiquement la progression de
la forme onciale (fig. XIX). Les chartes non datées projetées dans le même
espace se répartissent distinctement et s'organisent autour d'une frontière qui
correspond à un facteur temporel. Dans cet exemple, des indices internes permettent de confirmer les datations, en particulier l'évolution morphologique
de l'écriture, partiellement distincte de celle du système graphique, et, parfois,
la présence de témoins[54].

L'on peut néanmoins aller plus loin et proposer d'observer plus largement
un profil scribal collectif, c'est-à-dire des habitudes partagées par différents
scribes. En faisant porter l'analyse sur les allographes de position de **d** et **s** (et

---

[53] M. Exbrayat/L. Martin, Explorer3D (2004–2013), en ligne: <http://www.univ-orleans.fr/lifo/software/Explorer3D/>.

[54] Stutzmann, Paléographie statistique p. 255–257.

non plus sur les liens avec les voyelles qui suivent les lettres), l'on peut mettre en évidence la cohérence graphique des différents scribes de chartes actifs dans le scriptorium de Fontenay dans la seconde moitié du XIIᵉ siècle. La figure XX représente un espace où l'on projette le résultat d'une analyse en composante principale des systèmes graphiques de chartes produites en Bourgogne (chaque boule représente une charte positionnée selon ses caractéristiques graphiques). Les chartes produites hors du scriptorium de Fontenay dans le deuxième tiers du XIIᵉ siècle sont représentées par des boules bleues; celles du dernier tiers du XIIᵉ siècle et du début du XIIIᵉ siècle, par des boules turquoise et vertes. Cette image montre que les pratiques sont extrêmement diverses dans le deuxième tiers du siècle et couvrent tout l'axe 1 de droite à gauche, tandis que les productions textuelles de la fin de ce même siècle se concentrent à une extrémité de l'axe (ici, dans la partie gauche).

Dans cet espace polarisé par les pratiques bourguignonnes du XIIᵉ siècle, les chartes de Fontenay des années 1150–1170 (ici, fig. XX, en jaune) montrent qu'elles forment un groupe homogène, peu dispersé, et correspondant, y compris dans les années 1170, aux pratiques les plus éloignées de celles qui se généraliseront à la fin du siècle. Dans la seconde période, les pratiques graphiques de Fontenay rejoignent les usages généralisés en dehors du scriptorium, mais pas immédiatement. Dans une première phase, couvrant les années 1170–1190 (ici, fig. XXI, en rouge), la distinction des allographes de position reste très conservatrice et bien plus proche de la production antérieure que des pratiques contemporaines en dehors du scriptorium. Ce n'est qu'après 1190 que l'ensemble des scribes de chartes de Fontenay rejoignent les usages majoritairement attestés depuis une vingtaine d'années dans l'environnement de l'abbaye, en rejetant l'emploi de s long en fin de mot et en imposant le d oncial à presque toutes les positions (ici, fig. XXI, en rose).

Le caractère conservateur des pratiques d'écriture à Fontenay apparaît comme une forme spécifique de «canonisation»; des analyses similaires sur d'autres *scriptoria* monastiques des mêmes époques devraient montrer s'il s'agit d'une tendance générale des milieux réguliers, éventuellement influencés par une copie essentiellement tournée vers les écritures livresques, plus stables.

Cette évolution progressive, formant des groupes successifs homogènes, porte le témoignage d'une discipline collective et caractérise un scriptorium au-delà des individualités des copistes. Ce phénomène autorise à étendre les remarques précédentes de l'individu au groupe et à ouvrir l'enquête vers les formes sociales de l'écriture. Un rassemblement d'individus peut en effet se comporter de façon cohérente et présenter des conditions favorables à l'apparition d'un «profil scribal collectif». Ce faisant, il autorise une analyse des systèmes graphiques et offre à l'historien des indices nouveaux pour dater.

Cote (Archives départementales de Côte d'Or, 15 H)	Formes en position initiale		Formes en position médiane		Formes en position finale		Formes devant «a»		Formes devant «e»		Formes devant «i»		Formes devant «o»		Formes devant «u»		Proportion de δ initial	Proportion de δ médian	Proportion de δ final	Proportion de δa	Proportion de δe	Proportion de δi	Proportion de δo	Proportion de δu
	d	δ	d	δ	d	δ	da	δa	de	δe	di	δi	do	δo	du	δu								
199, n° 2	12	2	10	3	0	2	3	0	12	1	2	4	1	0	4	0	14,3	23,1	100,0	0,0	7,7	66,7	0,0	0,0
156, n° 2	10	1	12	4	1	2	2	0	10	3	2	1	3	0	2	0	9,1	25,0	66,7	0,0	23,1	33,3	0,0	0,0
163, n° 1	12	4	7	6	0	7	0	1	13	3	2	3	2	0	1	0	25,0	46,2	100,0	100,0	18,8	60,0	0,0	0,0
163, n° 3	12	4	7	2	0	4	0	1	12	1	4	2	1	0	1	0	25,0	22,2	100,0	100,0	7,7	33,3	0,0	0,0
190, n° 7	22	5	27	16	3	8	2	0	29	12	7	2	6	5	0	1	18,5	37,2	72,7	0,0	29,3	22,2	45,5	100,0
193, n° 2	7	2	11	1	1	2	1	0	10	2	5	1	1	0	1	0	22,2	8,3	66,7	0,0	16,7	16,7	0,0	0,0
243, n° 2	40	5	18	16	7	19	9	3	29	8	5	1	6	1	3	3	11,1	47,1	73,1	25,0	21,6	16,7	14,3	50,0
190, n° 2	6	2	5	3	2	4	1	0	8	2	2	1	0	0	0	1	25,0	37,5	66,7	0,0	20,0	33,3	NA	100,0
190, n° 4	5	3	8	1	3	3	1	1	7	2	3	0	0	0	2	0	37,5	11,1	50,0	50,0	22,2	0,0	NA	0,0
357, n° 2	12	4	15	10	5	9	2	2	15	4	7	3	2	2	0	1	25,0	40,0	64,3	50,0	21,1	30,0	50,0	100,0
148, n° 1	11	2	14	3	2	2	4	1	5	0	2	1	7	1	1	2	15,4	17,6	66,7	20,0	0,0	33,3	12,5	66,7
163, n° 2	11	2	14	1	1	3	5	1	10	2	4	0	3	0	1	0	15,4	6,7	60,0	16,7	16,7	0,0	0,0	0,0
199, n° 1	15	1	11	0	1	2	3	0	11	0	4	0	4	0	3	0	6,3	0,0	66,7	0,0	0,0	0,0	0,0	0,0
249, n° 2	17	18	17	27	3	21	1	7	18	22	10	8	2	3	2	1	51,4	61,4	87,5	87,5	55,0	44,4	60,0	33,3
249, n° 3	14	9	15	13	1	11	1	6	17	9	5	1	4	0	1	6	39,1	46,4	91,7	85,7	34,6	16,7	0,0	85,7
193, n° 1	6	1	1	0	0	0	1	0	5	1	0	0	0	0	1	0	14,3	0,0	100,0	0,0	16,7	NA	NA	0,0
203, n° 1	12	5	24	6	5	11	4	2	19	2	7	2	6	3	0	2	29,4	20,0	68,8	33,3	9,5	22,2	33,3	100,0
249, n° 1	14	5	6	4	1	9	1	2	14	3	1	2	3	0	0	2	26,3	40,0	90,0	66,7	17,6	66,7	0,0	100,0
203, n° 2	9	6	9	10	0	15	1	3	14	8	0	2	2	1	1	2	40,0	52,6	100,0	75,0	36,4	100,0	33,3	66,7

Fig. 2: Tableau des proportions de «d» oncial dans le sous-ensemble considéré: répartition des chartes de Fontenay selon l'emploi de «d» oncial et de la voyelle subséquente (étude sur un sous-ensemble chronologique des chartes produites par le scriptorium au XIIe siècle).

Cette dernière conclusion est renforcée par l'analyse des systèmes graphiques pour les actes conservés dans le chartrier de La Bussière. Cette abbaye présente la particularité d'avoir deux chartes datées de 1131, année de sa fondation et décrivant ses possessions initiales[55]. Si on les projette dans le même espace que précédemment, l'une vient se loger tout à droite et la seconde tout à gauche. Nous avons déjà dit, ci-dessus, que les pratiques du début du siècle sont extrêmement diverses et il ne peut donc pas être question de rejeter une date uniquement sur le critère du système graphique. Néanmoins, cette différence permet de soumettre à une nouvelle interrogation critique ces deux actes. Si l'absence de discipline commune et de profil scribal collectif à la naissance de l'abbaye n'étonne guère, puisqu'elle n'a pas encore pu organiser de scriptorium (son existence reste douteuse même pour les époques ultérieures[56]), la position de l'une des deux chartes au milieu de celles qui furent produites dans le dernier tiers du XIIe siècle permet néanmoins de rouvrir l'enquête d'attribution et de *discrimen veri ac falsi*: au terme d'une étude approfondie, il devient possible de démontrer que cet acte n'est pas des années 1130 ou 1140, mais des années 1170[57]. Ce n'est pas la divergence des systèmes graphiques qui apporte une preuve définitive. Seule l'étude approfondie des groupes et des contextes de production permet des analyses validées. Conjointement avec les autres méthodes de la critique interne et externe, cet apport de la paléographie systématique fait toutefois naître un nouveau regard sur le document et contribue à dater et à attribuer.

Conclusion

La pratique collective de l'écriture, les effets d'école et les cohérences des *scriptoria* sont à l'origine de morphologies distinctes et caractéristiques, et s'incarnent également dans des systèmes graphiques communs. Ces derniers permettent de distinguer un «profil scribal collectif». Ce concept se prête davantage que la morphologie aux études comparées et ouvre la voie à des enquêtes plus larges sur l'écriture et ses milieux sociaux, sur les archaïsmes ou les conservatismes possibles de groupes religieux et de réseaux sociaux, soit en

---

[55] Les deux actes sont conservés sous la même cote: Dijon, Archives départementales, 12 H 36.

[56] A. BONDÉELLE-SOUCHIER, Bibliothèques cisterciennes dans la France médiévale: répertoire des abbayes d'hommes (Documents, études et répertoires publiés par l'IRHT 41, 1991) p. 146–147. La Bussière ne semble pas avoir hébergé de scriptorium actif et sa bibliothèque a complètement disparu.

[57] D. STUTZMANN, Écrire le récit des origines: les chartes de fondation de La Bussière et l'enjeu mémoriel des actes diplomatiques (1131-vers 1170), in: Cîteaux. Commentarii Cistercienses 64/1–2 (2013) p. 5–40.

raison d'une dynamique collective, soit sous l'influence du système graphique de l'écriture livresque.

Le XIIe siècle constitue une période particulière où les écritures livresques et diplomatiques sont morphologiquement presque identiques et qui offre à la production diplomatique une invention formelle par artifice calligraphique. Ces conditions font de ce siècle un objet d'étude privilégié pour l'historien de l'écriture: les exemples de Fontenay et La Bussière montrent à quel point l'analyse des systèmes graphiques peut se révéler un outil heuristique puissant tant pour la paléographie que pour la diplomatique.

Malgré des travaux antérieurs[58], les corpus de chartes dont un encodage allographétique autorise l'analyse du système graphique sont encore trop maigres. Aussi est-il encore trop tôt pour tirer des conclusions générales sur ces systèmes et sur la perception qu'avaient les scribes eux-mêmes de leur pratique. Avec des outils ergonomiques et des corpus plus abondants et enrichis, l'on pourra sans nul doute tester de nouvelles hypothèses[59].

---

[58] A. FIEBIG, Urkundentext: computergestützte Auswertung deutschsprachiger Urkunden der Kuenringer auf Basis der eXtensible Markup Language (XML) (Schriften zur südwestdeutschen Landeskunde 33, 2000).

[59] L'enrichissement permettra d'étudier l'influence du discours diplomatique, de la mise en page et du sens sur les pratiques d'écriture (par exemple, comportements graphiques particuliers dans l'invocation, sur la première ligne, dans les noms de personnes, etc.). Un corpus plus abondant permettra de voir si certaines formes sont corrélées ou assimilables: un s long ondulé passant sous la ligne en fin de mot est-il tracé comme forme alternative d'un s rond passant sous la ligne ou reste-t-il perçu comme un s long? Une lettre portant une abréviation comme le signe tironien –us se comporte-t-elle comme une lettre en fin de mot ou faut-il distinguer un cas spécifique, ou faut-il distinguer selon les scribes?

Poor tools to think with
The human space in digital diplomatics

JONATHAN JARRETT

1. Introduction

It is hard to generalise too far about the new digital space in diplomatics for a number of reasons. First and most obvious of these is the great differences between the documents that may be involved from area to area, although such generalisations must be faced by projects like Monasterium.net whose intended coverage is global[1]. Perhaps second, though, is the great difference in scale between different researchers' projects and the expertise they require. An effort like Monasterium.net involves, in its own words, 'a Consortium of more than 50 institutions from 10 countries'; the present writer, however, took his first steps into digital diplomatics by himself, because of a particular question about the history of tenth-century Catalonia that was best so answered[2]. My enquiries involve a lot of charters, far too many to use accurately with no computerised help, and only thus have I come to work on diplomatics, digital or otherwise. This backdoor route into the field may, however, place me in a position to examine some issues that arise in the digital treatment, and indeed the digital generalisation, of our material.

---

[1] On this variety see e.g. R. Härtel, Notarielle und kirchliche Urkunden im frühen und hohen Mittelalter (Historische Hilfswissenchaften, 2011) p. 51–210 with examples 329–402; on its problems for scholarship, see J. Jarrett, Introduction, in: Problems and Possibilities of Early Medieval Charters, ed. by J. Jarrett/A. S. McKinley (International Medieval Research 19, 2013) p. 1–18, here p. 2–7. On digital diplomatic as a field see first of all Digitale Diplomatik: neue Technologien in der historischen Arbeit mit Urkunden, ed. by G. Vogeler (AfD Beiheft 12, 2009). Monasterium: MÕM: Europe's virtual documents online, ed. by ICARUS – International Centre for Archival Research, <http://www.monasterium.net>.

[2] Quote from Goals, in MÕM, <http://monasterium.net/pages/en/about-the-project.php>. My work emerged as J. Jarrett, Rulers and Ruled in Frontier Catalonia, 880–1010: pathways of power (Studies in History, 2010).

2. Initial Aims

My initial project, when I began my doctorate more than a decade ago, was to try and work out what social interactions were like on the well-documented but little-studied Spanish March of the Carolingian Empire. Although I did not immediately realise it, my work rapidly acquired characteristics of a network approach, plotting what I called 'pathways of power' through this society by finding groups of regular collaborators with persons and with institutions in the charters and placing them in their local contexts. In this way, I could say something about these pathways along which power and authority moved. I spoke of social networks when advertising my work, but in reality I was largely unaware of technical work on networks that might have helped me. My enquiry was analytically far more primitive: I did construct networks, but only so as to draw particular paths through them, not to study the network in its totality[3]. Large parts of each network were, in short, data, not information. These limits were at least partly those of technology, because the primary technology mapping these pathways was my own brain, which, alas, is far from infallible.

3. Uninformed and informed applications of technology

There were, obviously, ways in which technology would have helped this enquiry right from the start. I now suspect that a better approach would have been to have recorded each document in something like a wiki, with an entry for each document, from which each was linked to an entry for its archive, an entry for each participant, an entry for each place mentioned, and perhaps many more[4]. The possibilities of such an approach have since been demonstrated, indeed, on a purely unpaid basis, by an independent scholar by the name of Joan Vilaseca. His website at Cathalaunia.org, besides being an impossibly rich bibliographical resource, by now has most of the charters from the area of the turn of the ninth and tenth centuries digitised and atomised into personal names and place-names, with references to literature and digital texts taken from editions[5]. Each document has a page with links to the source

---

[3] One might now contrast R. BOULET et al., Batch Kernel SOM and Related Laplacian Methods for Social Network Analysis, in: Neurocomputing 71 (2008) p. 1257–1273, doi:10.1016/j.neucom.2007.12.026.

[4] Cf. A. IVANOVS/A. VARFOLOMEYEV in this volume. Since sending this chapter to press I have had some success in this with Zim, which can be downloaded from <zim-wiki.org>.

[5] Cathalaunia. La Catalunya abans de Catalunya, ed. J. VILASECA, <http://www.cathalaunia.org/>. See also the site blog, including accounts of data visualisation ex-

of the text and to each anthroponym and toponym[6]. These each link to a file per person or place with a list of his, her or its occurrences, each of course linked to the page of the respective document[7]. It is very simple therefore to rapidly see a list of all occurrences of a certain person or place. There is some difficulty with the word 'certain', however, to which I will return. I would not build things in quite the same way if I had to start over, but nonetheless this is very like what I probably should have done.

4. Improvements to the uninformed approach

Senyor Vilaseca, however, is a programmer, and I am not. Furthermore, as I began the project in 2000, neither my available hardware nor its software made a proper, scaled, database approach viable. Instead I read my charters in their editions and made extensive long-hand notes, which I marked in the margin whenever I saw something I thought was interesting. On reaching the end of such an edition, I would create a list – in Microsoft Word 6.0 – of those inter-esting data. Very quickly these lists became database-like. Certain persons re-curred; their entry therefore included all their occurrences. When I started to deal with people who occurred in several archives, I discovered that Word contained the ability to make links between files using DDE or OLE, and so I anchored their occurrences together like that, and tried to ensure that each file contained a full list of the person's occurrences in all archives checked[8].

This was, of course, neither well-advised nor very successful. Unfortunately I did not have time to retype all the documents I had dealt with in this way later in the project, and so those files persist, and I still try to keep them up to date. But the offhand nature of the files and their contents has also often been a great virtue. For example, here is an excerpt from one about the consecra-tion of a church:

---

periments, <cathalaunis.wordpress.com>.

   [6] E.g. his Documents / D00001, <http://cathalaunia.org/Documentia/D00001>, the document elsewhere published in Catalunya Carolíngia II: els diplomes carolingis a Catalunya, ed. R. D'ABADAL I DE VINYALS (Memòries de la Secció Històrico-Arque-ològica 2 & 3, 1926–55), Girona 2.

   [7] E.g. his Gents / G00002, <http://cathalaunia.org/Gents/G000002>, which is Bishop Wimar of Girona, recipient of Documents / D00001 as above.

   [8] Some more detailed description of this process, with examples and illustrations, as J. JARRETT, Take notes(s) II: re-examining Sant Pere de Casserres, in: J. JARRETT, A Corner of Tenth-Century Europe, <http://tenthmedieval.wordpress.com/2011/04/06/take-notes-ii-re-examining-sant-pere-de-casserres/>.

10 = CDCB MMXXIII & Cat. Car. IV 37: is the consecration of Sant Martin de Congost, including an unusually full description of its parish, including a dependent church of St Stephen at Castell de Centelles, which was presumably up till then the chief one in the area, and is we may note in a castle term; Emma gives an *aprisio* made by her uncle Sunifred, though which side of her family he was on is not made clear; what is clear is that she held personal property even after oblation ...; its penalty clause sets fine of a 'talent' of gold, very Old Testament but possibly not very useful. Its last line is in strange characters, which may be a mixture of Greek and numeric characters; it is seemingly by the Vic chapter priest Athanagild, seen in Cat. Car. IV 9, 10, 16, 283 & 285 & Vic 8, 10, 11, 16, 22 & 31. The only other charter I know with Greek characters in it is the much later Vic 533 by Altemir, which cannot be related. Plate 4[9].

Someone who had watched me work over the years would be able to tell that this is an early entry, because before very long I stopped making entries within entries; the priest Athanagild, whose annotation here was in fact in Coptic (and who also once signed with musical notation) would have had his own, as he entirely deserves[10]. Nonetheless, it is not a redundant exercise to consider what sort of data scheme would capture everything that is featured in this rather jumbled note. The locations, the properties and the participants would fit into most sensible diplomatic templates. The fine in the *sanctio* certainly could be databased, but it would be very hard to sort, given that a talent was not a unit of currency any more in this area, and was here mentioned largely for Biblical resonance. Should one convert it to *solidi* for informational compatibility, even though no real conversion between the units was in mind here, and although actual *solidi* were also long out of use?[11] Perhaps so.

[9] The *sigla* here relate to the following editions: CDCB: Colección Diplomática del Condado de Besalú, ed. F. MONSALVATJE Y FOSSAS (Noticias Históricas 11–13, 15 & 19, 1901–1908); Cat. Car. IV: Catalunya Carolíngia IV. Els Comtats d'Osona i Manresa, ed. R. ORDEIG I MATA (Memòries de la Secció Històrico-Arqueològica 53, 1999); Vic: Diplomatari de la Catedral de Vic (segles IX-X), ed. E. JUNYENT I SUBIRÀ, ed. by R. ORDEIG I MATA. The edition and document being abstracted was El Archivo Condal de Barcelona en los siglos IX-X. Estudio crítico de sus fondos, ed. F. UDINA MARTORELL (Textos 18, 1951), 10.
[10] Athanagild's notation, and the identification as Coptic, visible in UDINA, Archivo Condal lám. 4. The document with the musical notation is ORDEIG, Catalunya Carolíngia IV, 9, which also mentions an organ in the tiny frontier church that was being consecrated. See J. GARRIGOSA I MASSONA, L'acta de consagració de l'església del castell de Tona i la seva importància musical, in: Tona 889–1989. Mil cent anys de història, ed. by A. PLADEVALL (1989) p. 27–30.
[11] G. FELIU, La Moneda a Barcelona entre el 960 i el 1030, in: La Gènesi de l'Autonòmia Fiscal del Municipi (Quaderns d'Història 2–3, 1996) p. 103–115; J. JARRETT, Currency change in pre-millennial Catalonia: coinage, counts and economics, in: Numismatic Chronicle 169 (2009) p. 217–243.

The peculiar last line, however, except in the most encyclopaedic of data structures, would have to be relegated to notes.

Because there was no data structure here at all, however, all the contents are such notes such as this one, and, of course, they respond to electronic search, as long as I can imagine or recall suitable search terms. This means that although it is æsthetically and technically ugly, this system is not useless. It is, however, hard to keep updated, especially as even where changes are cascaded between documents successfully they become slower to open with each extra field, and extremely irregular.

It quickly became obvious that for some enquiries this would not do, and as more money and better computers became available to me, I investigated databases. Here I was aided by professional experience in Microsoft Access, not just in non-historical areas but in a project not unlike mine at University College London[12]. I customised the design that we created on that project for my purposes. Now in the closing stages of my doctorate, I had too little time to enter all the documents I had used into the database, and instead I dealt only with those that mentioned one particular count, Borrell II of Barcelona, Girona, Osona, and Urgell, who ruled from 947–993 and left us some 150 traces of his presence in charters[13].

The database in which these, and by now other, documents are stored is not very complex. Its front-end is a pair of forms, one of which is designed to display the charter's information in something like the sequence that it occurs in the original text, and the other of which is designed for speed of data entry. The actual workings are three main tables, one for documents, one for persons and one for places, along with look-up tables for certain values in these. One-to-many joins link Charters to Persons and Places and every single instance of a name is recorded individually in one or other of those tables, with a role recorded alongside it in the table which is then used to filter those names in the display form. Various queries run on this, or rather on one of a set of filters selecting particular projects' datasets, that allow me to ask where names matching a certain pattern occur, and even what persons occur at a place of such and such a pattern, and so forth[14].

5. Resisting accuracy

This is, perhaps, not very rigorous. There are, for example, 6,400 entries in my Persons table at the time of writing. This comes from a sample of 419

---

[12] This project has not resulted in publication at the time of writing.

[13] Discussed in JARRETT, Rulers and Ruled p. 141–166.

[14] Limited illustration at id., Takes note(s) II.

documents, which typically feature three or four transactors, four neighbours, three witnesses and a scribe. I can say with certainty, however, that of
the 340 entries for persons called Borrell, at least 297 are the same man, the
count around whom the database was first compiled. (The certainty is justified below.) Why have I allowed for this duplication; why does he not have
one entry as my ideal plan above would suggest? There are two reasons, one
conceptual and one technical.

5.1 Technical issues

The technical issues revolve around the actual process of data entry. As is well
known by the readers of this series, medieval charters are not uniform records; they contain a great deal of variation even when supposedly formulaic,
and very often present difficult category decisions[15]. By this I do not mean
mere normalisation of terms, so as to ensure that a search for a known entity
returns all instances of that entity, however spelt or referred to in the original
source, but more basic difficulties about how to classify things.

A document that contains several transactions, for example, presents the
obvious issue: are we to count documents, or transactions?[16] Or both? The
opposite case arises when we have two versions of a document recording the
same transaction, perhaps honestly but perhaps not (and often with no means
to tell)[17]. These are questions which will, to a considerable extent, be answered by the original aims of each research project, but it is hopefully obvious that there are advantages to each choice, and a person with a different
project might prefer the alternative.

Dates, often missing or vague, present a particular problem, especially in
an area such as this where one cannot, *a priori*, be sure when the royal reigns
that determined dating clauses were being counted from[18]. For diplomatists

---

[15] See e.g. A. Rio, Charters, law codes and formulae. The Franks between theory
and practice, in: Frankland: the Franks and the world of the early middle ages. Essays
in honour of Dame Jinty Nelson, ed. by P. J. Fouracre/D. Ganz (2008) p. 7–27, and
for Catalonia specifically M. Zimmermann, Écrire et lire en Catalogne (IXe-XIIe siècle)
(Bibliothèque de la Casa de Velázquez 23, 2003) p. 246–284.

[16] One such can be seen in Udina, Archivo Condal, 37, where the three transactions
obviously took place at the same ceremony but bear no relation to each other.

[17] E.g. Ordeig, Catalunya Carolíngia IV, 995A & 995B, to which cf. also Nr. 996;
for analysis and a side-by-side comparison of the texts see J. Jarrett, Pathways of
Power in Late-Carolingian Catalonia (phil. Diss. Birkbeck 2005) <http://www.chiark.
greenend.org.uk/~jjarrett/thesis.html>, p. 38–48.

[18] This subject has of course received a considerable amount of attention thanks to
the DEEDS Project of the University of Toronto: see Dating Undated Medieval Charters, ed. by M. Gervers (2000). For the Catalan material the question is taken up in

of a certain training the obvious distinction might be the type of charter, its *actio iuris*, and many of them indeed proclaim *'hic est venditio'* or similar so that this approach has something to use[19]. Sometimes, however, the scribes were not sure, recording *donatio seu venditio*, donations with prices mentioned or sales without[20]. Do we enter the document twice, once as each, messing with counting later on, or else create a deeper reference hierarchy in which a term 'gift/sale' exists that is a superset of both 'gift' and 'sale'? How many such special terms might this sample require ...? How many look-up tables, to make sure every such question is always answered the same way? What about when, despite our previous decisions, we find a case that seems to require the opposite answer?

To show that such issues are not just the author's hyperbole, I demonstrate with an extreme example, a document that presents an unusual number of such complexities. This huge single-sheet is a sort of *pancarta* from the monastery of Sant Pere de Casserres, in Catalonia near the city of Vic[21]. It firstly presents the problem that it contains five separate transactions on one parchment, but we have probably foreseen this in our notional database. The real problem is the first transaction. This lengthy and scribbled-over occasion saw, it tells us, the sale – though no prices are recorded – of 23 separate properties by 32 persons (two of whom were later crossed out and who recur at the end of one of the lists of names, but not the other). Reading more deeply, however, exposes that these transactions were being copied up from previous charters, some of which we have, and those documents reveal that the properties were then being sold not to the monastery, as here, but to the viscountess who is supposed to have founded the place[22]. The explanation may be that she

---

UDINA, Archivo Condal p. 44–80 and G. FELIU I MONTFORT, La cronología según los reyes de francos en el condado de Barcelona (siglo X), in: Anuario de Estudios Medievales 6 (1969) p. 441–463.

[19] For this and other means of categorisation see HÄRTEL, Urkunden p. 24–39.

[20] E.g., as well as the large example below, Col·lecció diplomàtica de Sant Pere de Casserres, ed. I. LLOP, I (Diplomataris 44, 2009), 100, a self-proclaimed sale with no price or any indication that one has been omitted, as opposed to the numerous cases of the reverse from England discussed in J. CAMPBELL, The Sale of Land and the Economics of Power in Early England. Problems and possibilities, in: Haskins Society Journal 1 (1989) p. 23–37.

[21] Barcelona, Biblioteca Universitària, Biblioteca de la Reserva, Pergamins C/3. The text is edited as LLOP, Col·lecció diplomàtica, 62, 63 & 65–67. I hope to study this document and its context further in a future paper.

[22] Thus, Riquel, Teuderic, Ermetruit, Guifré and Livul, the first sellers not struck out in LLOP, Col·lecció Diplomàtica, 62, can be found making the same sale to the viscountess in 56 there. Reinard and Alena, 13th and 14th sellers in 62 as it stands, sold the same lands to the viscountess in 59, which shares a parchment with 60, another sale to the viscountess that is also repeated by its sellers, Durabile, Oliba, Sesnanda and Er-

(Barcelona, Biblioteca
Universitària, Pergamins C/3,
image copyright the author.)

had died without passing these lands on to the monastery, and that the house's
managers, and in some cases the original sellers, since several of them went on to
appear in monastery transactions hereafter and therefore must have been com-
plicit, then confected a supposed occasion on which the properties had all been
sold to the monastery instead. The signatures, however, are all by the scribe, and
the fourth points in the *signa*, in this area sometimes left for transactors to put
in themselves, were never supplied, so we may doubt that the occasion really
took place[23]. If it did, it must have been before the charter was written, or the

---

menard, in 62 where they are 39th to 42nd sellers. More interestingly, 71 and 72, again
sharing a parchment, are sales to the viscountess that postdate the *pancarta*, where the
same sellers and lands occur selling to the monastery (Abo, Ranlo, Sentemir, Gro,
Amalric and Bero in 71, sellers 19 through 24 in 62 as it stands, and Guisad, Emma,
Miró and Fruio in 72, sellers 25 to 28 in 62 as it stands). This obviously calls the *pancarta*'s purported date into question.

[23] On this practice see ZIMMERMANN, Écrire et lire p. 81–90. Cf. for France B.-M.
TOCK, Scribes, souscripteurs et témoins dans les actes privés en France (VIIe – début XIIe
siècle (ARTEM (Atelier de Recherche sur les Textes Médiévaux) 9, 2006) p. 360–363.

signatures would presumably have been completed. In other words, we have something like ten transactions, some of known dates, here turned into one false one under another date that actually refers to an event that did not happen. The data scheme that can represent this is a complex one indeed![24]

5.2 Concepts of enquiry

All of these are technical headaches with which many digital practitioners will be familiar, but they are not necessarily ones that have to be solved. We can take as a conceptual example the original purpose of my database, to identify recurrences of persons in the documents that concerned Count Borrell. Since I needed the database to identify these recurrences, it was axiomatic that I could not link persons at data entry stage. (One could in theory be a bit more certain with places, until one realises how often names like *vinea*, *ad fontem* and so forth recur ...[25]) Otherwise, in order to find out who they were, I would already have had to know.

In some cases, of course, one can know this. When I say with confidence that 279 of my 340 Borrells are the count, this is possible because that is the number that occur with a comital title. There are in fact three other occurrences of counts called Borrell in my sample, but they are identifiable either by date or the details of their ancestry[26]. However, there are instances of Count Borrell appearing without his title, before his elevation[27]. Here he can

---

[24] It should be noted that even by editing the transactions on the document separately, LLOP has consciously or unconsciously opted to reduce their association, and perhaps because of this, she has not observed the difficulty with its date.

[25] The geographical proximity of la Vinya de Vallfogona and la Vinya de la Vall de Sant Joan, on opposite sides of the Serra de Vallfogona in the Ripollès and seen in documents which do not always provide more geographical context than the Ripollès itself, was especially problematic; see JARRETT, Rulers and Ruled p. 30–32 and references at n. 34.

[26] One is a forged instance confusing Borrell II with his homonymous predecessor of Urgell (ORDEIG, Catalunya Carolíngia IV, IV), and obvious by its date; one is his uncle Guifré II Borrell, Count-Marquis of Barcelona, Girona and Osona 898–911, identified only by *cognomen* on this occasion (Diplomatari de la Catedral de Barcelona: documents dels anys 844–1260. Volum 1: documents dels anys 844–1000, ed. A. FÀBREGA I GRAU (Sèries 4: Fonts Documentals 1, 1995), 30) and distinguishable by being specified as the brother of Count-Marquis Sunyer (911–947) rather than his son; the third is Borrell Count of Pallars, distinguishable because of appearing (in Els documents, dels anys 981–1010, de l'Arxiu Capitular de la Seu d'Urgell, ed. C. BARAUT, in: Urgellia 3 (1980) p. 7–166, no. 232) as a nephew and executor of the older count in that man's will.

[27] E.g. Catalunya Carolíngia V. Els comtats de Girona, Besalú, Empúries i Peralada, ed. S. SOBREQUÉS I VIDAL/S. RIERA I VIADER/M. ROVIRA I SOLÀ, ed. by R. ORDEIG I

be identified because he is said to be son of Count Sunyer, an identification repeatedly made throughout his subsequent career in bequests for his father's memory and the like.

What I needed the database to do, therefore, was to present me with all of the kinds of information which might make such decisions about identities possible, but without having effectively decided them already. This is why all the instances must appear. If I search my database, for example, for persons called Miró in the sample I have for documents relating to that monastery of Sant Pere de Casserres, I get forty-eight results[28]. Twelve of these appear with some kind of title; in six cases it is *presbiter*, in three *sacerdos* and in one, a seventeenth-century notice of a lost document, *sacerdot* in Catalan[29]. In two of these cases such a person occurs as scribe, and here one can actually compare the signatures and say that this is the same man[30]. However, the institutional context and the frequency with which the priests in this record appeared as landholders in the immediate area make it likely that all the occurrences except the earliest, distanced by nearly eighty years from the next, are also this person[31]. Likewise, four occurrences in the space of ten years by a Miró without any title, but all as witnesses for property in the nearby town of Roda de Ter being transferred, seem very likely to be the same person as each other, but one forty years before this is unlikely to be[32]. Whether the landowner in the same area who appears in intermediate documents as neighbour should be reckoned with the witness, however, I would prefer not to say[33].

Mata (Memòries de la Secció Històrico-Arqueològica 61, 2003), 260.

[28] From Ordeig, Catalunya Carolíngia IV, 302, 1393 & 1681 & Llop, Col·lecció diplomàtica, 3, 4, 11, 48, 54, 55, 59, 60, 62, 63, 72, 73, 76, 78, 88, 90, 93, 96, 100, 104, 110, 115, 116, 118, 119, 124, 125, 128, 131, 139 & 145, in some of which such a person occurs in more than one role.

[29] *Presbiter*: Llop, Col·lecció diplomàtica, 60, 73, 76, 90 & 116, in 73 in two roles; *sacerdos*: Ordeig, Catalunya Carolíngia IV, 302 & Llop, Col·lecció diplomàtica, 54 & 78; *sacerdot*: 55.

[30] Ibd., 60 & 73. Cf. Tock, Scribes, p. 311–322, for concerns about such methods, and in particular the possibility of scribes accurately imitating others' handwriting.

[31] That one Ordeig, Catalunya Carolíngia IV, 302 (927); the next Llop, Col·lecció Diplomàtica, 90, the first part of which dates to 999 (and so indexed as Ordeig, Catalunya Carolíngia IV, 1828).

[32] The four: Llop, Col·lecció diplomàtica, 124, 125, 128 & 145; the one: Ordeig, Catalunya Carolíngia IV, 1393.

[33] Visible in Llop, Col·lecció diplomàtica, 63, 100 & 119. On digital methodologies for such questions see also F.-W. Westerhoff, Gruppensuche. Ein Verfahren zur Identifizierung von Personengruppen in mittelalterlichen Namen-Quellen. Beschreibung des Verfahrens und der Programme (Schriftenreihe des Rechenzentrums der Universität Münster 61, 1988); F. Tinti, The Prosopography of Anglo-Saxon England:

6. Accurate inaccuracy

I think that, where I have been prepared to deduce here, the deductions are all reasonable, but of course they are not certain. This is not a failing of the database, however; it is an accurate result. There is not enough information to make those judgements, and the data returned from the query accurately reflects that. This design is set up to require the human user to make the final decision, or not. This subset is small enough that I can, even without a computer, establish accurately that we cannot tell which of these Miros are the same on a logical basis, and I ought not, therefore, to entertain data schemas that would make me do so. We do not, in fact, have to make technical solutions for these problems, because the historian can do as much with the information presented this way as he or she can with it anchored to look-up tables and so on.

On the other hand, one needs to know about the possibilities. Senyor Vilaseca, faced with an immensely variable orthography, opted in his Cathalaunia database to follow the spellings of names in documents rigorously. Thus, in his index of persons, there appear one Ansolfus, three Ansulfos, and one Ansulfus, all of which represent the same personal name[34]. One of these two Ansulfs (to normalise to modern Catalan) was a priest, who represented the bishop of Urgell in court in 910 and is therefore likely also to have been the priest who gave land to Urgell cathedral the year before[35]. Was he, however, also Ansolfus, who witnessed the will of an Urgell priest in 901?[36] That one uses no clerical title and we may think not, but with this set-up it is not obvious that the choice exists to be made. My feeling is, therefore, that by choosing to unite information about persons where they can be certainly identified but not otherwise, Senyor Vilaseca's database was then operating with an

---

facts and factoids, in: Prosopography approaches and applications: a handbook, ed. by K. S. B. KEATS-ROHAN (2007), p. 197–209; J. VILASECA i CORBERA, Detecció de grups d'homònims en documents de l'Alta Edat Mitjana, in: VILASECA, Recerques sobre l'Alta Edat Mitjana Catalana (II) (2013), p. 119–162.

[34] Ansolfus: J. VILASECA, Gents / G000938 <http://cathalaunia.org/Gents/G000938>. Ansulfo [1]: Gents / G002640 <http://cathalaunia.org/Gents/G002640>. Ansulfo [2]; Gents / G003018 <http://cathalaunia.org/Gents/G003018>. Ansulfo (jutge, reedificador): Gents / G000862 <http://cathalaunia.org/Gents/G000862>. Ansulfus (prevere, mandatari): Gents / G01994 <http://cathalaunia.org/Gents/G001994>.

[35] Gents / G01994 as in n. 33 above, seen so in Els documents, dels segles IX i X, conservats a l'Arxiu Capitular de la Seu d'Urgell, ed. C. BARAUT, in: Urgellia 2 (1979) p. 78–143, 66 & 67.

[36] Gents / G000938, as in n. 33 above, and so seen in Les actes de consagracions d'esglesies del bisbat d'Urgell (segles IX-XII), ed. C. BARAUT, in: Urgellia 1 (1978) p. 11–182, 14. See now VILASECA, Detecció de grups.

embedded double data standard. Given its structure, with entries per person that aim to aggregate data, it could not of course be otherwise, but his choices, and the choices of anyone who might set their data up similarly, would be challengeable. I make no claims of rigour for my set-up, where I make just such choices outside the database, but there is a difference between the tool and the results that is preserved that way, and that difference is important.

7. Conclusion

When we set out to manipulate information from medieval charters, we are not facing raw information. In extreme cases, the data in a charter may not have been accurate when they were recorded for writing up, whether because of malice or because of incompetence. Every stage of transmission multiplies this possibility, distorting not just by scribal error but by filtering and recasting of the information to suit the agendas, political, personal or administrative, of the copyists. Cartulary copies which omit witnesses stand at an end of this continuum of degradation much closer to us than to the people who originally generated the need for a record with their actions[37]. Obviously, when we have to manipulate such truly large data samples, we have to create processes and schemes that make the whole venture possible. We should, however, avoid letting those schemes add a further layer of degradation to our data by imputing uncertain characteristics or identifications to the data. For this historian's purposes, at least, rigour can be unhelpful, and what is really needed is a data scheme that preserves the flexibility of interpretation that was open to the participants and needs to be open, too, to those who now analyse their actions[38].

---

[37] On which see P. J. GEARY, Phantoms of Remembrance: memory and oblivion at the end of the first millennium (1994).

[38] The initial research which is recounted in this article was carried out with the aid of an Arts and Humanities Research Board Post-Graduate Scholarship and two Birkbeck College Graduate Bursaries, as well as other support from Birkbeck College, University of London; it would not have been possible without these awards, for which I remain very grateful. I must thank for their help towards the creation of this article Professor Wendy Davies, for whom I first attempted to apply my database knowledge to these problems, and Senyor Joan Vilaseca, my debt to whom is obvious by citation. My views are, of course, not necessarily theirs, but I could not have formed mine without interacting with them. I should also thank Dr Georg Vogeler and the organisers of the Digital Diplomatic 2011 conference, where the first version of this piece was given, for their work in making that conference possible and for encouraging me to write this article up for submission, and the commentators there and Professor Antonella Ambrosio for their suggestions for improvements; again, the blame for any failure to adapt myself to their views must be mine alone.

Appendices

Abstracts

I. Technical and theoretical models

BENOÎT-MICHEL TOCK

La diplomatique numérique, une diplomatique magique?

Les nouvelles possibilités offertes par les techniques modernes ont donné à la diplomatique un aspect que l'on pourrait qualifier de «magique». L'on accède facilement à un nombre de documents encore impensable il y a quelque années de cela, l'on dispose d'outils renouvelés pour leur étude ... Pour autant, l'on peut encore améliorer la chose, en affinant les instruments ainsi mis à notre disposition, et en profitant de ces nouvelles possibilités pour ne pas hésiter à donner des éditions et des outils différenciés, avec des niveaux d'élaboration correspondant aux situations et aux besoins. Il convient en outre de s'assurer de la pérennité des données ainsi produites, et de ne pas négliger pour autant les compétences de base qui sont traditionnellement celles du diplomatiste.

Digital Diplomatics: Magical Diplomatics?

The new possibilities which modern technologies offer have given diplomatics what might be called a "magic touch". One has easy access to a number of documents which would have been absolutely inconceivable a few years ago. We now have renewed tools at our disposal for their study ... Yet, things could still be improved by making these tools more efficient; the opportunity these new possibilities give us could be taken to resolutely create differentiated editions and tools, whose degree of elaborations would correspond to the situations and needs encountered. Moreover, the durability of the data which is thus produced is a question which should be considered; and for all this, the basic competencies which are traditionally those of a diplomatist should not be neglected.

CAMILLE DESENCLOS, VINCENT JOLIVET

Diple, propositions pour la convergence de schémas XML/TEI
dédiés à l'édition de sources diplomatiques

La complexité des normes de l'édition critique et la singularité de chaque projet éditorial semblent faire obstacle aux tentatives de standardisation que l'informatisation exige. La TEI, davantage adaptée aux sources littéraires que diplomatiques, permet de définir des schémas très différents et parfois difficilement interopérables pour des projets similaires. Solution alternative, la CEI (Charters Encoding Initiative) promeut des éléments spécifiques, au risque d'empêcher l'interopérabilité avec d'autres types de sources. L'École des chartes, à travers le développement de Diple, s'est engagée dans une voie médiane qui consiste à définir des schémas XML conformes à la TEI et dédiés à l'édition critique et à ses spécificités (tableau de la tradition, apparat critique, etc.).

Diple, en associant systématiquement à ses schémas des fonctionnalités pour les exploiter (affichage HTML, exports divers), facilite la mise en ligne des corpus, résout les problèmes de présentation des structures textuelles récurrentes et permet à l'éditeur de se concentrer sur les particularités de son corpus (développement des abréviations, repérage des parties du discours, etc.). Par ses schémas partagés et ses outils d'édition, Diple pourrait permettre une convergence des usages de la TEI pour l'édition de sources diplomatiques. Une telle convergence ouvrirait des perspectives scientifiques en facilitant l'interrogation croisée des corpus édités.

Diple, a proposal for the convergence of XML/TEI schemas dedicated to the edition
of diplomatic sources

The complexity of norms for a critical edition and the singularity of each editorial project seem to prevent any standardisation required by the computerisation. TEI, better adapted to literary texts than to diplomatic sources, allows, even for projects similar to each other, the building of very different schemas which are thus hardly interoperable. Another option, CEI (Charters Encoding Initiative) enhances specific elements but could impair interoperability with other kind of sources. The École nationale des chartes, through Diple's development, has chosen a middle path: defining XML schemas which are consistent to TEI and dedicated to specific elements of critical edition (tradition, critical apparatus, etc.).

The systematical association between Diple's schemas and the functionalities intended to exploit them (HTML display, various exports) facilitates corpora uploading, resolves the display problems of recurrent text structures and allows the editor to concentrate on his corpus' specificities (abbreviations development, diplomatic formulas, ...). Its shared schemas and edition tools could allow a convergence of TEI practices for the edition of diplomatic sources. Such a convergence would make cross-searching within edited corpora easier, thus opening new scientific perspectives.

FRANCESCA CAPOCHIANI, CHIARA LEONI,
ROBERTO ROSSELLI DEL TURCO

Codifica, pubblicazione e interrogazione sul web di *corpora* diplomatici per mezzo di strumenti *open source*

La consultazione di testi diplomatici costituisce uno strumento di lavoro insostituibile per gli storici e gli archivisti. La loro disponibilità online offre il massimo della flessibilità e della diffusione, permettendo allo studioso di accedere a questo materiale prezioso senza barriere spaziali o temporali: alcuni progetti, come *The Electronic Sawyer* (http://www.esawyer.org.uk/) e l'attività della *École nationale des chartes* (http://www.enc.sorbonne.fr), mostrano come sia possibile offrire testi di alta qualità scientifica sul web usando una codifica XML delle fonti. La loro creazione, tuttavia, richiede risorse non indifferenti: è possibile digitalizzare e mettere online questo materiale, per le proprie ricerche e per il beneficio della comunità accademica, in maniera (relativamente) semplice ed efficace? Inoltre una pubblicazione sul web è incompleta se non consente un'agevole consultazione e il *data mining* delle risorse offerte: come facilitare l'accesso e la ricerca all'interno dei testi?

Questo articolo si propone di mostrare come, grazie all'uso di software *open source*, il singolo studioso o un piccolo team di ricercatori possa digitalizzare un corpus di documenti usando il formato TEI (http://www.tei-c.org/), pubblicarlo sul web e inserire nell'interfaccia un motore di ricerca come eXist (http://exist-db.org/) o XTF (http://xtf.cdlib.org/) per effettuare ricerche complesse.

Open source tools for online publication of charters

Diplomatic texts consultation is an indispensable tool for historians and archivists. Their online availability offers maximum flexibility and dissemination, allowing the scholar to access this valuable material unimpeded by spatial or temporal barriers: some projects, such as *The Electronic Sawyer* (http://www.esawyer.org.uk/) and the encoding activities of the *École nationale des chartes* (http://www.enc.sorbonne.fr), show how it is possible to offer high quality scientific texts on the Web based on an XML mark-up of the archival sources. Their creation, however, requires substantial resources: is it possible to digitise and to put online this type of document collections for personal research, or to benefit the whole Academic community, in a (relatively) simple and effective way? Furthermore, Web publishing is only effective if it allows easy document browsing and a way to perform powerful data mining of the resources it offers: which methods are best to allow easy text access and search?

This paper aims to show how, through the use of open source software, single scholars or a small team of researchers can encode a corpus of documents using the TEI (http://www.tei-c.org/) standard, publish it on the Web, and provide a search engine such as eXist (http://exist-db.org/) or XTF (http://xtf.cdlib.org/) for complex queries.

SERENA FALLETTA

Dalla carta al bit. Note metodologiche sull'edizione digitale
di un cartulario medievale

Il testo presenta un modello ipertestuale e sperimentale di edizione di fonti storiche codificate adottando la sintassi XML e uno schema di marcatura calibrato sulle caratteristiche specifiche della documentazione e sulle classiche esigenze e categorie di analisi critica della ricerca storica, nel tentativo di superare i problemi concettuali e metodologici riscontrati dagli storici nell'utilizzo dei database, inadeguati ad esprimere la complessità di dati qualitativi.

L'esperimento condotto, basato sull'edizione quattrocentesca del *Liber Privilegiorum Sanctae Montis Regalis Ecclesiae*, è stato pensato come un laboratorio attraverso cui comprendere con più precisione le profonde implicazioni epistemologiche dell'applicazione delle tecnologie informatiche nel trattamento delle fonti storiche. Superando il tradizionale discorso storico, caratterizzato da linearità, l'ipertesto codificato è stato infatti in grado di incorporare la fonte e gli strumenti d'indagine, riconfigurando così strumentazione tecnica e prassi accademica. Si tratta, chiaramente, di una *sperimentazione sostenibile,* basata su un'ampia ragnatela ipertestuale i cui nodi sono sia i documenti prodotti da uno specifico soggetto istituzionale che la loro storia.

From paper to bit. Methodological notes on a medieval cartulary digital edition

The paper introduces a model of an historical sources hypertext edition encoded adopting the XML syntax and a markup pattern tailored to the specific characteristics of the documentation and the categories of critical analysis of historical research. The aim of the project is the attempt to overcome the conceptual and methodological problems experienced by historians in the use of databases, inadequate to express the complexity of qualitative data.

The experiment, based on the issue of *Liber Privilegiorum Sanctae Montis Regalis Ecclesiae*, was designed as a workshop for the comprehension of the deep epistemological implications of computer technology in the treatment of historical sources. Going beyond the traditional historical discourse, characterised by linearity, the encoded hypertext has been able to incorporate source and survey instruments, thus reconfiguring the technical equipment of academic practice. It is, of course, a sustainable experiment, based on extensive web hypertext whose nodes are both the documents produced by a specific institution and their story.

GUNTER VASOLD

Progressive Editionen als multidimensionale Informationsräume

Dynamischen Editionen ermöglichen Änderungen nach dem Zeitpunkt ihrer Publikation. Dadurch werden einige Grundprinzipien von Edition in Frage gestellt, etwa dass eine Edition eine stabile und zitierbare Ressource darstellt, oder dass es nur einen oder einige wenige Editoren gibt, die autoritative Textversionen produzieren. Einen möglichen Ausweg bietet die progressive Edition. Diese ist grundsätzlich offen und ohne definiertes Ende gedacht, kann also jederzeit verändert und erweitert werden. Voraussetzung dafür ist, dass die Edition nicht nur als Produkt gesehen wird, sondern als Prozess, der zu einer stetig wachsenden Menge von Teilresultaten und Versionen führt. Daraus lassen sich statische (und damit zitierbare) Editionen ableiten; diese sind aber immer nur Momentaufnahmen, die den Status zu einem bestimmten Zeitpunkt festhalten. Resultate, Versionen und die vielfältigen Beziehungen zwischen diesen bilden einen komplexen Informationsraum, der sich mit jeder Änderung der Edition erweitert. Die Beherrschung dieses Raumes ist nur möglich, wenn zusätzlich Prozessdaten generiert werden, die alle Änderungen dokumentieren. Auf Basis dieser Prozessdaten können Beiträge überprüft, bewertet, verwaltet und für bestimmte Ansprüche aufbereitet werden. Prozessdaten sind somit wesentlicher Bestandteil einer progressiven Edition, weil sie deren Dynamik für (Mit)Editoren und Benutzer transparent machen.

Progressive editions as multidimensional information space

Dynamic forms of critical editions allow the modification of texts after the edition has been published. But how can we implement dynamic editions without breaking basic principles of critical editions, such as the assumption that an edition does not change after publication or that an edition has only one or very few editors who produce a single authoritative text version? The concept of progressive editions might be a solution, because it does no longer conceive of critical editions as products, but as perpetual processes which lead to accumulating sets of distinct results, versions, and relations between these. It is still possible to generate traditional editions, but these are merely snapshots, each representing a certain (citeable) state of the steadily growing and shifting progressive edition. Such an edition forms a multidimensional information space, which becomes more complex with every change made to the edition. Keeping track of a progressive edition requires putting a stronger focus on the processes involved. Therefore process data documenting the changes has to be considered a relevant part of the edition, as it provides opportunities to organise, analyse, and evaluate data, and to make progressive editions transparent to fellow editors and users.

LUCIANA DURANTI

The return of diplomatics as a forensic discipline

Research has proven that digital documents/records, whether born digital or digitised, cannot be preserved. It is only possible to maintain the ability to reproduce them time after time. The most complex aspects of this ongoing preservation involve those activities that aim to counteract system and format obsolescence or to extract documents from their original environment when obsolescence has occurred before any measure could be taken to avoid it. To maintain and assess the authenticity of entities that no longer exist in their native environment requires the strong theoretical and methodological framework which, for traditional documents, has been provided by diplomatics. Although such framework is still valid when examining documents in digital form, it is no longer sufficient, and needs to be integrated with a tested robust practice that allows the certain authentication of what we keep in digital form, such as the digital objects – metadata – we link to digitised medieval documents to make them accessible and analyse them. This article will discuss the integration of digital diplomatics with digital forensics, a discipline that originated a decade ago and developed into a rigorous body of concepts, principles and procedures used internationally to fight cybercrime and identify, retrieve, and make accessible authentic digital objects as evidence of the facts and acts they reveal or to which they attest.

Il ritorno della diplomatica come scienza forense

La ricerca ha dimostrato che i documenti digitali non si possono conservare. È solo possibile mantenere la capacità di riprodurli. L'aspetto più complesso di questo tipo di conservazione è estrarre i documenti dal loro ambiente nativo quando esso è diventato obsoleto. Per determinare o mantenere l'autenticità di oggetti digitali che non esistono più nel loro ambiente originale è necessario fare uso dei concetti e del metodo di analisi della diplomatica, che tuttavia devono essere integrati con le pratiche sviluppate da una nuova area di conoscenze, digital forensics. Questo articolo discute l'integrazione della diplomatica con digital forensics, una disciplina che ha avuto origine dalla necessità di combattere il cybercrime e rendere accessibili oggetti digitali come prova autentica degli atti e fatti che essi attestano.

II. Projects for the edition of texts and the publication of information

DANIEL PIÑOL ALABART

Proyecto ARQUIBANC – Digitalización de archivos privados catalanes:
una herramienta para la investigación

En Cataluña se conserva un notable patrimonio documental privado que es fundamental para estudiar la historia del país. La mayoría de archivos privados se conservan en manos privados, aunque algunos están depositados en archivos públicos. Pero uno de los mayores problemas que revisten estos fondos documentales es el difícil acceso para los investigadores. Atendiendo a esta situación el proyecto ARQUIBANC, gestionado desde el Departamento de Historia Medieval, Paleografía y Diplomática de la Universitat de Barcelona tienen como objetivo facilitar el acceso a algunos de estos archivos. Para ello el proceso de investigación sigue diferentes pasos entre los que destaca la digitalización de algunos documentos. Las imágenes de éstos se introducen en unas bases de datos accesibles desde internet con la descripción de cada documento. Para poder llevar a cabo la descripción archivística es necesario un estudio individualizado de cada documento, incluyendo estudios diplomáticos y paleográficos, así se puede dotar de información cada una de las fichas introducidas en las bases de datos.

The ARQUIBANC project – Digitisation of private archives in Catalonia:
a research tool

Catalonia preserves a significant private documentary heritage which is essential for studying the country's history. Most of the private archives remain in private hands, although some are placed in public archives. One of the biggest problems of these documents is the difficult access for researchers. In response to this situation, the ARQUIBANC project, managed by the Department of Medieval History, Palaeography and Diplomatics of the University of Barcelona, intends to give access to some of these files. The research process follows different steps, among which is the digitisation of some documents. These images are entered into a database available on the Internet with the description of each document. To create the archival description, and in order to provide each of the cards introduced in the databases with the necessary information, an individualised study of each document is necessary, including diplomatic and palaeographical study.

ANTONELLA GHIGNOLI

Sources and persons of public power in 7th–11th century Italy
The idea of *Italia Regia* and the *Italia Regia* project

Italia Regia is an on-line system whose purpose is the digitalisation and restitution on the web of the documents issued by the rulers (kings, emperors) in the Italian kingdom between the 7th and the end of the 11th century. Its elaboration is the result of an international cooperation involving French, Italian and German researchers. The core of the work is a relational and dynamic database enabling corrections and amendements at any time, providing four types of forms: royal charters, records of legal disputes, individuals, and bibliography. Since the technical infrastructure was created in recent years of the project and is already operational (tested successfully on the documentation of Tuscany), the project now intends to cover the whole of the north of Italy (the main region of the Italian kingdom), in order to give access to new information about all public documents during the period. By using this tool, researchers will be able to discern a number of phenomena simultaneously: 1) the global distribution, on the territory of the Italian kingdom, of the documentation issued by the royal power or by public agents; 2) the recipients as a whole of the entirety of the preserved public documents; 3) the individuals as a whole involved in the genesis of public writings, at any level, with or without an official title. Finally, *Italia Regia* offers a technical and scientific model which could be extended to other European regions.

Les sources et les personnages de la puissance publique dans l'Italie des VIIe-XIe
siècles. L'idée et le projet de l'*Italia regia*

Italia Regia est un système en ligne pour la numérisation et la restitution sur le web des documents émis par le pouvoir royal ou impérial dans le royaume d'Italie entre le VIIe et la fin du XIe siècle. Conçu dans le cadre d'une collaboration entre des équipes française, italienne et allemande, il fonctionne grâce à une banque de données relationnelle dont les informations sont en permanence modifiables, mettant en jeu quatre catégories de fiches: les diplômes des souverains, les comptes rendus judiciaires, les personnes, la bibliographie. Disposant déjà d'une infrastructure technique et ayant déjà couvert la Toscane, le projet compte étendre le traitement du matériel à l'ensemble de l'Italie du Nord (c'est-à-dire la région la plus importante du royaume), de manière à donner accès à des informations renouvelées sur l'ensemble de la documentation publique pour la période considérée. Comme instrument de recherche, il permettra de percevoir plusieurs phénomènes en même temps: 1) la distribution globale, sur le territoire du royaume d'Italie, de la documentation émise par le pouvoir royal ou délégué; 2) l'ensemble des destinataires de toute la documentation publique conservée; 3) l'ensemble des personnes qui, à un niveau ou un autre, avec ou sans titre, sont impliquées dans la genèse des écritures publiques. *Italia Regia* fournit enfin un modèle technique et scientifique applicable à d'autres régions européennes.

RICHARD HIGGINS

The Repository view. Opening up medieval charters

As custodians of a broad range of collections we require a system that enables cataloguing and presentation of related digital material that is flexible enough to cope with all materials. We have been using EAD as a data storage format since 1996, and in combination with our Fedora-Commons digital repository we have a powerful, adaptable tool. It is imperative that one system includes all our collections, so that enhancements and migrations apply to the whole and do not break or drop the more complex data. EAD has proven hugely adaptable and scalable, ranging from brief description of collections to the calendaring of individual charters. As one of hundreds of collections in our care, the archive of Durham Priory and Cathedral includes thousands of charters, as well as cartularies and a full range of medieval documents. EAD has been able to accommodate descriptions of all of these – even 3,000 seals. The digital repository also stores images and transcripts of the documents. It enables the association of description and image using index terms, hyperlinks, and RDF, producing a more permanent linking between data within the catalogue, and offering researchers the ability to make reliable citations of online representations of individual documents. This enables investigation of not just additional versions of the charter, but also other documents witnessed by the same parties and other common features.

ŽARKO VUJOŠEVIĆ, NEBOJŠA PORČIĆ, DRAGIĆ M. ŽIVOJINOVIĆ

Das serbische Kanzleiwesen. Die Herausforderung der digitalen Diplomatik

Die zunehmende Anwendung von Informationstechnologien bei der wissenschaftlichen Bearbeitung und Darstellung der Urkunden findet die serbische Diplomatik in der Lage vor, immer noch keine einheitliche Edition ihres nicht allzu umfangreichen Bestands von mittelalterlichen Dokumente zu haben. In diesem Zusammenhang stellt sich die Frage, ob die Entscheidung zugunsten der Herstellung eines digitalen Urkundenkorpus statt einer gedruckten Edition die bessere Lösung wäre. Hinsichtlich der Einfachheit, Schnelligkeit und Zuverlässigkeit des Datenzugangs würde ein solches Ergebnis die Benutzbarkeit der diplomatischen Quellen bei der Forschung aller Aspekte des serbischen Mittelalters erheblich erhöhen. Der wichtigste Beitrag des *born digital* Vorhabens ist in der Anregung zu sehen, die in der serbischen Diplomatik bisher oberflächlich geklärten Schlüsselfragen des Kanzleiwesens, d. h. des Entstehungsprozesses von Urkunden, leichter erforschbar zu machen. Durch eine Darstellung der Daten in nach einzelnen Urkundenelementen aufgegliederten Feldern der Datenbank und ihre kombinierte Durchsuchbarkeit könnte induktiv die bürokratische Formalitätsstufe der serbischen diplomatischen Produktion untersucht werden. Als Ergebnis wäre festzulegen, inwiefern dabei von einem System die Rede sein kann, also von einer Einrichtung, die die Forschung „Kanzlei" zu nennen pflegt, oder es sich um für die mittelalterliche Gesellschaft typische Improvisation und *ad hoc* Lösungen handelte.

The medieval Serbian chancery. Challenges of digital diplomatics

At a time when digital information technologies are increasingly entering the field of processing and presentation of documentary heritage, Serbian diplomatics still has not published its comparatively modest corpus of medieval documents within one all-encompassing collection. The question therefore arises as to whether it would be better to shift the efforts aimed at producing a traditional printed edition towards producing a digital one. Simple, quick and reliable access to digitised data would considerably enhance the use of diplomatic sources in research of almost all aspects of medieval Serbian past. Most importantly for Serbian diplomatics as a scholarly discipline, this *born digital* project would give strong encouragement to dealing with the inadequately studied key issues relating to the functioning of the chancery, that is, the process of document creation. Fitted into separate cross-searchable fields of a digital database, the ample and diverse information about diplomatic features of Serbian charters would enable a comprehensive inductive study of the actual degree of bureaucratic formalisation of Serbian documents. Through this, it should be possible to establish whether they were indeed products of a system, represented by an institution commonly termed 'the chancery', or improvisation and *ad hoc* solutions typical of medieval society.

ALEKSANDRS IVANOVS, ALEKSEY VARFOLOMEYEV

Some approaches to the semantic publication of charter corpora
The case of the diplomatic edition of Old Russian charters

The paper discusses the basic principles that can be applied to semantic publications of electronic scholarly editing of charter corpora. In order to reveal the advantages of such editions in diplomatics and historical research on medieval charters, it presents a multifunctional prototype of a semantic publication of the 13th-century Old Russian charter corpus – a constituent part of the vast collection of medieval and early modern records "Moscowitica – Ruthenica" in the Latvian State Historical Archives (Riga). It uses the «Semantic MediaWiki» software which provides a special markup for semantic links. In addition the paper explores the possiblities of translating the tenor of the charters into Attempto Controlled English. The prototype of the semantic publication is designed as a comprehensive diplomatic edition of Old Russian charters; the transcription of the texts represents palaeographic features of the charters. At the same time, the semantic edition provides the texts with additional information. Firstly, information about persons, sites, events, etc. provided by the charters is given and linked with corresponding data reflected in different specialised ontologies. As a result, the semantic publication creates a specific model of historical reality. Secondly, the semantic publication provides appropriate tools for an in-depth pattern analysis of the charters, because it is based on a detailed markup of the texts. Thus, the semantic edition is designed as a specific Web information system that incorporates medieval charters, research tools, and research results into a knowledge-based system, which is specially created for a network community.

Quelques approches de la publication sémantique des corpus des chartes
Le cas d'une édition diplomatique des anciennes chartes russes

Cet article discute des principes de base des publications sémantiques et leur application à l'édition savante électronique d'un corpus des chartes. Afin de révéler les potentialités de ces éditions, l'article présente un prototype multifonctionnel d'une publication sémantique du corpus des anciennes chartes russes du XIIIᵉ siècle. Ces chartes font partie intégrante de la vaste collection de documents historiques, médiévaux et plus modernes, 'Moscowitica–Ruthenica', conservée aux Archives Historiques d'État de Lettonie (Riga). Le prototype de la publication sémantique est conçu comme une édition diplomatique globale des chartes. Dans cet article, une attention particulière est accordée au système «Semantic MediaWiki», qui fournit des outils de balisage spéciaux pour la création de couches sémantiques dans des publications sémantiques. Dans le même temps, les auteurs affirment que la teneur des chartes peut être pleinement représentée dans le Web sémantique par le biais d'Attempto Controlled English. Le prototype développe une approche orientée sur le document de la représentation des données historiques récupérées à partir des chartes. Par conséquent, dans ce prototype, les relations entre les divers objets (lieux, personnes, événements, etc.) reflètent réellement les liens entre les documents qui fournissent des informations sur les objets. La publication sémantique, qui révèle ces relations, peut être utilisée comme base pour un système d'information Web spécifique qui intègre des textes de chartes, des outils et des résultats de recherche dans un système fondée sur connaissance, et fournit aux chercheurs des outils appropriés de critique des sources historiques.

III. Digital diplomatics in the work of the historian

ELS DE PAERMENTIER

Diplomata Belgica. Analysing medieval charter texts (dictamen) through a quantitative approach. The case of Flanders and Hainaut (1191–1244)

The ongoing process of digitisation has obviously not bypassed the auxiliary science of diplomatics. This contribution focuses on the opportunities offered by the digital source collection *Diplomata Belgica* to analyse medieval charter texts through a quantitative approach. Starting from a case study on the charters and chancery of the count(esse)s of Flanders and Hainaut during the period between 1191 and 1244, this contribution will explain how the diplomatic method of analysis elaborated by L. Delisle and Th. von Sickel (the so-called *Stilvergleichung*), and refined by Walter Prevenier in the early 1960s, was extended with a whole new dimension of word statistics within a corpus of over 16,000 digitised charter texts. Until now, the existing method of diplomatic analysis has been limited to a 'manual' comparison of the Latin protocol formulas, and only juxtaposed the text of the charters issued by the count(esse)s with other texts from the archives of their recipients. However, the new research criteria and standards which were developed, gathered into a so-called 'three step action plan of determination', made it possible for the first time also to draw the dispositive text parts into the analysis, and to examine them from a much more comparative and creative perspective. Consequently, this 'modern' methodology was not only elaborated in order to find out the editorial origin of the comital charter texts. Gradually, it also offered new insights on the editorial traditions and 'innovations' within the chancery of the count(esse)s, on the extent to which this chancery tended to differentiate itself from other secular or ecclesiastical editorial centres, and on the direct influence some important chancery clerks had on the organisation and the editorial customs within the administrative entourage of the count(esse)s.

Diplomata Belgica: analyser le dictamen des chartes médiévales au moyen d'une approche quantitative

Grâce à l'«évolution numérique», de nouvelles approches du dictamen des actes médiévaux deviennent possibles. En se focalisant sur la chancellerie et les actes des comtes et comtesses de Flandre et de Hainaut (1191–1244) retenus dans la base *Diplomata Belgica*, cette contribution vise à montrer que grâce aux *Diplomata Belgica*, la méthode de la *Stilvergleichung*, élaborée au XIXᵉ siècle par L. Delisle et Th. von Sickel, et affinée dans les années 1960 par Walter Prevenier, a pu être approfondie et adaptée aux nouveaux moyens de recherche. Dans le cadre de l'analyse du dictamen des actes comtaux, la procédure d'identification se déroule en trois phases, à savoir la recherche de fréquences significatives, l'ajout de critères additionnels de nature «quantitative» (et la confrontation avec des contre-épreuves) et, enfin, l'identification finale d'un acte comtal en tant que produit rédactionnel de la chancellerie. En outre, il devient clair qu'une approche «quantitative» basée sur le calcul de la fréquence des mots dans un ensemble d'environ 16.000 textes d'actes de la période 1191–1244 n'aboutit pas seulement à des résultats bien fondés concernant la production rédactionnelle à la chancellerie comtale; en outre, elle nous renseigne sur les traditions diplomatiques en usage pendant les règnes successifs, sur les conséquences possibles d'une union personnelle de deux comtés concernant les tâches administratives, et même sur la mesure dans laquelle certains cadres actifs au sein de la chancellerie, ou du moins dans l'entourage administratif des comtes, ont exercé une influence personnelle sur la production des actes et sur les habitudes dominantes. Enfin, elle nous permet d'appréhender la manière dont la chancellerie comtale, en utilisant «ses» actes comme instruments, a tenté de se profiler et de se différencier par rapport à la concurrence d'autres centres de rédaction contemporains.

NICOLAS PERREAUX

De l'accumulation à l'exploitation? Expériences et propositions pour l'indexation et l'utilisation des bases de données diplomatiques

Depuis maintenant plusieurs décennies, les diplomatistes disposent de bases de données remarquables, dont le contenu est propre à révolutionner nos connaissances concernant le Moyen Âge. Pour autant, force est de constater que l'exploitation de ces vastes *corpus* reste encore largement à faire, les entreprises dans le domaine restant pour le moment embryonnaires. Il est donc intéressant de s'interroger sur l'origine des blocages structurels qui empêchent encore, à l'heure actuelle, l'utilisation massive de ces ressources. L'article fait l'hypothèse qu'une partie de ces problèmes naît d'une difficulté à concevoir le dispositif numérique comme un tout, impliquant à la fois le matériau, la création de schémas abstraits et techniques, mais aussi le questionnaire scientifique. Une thèse en cours, visant à exploiter une base de 150 000 chartes, servira d'exemple concret. On présentera un dispositif d'indexation/de classification automatique des actes, basé sur le data/text mining et l'intelligence artificielle. Une exploitation plus efficace du matériau numérisé passe en effet par une «mise en ordre» des actes, aussi bien au plan typologique, que géographique ou chronologique. On présentera aussi une première expérience, concernant la dynamique de la production diplomatique à l'échelle européenne, visant à mettre en lumière, à terme, les liens entre les différentes zones productrices de documents. Le but de cette démarche globale est de faire apparaître des structures restées invisibles à l'œil nu.

From data accumulation to data exploitation: proposals and experiments for indexing and using digital diplomatic databases

For several decades now, diplomatists have had at their disposal remarkable digitised databases, whose contents are now about to revolutionise our knowledge of the Middle Ages. However, it is clear that the exploitation of this vast *corpus* remains largely to be done, while experiments in this field are still in an embryonic state. It is time now to question ourselves about the structural obstacles that still prevent, at least until now, the massive use of these resources. This article makes the assumption that a part of these problems stems from the difficulty to conceive the numeric device as a whole, involving at the same time charters, the creation of an abstract, but also technical schemas, as well as the scientific enquiries. A PhD thesis in progress on the exploitation of a corpus made from 150 000 charters will be used as a concrete example. I will describe a system dedicated to the automatic indexation/classification of charters, based on data/text mining and artificial intelligence. Indeed, a more efficient use of digitised material implies an "arrangement" of it, on the typological, geographical as well as on the chronological levels. I will also present a first experiment, regarding the dynamics of the documentary production, at the scale of medieval Europe, aimed at finally highlighting the links and discrepancies between the different areas of this production. The purpose of this global approach is to show structures that remained invisible to the naked eye.

GELILA TILAHUN, MICHAEL GERVERS, ANDREY FEUERVERGER

Statistical methods for applying chronology to undated English medieval documents

A primary objective of ongoing research at the DEEDS Project (Documents of Early England Data Set) at the University of Toronto is to develop statistical methods for the dating of undated English private (as opposed to royal) charters. Of such documents issued between 1066 and 1307, only about five per cent were dated internally. Researchers at DEEDS have developed a database of over 10,000 dated charters from the period and used it to recognize chronological differences in word order and vocabulary which, through the application of statistical methodology, have enabled us to establish a temporal „footprint" for undated charter sources. In this paper, we present two such statistical methodologies that rely on usage patterns of words and phrases, and on the notion of „distances" between documents. Both methods are computer automated and use the DEEDS database as their source.

In the first method, we define a notion of „distance" between two documents. A kernel weight on the distance between an undated document and a dated document is defined, and the date of an undated document is estimated as a weighted sum of the dates from the dated documents. The second method is based on estimating from dated documents the probability of occurrence of words and phrases through time.

The procedure for dating an undated document involves combining the estimated probabilities of the occurrences of words and phrases from the document evaluated at every point in time. The time value that maximises the combined probabilities is taken to be the date estimate for the undated document. These methods could also be adapted to a setting in which we are estimating features of documents that are not necessarily dates. We could, for example, use these methods to identify the religious house which composed a charter or the geographical location from which a charter originates.

This paper is a review of the research which has led to the publication of the papers by A. FEUERVERGER, M. GERVERS, P. HALL and G. TILAHUN as they appear in the bibliography of the contribution.

MICHAEL HÄNCHEN

Neue Perspektiven für die Memorialforschung. Die datenbankgestützte
Erschließung digitaler Urkundencorpora am Beispiel der Bestände von Aldersbach
und Fürstenzell im 14. Jahrhundert

Die Diplomatik erfährt durch die Möglichkeiten der modernen Informationstechnologie einen wesentlichen Wandel. Die digitale Fotografie großer Urkundenbestände ermöglicht einen raum- und zeitunabhängigen Zugriff auf große Urkundencorpora mittels hochauflösender Digitalisate. Das Ziel des vorgestellten Projektes ist die datenbankgestützte Untersuchung von Seelgerätstiftungen bestimmter sozialer Gruppen während des „krisenhaften" 14. Jahrhunderts im Bistum Passau.

Eine Datenbank erlaubt es uns, digitale Urkundenbestände für spezifische Fragestellungen weiter zu fokussieren. Für das Forschungsprojekt werden die Urkunden betrachtet, gelesen und die Informationen der digitalen Abbildungen in eine Erfassungsmatrix übertragen. Die Matrix ist den Erkenntnisperspektiven entsprechend in elf Kategorien untergliedert und bündelt formale sowie inhaltliche Aspekte der Digitalisate in Form von abfragbaren Datensätzen. Hierbei ist es weiterhin vorgesehen, die Informationen der Digitalisate zu formalisieren und zu normieren, um die Abfragen stets unter gleichen terminologischen Voraussetzungen zu ermöglichen. Um dies zu illustrieren, stellte der vorliegende Beitrag Auswertungsmöglichkeiten anhand der Zisterzienserklöster Aldersbach und Fürstenzell vor.

Hinsichtlich der formalen Urkundenaspekte kann konstatiert werden, dass alle Stücke den voll entwickelten Urkunden des Spätmittelalters mit Intitulatio, Publicatio, Dispositio, Corrobatio und Datatio entsprechen. Die vorherrschende Sprache ist die Volkssprache, und es wurden nur geringe Abweichungen bei den äußeren und inneren Merkmalen durch die sozialen Gruppen ersichtlich. Bezüglich des historischen Kontextes konnte ein signifikantes Absinken der Stiftungszahlen gegenüber beiden Häusern bereits vor dem Ausbrechen der Pest festgestellt werden. Leicht unterscheiden sich die Stiftungsmaterien und die sozialen Schichten der Stifter bei beiden Klöstern. So wurde Aldersbach vornehmlich mit dauerhaften und einmaligen Geldzuwendungen bedacht und Fürstenzell mit Zehntrechten. Nahezu gleich sind die Gaben an Naturaleinkünften bei beiden Klöstern. Während Aldersbach sowohl durch den niederen und fürstlichen Hochadel als auch durch Bürger verschiedener Städte bestiftet wurde, ist Fürstenzell nur durch den landsässigen Adel und Bürger der Stadt Passau bedacht worden.

Mittels der Untersuchung großer Quantitäten kann die Nutzung und Auswertung einer solchen Datenbank Tendenzen und Entwicklungen entlang einer spezifischen Fragestellung aufzeigen, und es ist ein vielversprechender Weg, digitale Urkundencorpora für die Memorialforschung zu öffnen.

New perspectives for commemoration research. The database-assisted
development of digital charter corpora: the examples of the
14th-century collections of Aldersbach and Fürstenzell

With the capacities of modern information technology, diplomatic studies have experienced a fundamental change. The digital photography of great charter collections enables immediate research using high resolution images. The main goal of the present database-assisted project is the investigation of the mentality of benefactors from different social groups in the diocese of Passau having issued commemoration charters during the 14th century, the so-called "century of crisis".

A database allows us to concentrate on digital charters for further specified evaluations. Such evaluations assess, read, and transfer the information contained in the digital images into a database matrix. Structured in 11 categories, the matrix registers formal and contextual aspects of the images as consultable data sets. With the help of this matrix, it is intended to formalise and to normalise the images as much as possible in order to query the database under similar terminological conditions. In order to illustrate this, the article presents selected examples based on two Cistercian monasteries, Aldersbach and Fürstenzell.

Concerning the formal aspects we can say that all pieces constitute fully developed charters of the late Middle Ages with *Intitulatio, Publicatio, Dispositio, Corroboratio* and *Datatio.* The preferred language is German with a few variations of the inner and outer features depending upon the social groups. Regarding contextual aspects we can say that there was a significant decrease of donations before the plague, and we have differentiated the type of donations and the benefactors. Aldersbach was granted more permanent and singular endowments in currency than Fürstenzell, which received more donations in tithe. Nearly equal are the number of natural product donations to both monasteries. While both the lower and higher nobility and citizens from cities donated to Aldersbach, only lower nobility and citizens from the city of Passau donated to Fürstenzell.

With a great number of charters, the use and evaluation of a database can show tendencies and developments according to a defined question, and is a useful way to open up digital corpora for further historical research.

MARTIN ROLAND

Illuminierte Urkunden im digitalen Zeitalter – Maßregeln und Chancen

Illuminierte Urkunden standen bisher – abgesehen von der Dotalurkunde für Theophanu von 972, die als UNESCO-Weltkulturerbe vorgeschlagen wurde – nur vereinzelt im Fokus der Forschung. Der Beitrag stellt zuerst einige charakteristische Beispiele vor und behandelt eine 1028 in Bari ausgestellte Hochzeitsurkunde ausführlicher, um die Möglichkeiten der interdisziplinären Erforschung illuminierter Urkunden exemplarisch vorzuführen.

Kernstück ist eine Definition des Untersuchungsgegenstandes. Anschließend werden der Stand der Forschung und die Schwierigkeiten bei der Auffindung illuminierter Urkunden in den Archiven thematisiert. Die ungeheuren Möglichkeiten, die die Digitalisierung großer Urkundenbestände bietet, werden hervorgehoben und einige Maßregeln zur Erschließung des Materials formuliert. Anschließend wird ein praktischer Versuch auf Grundlage von *monasterium.net* beschrieben und der Nutzen für Kunstgeschichte, Archive und Diplomatik beleuchtet. Abschließend werden die Zukunftsperspektiven benannt: Hervorzuheben ist die gesamteuropäische Dimension des Phänomens und das kreative Potential, das sich aus der impliziten Spannung zwischen der Urkunde als Rechtsdokument und dem Bild bzw. Kunstwerk mit dessen medienspezifischer Ausrichtung auf den Betrachter ergibt.

Illuminated charters in the digital age – rules and opportunities

With the exception of the dowry charter for Theophanu from 972 (proposed as UNESCO-World Heritage), illuminated charters have only rarely been the subject of scientific research. This paper presents some characteristic examples, dealing more extensively with a marriage contract (issued in Bari in 1028) to demonstrate the interdisciplinary potential of the matter.

The central point is a definition of what "illuminated charter" exactly means. Subsequent topics focus on the current state of research, and the problems of finding illuminated charters in the archives. The substantial opportunities offered by mass digitisation are highlighted alongside a number of rules to be observed. In addition, a practical test using *monasterium.net* are described, revealing the numerous benefits for the history of art, archives and diplomatic research. As a final point some future prospects are discussed: illuminated charters have a pan-European dimension and a creative potential resulting from the implicit tension between the charter as legal document and the image/work of art with its media-specific orientation towards the observer.

DOMINIQUE STUTZMANN

Conjuger diplomatique, paléographie et édition électronique. Les mutations du
XIIᵉ siècle et la datation des écritures par le profil scribal collectif

L'apparente unité graphique retrouvée de l'Occident latin au XIIᵉ siècle et l'hégémonie incontestée de la minuscule caroline «prégothique» ouvrent aux scribes la voie de l'inventivité par artifice. Ils développent des systèmes graphiques variés et des profils scribaux collectifs émergent au sein de groupes restreints (chancelleries, scriptoria). Ceux-ci se caractérisent par leur emploi variable, mais spécifique, des différents allographes d'une même lettre. L'édition électronique permettant de conserver et montrer différentes formes d'un même texte, il est désormais possible d'éditer les textes médiévaux en en conservant l'information graphique ou allographétique et, en même temps, d'étudier les cohérences et les variations des systèmes graphiques. Ce faisant, émergent de nouvelles pistes de datation et d'attribution des actes, dans un dialogue renforcé entre diplomatique et paléographie.

Diplomatik, Paläographie und digitale Edition. Nutzung von schriftlichen Profilen
für die Datierung und Lokalisierung von Urkunden

Die scheinbare schriftliche Einheitlichkeit des lateinischen Abendlands im 12. Jahrhundert wurde durch den Sieg der „vorgotischen" karolingischen Minuskel vollzogen. Sie ebnete den Schreibern den Weg einer künstlichen Kreativität. Es wurden unterschiedliche graphische Systeme entwickelt, und gemeinsame schriftliche Profile bildeten sich in gewissen Milieus wie Kanzleien und Skriptorien auf. Diese Profile kennzeichnen sich durch den zwar unstabilen, aber spezifischen Gebrauch der verschiedenen Allographen der jeweiligen Buchstaben. Da die digitale Edition die Koexistenz verschiedener Textformen erlaubt, ist es möglich geworden, auch die graphetische Information während der editorischen Phase zu speichern, und die graphischen Systeme zu analysieren. Dadurch öffnen sich neue Wege für die Datierung und Zuschreibung von Urkunden im Dialog zwischen Diplomatik und Paläographie.

JONATHAN JARRETT

Poor tools to think with. The human space in digital diplomatics

The huge potential of the many new digital resources for work in diplomatics, and for historical work of a less technical nature, has so far remained largely potential, while on the other hand many projects continue to come forth in which researchers constructed their own digital resource rather than use an existing one. As such a researcher, the author here presents an anecdotal account of his progress into the field of digital diplomatics, and uses several detailed cases from his own research to argue that, although some of his choices were bad ones and made on the basis of inadequate information, the relatively unstructured systems that he has come to use have the virtue of requiring minimal interpretation to create a database, meaning that the human task of interpretation can be kept outside the data itself. Since the basic requirement of much historical work using such corpora is simply to put the information before the researcher in a comprehensible form without making judgements on it, such low-structure resources may have wider applicability and use for researchers than more heavily-structured resources in which more interpretation has had to precede the data entry.

Poor tools to think with: Der menschliche Raum in der digitalen Diplomatik

Das große Potential der zahlreichen neuen digitalen Ressourcen für die Urkundenforschung und für die – weniger technische – historische Arbeit ist bisher größtenteils nur Potential geblieben, während zugleich jedoch viele neue Projekte entstehen, bei denen Wissenschaftler die Entwicklung eigener digitaler Ressourcen der Nutzung existierender Werkzeuge vorziehen. Als ein solcher Forscher stellt der Autor hier einen anekdotischen Bericht über sein Eindringen in die digitale Diplomatik vor und zeigt anhand einiger Beispiele aus seiner Arbeit, daß, obwohl einige seiner Entscheidungen auf unzulänglichen Informationen gegründet waren, die von ihm genutzten relativ unstrukturierten Systeme mit nur wenig Interpretationsaufwand in eine Datenbank überführt werden können. Das bedeutet, daß die Interpretationsleistung des Forschers außerhalb der eigentlichen Daten bleiben konnte. Weil es eine der Grundvoraussetzungen historischen Arbeitens mit derartigen Corpora ist, Daten in einer übersichtlichen Form bereitzustellen, ohne im Vorhinein zu Urteilen zu gelangen, könnten derartige kaum strukturierte Ressourcen breitere Anwendbarkeit und Nützlichkeit für die Wissenschaft haben als stärker strukturierte Systeme, bei denen der Dateneingabe mehr Interpretationsarbeit vorausgeht.

Colour plates

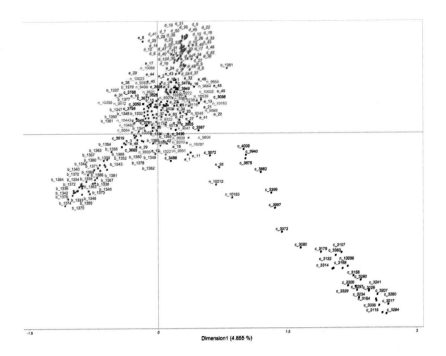

Fig. I: Analyse factorielle (AFC – Axe 1–2) de la matrice lexicale, réalisée grâce à Text-to-CSV, d'une série d'actes sélectionnés aléatoirement dans notre base. Légende: d_ (vert) = diplômes; b_ (bleu) = bulles; e_ (rouges) = actes épiscopaux; n_ (orange) = notices; c_ (noir) = chartes ne rentrant pas dans les catégories précédentes (hors pancartes)

Fig. II et III : (ci-dessus): Analyses factorielles (Axe 1–2) d'une matrice lexicale, réalisée grâce à Text-to-CSV, d'une série d'actes diplomatiques contenant a. Des bulles (b_). b. Des actes épiscopaux (e_). c. Des diplômes royaux et impériaux (d_).

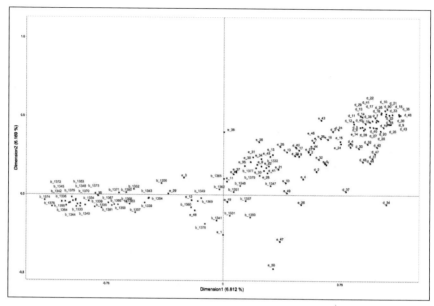

Fig. II

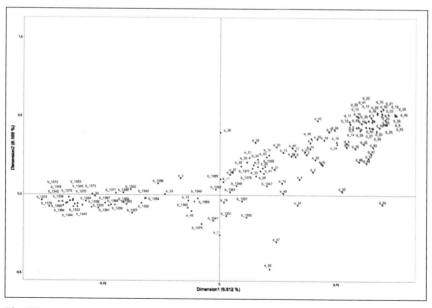

Fig. III

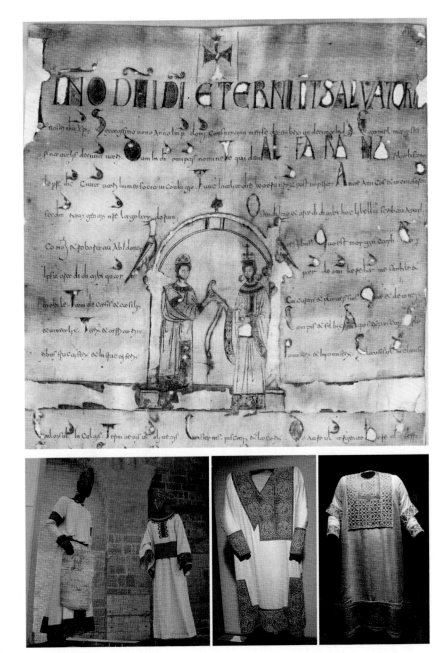

Abb. IVa: Detail der Hochzeitsurkunde des Magister Mel und der Alfarana mit der Darstellung des Brautpaares (1028 XII, Bari – siehe Anm. 4) – Abb. IVb: Rekonstruktion anläßlich einer Ausstellung in Bari 2011 (siehe Anm. 29) – Abb. IVc: Sogenannte Tunika Heinrichs II. (wohl 1. Viertel 11. Jh.; Bamberg, Domschatz) – Abb. IVd: Sogenannte Alba der Reichskleinodien (Sizilien, 1181).

Abb. Va: Detail der Urkunde König Karls V. von Frankreich und Herzog Philipps von Orléans mit der historisierten Dracheninitiale mit Büste des Königs (1367 I, Paris – siehe Anm. 37) – Abb. Vb: Portrait, wohl irrig bezeichnet als *Jehan roy de France* (Paris, Louvre).

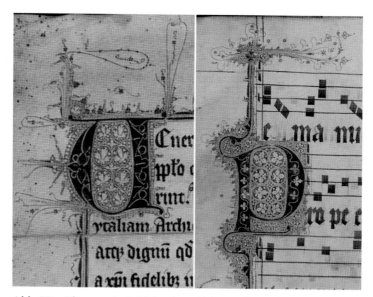

Abb. VIa: Fleuronnée-Initiale eines Ablasses des Kölner Erzbischofs Heinrich II. von Virneburg (1307 XII 28, Köln – siehe Anm. 49) – Abb. VIb: Wettinger Graduale, Fleuronnée-Initiale, Köln wohl nach 1334 (Aarau, Aargauer Kantonsbibliothek, MsWettFm1, fol. 4v – siehe Anm. 51).

Abb. VII: Detail des Stiftbriefes des Kaspar von Roggendorf für die Pfarrkirche Pögg-stall in Niederösterreich (1494 XI 11, Wien – St. Pölten, Diözesanarchiv, Pergament-urkunde sub dato – siehe Anm. 41).

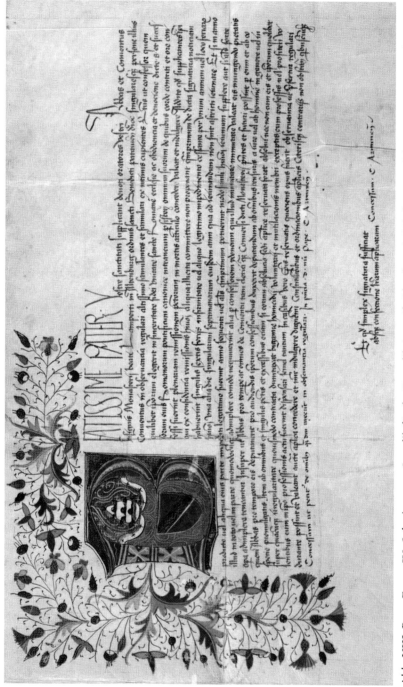

Abb. VIII: Papst Eugen IV., Sola signatura-Supplik für das Benediktinerstift Altenburg in Niederösterreich (1435/44, Rom – Altenburg, Stiftsarchiv, sub dato 1330 – siehe Anm. 40).

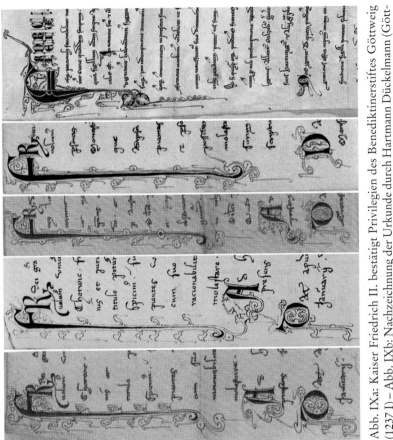

Abb. IXa: Kaiser Friedrich II. bestätigt Privilegien des Benediktinerstiftes Göttweig (1237 I) – Abb. IXb: Nachzeichnung der Urkunde durch Hartmann Dückelmann (Göttweig, Stiftsbibliothek, Cod. 895 [rot], fol. 30r) – Abb. IXc–e: weitere Privilegienbestätigungen (jeweils 1237) für Erla, Lambach und Raitenhaslach (siehe Anm. S. 263 f.).

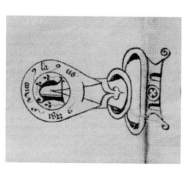

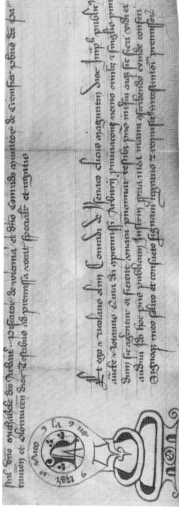

Abb. X: Notarssignet des in Wien tätigen Nicolaus olim Conradi de Ysenaco: a) 1381 VI 26 – Zwettl, Stiftsarchiv b) 1385 XII 20 – St. Pölten, Diözesanarchiv c) 1385 I 26 – Wien, Wiener Stadt- und Landesarchiv, Hauptarchiv, Urk. 1082bis d) 1385 VIII 03 – ebendort, Urk. 1093 bis (Siehe S. 265).

Abb. XI: Photomontage aus zwei Fahrzeugen mit unterschiedlichem sozialem Status und zwei Wappenbriefen für Kaschau/Kosice von 1369 und 1423, der ältere schmucklos, der jüngere mit Wappendarstellung in Deckfarbenmalerei und umgebenden Arkanthusfortsätzen (siehe S. 269).

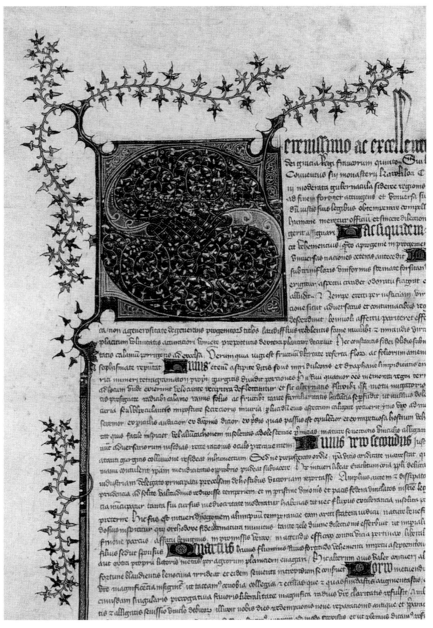

Abb. XII: Der Abt von Chaalis bestätigt eine Meßstiftung Karls V. von Frankreich (1379 IV 2, Chaalis – siehe Anm. 53).

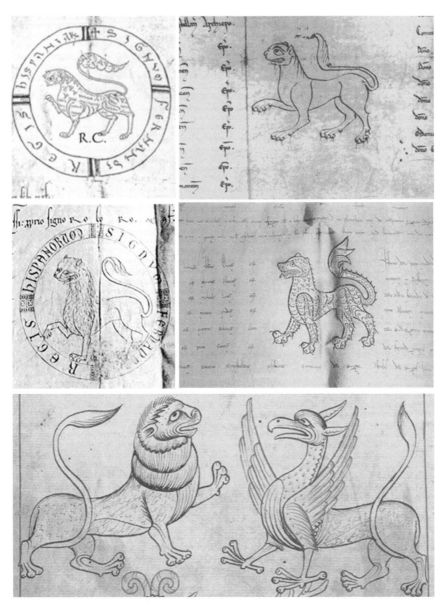

Abb. XIII: Rotae aus vier Königsurkunden aus Leon (zwei mit [1165, 1186] und zwei ohne umgebende Kreise [1219, 1229]) und Detail aus dem Musterbuch von Rein (Wien, Österreichische Nationalbibliothek, Cod. 507, fol. 8v), Österreich, wahrscheinlich ein Heiligenkreuzer Zeichner, um 1220/30 (siehe S. 266).

Abb. XIV: Bearbeiteter Screenshot der Urkundengruppe H 52 (bemalte Urkunden) aus dem Hauptstaatsarchiv Stuttgart. Die Kombination von Thumbnail und Kurzbeschreibung ermöglicht die effiziente Durchsicht von Beständen (siehe Anm. 76).

Abb. XV: Kaiser Ludwig der Bayer für das Nürnberger Heilig Geist-Spital (1341
II 24 – Nürnberg, Staatsarchiv, Rep. 1a, Kaiserl. Priv. Nr. 51 – siehe Anm. 79).

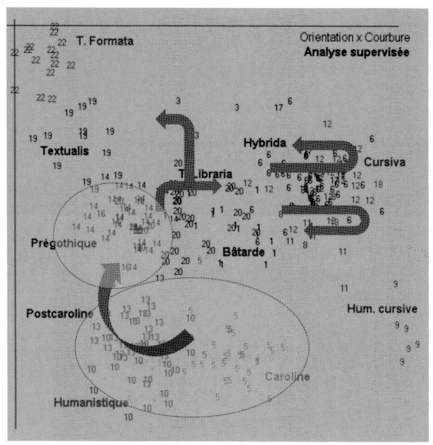

Fig. XVI: Un carrefour des écritures: la «pré-gothique». Cette figure représente les résultats d'une analyse semi-supervisée des cooccurrences des orientations et des courbures selon la méthode développée par I. Moalla et F. Lebourgeois dans le cadre du projet ANR GRAPHEM[1]. Cette analyse porte sur 313 images de manuscrits médiévaux sélectionnée dans le *Catalogue des manuscrits datés* de France. Chaque nombre représente une image; la valeur du nombre correspond à des classes d'écritures (par ex., «1» pour «Bâtarde bouclée» et «22» pour «Textualis Formata (quadrata)»). La clé d'interprétation des nombres n'a pas été transmise avant l'expérience, de façon à s'assurer que des interprétations historiques (ressemblance des écritures humanistiques et post-carolines) ne soient pas ajoutées à l'interprétation graphique.

[1] F. LEBOURGEOIS/I. MOALLA, Caractérisation des écritures médiévales par des méthodes statistiques basées sur les cooccurrences, in: Gazette du livre médiéval 56–57 (2011) p. 72–100.

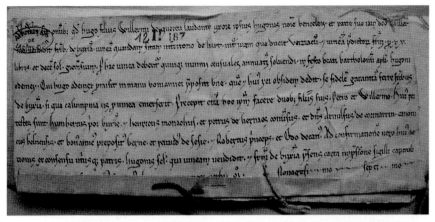

Fig. XVII: Dijon, Archives départementales de Côte d'Or, 12 H 187. Acte du chapitre de Beaune daté de 1197.

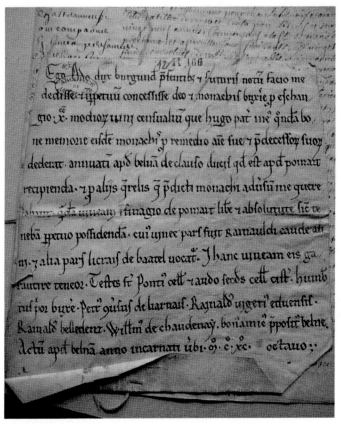

Fig. XVIII: Dijon, Archives départementales de Côte d'Or, 12 H 166. Acte du duc Eudes de Bourgogne, daté de 1198.

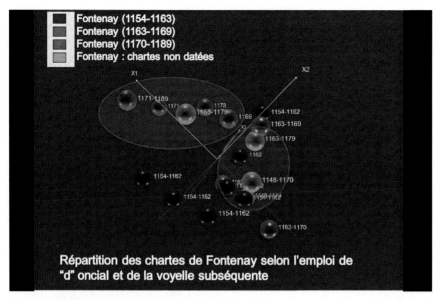

Fig. XIX: Analyse en composante principale et projection dans un espace à trois dimensions (interface du logiciel Explore3D de Matthieu Exbrayat).

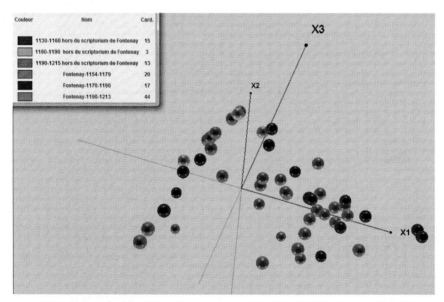

Fig. XX: Répartition des chartes de Fontenay selon l'emploi de «d» oncial et de «s» long pour la période 1150–1180.

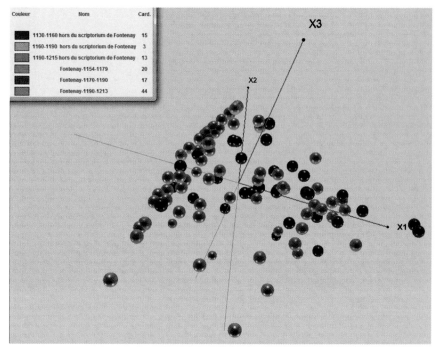

Fig. XXI: Répartition des chartes de Fontenay selon l'emploi de «d» oncial et de «s» long pour la période 1150–1210.

Glossary of technical terms

This glossary collects technical terms used in the contributions of this volume, and tries to give a short definition in order to help the reader with less technical expertise to understand them better. The contributions to this volume certainly were the first place to check for the explanations. Additionally we used publicly available sources like the original websites of the software and standards, or Wikipedia articles checked against other sources.

ACE, *Attempto Controlled English*: a *controlled natural language*, based on English.

ACP, *Analyse en composantes principales = principal component analysis*: mathematical method to reduce a set of correlated observations to their uncorrelated principal components.

AFC, *Analyse factorielle des correspondances = correspondence analysis*: statistical method to identify connections between items in a dataset, and summarise the data for a two dimensional display.

AI::Categoriser: an *open source* collection of software, written in the programming language *PERL*, used to categorise data automatically.

AJAX, *Asynchronous JavaScript and XML*: a group of software development techniques for web applications.

Algorithme, *algorithm*: a step-by-step procedure for calculations for data processing and automated reasoning.

Apache Xindice: *open source* database software for *XML* data.

Apache: Apache HTTP server, a Web server software system.

APE, *Attempto Parsing Engine*: a *parser* for translating *ACE* to *DRS*.

ATM, *Asynchronous Transfer Mode*: basic telecommunications concept for the carriage of voice, video and data signals in the network.

Atom Publishing Protocol: a set of rules to automatically distribute essential information on the creation and updates of websites.

Attribute: a part of the *XML* data structure which defines an *XML element* more precisely

Balises: see *tag*.

BaseX: a database software for *XML* data developed at Konstanz University.

Berkeley: *open source* database software which can handle *XML* data.

Catégorisation, *categorisation*: method used to group single items into categories, i.e. groups implying relationships between the members of the group representing an intellectual concept, for which computer science is developing specialised software.

CEI, *Charter Encoding Initiative*: charter-specific dialect of the *TEI*.

CELT, *Controlled English to Logic Translation*: a tool for converting controlled English (a *controlled natural language*) to formal logic expressions.

Cgi, *Common Gateway Interface*: interface between browser and web server to create dynamic web content by the server.

Checksum: a number calculated from the digital data of a file used to detect errors.

CIDOC-CRM, *Conceptual Reference Model of the International Comitee for Documentation in the International Council of Museums*: formal *ontology* for categories to describe cultural objects.

Clustering: method used to group single items by features for which computer science is developing specialised software.

CMA, *Content Model Architecture*: a model for describing digital objects in the *Fedora* environment.

CMS, *Content Management System*: software system for the publication of content (text, images), often on the web.

Controlled natural language: a restricted version of an existing language aimed at being simple and non-ambiguous, in our case for automated text processing.

Co-ocurrence: the simultaneous occurrence of two terms within a given space of text, used as the basis of statistical analysis and interpretation of texts.

CPL, *Computer-Processable Language*: a *controlled natural language*, based on English.

CQP/CWB, *Corpus Workbench*: *open source* software collection for computer linguistic analysis.

CrossQuery: the search module of the *XTF* software package.

CSS, *Cascading style sheets*: the standard codes to describe the display of *HTML/XML* data in web browsers.

CSV: a representation of table structured data as a pure text file.

Data Mining: see *Text Mining*.

DBMS, *Data Base Management System*.

dbXML Core: former database software to store and retrieve *XML* data.

DDE, *Dynamic Data Exchange*: a communication method between software applications developed by Microsoft® for the sharing and linking of data by several applications.

DHTML, *dynamic HTML*: a collective term for an open set of technologies used to manipulate *HTML* in the browser to create interactive and animated websites.

Digital forensics: expertise to fight cybercrime and identify, retrieve, and make accessible authentic digital objects as juridical evidence.

Dirty-OCR: *OCR* process whose results are not checked by a human.

Distance Based Method: statistics based machine learning method developed by the DEEDS project at the University of Toronto.

DOD 5015.2, *Design Criteria Standard for Electronic Records Management Software Applications*: a standard for electronic records in the United State Department of Defense adopted at the US federal level.

DOM, *Document Object model*: the hierarchical model for the parts of a text described in *HTML* and *XML*.

DRS, *Discourse Representation Structures*: formalized representation of linguistic structures like sentences, and their relationships.

Dublin Core: reduced metadata categories assumed to be common to many different kinds of documents, created to facilitate cross-research search, data aggregation and interoperability.

DynaXML: the presentation module of the *XTF* software package.

EAC, *Encoded Archival Context:* a standard used to describe the producers of archival material in *XML*.

EAD, *Encoded Archival Description*: a standard used to describe archival holdings in *XML* following the categories defined by *ISAD(G)*.

Editor: a software tool used to create and manipulate computer stored texts in a specific format.

e-learning: digital and mostly web-based teaching and learning procedures.

Element: the basic entity in the *XML* structure of a text, consisting of its *tags* and its content.

Encodage: see *markup, tag*.

Entities, character entities: in *markup languages* like *SGML, HTML* or *XML*, the association of a given character with its representations through a fixed character sequence.

ePub, *Electronic Publication*: format for e(lectronic)-books.

Espace de noms, *namespace*: extension of a tag referring to the context of its definition, allowing disambiguation in the presence of homonymous tags in a *XML* document.

EVT, *Edition Visualization Technology*: a software package to present digital scholarly editions with *XML* online, currently in development at Pisa University.

eXcelon XIS: a commercial database software to store and manipulate *XML* data.

eXist / eXist-DB: a major *open source* database to store *XML* and execute *XQuery* programmes.

Explorer3D: a three-dimension classification and visualization software application.

Expressions régulières: see *Regex*.

Fedora Commons, *Flexible Extensible Digital Object Repository Architecture*: *open source* software system for management of digital *repositories*.

First-order logic: formal system to make logical statements including quantified variables and predicates.

Fuzzy C-means/FCM: *algorithmic* method used to cluster items using fuzzy logic i.e. attributing the item to cluster not in a binary way but by expressing probability.

Gaiji: The *TEI*-module for the description and encoding of non-unicode characters.

gBank: online *repository* of non-standard characters suggesting encoding in TEI.

GIF, *Graphic Interchange Format*: proprietary format for (possibly animated) images, very popular for web applications.

GoXML DB: a commercial database software used to store and manipulate *XML* data.

GUI: *Graphical User Interface*, an interface allowing human-computer interaction through the manipulation of graphical components, as in today's most common operating systems.

Hash: *algorithm* used to map data to a short unique (at least in a specific context) representation, which can be used to identify the piece of data.

HCI, *Human Computer Interaction*: the discipline which considers the way in which a human can best interact with the computer.

HTML, *HyperText Markup Language*: a markup language used to create text which contains fragments linked to other texts, based on *SGML*. Currently the basic standard of all web pages in the internet.

Implementation: the realisation of a software concept into program code.

IMT see *UVic IMT*.

Information Retrieval: the computer supported finding of relevant information in a database or a collection of documents.

Interopérabilité, *interoperability*: the ability for several data systems, databases etc. to exchange information or be subject to joint queries.

ISAD(G), *General International Standard Archival Description*: standard for the description of archival items published by the International Council on Archives.

Java Virtual Machine: software which allows the execution of programs written in the Java programming language on different computer operating systems.

JavaScript: a language used to write software which can be executed directly in the major current web browsers.

JPEG, *Joint Photographic Expert Group*: format and *algorithm* for compressing images, defined by the said group.

jQuery: a collection of software written in JavaScript which reduces the need to take care of vendor specific implementations of JavaScript on different computer platforms, and offers prefabricated programs for frequent tasks in the development of web applications.

JSON, *Javascript Object Notation*: a data exchange format designed for easy use in Javascript.

Kernel: the core of a program to which several programs for special purpose can be attached.

Knime, *Konstanz Information Miner*: software and platform for data analysis.

LaTeX: markup language and "document preparation system" for typesetting.

Lexico3: a statistical text analysis software.

Library: in computer science, used for a collection of digital data or software.

Mapping: define rules to connect data description categories from different systems.

MARC, *MAchine-Readable Cataloging*: a standard for the electronic cataloguing of library holdings, with MARCXML being the corresponding *XML* schema, developed by the Library of Congress.

Markup: adding computer readable structure and annotation to a document with the help of *tags*, using markup languages such as *XML* or *HTML*.

Maximum Prevalence Method: statistics based machine learning method developed by the DEEDS project at the University of Toronto.

Metadata: data describing and accompanying other data.

METS, *Metadata Encoding and Transmission Standard*: a Library of Congress standard for encoding metadata in a digital library.

MoReq, *Model Requirements for the Management of Electronic Documents and Records*, later *Modular Requirements for Records Systems*: European Union standard for keeping and managing electronic records.

MS SQL Server, *Microsoft® SQL server*: commercial relational database management system.

MUFI, *Medieval Unicode Fonts Initiative*: group providing recommendations and encoding suggestions for integrating medieval characters into the Unicode standard.

MySQL: open-source relational data management system.

Naïve Bayes: a method for *classification* based on the probability of features attributed to a specific class in a training set.

NXD, *Native XML Database*: a database designed to store and manipulate data in *XML* format.

ODD, *One Document Does it all*: a method used to describe project specific modifications of the general rules of the *TEI* in a machine readable form and in one document.

OLE, *Object Linking and Embedding*: a communication method between software applications developed by Microsoft® for the sharing and linking of data by several applications.

Ontologie, *Ontology*: the formal, abstract representation of a given sector of knowledge, often expressed in related concepts.

Open Source Software: software giving access to its source code, and thus allowing free use and modifications.

Oracle DB, *Oracle Database*: a commercial relational database management system.

OWL, *Web Ontology Language*: a *RDF*-based language used for formal ontologies.

Oxygen: commercial *XML editor* with good *TEI* support.

Parser: a software tool or *algorithm* for the automated, formal analysis of text.

PENG, *Processable ENGlish:*, a controlled natural language.

Perl: a programming language.

Philologic: a software developed in Chicago, allowing the creation of a textual database and statistical interrogation of the texts.

PHP, *Hypertext PreProcessor*: programming language frequently used for creating dynamic web pages.

PID, *Persistent IDentifier*: permanent identifier for objects stored in *repositories*.

Plugin: small software component added to an existing structure, aimed at fulfilling a special function.

PNG, *Portable Netwok Graphics*: open format for images, specially designed for internet use.

Precision: the degree to which the result of a query is relevant to the search goals.

Proprietary software: software not displaying its source code, thus making modifications and further development impossible.

Protocolli di rete, *Web protocol*: set of rules for diverse types of communication and exchanges through the internet (such as *HTTP*, POP3, FTP, *SOAP* etc.).

Python: a programming language.

Q-GIS, *Quantum GIS: open source* geographic information system software.

Query: a specifically formulated "question" aiming to find data in any structure containing it.

R: major *open source* programming language and software for statistical analysis.

RACE, *Reasoning in ACE, Attempto ACE Reasoner*: software tool used to extract logic from *ACE* texts and check consistency between *ACE* texts.

Rapidminer: *open source* software system for data mining.

RDF, *Resource Description Framework*: a World Wide Web Consortium standard for describing data.

Recall: the number of answers to a query returned by a search engine.

Regex, *Regular expression*: a character sequence defining a pattern for a search in textual data, including wildcards and character ranges allowed at a specific position.

Relax-NG, *REgular LAnguage for XML Next Generation*: a language for describing the generic structure of a *XML* document, defining the allowed *tag* names and their relationships.

Repository: a storage structure for digital data and objects.

RESTful Web API: a standard for the communication of computer software over the internet.

ROMA: a *TEI* tool to create customisations of the *TEI* for specific uses.

RuleML, *Rule Markup Language*: a *XML markup*-language for expressing logical rules to deduce and infer between statements.

Rumore, *noise*: answers which a search engine gives to a query, which are not relevant to the search goal.

SARA, *SGML-Aware Retrieval Application*: a former search engine, predecessor of *Xaira*.

SAX, *Simple API for XML*: application programming interface for treating *XML* files.

Semantic Media Wiki: software extension to the MediaWiki software (the content managing system used e.g. for Wikipedia) allowing to add semantic annotations to *wiki* pages.

Semantic web: an initiative and a set of recommendations from the World Wide Web Consortium aiming at publishing structured data on the internet allowing their interconnection through the use of common descriptive languages such as *RDF*, *OWL*.

Semi-structured data: data mixing structures and simple strings, typically a text *tagged* with *XML*.

Servlet: a *Java* program executed on an internet server called by software on a remote computer.

SGML, *Standard Generalised Markup Language*: a markup language for describing documents, predecessor of *XML*.

Shingle: given sequence of words used as a basis for statistical analysis of texts.

SIG, *Special Interest Group*: a group of people wishing to share ideas and solutions within the *TEI*.

Silenzio, *Silence*: the absence of answers to a query, due to a problem in the formulation of the query or in the shaping of the database; the proportion of relevant documents ignored by a query.

SOAP: originally *Simple Objects Access Protocol*, a *XML*-based protocol for web services.

Sourceforge: online platform hosting (mostly *open source*) software and software projects.

Structured data: data in a very strict form, usually in a table-like form used in relational database systems.

SVG, *Scalable Vector Graphics*: a *XML*-based data format for vector images.

SVM, *Support Vector Machines*: a set of supervised automated machine learning techniques aimed at resolving questions of (statistical) regression and discriminant analysis.

SWRL, *Semantic Web Rule Language*: a rule language for the *semantic web*, combining *OWL* and a subset of *RuleML*.

Tag: "mark" used by *markup* languages to qualify a given portion of data (text, but also image, sound ...) according to a specific "vocabulary" and "grammar".

Tamino, *Tamino Information Server*: commercial *XML*-based information server for the Internet.

Tanagra: *open source data mining* software.

TEI Lite: simplified version of the *TEI* using a specific set of tags, designed for beginners or non-specialists, and aiming at covering "90 % of the needs of 90 % of the TEI user community".

TEI SGML: former *SGML*-based form of the *TEI* before the transition of the TEI to *XML* standard was adopted.

TEI, *Text Encoding Initiative*: consortium aiming at defining a standard for encoding and representing texts in digital form. Its guidelines are based on *XML* and are currently forming the TEI P5, version 2.5.0. "TEI" can be used to refer to either the consortium or the guidelines.

Test set: set of data used to control whether an automated machine learning procedure comes to a satisfying result.

Text Mining: the extraction of data and information from textual corpuses, through the use of computerised statistics and linguistics.

TextGrid: German project aiming at the construction of a virtual research environment for the Humanities.

TextGridLab: software and tool suite from *TextGrid*, designed to support digital humanists, above all in the creation of digital editions.

TextIndexer: module of the *XTF* software package used to create indexes for fast access to the texts.

TEXTML: commercial database and search engine used to process *XML* data.

Textométrie: set of methods for textual analysis based on the semantic and statistical approach of texts and same-named software platform.

TF-IDF, *Term Frequency-Inverse Document Frequency*: statistical measure for the importance of a word within a given corpus.

Thesaurus: organized and structured list of terms.

TIFF, *Tagged Image File Format*: public but proprietary format for images widely used as archival format of image files.

TILE, *Text-Image Linking Environment*: software tool used for connecting transcriptions with images of the texts.

Tokenisation: the (automated) division of text in units (token) chosen for their meaning and relevance before further processing.

Training set: set of data used to train a computer in automated machine learning.

Txt: most basic file format text.

UI, *User Interface*: the structure allowing human and computer to interact.

Unicode: standard to represent up to 2^{32} character types in the computer. It includes currently over 110.000 codes for characters ranging from Linear B script to modern Chinese.

UVic IMT: *Image Markup Tool* (project) from the University of Victoria: tool for marking up images in conformity with the *TEI* (P5).

Validation set: set of data used to test the usefulness or function of parameters during an automated machine learning procedure.

W3C DOM, *Document Object Model* of the World Wide Web Consortium: standard for the description for the parts of *HTML* and *XML* documents.

WebDav, *Web-based Distributed Authoring and Versioning*: extension of *HTTP* allowing use of a web server as file storage in a file system on a remote computer.

Weka, *Waikato Environment for Knowledge Analysis*: software suite for automated machine learning.

Widget: usually a *web widget*, i.e. a piece of software that can be integrated into a webpage.

Wiki: website whose pages can be written and modified by the users, thus allowing collaborative work.

Xaira, *XML Aware Indexing and Retrieval Architecture*: *XML* search engine.

XEP: commercial software processor for the conversion of *XML* to PDF using *XSL-FO*.

XHTML, *eXtensible HyperText Markup Language*: the version of *HTML* compliant to the strict rules of XML.

XML, *eXtensible markup language*: *markup* language designed to facilitate interoperability and flexibility.

XML: DB API: general definition of the possible methods of interaction between any kind of software to a *XML* enabled database/native *XML* database.

XMLObjects: any part of data described as a *XML* structure.

XML-RPC: *XML*-based protocol for remote procedure calls through Internet.

XPath: query language used to locate parts in a *XML* document.

XQuery Update Facility: *XQuery* extension introducing update functionality to *XQuery* and *XPath*.

XQuery: *query* language used to extract and process data from a *XML* database.

XREM: *Diple*-specific module used for the documentation of *XML* files (see the contribution by Desenclos/Jolivet).

XSL, *eXtensible Stylesheet Language*: group of languages for the rendering of *XML* documents.

XSL-FO, *eXtensible Stylesheet Language – Formatting Objects*: *markup* language for producing documents in displayable or printable formats such as PDF, after they have been transformed by *XSLT* from *XML* into XSL-FO and then processed.

XSLT, *eXtensible Stylesheet Language for Transformations*: language for turning XML documents into other documents, in *XML*, *HTML* or text, or into *XSL-FO*.

XTF, *eXtensible Text Framework*: collection of *open source* software to store, search and display texts in *XML* format.

XUpdate: *XML* language for updating *XML* documents.

The Authors

Antonella AMBROSIO
Università degli Studi "Federico II", Napoli
Dipartimento di Studi Umanistici
antonella.ambrosio@unina.it

Sébastien BARRET
Institut de recherche et d'histoire des textes
CNRS, Orléans
sebastien.barret@cnrs-orleans.fr

Francesca CAPOCHIANI
Università degli studi di Pisa
Informatica Umanistica
f.capochiani@gmail.com

Els DE PAERMENTIER
Ghent University
Department of History
els.depaermentier@ugent.be

Camille DESENCLOS
École nationale des chartes, Paris
camille.desenclos@enc.sorbonne.fr

Luciana DURANTI
The University of British Columbia
School of Library, Archival, and Information Studies
luciana.duranti@ubc.ca

Serena FALLETTA
Università degli Studi di Palermo
Dipartimento DSGSS – Sezione di Storia del diritto
serefalletta@hotmail.com

Andrey FEUERVERGER
University of Toronto
Department of Statistics
andrey@utstat.utoronto.ca

Michael GERVERS
University of Toronto
DEEDS Project
m.gervers@utoronto.ca

Antonella GHIGNOLI
La Sapienza – Università di Roma
Dipartimento di Storia Culture Religioni
antonella.ghignoli@mclinknet.it

Michael HÄNCHEN
TU Dresden
Forschungsstelle für Vergleichende Ordensgeschichte
michael.haenchen@tu-dresden.de

Richard HIGGINS
Durham University Library Special Collections
r.i.higgins@durham.ac.uk

Aleksandrs IVANOVS
Daugavpils University
Institute of Regional Studies (REGI), Rezekne Higher Education Institution
aleksandrs.ivanovs@du.lv

Jonathan JARRETT
University of Birmingham
School of History and Cultures
j.jarrett@bham.ac.uk

Vincent JOLIVET
École nationale des chartes, Paris
vincent.jolivet@paris-sorbonne.fr

Chiara LEONI
Università degli studi di Pisa
Informatica Umanistica
leoni.chia@gmail.com

Nicolas PERREAUX
Université de Bourgogne
UMR 6298, ARTeHIS
UFR Sciences de la Terre et Environnement
nicolas.perreaux@orange.fr

Daniel PIÑOL ALABART
Universitat de Barcelona
Departament d'Història Medieval, Paleografia i Diplomàtica
danielpinol@ub.edu

Nebojša PORČIĆ
Universität Belgrad
Philosophische Fakultät
nebojsa.porcic@f.bg.ac.rs

Martin ROLAND
Österreichische Akademie der Wissenschaften
Institut für Mittelalterforschung
Abteilung für Schrift- und Buchwesen
martin.roland@oeaw.ac.at

Roberto ROSSELLI DEL TURCO
Università di Torino
Dipartimento di Studi Umanistici
rosselli@ling.unipi.it

Dominique STUTZMANN
Institut de Recherche et d'Histoire des Textes (CNRS, UPR 841)
dominique.stutzmann@irht.cnrs.fr

Gelila TILAHUN
University of Toronto
DEEDS Project
gelila.tilahun@utoronto.ca

Benoît-Michel TOCK
Université de Strasbourg
EA 3400 – ARCHE (Arts, civilisation, histoire de l'Europe) France
btock@unistra.fr

Aleksey VARFOLOMEYEV
Petrozavodsk State University
Faculty of Mathematics
avarf@psu.karelia.ru

Gunter VASOLD
Universität Graz
Zentrum für Informationsmodellierung – Austrian Centre for Digital Humanities
gunter.vasold@uni-graz.at

Georg VOGELER
Universität Graz
Zentrum für Informationsmodellierung – Austrian Centre for Digital Humanities
georg.vogeler@uni-graz.at

Žarko VUJOŠEVIĆ
Universität Belgrad
Philosophische Fakultät
zarko.vujosevic@f.bg.ac.rs

Dragić M. ŽIVOJINOVIĆ
Institut für Geschichte Belgrad
dragic.zivojinovic@iib.ac.rs

BEIHEFTE ZUM ARCHIV FÜR DIPLOMATIK, SCHRIFTGESCHICHTE, SIEGEL- UND WAPPENKUNDE

HERAUSGEGEBEN VON WALTER KOCH UND THEO KÖLZER

böhlau

EINE AUSWAHL

BD. 6 | CHRISTIAN HANNICK (HG.)
**KANZLEIWESEN UND KANZLEI-
SPRACHE IM ÖSTLICHEN EUROPA**
1999. XIV, 232 S. GB.
ISBN 978-3-412-13897-4

BD. 9 | OTFRIED KRAFFT
**PAPSTURKUNDE UND
HEILIGSPRECHUNG**
DIE PÄPSTLICHEN KANONISATIONEN
VOM MITTELALTER BIS ZUR REFOR-
MATION. EIN HANDBUCH
2005. XII, 1247 S. GB.
ISBN 978-3-412-25805-4

BD. 10 | THOMAS LUDWIG
**DIE URKUNDEN DER BISCHÖFE VON
MEISSEN**
DIPLOMATISCHE UNTERSUCHUNGEN
ZUM 10.–13. JAHRHUNDERT
2008. IX, 337 S. 21 S/W- ABB. AUF 8 TAF.
GB. | ISBN 978-3-412-25905-1

BD. 11 | SEBASTIAN GLEIXNER
SPRACHROHR KAISERLICHEN WILLENS
DIE KANZLEI KAISER FRIEDRICHS II.
(1226–1236)
2006. XII, 580 S. 600 S/W-ABB. GB.
ISBN 978-3-412-03906-6

BD. 12 | GEORG VOGELER (HG.)
DIGITALE DIPLOMATIK
NEUE TECHNOLOGIEN IN DER
HISTORISCHEN ARBEIT MIT URKUNDEN
2009. VII, 362 S. 101 S/W-ABB. GB.
ISBN 978-3-412-20349-8

BD. 13 | IRMGARD FEES,
PHILIPPE DEPREUX (HG.)
**TAUSCHGESCHÄFT UND TAUSCH-
URKUNDE VOM 8. BIS ZUM
12. JAHRHUNDERT / L'ACTE
D'ÉCHANGE, DU VIIIᵉ AU XIIᵉ SIÈCLE**
2013. 508 S. 22 S/W-ABB. GB.
ISBN 978-3-412-21001-4

BD. 14 | ANTONELLA AMBROSIO,
SÉBASTIEN BARRET, GEORG VOGELER
(HG.)
DIGITAL DIPLOMATICS
THE COMPUTER AS A TOOL FOR
THE DIPLOMATIST?
2014. 347 S. 59 S/W- UND 21 FARB. ABB.
GB. | ISBN 978-3-412-22280-2

BÖHLAU VERLAG, URSULAPLATZ I, D-50668 KÖLN, T:+49 221 913 90-0
INFO@BOEHLAU-VERLAG.COM, WWW.BOEHLAU-VERLAG.COM | WIEN KÖLN WEIMAR

böhlau

ARCHIV FÜR DIPLOMATIK, SCHRIFTGESCHICHTE, SIEGEL- UND WAPPENKUNDE

HERAUSGEGEBEN VON
WALTER KOCH UND THEO KÖLZER

Die Zeitschrift bietet ein internationales Forum für Forschungen und Darstellungen zu den historischen Grundwissenschaften und zu ihren Nachbardisziplinen vom Frühmittelalter bis zur Gegenwart. Das Schwergewicht der Aufsätze und Miszellen liegt auf den Gebieten des Urkunden-, Akten-, Amtsbuch- und Archivwesens sowie der Schriftgeschichte. Gleiche Aufmerksamkeit gilt Untersuchungen zum Siegel- und Wappenwesen sowie zur Genealogie.

ERSCHEINUNGSWEISE: JÄHRLICH
JAHRGANG: PREIS AUF ANFRAGE
ERSCHEINT SEIT: 1955
ISSN 0066-6297

ZULETZT ERSCHIENEN:
BD. 59 (2013)
€ 94,90 [D]#€ 97,60 [A]
ISBN 978-3-412-22200-0

BÖHLAU VERLAG, URSULAPLATZ I, D-50668 KÖLN, T:+49 221 913 90-0
INFO@BOEHLAU-VERLAG.COM, WWW.BOEHLAU-VERLAG.COM │ WIEN KÖLN WEIMAR

Urkunden
und ihre
Erforschung

Zum Gedenken an Heinrich Appelt

Herausgegeben von
Werner Maleczek

Böhlau

WERNER MALECZEK (HG.)

URKUNDEN UND IHRE ERFORSCHUNG

ZUM GEDENKEN AN HEINRICH APPELT

(VERÖFFENTLICHUNGEN DES INSTITUTS FÜR ÖSTERREICHISCHE GESCHICHTSFORSCHUNG, BAND 62)

Der Band enthält zehn Beiträge, die das Urkundenwesen aus unterschiedlichen Perspektiven beleuchten:

Walter Koch: Heinrich Appelt und die Edition der Diplome Kaiser Friedrich Barbarossas – *Theo Kölzer*: Konstanz und Wandel. Zur Entwicklung der Editionstechnik mittelalterlicher Urkunden – *Irmgard Fees*: Zur Bedeutung des Siegels an den Papsturkunden des frühen Mittelalters – *Andreas Meyer*: Regieren mit Urkunden im Spätmittelalter. Päpstliche Kanzlei und weltliche Kanzleien im Vergleich – *Christian Lackner*: Die Vielgestaltigkeit der spätmittelalterlichen Herrscherurkunde – *Martin P. Schennach*: Mittelalterliche Urkunden in Staatsrecht, politischer Kommunikation und Historiographie in der Neuzeit – *Christoph Friedrich Weber*: Urkunden auf Bildquellen des Mittelalters – *Marie Bláhová*: Die Herrscherurkunden in den böhmischen Ländern in der Zeit der přemyslidischen Fürsten (bis zum Ende des 12. Jahrhunderts) – *Benoît-Michel Tock*: Actes confirmatifs et vidimus dans le Nord de la France jusqu'a la fin du XIIIe siecle – *Juraj Šedivý*: Deutschsprachige Beurkundung im Donaugebiet des mittelalterlichen Königreichs Ungarn.

2014. 284 S. 29 S/W-ABB. BR. 170 X 240 MM. | ISBN 978-3-205-78949-9

BÖHLAU VERLAG, WIESINGERSTRASSE I, A-IOIO WIEN, T:+43 I 330 24 27-0
INFO@BOEHLAU-VERLAG.COM, WWW.BOEHLAU-VERLAG.COM | WIEN KÖLN WEIMAR

böhlau

HISTORISCHE HILFSWISSENSCHAFTEN

HERAUSGEGEBEN VON ANTON SCHARER,
GEORG SCHEIBELREITER UND ANDREAS SCHWARCZ

BD. 1 | GEORG SCHEIBELREITER
HERALDIK
2. AUFLAGE 2014. 222 S. 280 S/W- U.
92 FARB. ABB. BR.
ISBN 978-3-205-78433-3 [A]
ISBN 978-3-486-59124-8 [D]

BD. 2 | WALTER KOCH
INSCHRIFTENPALÄOGRAPHIE DES
ABENDLÄNDISCHEN MITTELALTERS
UND DER FRÜHEREN NEUZEIT
FRÜH- UND HOCHMITTELALTER
2007. 264 S. MIT CD-ROM. BR.
ISBN 978-3-7029-0552-1 [A]
ISBN 978-3-486-58189-8 [D]

BD. 4 | REINHARD HÄRTEL
NOTARIELLE UND KIRCHLICHE
URKUNDEN IM FRÜHEN UND HOHEN
MITTELALTER
2011. 507 S. 30 S/W-ABB. BR.
ISBN 978-3-205-78578-1 [A]
ISBN 978-3-486-59775-2 [D]

BD. 3 | MICHAEL HOCHEDLINGER
AKTENKUNDE
URKUNDEN- UND AKTENLEHRE
DER NEUZEIT
2009. 292 S. 164 S/W-ABB.
MIT CD-ROM. BR.
ISBN 978-3-205-78296-4 [A]
ISBN 978-3-486-58933-7 [D]

BD. 5 | MICHAEL HOCHEDLINGER
ÖSTERREICHISCHE
ARCHIVGESCHICHTE
VOM SPÄTMITTELALTER BIS ZUM ENDE
DES PAPIERZEITALTERS
2013, 522 S. 281 S/W-ABB. FRANZ. BR.
ISBN 978-3-205-78906-2 (A)
ISBN 978-3-486-71960-4 (D)

BÖHLAU VERLAG, WIESINGERSTRASSE I, A-IOIO WIEN, T:+43 I 330 24 27-0
INFO@BOEHLAU-VERLAG.COM, WWW.BOEHLAU-VERLAG.COM | WIEN KÖLN WEIMAR

TR584